Ξ UNIV

# European Literature from Romanticism to Postmodernism

# European Literature from Romanticism to Postmodernism

A Reader in Aesthetic Practice

Edited by
**Martin Travers**

CONTINUUM

London and New York

Continuum
The Tower Building, 11 York Road, London SE1 7NX
370 Lexington Avenue, New York, NY 10017-6503

First published 2001
This selection and introductory material © Martin Travers 2001

**British Library Cataloguing-in-Publication Data**
A catalogue record for this book is available from the British Library.

ISBN 0–8264–4748–1 (hardback)
    0–8264–4749–X (paperback)

**Library of Congress Cataloging-in-Publication Data**
European literature from romanticism to postmodernism: a reader in aesthetic practice/
edited by Martin Travers.
    p. cm.
    Includes bibliographical references and index.
    ISBN 0–8264–4748–1 — ISBN 0–8264–4749–X (pbk.)
    1. Literature, Modern—History and criticism.   I. Travers, Martin.

PN710 .E88 2000
809′.03.—dc21

00–022684

Typeset by YHT Ltd, London
Printed and bound in Great Britain by Biddles Ltd, Guildford and King's Lynn

# CONTENTS

## Part II: Realism

## Part III: Modernism

## Part IV: The Literature of Political Engagement

## Part V: Postmodernism

# PREFACE

This book seeks to provide the reader with a collection of documents – essays, letters, prefaces, interviews, manifestos and other theoretical statements – in which some of the major voices of modern European literature have sought to define for themselves, and for others, the nature of their writing and the literary projects upon which they were engaged. This material helps us to understand not only the aesthetic frameworks within which their literature took shape, but also the broader intellectual ambit of that writing, those assumptions and values which may have been consciously or unconsciously held, regarding personal identity, the social and political realms, gender, and those many other attributes of knowledge that constitute the point of contact between literature and the world.

I have grouped these documents around the literary movements and schools with which many of these writers identified (or to which, with greater or lesser justice, they have since been attributed): Romanticism, Realism, Naturalism, Modernism, the Literature of Political Engagement, and Postmodernism. In approaching these writers in this fashion, my intention has not been to reduce them to mere epiphenomena of contemporary cultural trends, or to project them as unambiguous examples of some greater reality of which they were 'representatives'. The relationship between these writers and the larger cultural formations with which they are often associated was complex, as were the cultural formations themselves. Nevertheless, in spite of their amorphous parameters, these literary movements provide the modern reader with important points of reference, and make possible the identification of the larger conceptual frameworks that linked many of these writers, providing the contexts in which common projects, shared goals and aspirations, and intellectual and artistic convergences were initiated and consolidated.

I have endeavoured, as far as possible, to present these extracts as continuous wholes rather than as purple passages, *obiter dicta*, pregnant formulations and other forms of quotable morsels. I do this for two reasons: first, because my intention is to impart a sense of the developing logic of the arguments from which these extracts come; and second, because, just as, for example, Rousseau's unique projection of accentuated selfhood is inseparable from a grammar that continually draws the reader back to an almost oppressive first-person assertiveness and to a narrative line of unflagging self-reflexivity (*see* Part I, Reading 1), so too with the monolithic dogmatism of the 'On Guard' manifesto (Part IV, Reading 5), and the infinitely more subtle semantic play of Hélène Cixous (Part V, Reading 20), the style of these writings, including the repetitions, longueurs, *non sequiturs* and challenging obscurities that these documents contain, are an essential component of their discursive effect.

The reader, indeed, should look in these documents not only for unambiguous statements and clear avowals of literary intent (although such clearly exist: in the commitments to the cause, in the exhortations to read and to follow, and in the expressions of authorial probity), but also for the subtext of those aims, the stridency that betrays the sense of struggle, the hesitations and prevarications, the oscillations between assertive self-confidence and doubt, and the inner turmoil that emerges between a rejected (but all too solid) past, and a future which draws one into its potentiality, but does not, as yet, exist.

The contradictions are also revealing: Edward Young (Part I, Reading 2), for example, condemning the slavish adherence to the rules of a Classical past in language redolent with erudite allusion, impressive cultural capital (only four from the fifty pages of the standard edition do not contain at least one Classical reference or untranslated quotation from Latin or Greek), and the other essential baggage carried by the eighteenth-century exponent of 'good taste'; or Zola's much vaunted invocation of the scientific methodologies of the behavioural scientists (*see* Part II, Reading 12) within the arguably highly unscientific context of a novel of domestic melodrama and near Gothic horror; or, at the other end of the spectrum, John Fowles' ungainly advocacy of the cause of metafiction midway through a novel that has, both in narrative and plot, held almost slavishly to the markedly non-metafictional conventions of the nineteenth-century Realist novel (*see* Part V, Reading 8).

My approach has been to situate the author in question and his or her work within the broader literary movements of which they were a part, with the movements themselves receiving their own introductions at the beginning of each Part. These introductions are offered simply as broad grids intended to steer the reader through a complex area, and the comments on the individual authors viewed, at best, purely as nudges in the direction of understanding. To seek to have anything meaningful to say about Shelley's *Defence of Poetry* (Part I, Reading 12) or Sartre's *What Is Literature?* (Part IV, Reading 21) in the space of a paragraph must leave any author in danger of being caught between the Scylla of *lèse-majesté* and the Charybdis of scholarly suicide. It also needs to be said that the rationale that has governed my choice of extracts departs somewhat from that which informs the familiar 'novelists on the novel' or 'poets on poetry' genres. I have chosen not to go up that road, not because I adhere to some misplaced anti-auterism (we are surely now after three decades of theory able to see that the grain of the voice can depart from convention and grammar), but simply because the assertive self often misrepresents (does not see) the deeper values that have inspired its work. In order to uncover these values, it is often more useful to understand what the authors in question have written about someone or something else (a political development, a scientific innovation or even an art exhibition), rather than about their own projects, however privately or publicly they may have construed them.

The majority of texts published here have been newly translated into English, many for the first time. Most of these documents have been chosen either because they represent the major theoretical statement of a particular author, or because they were central texts within the literary movement in question (and seen as such), and highlight an essential aspect of the cultural and philosophical goals of that movement. I have not, however, slavishly followed any accepted canon in my choice of texts. On the contrary, I have deliberately included work from previously marginalized writers, such as the Spanish Romantic Mariano José de Larra (Part I, Reading 14), and the inspirational nationalist poet of Poland Adam Mickiewicz (Part I, Reading 17); or, in later chapters, from Realists such as Giovanni Verga (Part II, Reading 13), and Benito Pérez Galdós (Part II, Reading 16). Their writing has been included here not only to broaden the national base of these cultural formations, but to give a fuller picture of the ways in which literature can engage with the most complex desires of nations and individuals alike.

This book pays testimony to the self-aggrandizing, sometimes quarrelsome, frequently quixotic, but nonetheless creative, intellectually vital and essentially humane qualities of the writers represented here. These same qualities have been shared by many of the colleagues, students and mentors with whom I have studied and worked for the past thirty years, most notably at the University of East Anglia (Norwich), Gonville and Caius College (Cambridge) and Griffith University (Brisbane). They include Peter Bayley, Malcolm Bradbury, Pat Buckridge, John Casey, John Gatt-Rutter, Steve Giles, Chris Gooden, Michael Harvey, Chris Holmes, Franz Kuna, Paddy Lyons, Jock Macleod, John Milfull, John and Francie Oppel, David Punter, David Roberts, Elinor Shaffer, Max Sebald, Philip Thomson, Edward Timms and Nicholas Zurbrugg. I dedicate this book to them.

# ACKNOWLEDGEMENTS

Every effort has been made to trace or contact the copyright holders of original material contained in this volume. Grateful acknowledgement is made to the following for permission to translate or to reprint extracts from copyrighted material:

Anon, 'Manifesto of the "On Guard" group', from *Soviet Literature: An Anthology*, edited and translated by George Reavey and Marc Slonim. © 1934 Greenwood Press. Reprinted by permission of Greenwood Press.

Louis Aragon, Preface to *Le Paysan de Paris* © 1926 by Editions Gallimard. Translated by permission of Editions Gallimard.

Antonin Artaud, *The Theatre of Cruelty: First Manifesto*, from Antonin Artaud, *Le Théâtre et son double* © 1966 Editions Gallimard. Translated by permission of Editions Gallimard.

J. G. Ballard, Introduction to *Crash*. © 1974 Vintage Books. Reprinted by permission of Margaret Hanbury Literary Agency.

Roland Barthes, 'The death of the Author', from *Images, Music, Text*, essays selected and translated by Stephen Heath. English translation © 1977 by Stephen Heath. Reprinted by permission of Hill and Wang, a division of Farrar, Straus and Giroux, LLC.

Simone de Beauvoir, from *The Second Sex* by Simone de Beauvoir, translated by H. M. Parshley. © 1952 and renewed 1980 by Alfred A. Knopf, a division of Random House Inc. Reprinted by permission of Random House Inc.

Gottfried Benn, 'The new state and the intellectuals', from *Sämtliche Werke*, Stuttgarter Ausgabe. In Verb. m. Ilse Benn hrsg. v. Gerhard Schuster. Band 3: Prosa I. (1910–1932). Klett-Cotta, Stuttgart 1987. © J. G. Cotta'sche Buchhandlung Nachfolger GmbH, Stuttgart. Translated by permission of Klett-Cotta.

Ernst Bloch, 'Diskussionen über Expressionismus', from *Vom Hasard zur Katastrophe: Politische Aufsätze aus den Jahren 1934–1939*. © Suhrkamp Verlag. Frankfurt am Main 1972. Translated by permission of Suhrkamp Verlag.

Heinrich Böll, 'In defense of rubble literature', from *Essayistische Schriften und Reden, 1952–1963*, edited by Bernd Balzer. © 1979 Kiepenheuer and Witsch. Translated by permission of Kiepenheuer and Witsch.

Yves Bonnefoy, 'Image and presence', from *The Act and the Place of Poetry: Selected Essays*, edited and translated by John T. Naughton. © 1989 by The University of Chicago. Reprinted by permission of The University of Chicago Press and Yves Bonnefoy.

Bertolt Brecht, 'A short oragnum for the theatre,' from *Brecht on Theatre: The Development of an Aesthetic*, translated by John Willett. Translation © 1964, renewed 1992 by John Willett. Reprinted by permission of Methuen Publishing Ltd and Hill and Wang, a division of Farrar, Straus and Giroux, LLC.

André Breton, 'Manifesto of surrealism', from *Manifestes du surréalisme* © 1973 Editions Gallimard. Translated by permission of Editions Gallimard.

Italo Calvino, Preface to *The Path to the Nest of Spiders*, translated by Archibald Colquhoun. © 1947 Giulio Einaudi. Translation copyright © 1956 by William Collins and Sons, Co., Ltd. Preface translation copyright © 1976 by William Weaver. Reprinted by permission of HarperCollins Publishers, Inc.

Albert Camus, *The Myth of Sisyphus*. © 1942 Editions Gallimard. Translated by permission of Editions Gallimard and Alfred A. Knopf Inc.
*The Rebel*. © 1951 Editions Gallimard. Translated by permission of Editions Gallimard and Alfred A. Knopf Inc.

Hélène Cixous, *The Newly-Born Woman*. © 1975 Editions des Femmes. Translated by permission of Editions des Femmes.

Jacques Derrida, *Writing and Difference*, edited and translated by Alan Bass, published by Routledge and Kegan Paul, 1978. Reprinted by permission of The University of Chicago Press.

Pierre Drieu la Rochelle, *Notes pour comprendre le siècle*. © 1941 Editions Gallimard. Translated by permission of Editions Gallimard.

T. S. Eliot, 'Tradition and the individual talent', from *Selected Prose of T. S. Eliot*, edited by Frank Kermode. © 1975 Valerie Eliot. Introduction and notes copyright © 1975 by Frank Kermode. Reprinted by permission of Faber and Faber Ltd, and Harcourt, Inc.

Dario Fo, 'Dialogue with an audience', translated by Tony Mitchell, first published in *Theatre Quarterly*, no. 35 (1979). Reprinted by permission of Tony Mitchell and *Theatre Quarterly*. Originally published in Italian in *Teatro Politico di Dario Fo, compagni senza censura*, Vol. 1 (2nd edn), Gabriele Mazzotta Editore, Torino, 1977.

John Fowles, *The French Lieutenant's Woman*, published by Jonathan Cape. © John Fowles 1969. Reprinted by permission of Sheil Land Associates Ltd.

Ralph Fox, *The Novel and the People*. © 1937 Lawrence and Wishart. Reprinted by permission of Lawrence and Wishart.

Alfredo Giuliani, Preface to *The Newest Voices*. © 1961 Giulio Einaudi. Translated by permission of Giulio Einaudi.

Nicolai Gumilev, 'Acmeism and the legacy of symbolism', from *Nicolai Gumilev on Russian Poetry*, edited and translated by David Lapeza. Reprinted by permission of Ardis Publishers.

Peter Handke, Note on *Offending the Audience* and *Self-Accusation*, from *Offending the Audience and Self-Accusation*, translated by Michael Roloff. Reprinted by permission of Farrar, Straus and Giroux, LLC.

Ted Hughes, Introduction to Vasko Popa, *Collected Poems*. © The Ted Hughes Estate. Reprinted by permission of Faber and Faber Ltd.

Eugene Ionesco, *Notes and Counter-Notes*. © 1962 Editions Gallimard. Translated by permission of Editions Gallimard.

Arthur Koestler, 'The initiates', from *The God That Failed*, edited by Richard Crossman. © 1953 Hamish Hamilton. Reprinted by permission of Peters, Fraser and Dunlop Group Ltd.

Mariano José de Larra, 'Literature', from *Articulos Completos*. Translated by Douglas Pacheco.

D. H. Lawrence, Letter to Edward Garnett, from *The Letters of D. H. Lawrence*, edited by George J. Zytaruk and James T. Boulton, Cambridge University Press. Reprinted by permission of Laurence Pollinger Limited and the Estate of Frieda Lawrence Ravagli.

Preface to *Fantasia of the Unconscious* by D. H. Lawrence. © 1922 by Thomas Seltzer, Inc., and renewed 1950 by Frieda Lawrence. Used by permission of Viking Penguin, a division of Penguin Putnam Inc. (North America), and by permission of Laurence Pollinger Limited and the Estate of Frieda Lawrence Ravagli (world excluding North America).

Federico García Lorca, selected letters, from *Selected Letters, 1927–1928*, translated by David Gershator. © 1977 by The Estate of Federico García Lorca, 1980 by David Gershator. Reprinted by permission of Marion Boyars Publishers of London and New York, and New Directions Publishing Corp.

Georg Lukács, 'Es geht um den Realismus'. German copyright Luchterhand Verlag. Translated by permission of Agentur Artisjus.

Louis MacNeice, *Modern Poetry: A Personal Essay*. © 1968 Clarendon Press. Reprinted by permission of Clarendon Press and David Higham Associates.

Heinrich Mann, 'Zola', from *Geist und Tat: Franzosen von 1780–1930*. All rights reserved by S. Fischer Verlag GmbH, Frankfurt am Main. Translated by permission of S. Fischer Verlag.

Thomas Mann, 'An appeal to reason', from *Order of the Day* by Thomas Mann, translated by H. T. Lowe-Porter. © 1942 by Alfred A. Knopf Inc. Reprinted by permission of Alfred A. Knopf, a division of Random House Inc.

Filippo Tommaso Marinetti, 'The founding and manifesto of Futurism', and 'Beyond Communism', from *Marinetti: Selected Writings*, by F. T. Marinetti, edited by R. W. Flint, translated by R. W. Flint and Arthur A. Coppotelli. Translation © 1972 by Farrar, Straus and Giroux, LLC. Reprinted by permission of Farrar, Straus and Giroux, LLC.

Vladimir Mayakovsky, *How Are Verses Made?*, translated by G. M. Hyde. Reprinted by permission of G. M. Hyde and Bristol Classical Press.

Pierre Naville, *La Révolution et les intellectuels*. © 1975 Editions Gallimard. Translated by permission of Editions Gallimard.

George Orwell, 'Why I write', from *Such, Such Were the Joys* by George Orwell. US rights: © 1953 by Sonia Brownell Orwell and renewed 1981 by Mrs George K. Perutz, Mrs Miriam Gross and Dr Michael Dickson, Executors of the Estate of Sonia Brownell Orwell. Reprinted by permission of Harcourt, Inc. World rights excluding US: © George Orwell 1953. Permission to reprint from Bill Hamilton as the literary executor of the Estate of the late Sonia Brownell Orwell, Martin Secker & Warburg Ltd.

Georges Perec, 'Writing and the mass media'. Translated by permission of the Estate of Georges Perec.

Benito Pérez Galdós, 'Contemporary society as novelistic material', from George Becker (ed.), *Documents of Literary Realism*. © 1963 by Princeton University Press. Reprinted by permission of Princeton University Press.

Harold Pinter, 'Writing for the theatre', from *Plays One*. © 1962 Faber and Faber Ltd. Reprinted by permission of Faber and Faber Ltd and Grove/Atlantic, Inc.

Ezra Pound, 'Imagism: a retrospect', from T. S. Eliot (ed.), *The Literary Essays of Ezra Pound*. © 1935 by Ezra Pound. Reprinted by permission of New Directions Publishing Corp. and Faber and Faber Ltd.

Alain Robbe-Grillet, *Towards a New Novel*. © 1963 Editions de Minuit. Translated by permission of Editions de Minuit.

Nathalie Sarraute, 'What I am seeking to do', from *Oeuvres complètes*, edited by Jean-Yves Tadie. © 1996 Editions Gallimard. Translated by permission of Editions Gallimard.

Jean-Paul Sartre, *What Is Literature?* © 1946 Editions Gallimard. Translated by permission of Editions Gallimard, and Taylor and Francis Books Ltd.

August Strindberg, Foreword to *Miss Julie*, from George Becker (ed.), *Documents of Literary Realism*. © 1963 by Princeton University Press. Reprinted by permission of Princeton University Press.

Arthur Symons, 'A literature in which the visible world is no longer a reality, and the unseen world no longer a dream', from *The Symbolist Movement in Literature*. Reprinted by permission of Brian Read, MA (Oxon), Literary Executor to Arthur Symons.

Leon Trotsky, *Literature and Revolution*, translated by Rose Strunsky. © The University of Michigan Press. Reprinted by permission of The University of Michigan Press.

Paul Valery, 'Concerning "Le Cimetière marin"', from *Oeuvres*. © 1969 Editions Gallimard. Translated by permission of Editions Gallimard.

Virginia Woolf, 'Modern fiction', from *Collected Essays*. © 1966 The Hogarth Press. Reprinted by permission of The Society of Authors as the literary representative of the Estate of Virginia Woolf.

All further translations from the Italian are by Nicholas Everett, and from the French and German by myself, except where otherwise stated.

To Ann, Charlotte, Lucie and Isabel

# Part I
# Romanticism

# INTRODUCTION

Romanticism began in the late eighteenth century as a broad movement of protest against the aristocratic culture of the *ancien régime* and against the neo-classical aesthetic upon which that culture was based. The movement had its precursors in writers such as Samuel Richardson (*Pamela*, 1740, and *Clarissa*, 1748), George Lillo (*The London Merchant*, 1731), Denis Diderot (*Father of the Family*, 1758) and Gotthold Lessing (*Miss Sara Simpson*, 1755), whose work sought to give validity to the claims for power of a swiftly ascending mercantile middle class, its material base secured by the achievements of the Industrial Revolution and its moral self-image sustained by the Protestant Ethic. Against what was seen as an increasingly corrupt and parasitic aristocratic ruling class these writers pitted characters from humbler backgrounds who combined depth of feeling with a supreme moral probity – which, in its unflagging commitment to private virtue (and in its conviction to use this virtue to judge the mores of the public realm), could not but have, as subsequent historical events confirmed, implications of a social and ultimately political nature.

The early exponents of the Romantic movement, figures such as Edward Young, James Macpherson, Johann Gottfried Herder and Jean-Jacques Rousseau (the major names in what is now known as Pre-Romanticism), may have lacked the ideological momentum of these 'bourgeois' writers, but they did retain the emotive (*larmoyant*) rhetoric of their work, deepening Diderot and Richardson's idealization of heightened 'sensibility' (a term that combined for this generation both aesthetic and moral experience) into a more self-conscious ethos of personal and aesthetic authenticity. This was particularly true in the case of Rousseau. It was he who was largely responsible for providing the Romantics proper with much of the intellectual animus that motivated them in their campaign against what they saw to be the stultifying legacy of Enlightenment rationalism.

Rousseau was, above all, a fervent critic of the civic mores of his contemporary France, and throughout his estranged and peripatetic life launched repeated attacks upon its institutions – social (in the *Discourse on Inequality*, 1755), domestic (*The New Héloïse*), political (*The Social Contract*, 1762) and educational and religious (*Emile*, 1762). But it was through his concept of selfhood and psychology, formed in his more personal autobiographical writings, that Rousseau was to have the greatest impact upon the development of Romanticism. Here, in works such as *The Confessions* (1764–70) and *Reveries of a Solitary Walker* (1782), Rousseau projected an image of himself as a sensitive soul raised to near-martyrdom through the persecution of the public and the indifference of friends. It was in this highly personal, almost monomaniacal projection of a personality tortured and alienated, but at the same time 'purified in the crucible of adversity' and rendered almost clairvoyant by its hypersensitivity, that Rousseau was to have the deepest and most lasting effect upon the self-understanding of the Romantic mind (**Reading 1**).

The initiatives of the pre-Romantics emerged within a variety of cultural discourses. In the area of art theory and art criticism, for example, notions of 'refinement', 'good taste' and 'decorum', the key terms in the neo-classical aesthetic of the seventeenth and early eighteenth centuries, now gave way to the celebration of 'originality', 'nature' and 'genius'. Certainly, this did not represent an immediate rupture with the past. Works such as Richard Hurd's *Letters on Chivalry and Romance* (1762) and Joseph Warton's *History of English Poetry* (1774–81) (to name two important transitional texts from the English context) retain an unmistakable respect for the accomplishments of Augustan poetry, but they frame those accomplishments (and in a way that necessarily relativizes them) against the grandeur of Chaucer and Spenser, Tasso and Ariosto – 'Romance' writers whose epic achievements are granted both a generic and historical superiority. A similar duality is evident in Edward Young's highly influential *Conjectures on Original Composition* (1759); but here what remains as a pre-theoretical set of dispositions in Hurd and Warton is stated as a more consciously held aesthetic. Great art and literature, Young argues (playing Milton off against Pope), do not seek to imitate models or follow accepted conventions or rules. On the contrary, they emerge ('grow' was the preferred organic metaphor) directly from the internal sources of inspiration that lie within the creative 'genius'. That this quality of genius, this 'stranger within thee', belongs to a realm that must remain impervious to rational explanation is simply a fact that confirmed for Young, and for many of those who came after him, the depth of its creative potency (**Reading 2**).

To give support to their critiques of the neo-classical tradition, the pre-Romantics pointed to two figures whose work could not be assimilated to prevailing standards of good taste and propriety, but belonged instead to a transcendent realm of universal experience: Shakespeare and the Scottish bard, Ossian. From Johann Gottfried Herder's adulation in the 1770s, in an essay that established Shakespeare as the first great writer of the modern period, through to Stendhal's *Racine and Shakespeare* (1823) and Victor Hugo's polemics in the 1830s (*see* **Reading 13**), Shakespeare came to be invoked whenever it was necessary to provide a justification for breaking with established dramatic convention. Shakespeare's importance for this generation lay not only in the fact that he suspended the three unities of time, place and manner, and defiantly crossed genres such as tragedy and comedy, the epic and the pastoral, to produce plays of surpassing emotional and intellectual depth. His work also called up, according to Herder in his famous essay (**Reading 3**), those mythic reserves within the popular mind. Drawing upon these, Herder argued, Shakespeare, 'the interpreter of nature in all her tongues', was able to transform morality plays and chronicles, legend and homily into works of universal significance and unsurpassable artistic consummation.

Shakespeare was a true spirit of the people, the heart of the authentic, autochthonic culture of his nation, and, as such, could take his place beside the other great *Volksgeist* that inspired the Romantic imagination: the medieval Celtic bard, Ossian. Ossian's *Fragments of Ancient Poetry, collected in the Highlands of Scotland* (1760) spoke of a world lost in the mists of time, criss-crossed by noble heroes driven by conscience, fate and tribal custom, the denizens of wild and sublime landscapes. The contemporary interest in the Gothic and the supernatural, in dark mystery and transgression, is here divested of its origins in base melodrama and transformed, for the gentle reader of eighteenth-century *belles-lettres*, into a pagan but lofty sentiment. As James Macpherson, editor and translator of the volume, argued, in a 'dissertation' that accompanied the second edition of *The Works of Ossian* (1765), 'so well adapted are the sounds of [the poems] to the sentiments, that, even without any knowledge of the language, they pierce and dissolve the heart'. The poems of the ancient bard, in their selfless commitment to the values of Celtic chivalry, and in their readiness to sacrifice all in defence of those values, would, Macpherson was confident, appeal to readers of all dispositions, because such writings were the creations of a time and people that saw no distinction between nature and culture (**Reading 4**).

Doubts about the authenticity of Ossian's work did not prevent an entire generation of readers, both in Britain and on the Continent, from lauding the Celtic bard as the Homer of the North, as a poet whose direct depictions of the tragedies and the melancholy grandeur of life were all the more persuasive for lacking artifice and premeditation. The French critic and cultural historian, Madame de Staël, was one such reader. Around her reading of Ossian, Madame de Staël in fact elaborated an entirely new aesthetic, one that abandoned the categories of traditional aesthetics (with their concern to define the essential qualities of 'beauty' and 'goodness') in favour of a historicist perspective where the importance of ethnicity and local custom to the formation of national culture would receive full recognition. To this purpose she developed a simple but effective taxonomy. As de Staël made clear in her *On Literature Considered in Relation to Social Institutions* (1800), Classical literature belonged to the South, and was the product of the clear light of rationalism and order; the North, however, was subject to a harsher climate, dark and hostile, but it was precisely such an environment that enabled poets, such as Ossian, to produce verse of 'ardent enthusiasm and pure exaltation' (**Reading 5**). It was largely due to the popularity of Ossian (particularly in Germany) that the folk-songs and rustic tales rediscovered by, among others, the brothers Grimm (*Fairy Tales*, 1812–15), and Arnim and Brentano (*The Boy's Magic Horn*, 1805–8), could, almost half a century later, be assured of serious acceptance by their reading public (*see* **Reading 16**).

Neither Rousseau nor Herder elaborated a Romantic aesthetic in any formal terms; that would be the task of a younger generation, such as Novalis and the Schlegel brothers in Germany, Wordsworth and Coleridge in England, and others in France, Italy and Spain, who would consciously address the nature and ambit of the 'Romantic' and 'Romanticism'. In doing so, these writers succeeded in transforming the negative connotations that had adhered to previous uses of the term (where, in the hands of writers such as Boileau in France and Johnson in England, it had been conterminous with attributes such as 'absurd', 'incredible', 'fantastic') into a positive programme that would celebrate the role of the creative will in opening up the objective world to the active agency of the mind. This exploration of the subjective and psychological realms took many forms in the literature of the Romantics. It included the transfiguration of darkness and death in Novalis' *Hymns to the Night* (1800), and the fantasy world portrayed with a sense of the Gothic in the *Märchen* of Tieck and Hoffmann, through to the poems of the supernatural and the macabre of Coleridge's 'The Ancient Mariner' and 'Christabel', and the final hallucinatory works of Gerard de Nerval and Thomas de Quincey. These writers all constructed worlds of nocturnal ambience where dream and reality, madness and composure, the conscious and the unconscious eventually merge into one another, sometimes in tones that transport, at other times in ways that lead to horror and despair for those who (in Novalis' words) inhabit an inner realm where 'madness and truth' are one (**Reading 6**).

The cognitive faculty that allowed access to these diverse realms was the 'imagination'. It became the key term within Romantic epistemology. For Novalis, imagination ('Phantasie') alone guaranteed contact with the primary forces of myth and the mysteries of the dream world. Imagination, to those who possessed it, was able to restore that animistic feeling of oneness with the universe that had been destroyed through 200 years of mechanistic thinking and Rationalist philosophizing (*see* **Reading 6**). Similar sentiments were expressed by Coleridge, who likewise stressed the essentially animating and vitalistic characteristic of imagination (which he divided into 'primary' and 'secondary' forms). It had the power to bridge those divisions within an object world, which would otherwise, through its inaccessible facticity, remain distant and isolated from the perceiving self (*see* **Reading 10**). Shelley, on the other hand, granted the imagination the capacity to broaden the moral sympathies of mankind, making a claim for its egalitarian and all-embracing potency that clearly possessed for the author, as his *Defence of Poetry* (1821) indicates (*see* **Reading 12**), socially ameliorating and even political implications; while for Blake, who saw the world in 'one continued vision', the transforming agency of the imagination possessed a near mystical capacity which came close to dissolving the external world entirely (**Reading 7**).

For many Romantics, such as the German, August Wilhelm von Schlegel, this realm of pure inwardness was the chief characteristic of the modern mind. As he argued in his famous lecture of 1808 (one of the seminal formulations of the 'Romantic-Classical' taxonomy), Romanticism was the product of a mind-set which has lost that naive confidence in the tangibility of the outer world and the simple enjoyment in theoretically unmediated sensuality that previous generations, such as the great Classical writers of ancient Greece, had enjoyed. Schlegel argues that this confidence has been undermined by the advent of the Christian ethos of inner grace, which has installed the transcendent as the goal of all earthly happiness. Unable to reach such a realm of pure spirituality, the modern artist can do nothing more than persist in a state of 'Sehnsucht', an unrequited longing for a utopian world in which 'sensual impressions [will be] hallowed by a mysterious union with higher feelings, while the spiritual, on the other hand, will embody its intimations or ineffable perceptions of infinity in sensuous forms drawn from the physical world' (**Reading 8**).

As if to balance this realm of pure interiority, other Romantic writers sought to ground their work in a reappraisal of the more solid realm of the language and customs of rural life. William Wordsworth was one of them. As his friend and colleague Coleridge later noted, Wordsworth's importance lay in his radical break, both with the formal versification used by preceding poets such as Pope and Dryden, and with the narrow range of their subject matter. In the place of such versification, Wordsworth chose, as he explained in his famous preface to the second edition of the *Lyrical Ballads* (1800), subjects from 'humble and rustic life', because there 'the essential passions of the heart find a better soil in which they can attain their maturity, are less under restraint, and speak a plainer and more emphatic language'. Indeed, within this environment of unmediated sincerity poetry and prose become one, traceable back to the same linguistic matrix; for, as Wordsworth explained, 'poetry sheds no tears such as Angels weep, but natural and human tears; she can boast of no celestial ichor that distinguishes her vital juices from those of prose; the same human blood circulates through the veins of them both' (**Reading 9**).

Coleridge construed Wordsworth's break from the canon almost entirely as an aesthetic enterprise, which had been pursued largely in terms of the renewal of the cognitive and linguistic categories through which the world is grasped, in a process that, if successful, would awaken 'the mind's attention from the lethargy of custom'. As he explained in his *Biographia Literaria* (1817), the poet's goal had been to remove that 'film of familiarity and selfish solicitude' that obscures from vision the true meaning of the world (**Reading 10**). Coleridge, who had assigned himself the task of locating the supernatural in quotidian experience and commonplace things, was later in his *Biographia* to criticize Wordsworth's ambition to collapse the diction of poetry with that of prose; but he arguably overlooked the *strategic* effect of this rejection of the pastoral diction of the eighteenth century: the fact that it opened areas of new experience (admittedly more largely rural than urban in origin), and provided a voice for social classes and issues that had been previously deemed unworthy of poetic consideration.

This was the important point that the great Italian defender of Romanticism, Alessandro Manzoni, was later to make in his 'On Romanticism: letter written to the Marchese Cesare d'Azeglio' (1823). Here Manzoni argued that the broader focus of Romantic writing was intended to give expression to a new sense of humanism in literary subject matter, one that is free from doctrinaire dogmatism and studied convention (**Reading 11**). Romanticism alone, Manzoni contended here, is capable of 'introducing into literature the ideas, and the sentiments, which ought to inform every discourse', of providing avenues to the local, the historically specific and the socially modest, to all that embraces the entirety of human experience, qualities to which Manzoni himself would go on to give epic shape to in his novel *The Betrothed* (1842).

As Manzoni's essay clearly implies, the Romantic movement was also (albeit within the contemporary parameters of the term) a democratic one. This was reflected not only in its choice of subject matter and poetic diction, but, more explicitly, in its determination to undermine the continued dominance of the conservative status quo. Two writers, in particular, sought to unify the two realms of aesthetics and politics in their work: Percy Bysshe Shelley and Victor Hugo. It was Shelley, for example, who even in the midst of his most extended and eloquent promotion of the spiritualizing capacity of the imaginative faculty, in his *A Defence of Poetry* (1821) felt it important to remind his readers that his speculations were taking place within a context in which 'the rich have become richer, and the poor have become poorer; and the vessel of the state is driven between the Scylla and Charybdis of anarchy and despotism' (**Reading 12**). While Shelley does not identify the targets of his political ire, he nevertheless concludes his essay by investing all who would share his vision of the transforming agency of the poetic mind with a broad mandate to revolutionize the customs and values of his contemporary England.

Similar radical sentiments were held by Mariano José de Larra in Spain and Victor Hugo in France, two countries in which Romanticism had become an ally of progressive liberal movements. In the polemical preface to his play *Hernani* (1830), Hugo had exclaimed: 'Romanticism is liberalism in literature!', giving voice to a cultural politics that would become increasingly more radical (indeed would lead to the author's exile in 1851, following his participation in the protests against the anti-Republican government of Napoleon III). But the animus of Hugo's political stance, his determined opposition to non-liberal, anti-democratic forms of government can be clearly felt in his famous preface to the play *Cromwell* (1827) (**Reading 13**). Here Hugo, effectively writing the first French manifesto in support of the Romantic movement in France, sought to dislodge the cultural norms of the establishment by promoting the grotesque and the fantastic as forms of dramatic statement, whose greatest realization he saw in the plays of Shakespeare. By giving shape to these new dramatic principles (and Hugo energetically tried to show the way in his own plays), the French stage would be able to take its place alongside those other greater forces – social, technological and constitutional – that were swiftly bringing France into the modern period. For as Hugo confidently argued: 'The time for it has come, and it would indeed be strange if, in the present age, liberty, like light, should penetrate everywhere, except into that one place where freedom finds its most natural realm – in the world of ideas.'

In Spain also, after the dissolution of the absolutist Hapsburg regime of Ferdinand VII in 1834, Romanticism became synonymous with attempts to found a modern, progressive liberal state. Up until that point, Romanticism had been largely associated with monarchist traditionalism and the Roman Catholic Church in that country. This changed after 1834 when a second generation of Romantics, influenced by developments in France and elsewhere, started to project Romanticism as essentially a movement of the modern period. The political parallels were drawn, above all, by the Spanish poet and critic, Mariano José de Larra. In his essay 'Literature' (1836), subtitled (in some editions) 'a profession of faith', Larra consciously linked initiatives to renew Spanish literature to emancipatory social and political causes, to, as he explained, liberty 'in the arts, in industry, in commerce, in individual conscience', precisely those values that a restored Monarchist-Royalist Spain found potentially the most threatening (**Reading 14**).

What also emerges from Larra's essay (but is less evident in those by Shelley and Hugo) is a close symbiosis between the cultural politics of the Romantic movement and the promotion of national identity, a process that Larra helped foster through his *costumbrismo* (provincial writings). To a certain extent, national self-consciousness had been there from the very beginning of the Romantic movement, for example, in the rediscovery of ancient verse and bardic poetry made by Macpherson in his Ossian books, and by other authors of the arcane, such as Thomas Percy, whose *Reliques of Ancient English Poetry* (1765) had been almost equally influential. In their promotion of a native folk poetry, these works patently challenged, *nolens volens*, the cultural hegemony of France, whose neo-classical aesthetic had been disseminated through guides to 'good taste', such as Boileau's *The Art of Poetry* (1674). Many, such as the Italian poet Giovanni Berchet, argued that Romanticism was the sole force of breaking that hegemony, and providing a medium for national cultural unification. Romantic literature, irrespective of when it was created (and Berchet eclectically invokes figures as diverse as Homer, Pindar and Milton), represents the most vital part of a nation's culture, the 'poetry of the living', that heart of the past which has continued to beat into the present, and which is capable of transcending all divisions, cultural and social (**Reading 15**).

As is shown by the example of Herder, who published his *Volkslieder* [*Songs of the People* or *Folk*] between 1778 and 1779, German Romantic writers, in particular, felt liberated by the rediscovery of a previously neglected folk tradition in their poetry. When the military imperialism of Napoleon reinforced the cultural dominance of France in the years between 1803 and 1814, the antiquarian impulse began to merge with a powerful feeling of nascent German nationalism. The product of this convergence was a spate of publications, of which the most famous are the *Fairy Tales* collected by the brothers Grimm (1812–15) and *The Boy's Magic Horn*, edited by Clemens Brentano and Achim von Arnim (1805–08). As he explained in its postscript, Brentano saw the publication of the latter volume as a 'service to the nation'; not only would such a volume help remove the foreign taint that had spoiled German literature in the past but, by doing so, it would be instrumental in promoting a sense of national unity among the still disunited branches of the German people, who would now recognize themselves in a common language and common folk culture (**Reading 16**). The key term here was *Volk*, an almost mystical notion which combined linguistic, ethnic and cultural denominators into a powerfully emotive symbol, which could be employed to include some, as it was intended to exclude others from the ideal community of the German nation. As a cornerstone of the ideology of the neo-nationalist movement, the notion of *Volk* would reverberate throughout the early decades of the twentieth century, its rhetorical effect all the more powerful and dangerous for having its origins in the bucolic wonderland evoked by the fairy stories and songs of the brothers Grimm, and Arnim and Brentano.

In the work of the German Romantics, the imperative of national renewal possesses an intensity that borders upon religious revivalism; but the Germans were not alone in grasping the political potential that resided within the Romantic ethos. Many writers in the Scandinavian countries, such as Elias Lönnrot (see, for example, his epic *Kalevala*, 1835), in Greece (whose struggles against Turkey were celebrated by Dionysios Solomos in his 'Hymn to Liberty', 1823), and in Central Europe also saw in Romanticism a vehicle for national revival. In Poland, the poet and novelist, Adam Mickiewicz (author of *Master Thaddeus*, 1834), consciously developed this interaction between the aesthetic, the political and the religious, and in a way that was to give a seminal thrust to the notion of a Polish nation state. His theoretical writing, in particular, is infused with a pathos and a Messianic fervour that brings to full expression redeemerist qualities that remain only implicit in the writings of the other European Romantics. For Mickiewicz, Romanticism represented an ethos of both personal and national liberation. As he argued in his series of lectures, *The Slavs* (1844), literature is not simply the expression of a nation's suffering (and he is thinking here of a Poland forced into tutelage by Russia); it is also (and primarily) the means by which that suffering can be undone through cultural struggle. Mickiewicz' words are aimed at 'those souls who are the best tempered, the most noble, the strongest, those who communicate with Divinity, [and] reserve all their strength for action rather than for words' (**Reading 17**). The poet who seeks change, Mickiewicz exhorts, must align himself with the progressive forces in Europe (France, not Germany), in order to bring about the Heavenly Kingdom that was much promised by the Church, but now is only achievable through other means: radical politics, the promotion of national identity, and the cultural movement that will inspire both: Romanticism.

The writings of Blake and Shelley, Novalis and Mickiewicz exude a confidence, a faith in the power of the mind to meet the world and to mould it to its vision. Yet there was also a more hesitant, self-analytical side to the Romantic imagination, where this almost triumphalist sense of purpose was displaced or, at the very least, significantly modified by, a form of self-consciousness that was aware, at times painfully so (as, for example, Coleridge was) of the unbridgeable gap between self and world. A. W. Schlegel addressed precisely this aspect of the Romantic mind in his famous lecture of 1808 (*see* **Reading 8**), where he describes that quintessential Romantic disposition, *Sehnsucht*, a longing for that which cannot be attained. It was, however, the great dramatist and theoretician, Friedrich von Schiller, who most clearly defined this intellectual predicament in his study *On Naive and Sentimental Poetry* (1795–96). Here, Schiller identified two types of poet: the 'naive' and the 'sentimental'. The 'naive', Schiller argued, 'only follows simple nature and his feelings, and restricts himself merely to reproducing the external world, he can only have a single relationship to his subject.' The naive poet is thus secure in his world view; he is unpremeditative, someone who creates out of a natural vitality and instinctual sense of the security of self. The 'sentimental' poet, on the other hand, is the modern type of poet. He is introspective, self-analytical, an artist who requires a theoretical framework in order to make sense of the activity in which he is involved. As Schiller explains, in words that strikingly anticipate the self-image of the Modernists almost a century later: 'The sentimental poet is thus always involved in two conflicting intellectual and emotional states – with actuality as a limit and with his mind as infinitude; and the mixture of feelings that he excites will always bear a trace of these dual origins' (**Reading 18**).

Some Romantic writers, such as John Keats, were, as the latter's notion of 'negative capability' shows, aware of the problem, and glad that they belonged to the 'naive' rather than 'sentimental' type; but there were others who found it necessary to find a way out of this impasse. Friedrich Schlegel, younger brother of August Wilhelm, was one. Like Schiller, he also recognized that the quest for personal and aesthetic authenticity that many Romantic writers sought, and which many had hoped to see realized in transcendent (Novalis) or natural (Wordsworth) paradigms, was highly problematic, and that their search for intellectual surety beyond stale convention was doomed to failure. In the final analysis, a poet cannot choose not to know. On the contrary, the way forward was precisely to recognize this impasse. As Schlegel explained in his *Aphorisms* (1797–1800), the Romantic project could never be a finished object, but should be viewed as the product of a hermeneutic process that is always in the making. It was a multifaceted ideal rather than a single reality, and could contain a variety of positions on the world. Some Romantic writers might be naively 'natural', others might be analytical; some might exude a confidence that they had secured the proper image of their desired object, while others would remain tentative, hesitatingly self-conscious, and proud of their failure to achieve totality. For Schlegel, the sole means available for an author to avoid dissolution and debilitating inactivity between these various positions (an aporia already signalled in Schiller's famous distinction between the 'naive' and the 'sentimental') was irony, a mental facility that could transcend or sublimate ('*aufheben*' was the term that would later become famous) this dichotomy by finding a superior intellectual vantage point capable of holding these tensions in some sort of equilibrium. Irony would allow the Romantic poet to act and write *as if* he were 'naive'; but he would do so in a self-conscious, 'sentimental' way. As Schlegel explained in one of his *Athenäum* fragments, irony alone makes possible 'an absolute synthesis of absolute antitheses, the continually self-generating exchange of two conflicting thoughts'

(**Reading 19**). In Schlegel's concept of irony, the Romantic mind reaches a stage of epistemological sophistication that will find its apogee in the ambitious Idealist philosophy of Friedrich Wilhelm Hegel. In Hegel's *Phenomenology of the Spirit* (1807), self-consciousness is no longer condemned to that sad path inwards, a victim of its own achieved introspection, but has now returned as consciousness of consciousness, and learned to recognize itself as both subject *and* object, as a defining presence within the material culture of community and world.

1

---

## 'A new knowledge of my real self and my character'

Jean-Jacques Rousseau: *Reveries of a Solitary Walker* (1782)

*The main works of Jean-Jacques Rousseau (1712–78) were* Discourse on the Sciences and Arts *(1750),* The New Héloïse *(1761),* Émile *and* The Social Contract *(both 1762), and* The Confessions *(2 vols: 1782 and 1789). Rousseau articulated a number of tenets that were to remain central to the Romantic world view: a belief in the superiority of nature over society, of feeling over reason, of natural justice over the law, and of pantheistic religion over that of the Church. His* Reveries of a Solitary Walker, *written between 1776 and 1778 but not published until 1782 (four years after the author's death), reveals Rousseau at his most introspective. In its nine short sections (each devoted to a separate walk), Rousseau ranges over a variety of subjects, from the unpredictability of personal relations to the emotionally healing value of empathy with nature, from speculations on the divide between public and private morality to problems of botanical classification; but it is at all times the feeling, questioning, self-analytical Rousseau himself who is the real subject. In the following passage, taken from the final pages of the first walk, Rousseau outlines the nature of his project, projecting it as a vehicle not only for the recovery of past experiences, but also for the exploration of past and present states of mind.*

I am devoting my final days to a study of myself, preparing a personal account that I will soon deliver. I wish to give myself over entirely to the pleasure of conversing with my soul, since that is the one thing that

---

**Source:** Jean-Jacques Rousseau, *Les Rêveries du promeneur solitaire* (Paris: Garnier-Flammarion, 1964), pp. 39–42. **Standard translation:** *The Reveries of the Solitary Walker*, translated, with preface, notes, and an interpretive essay by Charles E. Butterworth (New York: New York University Press, 1979). **Further reading:** Huntington Williams, *Rousseau and Romantic Autobiography* (Oxford: Oxford University Press, 1983), esp. pp. 166–80 and 214–17.

cannot be taken away from me. If by reflecting upon my inner life, I am able to put it into better order and correct the evil that may remain there, my meditations will not have been entirely in vain, and although I may be good for nothing on this earth, I shall not have completely wasted my last days. The leisurely moments of my daily walks were often filled with charming moments of contemplation, most of which I now regret to having lost from memory. But I will set down in writing those that I can still summon up, and whenever I read them in the future, I will experience the pleasure anew. I will forget my unhappiness, my persecutors and my disgrace, while thinking of the prize my heart deserved.

These pages will be no more than a formless diary of my reveries. There will be much concerning myself in them, because a solitary person who thinks a lot necessarily reflects a great deal upon things concerning himself. But all the other thoughts that come to mind whilst I'm out walking will also find their place here. I will say what I thought just as it came to me, with as little connection as the ideas of yesterday have with those of today. But a new knowledge of my real self and character will result from this process through an understanding of those feelings and thoughts that my spirit daily feeds upon in this strange state that I am in. The following pages can, then, be seen as an appendix to my *Confessions*; but I do not call them that, for I no longer feel that I have anything to say that merits this title. My heart has been purified in the crucible of adversity, and I can scarcely find, examining it carefully, any remaining trace of reprehensible inclinations. What could I have still to confess when all earthly affection has been torn from my grasp? I have nothing to praise or condemn myself for; from now on, I am of no significance to my fellow creatures, and this is the way it has to be, since I no longer have any real relationship with them, nor any social contact. No longer being able to do any good which does not turn into evil, no longer being able to act without harming others or myself, my only duty now is to stand apart from society, and this I will do as much as it lies within my power. But although my body is inactive my mind remains alert, and continues to produce feelings and thoughts; indeed, its inner and moral life seems to have grown more intense with the loss of all earthly and temporal interests. My body is now no more than an encumbrance and an obstacle, and, right from the outset, I have done all I can to separate myself from it.

Such a strange situation surely deserves to be examined and described, and to this task I shall devote my last days of leisure. To do it successfully, I would have to proceed in an orderly and methodological manner; but I'm incapable of such work, and, indeed, this would divert me from my true goal, which is to make me aware of the modifications of my soul and their permutations. I shall perform on myself something like those sorts of tests that scientists conduct upon the air in order to gauge its daily condition. I will apply the barometer to my soul, and these measurements, carefully executed and repeated over a long period of time, may well provide results that are as accurate as theirs. But I won't extend my enterprise that far. I shall content myself with keeping a register of my tests, without trying to reduce them to a system. My enterprise is like Montaigne's, but my goal is entirely different, for he wrote his *Essays* only for others to read, whilst I am writing my *Reveries* for myself alone. If in my old age, as death approaches, I remain (as I hope) in the same mood as I am today, reading the reveries will recall to me the pleasures that I had in writing them. They will, also, by reviving past times, so to speak, add a second dimension to my existence. In spite of other people, I shall, thus, still be able to enjoy the conviviality of society, and in my decrepitude shall live with my earlier self as I might with a younger friend.

I wrote my first *Confessions* and my *Dialogues* in a state of constant anxiety, worried about how best to keep them away from the rapacious hands of my persecutors, so that I would be able, if possible, to pass them on to future generations. The same disquiet no longer torments me as I write these pages. I know that it would be useless, and the desire to be better understood has been extinguished in my heart; I am capable now only of a profound indifference to the fate of my writings and to testimonies regarding my innocence, which perhaps have gone forever anyway. Let them spy upon what I am doing, let them be alarmed by these pages; they can seize them, suppress them, falsify them – from now on all that is a matter of indifference to me. I will neither hide them nor publicise them. If, during my lifetime, they take them away from me, they can't take away from the pleasure of having written them, nor the memory of what they contain, nor the solitary meditations which inspired them, and whose source can be extinguished only when my soul has been. If from the moment of my first disasters, I had not tried to resist fate, but had taken the course that I take today, all those attacks against me, all the frightful intrigues, would have had little effect, and these people would not have troubled my soul with all their plots any more than they can trouble it in the future, should these plots be successful. Let them enjoy my disgrace to the full; they will not unsettle me in the conviction of my innocence, nor prevent me from spending my final days in peace, in spite of them.

# 2

# 'The vital root of genius'

## Edward Young: *Conjectures on Original Composition* (1759)

*Edward Young (1683–1765) was one of the major figures of the pre-Romantic movement. Although largely known for his* The Complaint, or Night Thoughts on Life, Death and Immortality *(1742–46), a series of nine interconnecting verse sequences, which offer now melancholic, now inspirational meditations on life, death and resurrection, it was his* Conjectures on Original Composition *(1759) which exerted the greatest influence upon the direction of Romantic theory. Young's essay, written in the form of a letter to Samuel Richardson, constitutes an erudite and lengthy disquisition on the aesthetic inauthenticity of imitation in the arts (he is thinking here of neo-Classicism and its dependency on fixed rules of composition drawn from Classical sources, such as Aristotle). True art requires originality, and that can only be drawn from internal not external sources, for, as he explains in one famous passage: 'an original may be said to be of a vegetable nature, it rises spontaneously from the vital root of genius; it grows, it is not made: imitations are often a sort of manufacture wrought up by those mechanics, art and labour, out of pre-existent materials not their own.' The artist should certainly draw upon past masters, but not to the detriment of his own individual 'vision'.*

Modern writers have a choice to make, and therefore have a merit in their power. They may soar in the regions of liberty, or move in the soft fetters of easy imitation; and imitation has as many plausible reasons to urge as pleasure had to offer to Hercules. Hercules made the choice of an hero, and so became immortal.

Yet let not assertors of classical excellence imagine, that I deny the tribute it so well deserves. He that admires not ancient authors betrays a secret he would conceal, and tells the world that he does not understand them. Let us be as far from neglecting, as from copying, their admirable compositions: sacred be their rights, and inviolable their fame. Let our understanding feed on theirs; they afford the noblest nourishment; but let them nourish, not annihilate, our own. When we read, let our imagination kindle at their charms; when we write, let our judgement shut them out of our thoughts; treat even Homer himself as his royal

**Source:** Edward Young, *The Complete Works, Poetry and Prose*, edited by James Nichols (London: William Tegg and Co., 1854, reprinted by Georg Olms Verlagsbuchhandlung, Hildesheim, 1968), pp. 554, 557–8, 559 and 564. **Further reading:** Harold Foster, *Edward Young: The Poet of the Night Thoughts, 1683–1765* (Alburgh Harleston: Erskine Press, 1986), pp. 302–25.

admirer was treated by the cynic, – bid him stand aside, nor shade our composition from the beams of our own genius; for nothing original can rise, nothing immortal can ripen, in any other sun.

*'Genius' is the key word here; and Young devotes much of his essay to elaborating both the nature and the provenance of those who have partaken 'of something Divine'.*

There is something in poetry beyond prose reason; there are mysteries in it not to be explained, but admired, which render mere prose-men infidels to their divinity. And here pardon a second paradox: namely, 'Genius often then deserves most to be praised when it is most sure to be condemned; that is, when its excellence, from mounting high, to weak eyes is quite out of sight'.

If I might speak farther of learning and genius, I would compare genius to virtue, and learning to riches. As riches are most wanted where there is least virtue, so learning where there is least genius. As virtue without much riches can give happiness, so genius without much learning can give renown. As it is said, in Terence, *Pecuniam negligere interdum maximum est lucrum*, so, to neglect of learning genius sometimes owes its greater glory. Genius, therefore, leaves but the second place, among men of letters, to the learned. It is their merit and ambition to fling light on the works of genius, and point out its charms. We most justly reverence their informing radius for that favour; but we must much more admire the radiant stars pointed out by them.

A star of the first magnitude among the moderns was Shakespeare; among the ancients, Pindar; who, as Vossius tells us, boasted of his no-learning, calling himself the eagle, for his flight above it. And such genii as these may, indeed, have much reliance on their own native powers. For genius may be compared to the natural strength of the body; learning to the superinduced accoutrements of arms. If the first is equal to the proposed exploit, the latter rather encumbers, than assists; rather retards, than promotes, the victory. *Sacer nobis inest Deus*, says Seneca. With regard to the moral world, conscience – with regard to the intellectual, genius – is that god within. Genius can set us right in composition without the rules of the learned, as conscience sets us right in life without the laws of the land; this, singly, can make us good, as men; that, singly, as writers, can sometimes make us great.

I say, 'sometimes', because there is a genius which stands in need of learning to make it shine. Of genius there are two species, an earlier, and a later; or call them infantine, and adult. An adult genius comes out of nature's hand; as Pallas out of Jove's head, at full growth, and mature: Shakespeare's genius was of this kind: on the contrary, Swift stumbled at the threshold, and set out for distinction on feeble knees. His was an infantine genius; a genius, which, like other infants, must be nursed and educated, or it will come to naught. Learning is its nurse and tutor; but this nurse may overlay with an indigested load, which smothers common sense; and this tutor may mislead with pedantic prejudice, which vitiates the best understanding.

*As Young explains, in a series of inspirational images that were to become recurrent tropes within the Romantic aesthetic, the gifts of 'genius' cannot be learnt; they are by their very nature intuitive and innate:*

By the praise of genius we detract not from learning; we detract not from the value of gold by saying that a diamond has greater still. He who disregards learning, shows that he wants its aid; and he that overvalues it, shows that its aid has done him harm. Over-valued, indeed, it cannot be, if genius as to composition is valued more. Learning we thank, genius we revere; that gives us pleasure, this gives us rapture; that informs, this inspires, and is itself inspired; for genius is from heaven, learning from man: this sets us above the low and illiterate; that, above the learned and polite. Learning is borrowed knowledge; genius is knowledge innate, and quite our own.

*Above all, Young decides, genius resides in that dark core of the self, being a product of those 'dormant, unsuspected abilities' that are impervious to the rational persuasions of the mind or intellect. He concludes this part of his discussion by exhorting the would-be author to make contact with this deeper self:*

Therefore dive deep into thy bosom; learn the depth, extent, bias, and full fort of thy mind; contract full intimacy with the stranger within thee; excite and cherish every spark of intellectual light and heat, however smothered under former negligence, or scattered through the dull, dark mass of common thoughts; and, collecting them into a body, let thy genius rise (if a genius thou hast) as the sun from chaos; and if I should then say, like an Indian, 'Worship it', (though too bold,) yet should I say little more than my second rule enjoins; namely, 'Reverence thyself'.

# 3

# 'Touched by divinity'

## Johann Gottfried Herder: 'Shakespeare' (1773)

*'When I think of a man who most corresponds to the following description — "High upon the edge of a cliff he sits, at his feet there are storms, tempests and the roaring of the waves, but his head is amongst the bright beams of the firmament" — I think of Shakespeare,' noted Johann Gottfried Herder (1744–1803) in the opening lines of his epochal essay on the great English dramatist. Herder was one of the leading voices in the dynamic, iconoclastic German variation of pre-Romanticism known as* Sturm und Drang *(Storm and Stress). In works such as* On Recent German Literature: Fragments *(1767),* Critical Forests, or Reflections on the Science and Art of the Beautiful *(1769),* Essay on the Origin of Language *(1772), and* Volkslieder *[Folk Songs] (1778–9), he emphasized the importance played by myth, symbol and indigenous custom in the development of national cultures. The essay on Shakespeare appeared in 1773 in a work entitled* On German Manners and Art *[Von deutscher Art und Kunst], a collection edited by Herder, which also included his eulogy of Ossian, and Goethe's essay on the style of the Gothic architecture of the North. Herder's image of Shakespeare as the great Nordic genius who, transcending the formal rules of drama, drew deeply upon the popular traditions and art-forms of his people influenced not only the Romantics but subsequent generations, who found the German Romantic's elevation of the bard to the level of an artistic godhead entirely appropriate. Midway through his essay, Herder addresses himself to the source of Shakespeare's plays.*

Shakespeare inherited no choric tradition, but he did have puppet plays and the chronicles. And he was able to make out of these puppet plays and chronicles, out of this raw clay, the noble creation that we see alive before us today! There was no simple folk or national character to be found, but rather people from a multitude of backgrounds, walks of life, temperaments, races and languages. It would have been futile to have bemoaned the demise of the former; so, he brought thus the various estates and their representatives, the peoples and their languages, the king and his fool, the fool and the king, into an artistic whole. He did not inherit a simple view of history, or of plot and action; he took history as he found it, and with the power of his creativity shaped the most diverse

**Source:** *Herders Werke in fünf Bänden* (Berlin and Weimar: Aufbau Verlag, 1969), vol. 2, pp. 247–8 and 250–1. There is no standard translation. **Further reading:** Robert E. Norton, *Herder's Aesthetics and the European Enlightenment* (New York: Cornell University Press, 1991), esp. pp. 75–81.

material into a wonderful unity, into something that we call, if not 'plot' in the Greek meaning of the word, 'action', in the sense that the word was used in the Middle Ages and is used now in the modern period under the designation of 'events' ('événements'), or 'noteworthy happenings'. Oh, Aristotle, if you came back, how would you canonize this new Sophocles; you would write a new theory to account for him, a theory that his countrymen, Home and Hurd, Pope and Johnson, have not yet written! You would take pleasure in drawing a line, as between the points of a triangle, in each of his plays between plot, character, beliefs and expressions, points which would meet at the top in one point of purpose: perfection! You would say to Sophocles: 'Paint the holy image of this altar. And you, Oh Bard from the North, every wall in this temple, paint with your immortal frescos!'

Allow me to continue as his commentator and rhapsodist, for I am closer to Shakespeare than I am to the Greeks. If in the latter plot dominates, so the former deals with events, with action. If with the latter one type of character reigns, in the former all types of character, estates and ways of living are made to combine into the main motifs of his concert. If with the Greeks a melodious fine language can be heard, as if it is sounding out from a higher atmosphere, with Shakespeare we find a medley of languages drawn from every age, from all people and types of people, from him who is the interpreter of nature in all her tongues. And in their so different ways, both touched by divinity? And if those Greeks depicted and instructed and moved and educated, so too does Shakespeare instruct, move and educate Nordic people! When I read him, it is as if the theatre, the actors and the scenery all disappear. All that remains, blowing through the storms of the ages, are a few pages from the book of events, from the Providence of the world – particular features of all the peoples, of estates, of souls, the most varied and most isolated players on life's stage. All are (as we all are, in the hands of our Maker) ignorant, blind tools, which have become the totality of a theatrical image, a dramatic event of great proportions, which only the poet can survey. Who can think of a greater poet of Nordic mankind in this age of ours!

> But it was not the Greek dramatists (whom Herder essentially admired) who attracted his ire, but the French neo-Classicists, in whose hands the original dramatic forms, particularly the three unities of time, place and action, had, according to Herder, atrophied into a set of stultifying rules that had nothing in common with how space and time are experienced in reality:

That time and place, like the husk around the kernel, must always go together, should not even be worthy of consideration; and yet it has formed the shrillest clamour against him. If Shakespeare has found that God-like stroke of bringing an entire world of the most disparate scenes into a single event, then naturally it belongs exactly to the truth of the events described that he should imaginatively reconstruct time and place whenever it was necessary, so that they contribute to dramatic illusion. Have we all not had times when we have become quite indifferent to the petty considerations of time and place, particularly on those occasions when one's entire mind has been touched, formed and changed, as in youth, at moments of passion, indeed in all one's activities in life? It is certainly place, time and the plenitude of external circumstances that give our entire actions shape, duration and existence; but any child, youth, lover, or man in the course of his activities knows that local circumstance, that the how and where and when, can be occluded from his vision without it, in any way, damaging the faculty of his mind. It is here that Shakespeare is the greatest master, exactly because he is only and always the servant of nature. When he conceives the actions of his dramas, and turns them around in his head, so places and times turn around with them. From the scenes and periods chosen from throughout the world, there emerge, as if propelled by a law of fate, only those which impart to the feeling of the plot the most powerful, the most ideal aspect, in circumstances where the most singular, the most precarious circumstances most firmly support the illusion of truth, where changes of time and place, over which the poet alone exerts control, proclaim with the greatest confidence: 'Here is no artist; here is the creator, the history of the world!'

4

---

## 'Irresistible simplicity and nature'

### James Macpherson: *The Works of Ossian* (1765)

*James Macpherson (1736–96) was the editor (some might say inventor) of the poetry of the Celtic bard Ossian, whose work he published in* Fragments of Ancient Poetry, collected in the Highlands of Scotland, and translated from the Galic or Erse Language *(1760),* Fingal *(1762),* Temora *(1763), and* The Works of Ossian *(1765). Macpherson offered these works to the public as simple translations of (in the words of the original preface) the 'genuine remains of ancient Scottish poetry', as a body of work that had been originally composed by Ossian, and*

---

**Source:** *The Poems of Ossian and Related Works*, edited by Howard Gaskill with an introduction by Fiona J. Stafford (Edinburgh: Edinburgh University Press, 1996), pp. 213–15. **Further reading:** Fiona J. Stafford, *The Sublime Savage: A Study of James Macpherson and the Poems of Ossian* (Edinburgh: Edinburgh University Press, 1988).

*then passed down through the generations by word of mouth. In spite of the doubts expressed regarding its authenticity, this was, indeed, how the poetry of Ossian was read by a generation of readers throughout Europe, who, from Goethe to Napoleon, were impressed by the brooding melancholic and heroic sentiment of these epic narratives, and the way they combined elegiac depth with an apparent lack of stylistic premeditation. In the dissertation that accompanied the second volume of the* Works, *Macpherson established a genealogy for the legendary bard and his writing, emphasizing its autochthonic status, the fact that it has grown out of the indigenous folk culture of the Highlands, a culture concerned with tradition, ancestry and tribal history. In his presentation of Ossian, Macpherson anticipates some of the main tropes of Romantic theory: the valorization of the emotive effect of art and its source in local custom; its freedom from rule and convention, particularly as imposed by 'strangers'; and the artist's instinctive identification with nature. Macpherson begins this section by constructing a primitive Arcadian utopia for the native culture of the Highlands: 'The seats of the Highland chiefs were', he tells us, 'neither disagreeable nor inconvenient. Surrounded with mountains and hanging woods, they were covered from the inclemency of the weather. Near them generally ran a pretty large river, which, discharging itself not far off, into an arm of the sea, or extensive lake, swarmed with variety of fish. The woods were stocked with wildfowl; and the heaths and the mountains behind them were the natural seat of the red deer and roe.'*

In this rural kind of magnificence, the Highland chiefs lived, for many ages. At a distance from the seat of government, and secured, by the inaccessibleness of their country, they were free and independent. As they had little communication with strangers, the customs of their ancestors remained amongst them, and their language retained its original purity. Naturally fond of military fame, and remarkably attached to the memory of their ancestors, they delighted in traditions and songs, concerning the exploits of their nation, and especially of their own particular families. A succession of bards was retained in every clan, to hand down the memorable actions of their forefathers. As the era of Fingal, on account of Ossian's poems was the most remarkable, and his chiefs the most renowned names in tradition, the bards took care to place one of them in the genealogy of every great family. – That part of the poems, which concerned the hero who was regarded as ancestor, was preserved, as an authentic record of the antiquity of the family, and was delivered down, from race to race, with wonderful exactness.

The bards themselves, in the mean time, were not idle. They erected their immediate patrons into heroes, and celebrated them in their songs. As the circle of their knowledge was narrow, their ideas were confined in proportion. A few happy expressions, and the manners they represent, may please those that understand the language; their obscurity and inaccuracy would disgust in a translation. – It was chiefly for this reason, that I kept wholly to the compositions of Ossian, in my former and present publication. As he acted in a more extensive sphere, his ideas are more noble and universal; neither has he so many of those peculiarities, which are only understood in a certain period or country. The other bards have their beauties, but not in that species of composition in which Ossian excels. Their rhimes, only calculated to kindle a martial spirit among the vulgar, afford very little pleasure to genuine taste. This observation only regards their poems of the heroic kind; in every other species of poetry they are more successful. They express the tender melancholy of desponding love, with irresistible simplicity and nature. So well adapted are the sounds of the words to the sentiments, that, even without any knowledge of the language, they pierce and dissolve the heart. Successful love is expressed with peculiar tenderness and elegance. In all their compositions, except the heroic, which was solely calculated to animate the vulgar, they give us the genuine language of the heart, without any of those affected ornaments of phraseology, which, though intended to beautify sentiments, divest them of their natural force. The ideas, it is confessed, are too local to be admired, in another language; to those who are acquainted with the manners they represent, and the scenes they describe, they must afford the highest pleasure and satisfaction.

It was the locality of his description and sentiment, that, probably, kept Ossian so long in the obscurity of an almost lost language. His ideas, though remarkably proper for the times in which he lived, are so contrary to the present advanced state of society, that more than a common mediocrity of taste is required, to relish his poems as they deserve. – Those who alone were capable to make a translation were, no doubt, conscious of this, and chose rather to admire their poet in secret, than see him received, with coldness, in an English dress.

These were long my own sentiments, and accordingly, my first translations, from the Galic, were merely accidental. The publication, which soon after followed, was so well received, that I was obliged to promise to my friends a larger collection. In a journey through the Highlands and isles, and, by the assistance of correspondents, since I left that country, all the genuine remains of the works of Ossian have come to my hands. In the preceding volume compleat poems were only given. Unfinished and imperfect poems were purposely omitted; even some pieces were rejected, on account of their length, and others, that they might not break in upon that thread of connection, which subsists in the lesser compositions, subjoined to *Fingal*. – That the comparative merit of pieces was not regarded, in the selection, will readily appear to those who shall read, attentively, the present collection. – It is animated with the same spirit of poetry, and the same strength of sentiment is sustained throughout.

# 5

# 'The Nordic imagination'

## Madame de Staël, *On Literature* (1800)

*The main works of Anne-Louise-Germaine Necker, Madame de Staël (1766–1817), were the novels* Delphine *(1803) and* Corinne *(1807), and two theoretical treatises:* On Literature *(1800) and* On Germany *(1810). In* On Germany, *de Staël had followed her mentor, A. W. Schlegel, in viewing Romanticism as a cultural paradigm whose origins lay in the Christian chivalric traditions of the Middle Ages, and not, as with Classicism, in those of pagan Greece and Rome. In her earlier book* On Literature *(or, to give it its full title,* On Literature Considered in Relation to Social Institutions*), de Staël had given this famous dichotomy an even firmer geographical dimension, anchoring Romanticism in the customs and values of Northern Europe.*

There exist, in my opinion, two literatures which are quite distinct: one that comes from the South and one from the North; Homer is the prime source of the former, and Ossian of the latter. The Greeks, the Romans, the Italians, the Spanish, and the French of the century of Louis XIV are exponents of that type of literature that I will call the literature of the South. The works of the English and Germans, and certain works by the Danish and the Swedish, must be classified as literature of the North, which began with the Scottish bards, the fables of Iceland and the poetry of Scandinavia. Before characterising English and German writers, it seems to me to be necessary to consider, in general terms, the principal differences between the literatures of these two hemispheres.

English and German writers have undoubtedly often imitated ancients. They have drawn some useful lessons from their rich study; but the original beauties of their work, which bears the imprint of Northern mythology, possess certain common traits, a certain poetic grandeur, which first appeared in Ossian. The English poets, it might be said, are remarkable for their philosophical spirit; it manifests itself in all their works: but Ossian offers us few theoretical ideas; he simply narrates a series of events and impressions. My response to that objection is that the most common images and thoughts in Ossian are those that recall the

**Source:** Madame La Baronne de Staël-Holstein, *Oeuvres complètes*, 2 vols (Paris: Firmin Didot, 1871), vol. 1, pp. 252–4. **Standard translation:** *An Extraordinary Woman: Selected Writings of Germaine de Staël*, translated by Vivian Folkenflik (New York: Columbia University Press, 1987), pp. 172–200. **Further reading:** Charlotte Hogsett, *The Literary Existence of Germaine de Staël* (Carbondale: Southern Illinois University Press, 1987).

brevity of life, respect for the departed, glorification of their memory, and the adoration for those who have left this life by those that remain. If the poet has not added to these sentiments any moral maxims or philosophical reflections that is because, in that period, the human mind was not yet capable of the abstract ideas required to draw such conclusions. But the songs of Ossian arouse the imagination in such a way as to give rise to profound reflections upon life.

The poetry of melancholy is the closest in spirit to philosophy. Sadness goes deeper into the character and destiny of man than any other mood. English poets, who are the heirs of the Scottish bards, have incorporated into their portrayals the reflections and ideas that have been inspired by such portrayals; but they have retained the Nordic imagination, which delights in the seashore, in the sound of the wind, the wild heaths: precisely that which transports one into the future, towards another world, the soul borne down by destiny. The imagination of Northern man soars beyond this earth, whose confines it inhabits; it soars through the clouds that border their horizon, and which seem to form some dark passage from life into eternity.

*Although, for de Staël, the literature of the North has a uniquely supernatural dimension, it also possesses an inner resilience and fortitude that is the product of its geopolitical origins. As she explains:*

The peoples of the North are less concerned with pleasure than with pain, and their imaginations have become more fecund accordingly. The spectacle of nature affects them deeply; and the effect it makes is precisely the one that displays itself in their climate, which is always sombre and misty. Undoubtedly, this tendency towards melancholy might vary according to the material circumstances of individual lives; but this disposition alone bears the stamp of the national temperament. As with individuals, it is not necessary to search hard in a people for its characteristic trait: everything else may be the result of a thousand different accidents, but the former alone constitutes its true being.

The poetry of the North is more suited than that of the South to the spirit of a free people. The first known authors of the literature of the South, the Athenians, amongst all the peoples of the world, jealously guarded their independence. Nevertheless, it was easier to press into servitude the Greeks than the people of the North. Love of the arts, the beauty of the climate, all the many joys provided for the Athenians were accepted as compensation. Independence was the one and only happiness for the Northern nations. A certain haughtiness of spirit, a certain other-worldliness, brought about by the harshness of nature and the gloominess of the sky, made servitude insufferable; and long before the theory of constitutions and the advantages of representative government were known in England, that warrior spirit, extolled with such enthusiasm in the poetry of the Gaels and the Scandinavians, had endowed man with an elevated notion of his personal strength and will-power. Independence existed for the individual before liberty was established for all.

During the Renaissance, philosophy began in the Northern nations, in whose religious customs the rational mind found infinitely less prejudice to oppose than in those of the Southern peoples. The ancient poetry of the North possesses far less superstition than Greek mythology does. There are a few dogmas and a few absurd fables in the Edda; but the religious ideas of the North almost always sit well with reason in its elevated mode. The shadows that crouch in the gloom are nothing but memories animated by startling imagery.

The emotions that Ossian's poems give rise to might be reproduced in any nation, because the means that they use to move us are taken entirely from nature; but it would require a prodigious talent to introduce, without affectation, Greek mythology into French poetry. In general, nothing is so cold and so artificial as religious dogmas transported into a country where they can only be received as ingenious metaphors. The poetry of the North is rarely allegorical; its effects can strike the imagination without the help of local superstitions. Ardent enthusiasm and pure exaltation could likewise belong to any nation; that is the result of true poetic inspiration whose sentiment lies within every heart, but whose expression requires the gifts of a genius. It sustains a celestial dream-world, which inclines one to love the countryside and solitude; it can often incline the heart towards religious ideas, and must excite amongst those privileged beings the devotion of virtue and the inspiration of elevated thoughts.

6

## 'Inwards lies the path of mystery'

### Novalis: *Fragments* (1798)

*Novalis was the pseudonym of Friedrich von Hardenberg (1772–1801), whose main works include the historical-utopian tract* Christianity and Europe *(1799), the poems* Hymns to the Night *(1800), and the* Bildungsroman *(novel of personal development)* Henry from Ofterdingen *(published posthumously in 1802). Novalis' contribution to the formation of Romantic theory in Germany was*

**Source:** Novalis, *Werke und Briefe*, edited by Alfred Kelletat (Munich: Winkler-Verlag, 1953), pp. 530, 439, 530–1, 342, 479, 480, 465 and 351. There is no standard translation. **Further reading:** William Arctander O'Brien, *Novalis: Signs of Revolution* (Durham, NC: Duke University Press, 1995), esp. pp. 130–61.

*largely made through a series of pithy aphorisms known as* Pollen [Blütenstaub], *published between 1798 and 1800 in the journal* Athenäum, *edited by the brothers Schlegel, and an unpublished collection,* New Fragments, *written slightly later. In their terse form and in their expansive content, Novalis' fragments capture the Romantics' conviction that truth can only be grasped in brief but intense flights of the imagination* [Phantasie], *as* aperçus, *sudden disclosures, or epiphanies. Novalis' aphorisms have a vigour and a heuristic thrust that belong to the early days of the Romantic movement, when the very term needed clear and assertive definition.*

### New Fragment No. 470

The art of genial estrangement, of making an object seem strange and yet familiar and attractive, that is the poetic of Romanticism.

### New Fragment No. 86

The world must be romanticized. In that way, one will find its original meaning again. Romanticization is nothing other than a qualitative empowerment. In this process, the lower self merges with its higher state, just as we ourselves partake of such a sequence of empowerments. This process has as yet to be identified. By giving the everyday a higher sense, the familiar an unusual aspect, the known the value of the unknown, the finite the semblance of the infinite, thus do I romanticize it. And the process is the reverse for higher things, for the unknown, mystical, the eternal. These become through this contact logarithmitized. They acquire a common designation. Romantic philosophy. *Lingua romana.* Alternating elevation and abasement.

### New Fragment No. 474

A novel must be poetry through and through. Poetry, indeed, like philosophy, is the harmonious mood of our temperament, in which everything becomes more beautiful, where every thing possesses its fitting aspect – and everything finds its appropriate accompaniment and environment. In a truly poetic book all seems so natural – and yet so wondrous. One might believe that it could not be any other way, as if one had been just daydreaming up to that point and was only now awakening to the real significance of life. All remembrance and prescience seem to come precisely from this source. One often feels that just living in the present, on those occasions when one is trapped within illusions – lonely hours, where one is, so to speak, present within all the objects that one views, and experiences the unending, incomprehensible, simultaneous feeling of an harmonious plurality.

### Pollen No. 16

The imagination projects the future world either up into the heights or down into the depths, or into metempsychosis. We dream of travels through the universe: but is not the universe within us? The depths of our spirit remain unknown to us. – Inwards lies the path of mystery. Within us or nowhere is eternity with its worlds, the past and future. The external world is a world of shadows, which casts its shadows on to the realm of light. At present, it is true, that inner world seems to us so dark, lonely and without form, but how different will it appear when this darkness has gone, and those shadowy forms have been removed. We will be able to enjoy the world more than ever, for our spirit has become ethereal.

*New Fragment* No. 272
Imagination [*Einbildungskraft*] is the marvellous sense that can replace all our other senses – and which lies so much under our own discretion. If our external senses seem to stand so entirely under mechanical laws, so is the imagination equally clearly not bound to the present and to contact with external stimulation.

*New Fragment* No. 276
The distinction between madness and truth lies in the different contexts from which they arise. Truth is connected with the absolute, positive universe. Madness is related only to certain paradoxical parts of the universe, which are elevated to absolute totalities. For that reason, madness is construed as an illness, which is always distinctive, exclusive, paradoxically and polemically staked against everything through the infinite nature of its demands and assertions.

*New Fragment* No. 206
Everything visible adheres to the invisible – the audible to the inaudible – the tactile to the non-tactile. Perhaps even the thinkable to the unthinkable.

*Pollen* No. 51
Every object that is loved forms the centre of a paradise.

# 7

# 'As the Eye is formed, such are its Powers'

## William Blake: Letter (1799)

*William Blake (1757–1827) was the great visionary poet of the Romantic movement. His main works were* Songs of Innocence *(1789),* Songs of Experience *(1794),* The Marriage of Heaven and Hell *(1790),* Milton *(1802–8) and* Jerusalem *(1804–20). His attempts to mediate between conventional notions of the religious and his own heightened, almost mystical, sense of the other-worldly largely met with incomprehension, or at least suspicion, as the following letter indicates. It was written to a benefactor, the Revd Dr John Trusler, who had commissioned Blake to produce a water-colour for publication in one of the former's many edifying religious tracts. But what Blake produced both offended and mystified its recipient. Blake's letter to Trusler brings together many of the characteristic tropes of the visionary dimension of the Romantic mind: its insistence upon the reality of the intangible world; its pantheistic conflation of imagination with nature; and (characteristically for Blake) its respect for children and the childlike perspective.*

13 Hercules Buildings
Lambeth,

August 23, 1799

REVD. SIR,

I really am sorry that you are fall'n out with the Spiritual World, Especially if I should have to answer for it. I feel very sorry that your Ideas & Mine on Moral Painting differ so much as to have made you angry with my method of Study. If I am wrong, I am wrong in good company. I had hoped your plan comprehended All Species of this Art, & Especially that you would not regret that Species which gives Existence to Every other, namely, Visions of Eternity. You say that I want somebody to Elucidate my Ideas. But you ought to know that What is Grand is necessarily obscure to Weak men. That which can be made Explicit to the Idiot is not worth my care. The wisest of the Ancients consider'd what is not too Explicit as the fittest for

**Source:** *The Letters of William Blake,* edited by Geoffrey Keynes, third edition (Oxford: Clarendon Press, 1980), pp. 8–10. **Further reading:** Morton D. Paley, *Energy and Imagination: A Study of the Development of Blake's Thought* (Oxford: Clarendon Press, 1970).

Instruction, because it rouzes the faculties to act. I name Moses, Solomon, Esop, Homer, Plato.

But as you have favor'd me with your remarks on my Design, permit me in return to defend it against a mistaken one, which is, That I have supposed Malevolence without a Cause. Is not Merit in one a Cause of Envy in another, & Serenity & Happiness & Beauty a Cause of Malevolence? But Want of Money & the Distress of A Thief can never be alledged as the Cause of his Thieving, for many honest people endure greater hardships with Fortitude. We must therefore seek the Cause elsewhere than in want of Money, for that is the Miser's passion, not the Thief's.

I have therefore proved your Reasonings Ill proportion'd, which you can never prove my figures to be; they are those of Michael Angelo, Rafael & the Antique, & of the best living Models. I perceive that your Eye is perverted by Caricature Prints, which ought not to abound so much as they do. Fun I love, but too much Fun is of all things the most loathsom. Mirth is better than Fun, & Happiness is better than Mirth. I feel that a Man may be happy in This World. And I know that This World Is a World of IMAGINATION & Vision. I see Every thing I paint In This World, but Every body does not see alike. To the eyes of a Miser a Guinea is more beautiful than the Sun, & a bag worn with the use of Money has more beautiful proportions than a Vine filled with Grapes. The tree which moves some to tears of joy is in the Eyes of others only a Green thing which stands in the way. Some see Nature all Ridicule & Deformity, & by these I shall not regulate my proportions; & Some scarce see Nature at all. But to the Eyes of the Man of Imagination, Nature is Imagination itself. As a man is, So he Sees. As the Eye is formed, such are its Powers. You certainly Mistake, when you say that the Visions of Fancy are not to be found in This World. To Me This World is all One continued Vision of Fancy or Imagination, & I feel Flatter'd when I am told so. What is it sets Homer, Virgil & Milton in so high a rank of Art? Why is the Bible more Entertaining & Instructive than any other book? Is it not because they are addressed to the Imagination, which is Spiritual Sensation, & but mediately to the Understanding or Reason? Such is True Painting, and such was alone valued by the Greeks & the best modern Artists. Consider what Lord Bacon says: 'Sense sends over to Imagination before Reason have judged, & Reason sends over to Imagination before the Decree can be acted'. See Advancemt. of Learning, Part 2, p. 47 of first Edition.

But I am happy to find a Great Majority of Fellow Mortals who can Elucidate My Visions, & Particularly they have been Elucidated by Children, who have taken a greater delight in contemplating my Pictures than I ever hoped. Neither Youth nor Childhood is Folly or

Incapacity. Some Children are Fools & so are some Old Men. But There is a vast Majority on the side of Imagination or Spiritual Sensation.

To Engrave after another Painter is infinitely more laborious than to Engrave one's own Inventions. And of the size you require my price has been Thirty Guineas, & I cannot afford to do it for less. I had Twelve for the Head I sent you as a Specimen; but after my own designs I could do at least Six times the quantity of labour in the same time, which will account for the difference of price as also that Chalk Engraving is at least six times as laborious as Aqua tinta. I have no objection to Engraving after another Artist. Engraving is the profession I was apprenticed to, & Should never have attempted to live by anything else, If orders had not come in for my Designs & Paintings, which I have the pleasure to tell you are Increasing Every Day. Thus If I am a Painter it is not to be attributed to seeking after. But I am contented whether I live by Painting or Engraving.

I am, Revd. Sir, your very obedient servant,

WILLIAM BLAKE.

8

# Romantic longing

August Wilhelm von Schlegel: *Lectures on Dramatic Art and Literature* (1808)

*August Wilhelm von Schlegel (1767–1845), whose main works include* Lectures on Fine Arts and Literature *(1801), and* Lectures on Dramatic Art and Literature *(1808), was the elder brother of Friedrich Schlegel, and the foremost exponent of Romanticism among the first, Jena school of German Romanticism. His second series of lectures (published between 1809 and 1811) were translated into French in 1813, English in 1815 and Italian in 1817, giving a powerful impetus to the development of Romanticism in those countries (Madame de Staël in France, and Coleridge in England were particular acolytes). In his first lecture, Schlegel describes how Romanticism developed out of the spiritual, inward-looking ethos of Christianity, which had reached its first artistic peak in Gothic architecture, and*

**Source:** August Wilhelm von Schlegel, *Vorlesungen über dramatische Kunst und Literatur*, edited by Edgar Lohner (Stuttgart: W. Kohlhammer, 1966), pp. 24–6. **Standard translation:** *A Course of Lectures on Dramatic Art and Literature*, translated by John Black, and revised by A. J. W. Morrison (London: Bohn, 1846). **Further reading:** Ralph W. Ewton, *The Literary Theories of August Wilhelm Schlegel* (The Hague: Mouton, 1972).

*which had come to supplant the pagan sensualism of Classical art. Schlegel argues that this development represented a deepening moment in Western culture; but it also destroyed that harmony between self and world that the Ancients enjoyed, producing an inner division that the 'modern' (Romantic) writer can only (through that characteristic Romantic emotion of 'Sehnsucht') dream of bridging.*

Since Christianity, the development of Europe since the beginning of the Middle Ages has largely been determined by the Germanic race of Nordic conquerors, who have brought new life and vigour to a degenerate human race. The severe nature of the North forces man more back into himself, but what is lost in the free development of the senses is gained, in noble souls, in an increased seriousness of spirit. Hence the genial cordiality with which the Teutonic tribes embraced Christianity, so that nowhere else did it penetrate so deeply the inner self, prove so powerful an influence, or infuse so deeply human affection.

The unsophisticated but truly heroic spirit of the Nordic conquerors combined with the sentiments of Christianity to produce Chivalry, whose purpose it was, through oaths that were regarded as holy, to prevent the practice of weapons from degenerating into a violent and base misuse of force, which could so easily have happened.

With the virtues of chivalry was associated a new and purer spirit of love, an inspired homage of true womanhood, who only now came to be revered as the pinnacle of human kind, and, maintained by religion itself through the image of the Virgin Mother, infused into all hearts a sense for the divine mystery of love.

Since Christianity did not, unlike the religious worship of earlier times, limit itself to certain external practices, but made claims upon the entire inner life of man and the deepest movements of the heart, ethereal motion, that feeling for moral independence took refuge in the realm of Honour. This was, as it were, secular morality which, existing beside the religious, was often at variance with it, but which was, nevertheless, related to it, to the extent that it never calculated consequences but consecrated unconditionally certain principles of action, and elevated them as articles of faith beyond the scrutiny of demurring reason.

Chivalry, love and honour form, together with religion itself, the subject matter of the nature poetry which, in the Middle Ages, poured forth in unbelievable profusion, and which anticipated its more artistic cultivation by the Romantic spirit. This period also had its mythology, consisting of chivalric fables and legends; but its sense of wonder and its heroism set it entirely apart from classical mythology.

Some thinkers who share a similar understanding of the identity and the origins of the moderns have traced the essence of Nordic poetry to melancholy. To this, when it is interpreted in the correct way, we have no objection.

With the Greeks, human nature was all-sufficient; they felt they had no personal deficiencies, and aspired to no state of perfection other than that which they could effectively attain through the exercise of their native energies. We, however, are taught by a higher wisdom that man, through a grievous transgression, forfeited the place for which he was originally destined, and that the sole mission of his earthly existence is to regain that lost position, which, if left solely to his own powers, he can never do. The old religion of the senses sought only outer, transient blessings; and immortality, as far as people believed in it, stood like a shadow in the dark distance, a faint dream of this bright waking life. In the Christian view of things, it is absolutely the reverse: the contemplation of the infinite has destroyed the finite; life has become shadow and darkness; and only in the beyond does the eternal day of true existence dawn. Such a religion must awaken the foreboding which slumbers in every sensitive heart into a distinct conviction that the happiness that we strive for here on this earth is unattainable; that no external object can entirely satisfy our souls, that all enjoyment is but a fleeting illusion. And when now the soul, resting, as it were, under the weeping willows of exile, breathes out its longing for its distant home, what else but melancholy can be the key-note of its songs? Hence the poetry of the ancients was one of plenitude; ours is one of longing [*Sehnsucht*]; the former stood firmly with its feet on the ground of the here and now, the latter hovers between recollection and yearning. Let me not be understood as meaning that everything flows in one single strain of lament, and that the voice of melancholy must always be the loudest one. As the austerity of tragedy was not incompatible with the joyous mentality of the Greeks, so can romantic poetry (which has arisen from the temperament that I have described above) give voice to all kinds of tone, even the most joyful; but they will, nevertheless, retain in some mysterious way traces of the sources from which they came. Feeling amongst the moderns is, in general, more intense, their imagination more ethereal, and their thinking more meditative. (In nature, it is true, the boundaries between objects flow into each other, and things are not as distinct from one another as we make out in order to convey clear notions of them.)

The Greek ideal of humanity was of a perfect union and balance between all the forces of life – a natural harmony. Modern writers, on the other hand, have become conscious of a division within themselves, which makes reaching such an ideal impossible; hence, they strive in their poetry to reconcile these two worlds, by which we feel divided, the spiritual and the sensual, and to blend them indissolubly together. Sensual impressions are to be hallowed by a mysterious union with higher feelings, while the spiritual, on the other hand, will embody its intimations or ineffable perceptions of infinity in sensuous forms drawn from the physical world.

In the art and poetry of the Greeks, we find an original and unconscious unity of form and content; amongst the moderns, at least as far as they have remained true to their original spirit, an inner interpenetration of the two is sought as a union of contrary principles. Greek art fulfilled its aim to perfection; the moderns can satisfy their longing for the infinite only by distant approximation; and, because of a certain appearance of incompletion, they run the risk of being completely misunderstood.

9

---

# 'The passions of men are incorporated with the beautiful and permanent forms of nature'

## William Wordsworth: Preface to *Lyrical Ballads* (1800)

*In spite of his later drift towards conservatism (political and poetic), William Wordsworth (1770–1850) was both the most original and the most prolific writer of the early 'school' of English Romanticism, known as the Lake School. His main works were: (with Coleridge)* Lyrical Ballads *(1798, second edition, 1800),* Poems in Two Volumes *(1807),* The Excursion *(1814) and* The Prelude *(1850). It was not only the substantive qualities of Wordsworth's verse (its demotic subject matter, its unadorned vocabulary and colloquial speech rhythms) that were new; behind his writing existed a theory of poetic creation which, in arguing for the psychological fluidity and (at least) partial indeterminacy of the imaginative process, opened up insights into the creative act that subsequent figures, such as Shelley, among others, would more fully develop. In the famous preface to the second edition of the* Lyrical Ballads, *Wordsworth defended both the goals of his poetic and his methodology.*

The principal object, then, proposed in these Poems was to choose incidents and situations from common life, and to relate or describe them, throughout, as far as was possible in a selection of language really used by men, and, at the same time, to throw over them a certain colouring of imagination, whereby ordinary things should be presented to the mind in an unusual aspect; and, further, and above all, to make these incidents and situations interesting by tracing in them, truly though not ostentatiously,

---

**Source:** William Wordsworth, *Poetical Works*, edited by Thomas Hutchinson, in a new edition, revised by Ernest de Selincourt (Oxford: Oxford University Press, 1969), pp. 734–6.
**Further reading:** John H. Talbot, *The Nature of Aesthetic Experience in Wordsworth* (New York: Peter Lang, 1989).

the primary laws of our nature: chiefly, as far as regards the manner in which we associate ideas in a state of excitement. Humble and rustic life was generally chosen, because, in that condition, the essential passions of the heart find a better soil in which they can attain their maturity, are less under restraint, and speak a plainer and more emphatic language; because in that condition of life our elementary feelings coexist in a state of greater simplicity, and, consequently, may be more accurately contemplated, and more forcibly communicated; because the manners of rural life germinate from those elementary feelings, and, from the necessary character of rural occupations, are more easily comprehended, and are more durable; and, lastly, because in that condition the passions of men are incorporated with the beautiful and permanent forms of nature. The language, too, of these men has been adopted (purified indeed from what appear to be its real defects, from all lasting and rational causes of dislike or disgust) because such men hourly communicate with the best objects from which the best part of language is originally derived; and because, from their rank in society and the sameness and narrow circle of their intercourse, being less under the influence of social vanity, they convey their feelings and notions in simple and unelaborated expressions. Accordingly, such a language, arising out of repeated experience and regular feelings, is a more permanent, and a far more philosophical language, than that which is frequently substituted for it by Poets, who think that they are conferring honour upon themselves and their art, in proportion as they separate themselves from the sympathies of men, and indulge in arbitrary and capricious habits of expression, in order to furnish food for fickle tastes, and fickle appetites, of their own creation.

I cannot, however, be insensible to the present outcry against the triviality and meanness, both of thought and language, which some of my contemporaries have occasionally introduced into their metrical compositions; and I acknowledge that this defect, where it exists, is more dishonourable to the Writer's own character than false refinement or arbitrary innovation, though I should contend at the same time, that it is far less pernicious in the sum of its consequences. From such verses the Poems in these volumes will be found distinguished at least by one mark of difference, that each of them has a worthy *purpose*. Not that I always began to write with a distinct purpose formally conceived; but habits of meditation have, I trust, so prompted and regulated my feelings, that my descriptions of such objects as strongly excite those feelings, will be found to carry along with them a *purpose*. If this opinion be erroneous, I can have little right to the name of Poet. For all good poetry is the spontaneous overflow of powerful feelings: and though this be true, Poems to which any value can be attached were never produced on any variety of subjects but by a man who, being possessed of more than usual organic sensibility, had also thought long and deeply. For our continued influxes of feeling are modified and directed by our thoughts, which are indeed the representatives of all our past feelings; and, as by contemplating the relation of these general representatives to each other, we discover what is really important to men, so, by the repetition and continuance of this act, our feelings will be connected with important subjects, till at length, if we be originally possessed of much sensibility, such habits of mind will be produced, that, by obeying blindly and mechanically the impulses of those habits, we shall describe objects, and utter sentiments, of such a nature, and in such connection with each other, that the understanding of the Reader must necessarily be in some degree enlightened, and his affections strengthened and purified.

> *Wordsworth then turns his attention to the style of his poems, affirming that 'the Reader will find that personifications of abstract ideas rarely occur in these volumes; and are utterly rejected, as an ordinary device to elevate the style, and raise it above prose. My purpose was to imitate, and, as far as possible, to adopt the very language of men'. Wordsworth's fervent rejection of 'poetic diction' leads him to an inevitable conclusion.*

By the foregoing quotation [from Gray's sonnet 'On the Death of Mr Richard West'] it has been shown that the language of Prose may yet be well adapted to Poetry; and it was previously asserted, that a large portion of the language of every good poem can in no respect differ from that of good Prose. We will go further. It may be safely affirmed, that there neither is, nor can be, any *essential* difference between the language of prose and metrical composition. We are fond of tracing the semblance between Poetry and Painting, and, accordingly, we call them Sisters; but where shall we find bonds of connection sufficiently strict to typify the affinity betwixt metrical and prose composition? They both speak by and to the same organs; the bodies in which both of them are clothed may be said to be of the same substance, their affections are kindred, and almost identical, not necessarily differing even in degree; Poetry sheds no tears 'such as Angels weep', but natural and human tears; she can boast of no celestial ichor that distinguishes her vital juices from those of prose; the same human blood circulates through the veins of them both.

# 10

# 'Awakening the mind's attention from the lethargy of custom'

## Samuel Taylor Coleridge: *Biographia Literaria* (1817)

*Samuel Taylor Coleridge (1772–1834) was, with 'Kubla Khan' (1797), the 'Rime of the Ancient Mariner' (1798), and 'Christabel' (1816), the author of some of the most enigmatic poems of the Romantic mind. He was also the major theoretician of the Romantic movement in England. His major theoretical work, the* Biographia Literaria, *written over a period of fifteen years, does not, perhaps, entirely succeed in bringing Coleridge's diverse interests, which range from aesthetic speculation and religious mediation through to personal reminiscences and polemical thrusts against contemporary critics, into philosophical coherence, but it does provide many insights into the contemporary formation of the Romantic mind, none more significant than his account of the origins of his collaboration with Wordsworth on the* Lyrical Ballads. *In his retrospective account, Coleridge vividly captures the revolutionary significance of that epochal volume, which so decisively broke with the predictable diction and the refined pastoralism of the Augustan poets. Earlier in the* Biographia *he explained how, even as a schoolboy, he had harboured misgivings concerning the neo-classical style that dominated the poetry of his age.*

Amongst those with whom I conversed there were, of course, very many who had formed their taste and their notions of poetry from the writings of Mr Pope and his followers: or to speak more generally, in that school of French poetry condensed and invigorated by English understanding which had predominated from the last century. I was not blind to the merits of this school, yet as from inexperience of the world and consequent want of sympathy with the general subjects of these poems they gave me little pleasure, I doubtless undervalued the *kind*, and with the presumption of youth withheld from its masters the legitimate name of poets. I saw that the excellence of this kind consisted in just and acute observations on men and manners in an artificial state of society as its matter and substance – and in the logic of wit conveyed in smooth and strong epigrammatic couplets as its form. Even when the subject was addressed to the fancy or the intellect, as in the *Rape of the Lock* or the *Essay on Man*; nay, when it was a consecutive narration, as in that

**Source:** Samuel Taylor Coleridge, *Biographia Literaria*, edited with an Introduction by George Watson (London: Dent, 1960), pp. 9, 168–9 and 167. **Further reading:** Kathleen Wheeler, *Sources, Processes and Methods in Coleridge's 'Biographia Literaria'* (Cambridge: Cambridge University Press, 1980).

astonishing product of matchless talent and ingenuity, Pope's translation of the *Iliad*; still a *point* was looked for at the end of each second line, and the whole was as it were a sorites or, if I may exchange a logical for a grammatical metaphor, a *conjunction disjunctive* of epigrams. Meantime the matter and diction seemed to me characterized not so much by poetic thoughts as by thoughts *translated* into the language of poetry.

> Compared to the bland versification of the neo-classicists, the poetry of Wordsworth, encountered during a reading given by the latter in Bristol in 1795, came as a revelation to the young Coleridge. Wordsworth had that 'freedom from false taste' that Coleridge saw as the defect of Augustan verse, and with it 'the original gift of spreading the tone, the atmosphere and with it the depth and height of the ideal world, around forms, incidents and situations of which, for the common view, custom had bedimmed all the lustre, had dried up the sparkle and the dew-drops'. Their meeting led to a famous collaboration that was to produce the Lyrical Ballads of 1798. Coleridge explains what the two poets were trying to achieve, when, during the period 1797 to 1798, they lived close by in Somerset.

During the first year that Mr Wordsworth and I were neighbours our conversations turned frequently on the two cardinal points of poetry, the power of exciting the sympathy of the reader by a faithful adherence to the truth of nature, and the power of giving the interest of novelty by the modifying colours of imagination. The sudden charm which accidents of light and shade, which moonlight or sunset diffused over a known or familiar landscape, appeared to represent the practicability of combining both. These are the poetry of nature. The thought suggested itself (to which of us I do not recollect) that a series of poems might be composed of two sorts. In the one, the incidents and agents were to be, in part at least, supernatural; and the excellence aimed at was to consist in the interesting of the affections by the dramatic truth of such emotions as would naturally accompany such situations, supposing them real. And real in this sense they have been to every human being who, from whatever source of delusion, has at any time believed himself under supernatural agency. For the second class, subjects were to be chosen from ordinary life; the characters and incidents were to be such as will be found in every village and its vicinity where there is a meditative and feeling mind to seek after them, or to notice them when they present themselves.

In this idea originated the plan of the *Lyrical Ballads*; in which it was agreed that my endeavours should be directed to persons and characters supernatural, or at least romantic; yet so as to transfer from our inward nature a human interest and a semblance of truth sufficient to procure for these shadows of imagination that willing suspension of disbelief for the moment, which constitutes poetic faith. Mr Wordsworth, on the other hand, was to propose to himself as his object to give the charm of novelty to things of every day, and to excite a feeling analogous to the supernatural, by awakening the mind's attention from the lethargy of custom and directing it to the loveliness and the wonders of the world before us; an inexhaustible treasure, but for which, in consequence of the film of familiarity and selfish solicitude, we have eyes yet see not, ears that hear not, and hearts that neither feel nor understand.

With this view I wrote the 'Ancient Mariner', and was preparing, among other poems, the 'Dark Ladie' and the 'Christabel', in which I should have more nearly realized my ideal than I had done in my first attempt. But Mr Wordsworth's industry had proved so much more successful and the number of his poems so much greater, that my compositions, instead of forming a balance, appeared rather an interpolation of heterogeneous matter. Mr Wordsworth added two or three poems written in his own character, in the impassioned, lofty and sustained diction which is characteristic of his genius. In this form the *Lyrical Ballads* were published; and were presented by him, as an experiment, whether subjects which from their nature rejected the usual ornaments and extra-colloquial style of poems in general might not be so managed in the language of ordinary life as to produce the pleasurable interest which it is the peculiar business of poetry to impart.

*Coleridge had argued earlier in his book that the transformation of the quotidian world is only possible through the creative agency of the imagination, of which he offered the following famous definition.*

The imagination then I consider either as primary, or secondary. The primary imagination I hold to be the living power and prime agent of all human perception, and as a repetition in the finite mind of the eternal act of creation in the infinite I AM. The secondary I consider as an echo of the former, co-existing with the conscious will, yet still as identical with the primary in the kind of its agency, and differing only in degree, and in the mode of its operation. It dissolves, diffuses, dissipates, in order to re-create; or where this process is rendered impossible, yet still, at all events, it struggles to idealize and to unify. It is essentially *vital*, even as all objects (as objects) are essentially fixed and dead.

Fancy, on the contrary, has no other counters to play with but fixities and definites. The fancy is indeed no other than a mode of memory emancipated from the order of time and space; and blended with, and modified by that empirical phaenomenon of the will which we express by the word *choice*. But equally with the ordinary memory it must receive all its materials ready made from the law of association.

# 11

# 'Sentiments which ought to inform every discourse'

## Alessandro Manzoni: 'On Romanticism' (1823)

*Alessandro Manzoni (1785–1873) is largely known as the author of the epic historical novel,* The Betrothed *(1827, revised 1840–2); but he also wrote two important defences of Romanticism in the shape of his Preface to his tragedy,* The Count of Carmagnola *(1820), where he attacks the slavish adherence to the three unities practised by French dramatists, and his extended disquisition written in 1823 as a letter to the Marchese Cesare d'Azeglio, and known generally as 'On Romanticism'. Here, Manzoni aimed at a poised assessment of Romanticism, approaching the movement (which he largely sees as being of German extraction) through a form of Christian humanism that explicitly rejects the 'huddle of witches, of ghosts' that inspires the Gothic imagination, decrying the latter as 'a methodical mess, an eccentric quest, a repudiation of common understanding'. Manzoni offers a definition that seeks to balance its 'negative', in other words, its critical momentum, and its 'positive' side.*

With respect to the former, there is a tendency to exclude: the use of mythology, the servile imitation of the classics, the rules founded upon special events, rather than upon general principles, upon the authority of the rhetoricians, and not upon reasoning, especially the authority of the so-called dramatic unities, those of time and place, as proposed by Aristotle.

With respect to mythology, the Romantics have said that it is absurd to speak of certain things as being false, and others being true, simply because certain people, in earlier times, have held something to be true; that it is cold to introduce into poetry that which does not recall any memory, any feeling of real life; that it is boring to rehearse always this coldness and this falsity; that it is ridiculous to rehearse them with seriousness, with an air of reverence, with invocations which one might call 'ascetic'.

The Classicists have contended that, in removing mythology, one divests poetry of images, one takes the life out of it. The Romantics have responded that the mythological inventions drew, in their time, upon the conformity of a common belief, upon a spontaneity and a naturalness that

**Source:** Alessandro Manzoni, *Opere*, edited by Lanfranco Caretti (Milan: Ugo Mursia, 1973), pp. 1141–3, 1155–6 and 1156. There is no standard translation. **Further reading:** *The Reasonable Romantic: Essays on Alessandro Manzoni*, edited by Sante Matteo and Larry H. Peer (New York: Peter Lang, 1986), esp. pp. 73–83.

cannot be revived in modern compositions, where they are out of place. And in order to prove that these can live (and what a life!) without mythology, they cite those lauded inventions in which mythology peeps out, now here, now there, but always as though contraband or an escapee, and from which they could be removed without breaking up the structure or diminishing the beauty of the work. They cite, I say, especially the *Divine Comedy* and *Jerusalem*, in which miraculous supernaturalism plays an important part, indeed even a fundamental one, and which is anything but pagan; they cite also the spiritual rhymes of Petrarch, and the political ones, and his love rhymes. They also invoke the *Orlando* of Ariosto, in which, instead of gods and goddesses, magi and fates appear on the stage, not to mention all sorts of other things. And they cite various foreign works, which enjoy a good deal of fame, not only in the places where they were conceived, but also among cultivated people all over Europe.

Another argument of the Classicists is that in mythology one finds a complex collection of the wisest allegories. Romantics respond that if there really is an important and rational meaning underneath all this rubbish then it should be expressed directly; that if others in past times believed in saying one thing to mean another, they would have had reasons for doing so that are not relevant in our case, because there is no reason why this imagined exchange of ideas ought to become and remain a doctrine, a perpetual convention.

In order to prove that mythology is eminently acceptable, also in modern poetry, the Classicists argue that it has never ceased to be used right up until the present. To this the Romantics respond that mythology, which was at all times diffused among the works of the Greek and Latin writers, and co-mingled with the same, came naturally to partake of the beauty, of the culture, and the novelties of these works for the many educated readers who, during the Renaissance, turned to these works with curiosity, with enthusiasm, and also with a superstitious reverence, as was only too natural; and that, as though it were not a strange thing, such attractions from the very beginning will have tempted modern poets to give a little place to mythological inventions. It is not difficult to understand that such practices, transmitted from generation to generation with rudimentary studies, and transformed into doctrines, not only could maintain, but, as happens when such practices are abused, could also grow until they attacked all poetry, and becoming its foundation and its heart and soul. But, they conclude, certain absurdities can still keep us going, for some time at least, but cannot do so forever; the moment of the fall comes only once; and for mythology the moment has arrived.

'Where the opinions of the Romantics are unanimous,' Manzoni goes on to tell us, 'is in this: that poetry must put forward truth in place of the object, as though it were the

*only source of noble and lasting pleasure; indeed the false can well amuse the mind, but it*
*can not enrich nor elevate it; and this amusement is, by its very nature, unstable and*
*temporary, able to be destroyed (a desirable thing to do), or perhaps changed with a*
*whim, or by a sudden recognition of the truth, or by a love which the truth has nurtured.'*
*As Manzoni explains, the exact nature of Romantic truth is difficult to define.*

The truth, which must be present in every kind of imaginative work, *et*
*même dans la fable*, is therefore something different from that which we
ordinarily mean when we use the word, and, to put it more accurately, it
is something that has remained altogether undefined. Nor would defining
it be an easy task, if that is at all possible. Be it so, such uncertainty is not
particular to the principle I am trying to explain: it is common to all other
such principles, and it is ancient; the romantic system retains uncertainty
less than other literary systems, because the negative part, which specifies
the false, the useless, the damaging – the things to be excluded – indicates
and circumscribes, when faced with contrary ideas, something more
precise, a sense more lucid than that which we have had up until now. It
is also true that, with a new system, one does not wish to assess the
developments it has made as much as understand what it is capable of.
The formula which the term expresses is so general: the words have, if
nothing more than sound, a presentiment so beautiful and so wise; the
material of facts, which facilitates experimentation, is so abundant that
such a principle might receive by turns discussions, explanations, and
confirmations – all of which it is impossible to see now in any concrete
sense, in terms of numbers or of importance. Such is my opinion, or at
least I've come to think of the matter, and it also makes me smile, for in
this system I believe we can see a Christian tendency.

*Manzoni concludes, delineating the culturally progressive impact of Romanticism.*

The Romantic system, in emancipating literature from pagan traditions,
liberates it from a morality that is sensual, proud, ferocious, circumscribed
by time, and also improvident in this sense; antisocial where it is patriotic,
egoistic even when it ceases to be hostile; and it certainly tends to make it
less difficult to introduce into literature ideas and sentiments which ought
to inform every discourse. Moreover, by generally putting forward terms
like the truth, the useful, the good, and the reasonable, it concurs, it least
in words if not otherwise, with the vision of Christianity; at least the
terms do not contradict it.

# 12

# 'The great instrument of moral good is the imagination'

## Percy Bysshe Shelley: *A Defence of Poetry* (1821)

*Percy Bysshe Shelley (1792–1822), the poet of* Queen Mab *(1813),* Prometheus Unbound *(1820) and* Adonais *(1821), represents all that was radical about the second 'school' of English Romanticism: its energetic self-confidence, its intense lyricism and its forceful advocacy of its aesthetic and political causes. Shelley's* A Defence of Poetry *(written in 1821 but not published until 1840) was his most extensive theoretical statement. In an essay that is at once exordium, analysis and prophecy, Shelley seeks to define (and defend) the nature of poetry and the poetic activity. He does so both by highlighting the expansion of personal consciousness that poetry makes possible, and by stressing its humanizing effect upon social and political custom, which is achieved through the encouragement of empathy and the expansion of the moral sensibilities of mankind.*

The whole objection, however, of the immorality of poetry rests upon a misconception of the manner in which poetry acts to produce the moral improvement of man. Ethical science arranges the elements which poetry has created, and propounds schemes and proposes examples of civil and domestic life: nor is it for want of admirable doctrines that men hate, and despise, and censure, and deceive, and subjugate one another. But Poetry acts in another and deviner manner. It awakens and enlarges the mind itself by rendering it the receptacle of a thousand unapprehended combinations of thought. Poetry lifts the veil from the hidden beauty of the world, and makes familiar objects be as if they were not familiar; it reproduces all that it represents, and the impersonations clothed in its Elysian light stand thenceforward in the minds of those who have contemplated them, as memorials of that gentle and exalted content which extends itself over all thoughts and actions with which it coexists. The great secret of morals is love; or a going out of our own nature, and an identification of ourselves with the beautiful which exists in thought, action, or person, not our own. A man, to be greatly good, must imagine intensely and comprehensively; he must put himself in the place of another and of many others; the pains and pleasures of his species must become his own. The great instrument of moral good is the imagination;

**Source:** *The Complete Works of Percy Bysshe Shelley*, newly edited by Roger Ingpen and Walter E. Peck, 10 vols (New York: Gordian Press), vol. 7, pp. 117–18, 135–6 and 140. **Further reading:** Lucas Verkoren, *A Study of Shelley's Defence of Poetr[y]: Its Origin, Textual History, Sources, and Significance* (New York: Haskell House, 1970).

and poetry administers to the effect by acting upon the cause. Poetry enlarges the circumference of the imagination by replenishing it with thoughts of ever new delight, which have the power of attracting and assimilating to their own nature all other thoughts, and which form new intervals and interstices whose void for ever craves fresh food. Poetry strengthens that faculty which is the organ of the moral nature of man, in the same manner as exercise strengthens a limb. A poet therefore would do ill to embody his own conceptions of right and wrong, which are usually those of his place and time, in his poetical creations, which participate in neither. By this assumption of the inferior office of interpreting the effect, in which perhaps after all he might acquit himself but imperfectly, he would resign the glory in a participation in the cause.

*However, while poetry may impact upon the moral and civil realms its source lies in those areas of the mind that belong to the more inaccessible reaches of the self. Shelley explains, evoking one of his most famous images.*

Poetry is not like reasoning, a power to be exerted according to the determination of the will. A man cannot say, 'I will compose poetry.' The greatest poet even cannot say it: for the mind in creation is as a fading coal, which some invisible influence, like an inconstant wind, awakens to transitory brightness: this power arises from within, like the colour of a flower which fades and changes as it is developed, and the conscious portions of our natures are unprophetic either of its approach or its departure. Could this influence be durable in its original purity and force, it is impossible to predict the greatness of the results; but when composition begins, inspiration is already on the decline, and the most glorious poetry that has ever been communicated to the world is probably a feeble shadow of the original conception of the Poet.

*For the bulk of his essay, Shelley has sketched out his own cultural history of dramatic and poetic forms, seeking to refute the thesis advanced by the critic and satirical novelist, Thomas Love Peacock, in his* Four Ages of Poetry *(1820), that the poetic muse was in a state of decline. This is a thesis that Shelley determinedly rejects, turning in the final pages of his essay to his contemporary England to celebrate, in words that are famously triumphal, those creative personalities that he sees around him (and he is thinking of the Romantic generation), who embody that positive spirit of the poetic imagination that Shelley has so passionately espoused in his essay. The divine afflatus is not a distant Platonic ideal; it is a living force in the present.*

For the literature of England, an energetic development of which has ever preceded or accompanied a great and free development of the national will, has arisen as it were from a new birth. In spite of the low-thoughted envy which would undervalue contemporary merit, our own will be a memorable age in intellectual achievements, and we live among such philosophers and poets as surpass beyond comparison any who have appeared since the last national struggle for civil and religious liberty. The most unfailing herald, companion, and follower of the awakening of a great people to work a beneficial change in opinion or institution, is Poetry. At such periods there is an accumulation of the power of communicating and receiving intense and impassioned conceptions respecting man and nature. The persons in whom this power resides, may often as far as regards many portions of their nature, have little apparent correspondence with that spirit of good of which they are the ministers. But even whilst they deny and abjure, they are yet compelled to serve, the Power which is seated upon the throne of their own soul. It is impossible to read the compositions of the most celebrated writers of the present day without being startled with the electric life which burns within their words. They measure the circumference and sound the depths of human nature with a comprehensive and all-penetrating spirit, and they are themselves perhaps the most sincerely astonished at its manifestations; for it is less their spirit than the spirit of the age. Poets are the hierophants of an unapprehended inspiration; the mirrors of the gigantic shadows which futurity casts upon the present; the words which express what they understand not; the trumpets which sing to battle, and feel not what they inspire; the influence which is moved not, but moves. Poets are the unacknowledged legislators of the world.

## 13

## *'The grotesque and the sublime'*

### Victor Hugo: Preface to *Cromwell* (1827)

*The main works of Victor Hugo (1802–85) include his verse drama* Hernani *(1830), the novel* Notre Dame de Paris *(1831) and the epic poetry cycle* The Legend of the Centuries *(1859–83), and he established the Romantic movement in France with the Preface to his play,* Cromwell. *As a text, the Preface is a highly discursive and repetitive piece of writing, but it served, nonetheless, as a rallying call for an entire generation of young dramatists, such as Alfred de Musset, Alfred de Vigny and Alexandre Dumas, who were drawn to its energy and youthful self-confidence. Hugo argues here that European literature has evolved through the stages of lyrical poetry and epic verse into the modern period, where it is typified by a*

**Source:** Victor Hugo, *Théâtre complet*, 2 vols (Paris: Editions Gallimard, 1963), vol. 1, pp. 416–17, 422–3 and 434. There is no standard translation. **Further reading:** W. D. Howarth, *Sublime and Grotesque: A Study of French Romantic Drama* (London: Harrap, 1975), pp. 122–200.

*powerful eclecticism that can accommodate (as the neo-classicists could not) the broad and conflicting traits of human nature.*

Christianity leads the poets to the truth. Like it, the modern muse will see things from a higher and broader perspective. It will recognize that not all things in creation are beautiful in human terms, that ugliness exists beside beauty, the deformed alongside the graceful, that the grotesque is the obverse of the sublime, that evil coexists with good, dark with light. It will ask itself whether the narrow and restricted powers of reason that the artist has should have priority over the absolute and infinite reason of the Creator; whether it is for man to correct God; whether a mutilated nature will be more beautiful; whether art has the right, as it were, to duplicate man, life and creation; whether a thing will function better if its muscles and its vigour have been taken away from it; whether, in short, incompleteness is the means to harmony. It is, then, in the light of events both risible and imposing, and under the influence of that Christian melancholy and philosophical criticism that we noted above, that poetry will take a step forward, a decisive step, a step that, like the upheaval of an earthquake, will change the entire face of the intellectual world. It will set about doing as nature does, as it mixes the different aspects of creation (but without losing their differences), darkness and light, the grotesque and the sublime; in other words, body and soul, the animal and the spiritual; for the starting point of religion is always the starting point of poetry. All things are connected.

And through this process, there will come into existence a principle unknown to antiquity, a new mode of poetry; and, just as modifying one aspect of a thing may change it in its entirety, so here a new artistic form is coming into existence. This mode is the grotesque, and its form is comedy.

And we beg leave to dwell upon this point, for we are now coming to the characteristic trait, that fundamental difference which distinguishes, in our opinion, modern from ancient art, contemporary forms from defunct forms, or, to make use of less definite but better known terms, *romantic* literature from *classical* literature.

'Finally!', exclaim the people who for some time now *have seen us coming to this point,* 'at last, we have you! You are caught red-handed! So now you are recommending the ugly as something to imitate, and the grotesque as something that belongs to art! But what about the graces and good taste; don't you know that it is art's duty to rectify nature? That it is necessary to ennoble it? That it is necessary to exercise choice? Did the ancients ever display the ugly or the grotesque in their work? Did they ever mingle comedy and tragedy? Gentlemen, you should note the example of the ancients. And Aristotle, too, and Boileau, and La Harpe, by my word!'

These arguments are, without a doubt, sound ones, and, of course, of extraordinary novelty. But it is not our place to reply to them. We are not constructing a system here – God protect us from systems!; we are simply stating a fact. We are historians and not critics. Whether the fact pleases or displeases is of little significance; it remains a fact. Let us return to our argument, therefore, and try to prove that it is from the fruitful union of the grotesque and the sublime that the modern genius has been born, which is so complex, so varied in its forms, so inexhaustible in its creations, and because of that so fully opposed to the uniform simplicity of the genius of antiquity; let us show that this is the point from which we must set out to establish the real and radical difference between the two literatures.

> *One figure, above all, symbolized for Hugo the spirit of modern art: Shakespeare. His plays, performed in France in 1822 and again in 1827, became a cause célèbre on the French stage, and effectively manufactured a final rupture with the themes and style of eighteenth-century dramaturgy. Hugo, accordingly, attributes to the great dramatist epochal significance.*

We have now reached the poetic culmination of the modern period. Shakespeare is drama; and the author of a dramatic art which blends, in a single breath, the grotesque and the sublime, the terrible and the farcical, tragedy and comedy, – drama is the most fitting form for the third epoch of poetry, for contemporary literature.

So, to give a rapid summary of what has been said so far, poetry has three ages, each of which corresponds to an epoch in the development of society: the ode, the epic and drama. Primitive times were lyrical, ancient times epic, and the modern is dramatic. The ode sings of eternity, the epic consecrates history, whilst drama paints life. The defining quality of the first kind of poetry is naivety, of the second simplicity, and of the third truthfulness.

> *Hugo construed his project in largely dramaturgical terms, but that he was aware of the broader cultural politics which his radical break with convention entailed is clear from the following passage.*

Let us then speak boldly. The time for it has come, and it would indeed be strange if, in the present age, liberty, like light, should penetrate everywhere, except into that one place where freedom finds its most natural realm – in the world of ideas. Let us then take the hammer to theories, to poetics and systems. Let us pull down the old plastering that conceals the façade of art. There are neither rules nor models; or, rather, there are no other rules than the general laws of nature, which soar above the whole world of art, and then those particular rules which appertain to specific compositions in their treatment of individual subjects. The former are eternal, belong to the essence of the work, and are permanent; the latter are variable, external, and are transitory.

# 14

# 'Liberty *in literature as in Arts, industry, commerce and consciousness. This is the motto of our epoch.'*

## Mariano José de Larra: 'Literature' (1836)

*Mariano José de Larra (1809–37) was, along with Angel de Saavedra, Juan Eugenio Hartzenbusch and José Zorrilla, one of the leading figures of Spanish Romanticism. Although best known for his historical novel* The King's Page *(1834), and his sharply observed vignettes of local Spanish life and customs (the* 'costumbristas')*, Larra also wrote, under the sobriquet 'Figaro', many satirical and caustic essays attacking Spanish society on account of its hypocrisy and false values. His essay 'Literature' celebrates the new energies that are coming to transform Spanish society and literature alike.*

Politics, that interest which today is absorbed and fills the space offered by newspaper columns for the public's curiosity, has, so far, prevented us from pointing out the place that literature deserves. We have however, not forgotten that literature is the expression, or thermometer of the state of civilization of a people. We, unlike the foreigners, do not think that at the end of our Golden Age the passion for literature died in Spain. We do think that even in the apogee of the epoch our literature had a particular character that was either going to change in time or was going to lead to its own death if it did not compromise with the innovations and philosophical spirit that was beginning to emerge on the European horizon. Impregnated with the orientalism brought to us by the Arabs and influenced by religious metaphysics it can be said that it was brighter than it was solid; more poetic than positivist. At this moment, and when our ingenuity did not and could not do anything other than spin within a very tight circle, before our language could start to mould itself, there appeared in the world a cause that was in the beginning religious but in the end political in its consequences. As such it appeared in the world. And it is the same cause that gave the investigative drive to other peoples. Repressed and persecuted, Spain fixed within us the *nec plus ultra* that has made us static.

*Literature is, as Larra explains, 'the expression of the progress of a people and the word, spoken or written, is nothing more than the representation of ideas. That is to say, of progress itself.' As such, literature in Spain has reached a critical juncture.*

**Source:** Mariano José de Larra, *Articulos completos*, edited by Melchor de Almagro San Martin (Madrid: Aguilar, 1961), pp. 975–6 and 981–3. There is no standard translation. **Further reading:** Derek Flitter, *Spanish Romantic Literary Theory and Criticism* (Cambridge: Cambridge University Press, 1992), pp. 50–75.

If our reasons do not have enough weight then an example comes undoubtedly from those same nations that we have been forced to imitate, and while we have remained static with our language they have enriched theirs with voices from other places. They never asked of the words that they accepted *where do you come from?* Instead, they asked *what is your use?* Let's think about it. To be standing here while everyone is walking means not only to be standing, it means to be left behind, to lose ground. Besides the reason that brought so many obstacles to our improvement there was another: the number of those who adopted French taste and imported the new literature was very limited. These were, then, only a few progressive spirits from a general multitude still static in literature as well as in politics. We do not want to refuse the gratitude that rightly belongs to them. We would like to open up a vast space for the young Spain; our hopes are only that it might acquire one day its *own* standing, *assured and distinctly Spanish*, within European literature.

It is not our intention in this brief overview to start analysing the merits of the writers that have preceded us. This would be tiresome and inappropriate for our purposes and a little bit flattering to some of those still alive. After all, some of our idols, dear to the muses, failed to elevate our literature but instead introduced the French one into Spain. After imposing the yoke imposed by the theorists of the ostentatious and measured Age of Louis XIV, turbulent politics came to interrupt that same impulse, which we will call a good one, in the absence of any other.

Many years have passed since then without us even being able to realize our own condition, without knowing if we would have a literature at last of our own or if we would continue to be the left-over postscript of last century's classic French literature. We are still in that condition; in verse and in prose we are prepared to receive anything because we have nothing. Today a lot of young people eagerly rush towards the sources of knowledge. And when are they doing this? At a time when intellectual progress everywhere is breaking old chains, wearing down outdated traditions and bringing down idols. It proclaims to the world *moral liberty*, side by side with *physics*, because one can not live without the other.

Literature must look with resentment at this prodigious revolution and at this immense progress. In politics, men do not see beyond *interests and rights*, that is to say *truths*. Literature, therefore, cannot see anything else but *truths*. And we must not be told that the tendency of the century and its spirit, analytic and positivist, carries within itself the death of literature. Because passions in men will always be *truths*, because what is imagination itself but the most beautiful *truth*?

If our classic literature during the Golden Age was brighter than it was solid, it soon died at the hands of religious intolerance and political tyranny. If it had not been reborn with the help of French writers, finding itself cut off by the misfortunes of the fatherland, that same strange impulse, we hope very soon can build the foundations of a *new* literature, an expression of a *new* society that we compose all of which is *truth* as it is in our society without any rule other than that of *truth* itself, without any master other than *nature*, youthful in the end as the Spain that we are forming. *Liberty* in literature as in Arts, industry, commerce and consciousness. This is the motto of our epoch, this is our own, this is the yardstick with which we will measure. In our cultural judgements thus we will ask of a book: *Are you teaching us anything? Are you useful? If so, you are good.* We do not recognize masters of literature in any country, least of all in any man and even less in any epoch because taste is relative, we do not recognize an exclusively good school because there are none which are absolutely bad. Do not assume that we assign to whoever wants to follow an easier task. We urge him to study the knowledge of men. It is not enough as the *classics* did, to open Horace and Boileau and snub Lope or Shakespeare. It will not be enough, as the romantics did, to locate themselves under the banners of Victor Hugo and to make the rules using Molière and Moratín. This will not be because in our library we keep Ariosto beside Virgil, Racine next to Calderon, Molière next to Lope, sitting next, in one word, to Shakespeare, Schiller, Goethe, Byron, Victor Hugo, and Corneille, Voltaire, Chateaubriand and Lamartine.

What we are refusing, then, is what is nowadays called Literature amongst us; we do not want that literature to be reduced to the galas of sayings, to the rhythms of song, to the tune of a sonnet and odes to circumstances that concede everything to expression and nothing to the idea. We want a literature, a daughter of experience and history. Beacon of the future, studious, analytical, philosophical, deeply thinking everything through, saying everything in prose, in verse, within the reach of the yet ignorant multitudes, apostolic and propagandistic. Teaching *truths* to those who wish to know, showing man *not as he should be but as he is*, in order to know him. Literature in the end is the total expression of the science of the period, of the intellectual progress of the century.

# 15

# 'For the spirit comes alive'

## Giovanni Berchet: 'The semi-serious Letter' (1816)

*Giovanni Berchet (1783–1851), with his contributions to the periodical* Il
Conciliatore *[The Peacemaker] (1818–19), and his 'Semi-serious Letter', was
one of the foremost theoreticians of Romanticism in Italy. Berchet's 'letter' (or, to give
it its full title, 'On the "Fierce Hunter" and "Leonora" of G.A. Bürger: The
semiserious Letter from Chrysostom to his Son') is, in fact, a detailed study (with
translations) of the work of the Storm and Stress German poet, Gottfried August
Bürger, whom Berchet praised for being among the first to abandon neo-classical
models for the patterns and forms of popular literature. Berchet begins his letter by
justifying his translation of Bürger's poetry into Italian prose. He then goes on to
define three 'classes' of archetypal audiences for poetry, two of which are the subject of
high caricature: the stupid and ignorant 'Hottentot' or savage, whose simple life,
inextricably linked with the natural environment, does not permit the development of
any poetic tendency; and the over-civilized and cynical Parisian, whose intellect and
senses have been saturated with stimulus and whose tendency to philosophize spoils
the poetic. It is to a third class, 'the people', that Berchet believes all modern poets
should direct their work.*

The praise which the poet receives from this small part of his own nation
indeed cannot lead to haughtiness on his part: therefore the blame that is
laid upon him should not frighten him greatly. The people which the
poet seeks, his true readers, are found in millions in the third class. It is
this class, I believe, that the modern poet ought to admire, ought to know
well, ought to endeavour to enjoy, both in support of his own interests
and, at the same time, the true interests of art. We can conclude, then,
that the only true poetry is popular poetry: notwithstanding the
exceptions, as always, as I have already said; and notwithstanding
reasonable discretion, with which this rule should be interpreted.

If the modern poets from one part of Germany have made so great a
noise in their own house and in all the lands of Europe, we may attribute
that to the popularity of their own poetry. And the healthy direction that
their art took was the product of their profound study of the human heart
and of the purpose of art, of its history, and of the works which it has
produced in every epoch: it was the product of that division between the

**Source:** Giovanni Berchet, *Opere*, edited by Marcello Turchi (Naples: F. Rossi, 1972),
pp. 462–4. There is no standard translation. **Further reading:** Rene Wellek, *A History of
Modern Criticism: 1750–1950*, 4 vols (London: Jonathan Cape, 1955), vol. 2, pp. 259–60.

'classical' and the 'romantic', to which they have given shape in their poetry.

Remember, however, in parenthesis, that this division is not due to the mere whim of strange minds, taking pleasure in mumbling certain judgements which are sentenced without trial; to escape the rules upon which every genre of poetry agrees is not subterfuge, given that Tasso is one of the poets called 'Romantic'. And amongst the accusations they hurl at *Jerusalem*, who has ever heard it said that it transgresses any rules? What other poem has conformed more to the algebraic speculations of the Aristotelians?

Nor should you believe, my dear boy, that with this division (of which I speak) the Germans expected to take one art which is unique, indivisible, and split it into two. They were not stupid. But if the productions of this art, following the different nature of epochs and civilizations, have assumed different faces, why can I not distribute them to different tribes? And if those of the second tribe have in themselves something that the character of the present European civilization can express more intimately, shall I reject using them in this epoch because they do not have a face similar to that of the first tribe?

Now that the European nations have, one by one, been roused from sleep and from discontent (blocked up as they were by the irruption of the barbarians after the fall of the Roman empire), poets have emerged here and there to re-gentrify (or re-civilize) them. Willing companion of thought and ardent daughter of passions, the art of poetry, like the phoenix, has revived itself in Europe, and strives for the height of perfection. The miracles of God, the trials and tribulations of love, the joy of the victorious, bitter hatred and the splendid deeds of knights stirred the poetic power in the spirit of the troubadours. And the troubadours, educated neither by Pindar nor by Horace, rushed to the harp, burst into spontaneous songs, and communicated to the spirit of the people the sentiment of beauty, a long time before the invention of the printing press and before the refugees from Constantinople disseminated the Greek and Latin poetry. The poetic tendency having been steered so in the nations of Europe, a desire grew in the poets to honour it more worthily. They strove to rescue it in a thousand ways, and in celebrating the occasion, they also turned to the study of ancient poetry, initially as though it were a mysterious sanctuary, accessible only to them, and then as though it were a common spring of fantasy, one from which all readers could draw. But, to the shame of scholarship and erudition, the poets who have enlightened Europe from the renascence of literature up until our times and who bear the title 'modern' have chosen to take different paths. Some, hoping to reproduce the esteemed beauty found in the Greeks and Romans, have merely repeated, or often imitated with slight modifications, the customs, the opinions, the passions and the mythology of ancient peoples. Others interrogated nature directly, and nature neither dictated to them thoughts nor ancient affectations, but rather feelings and modern maxims. They examined the beliefs of the people: and in response found the mysteries of the Christian religion, the tale of a regenerating God, the certainty of an afterlife, the fear of an eternity of suffering. They interrogated the living human mind, and it told them things never before heard by them or their contemporaries: things that derive from custom, now chivalric, now religious, now ferocious, practised or present, or commonly known; things which derive from the entirety of the civilization of the century in which they live.

The poetry of the former group is classical, that of the latter is 'romantic'. This was what it was called by all the learned persons in one part of Germany, who recognized before all others the diversity of paths taken by modern poets. Whoever might mock these terms can change them to their own liking. However, I believe we can rightfully label the first the 'poetry of the dead', and the second the 'poetry of the living'. Nor do I fear deceiving myself in saying that Homer, Pindar, Sophocles, Euripides, etc. etc., were in their own times 'romantics', because they did not sing of things Egyptian or Chaldeian, but of things pertaining to their own Greeks: just as Milton did not sing Homeric superstitions, but rather Christian traditions. Whoever might wish to add that, amongst the modern poets who practise the classical genre, the best are those who manage to combine it with the romantic, and that these should indeed be grateful to the romantic spirit that their works are saved from oblivion – it seems to me that this person is not deserving of the stake. And why should this person be saved from such a fate, when he attempts to teach us by screaming that poetry ought to mirror that which moves our spirit the most? For the spirit comes alive when stirred by the things that surround us, not by the things of ancient or other peoples, which we know only through the means of books and history.

When you shall see deeply into these doctrines, which will not be found in the journals, you shall learn how the frontiers of poetic beauty are as broad as those of nature, and that the rock of comparison, with which we judge this beauty, is again nature itself, and not a sheaf of parchment; you shall learn how well-obeyed is the literature of the Greeks and the Latins; and you shall learn indeed how to make use of it. But you shall also hear how the proposed division helps to liberate you from the ever-noxious predominance of authority. You shall no longer swear on the word of anyone when it is a matter of the intellect.

You shall make your poetry an imitation of nature, not an imitation of an imitation. To the disrespect of your teachers, your conscience shall free you from the obligation of blindly venerating the oracles of an old and moth-eaten manuscript, in order to subject you to the obligation of perpetual and most lucid reason. And you shall laugh at your teachers who, with lenses perched upon their noses, continue to rummage around in old and moth-eaten manuscripts, and who read that which is not even written.

16

---

# *The poetry of the* Volk

## Ludwig Achim von Arnim and Clemens Brentano: *The Boy's Magic Horn* (1805–8)

*Ludwig Achim von Arnim (1781–1831) wrote the novel* The Poverty, Riches, Guilt and Expiation of the Countess Delores *(1810) and the fantastic story 'The mad invalid in Fort Ratonneau' (1818); Clemens Brentano (1778–1842) is best known for his novel* Godwi, or the Stone Image of the Mother *(1801), 'The story of bold Kasperl and the beautiful Annerl' (1817), and 'From the chronicle of a wayfaring pilgrim' (1818). Arnim and Brentano were two minor writers of the later school of German Romanticism, the producers of tales of fabulation and fantasy (*Märchen*), which, although striking, never quite reach the heights of the work of Tieck or Hoffmann. Where they did touch the heart of the nation was in their collection of antiquarian songs and poems gathered from their wanderings around rural Germany in the years between 1804 and 1807. What they produced here was more than just a German version of Percy or Ossian; written at the time of Napoleon's greatest military successes,* The Boy's Magic Horn *[Des Knaben Wunderhorn] is work of national (even nationalist) defiance, a rallying call to all who believe in the essential unity of the German people and harbour hopes for its future. The postscript to the first edition paints a picture of a country dominated by foreign taste and decadent mores, of a nation that can only be saved by the rediscovery of its traditional roots in folk art and literature. 'We looked around us, and everything appeared so wretched and decrepit', the authors tell us, describing a Germany (indeed, a Europe) caught in a process of cultural decline.*

New had to follow new, not because the new really had anything new to offer, but simply because that was what was required. In this fashion cheap popular tunes that could never be genuine folk songs [*Volkslieder*] made their way to the people. In this whirlwind of novelty, in this supposed immediate paradise on earth, true folk songs had been

---

**Source:** Ludwig Achim von Arnim and Clemens Brentano, *Des Knaben Wunderhorn: Alte Deutsche Lieder* (Munich: Winkler, 1957), pp. 861, 877 and 885. There is no standard translation. **Further reading:** Roland Hoermann, *Achim von Arnim* (Boston: Twayne, 1984), esp. pp. 19–43.

extinguished, even in France (and even before the Revolution, which perhaps it had helped make possible); and since they are still without them – what can unite them with that which gives them permanence as a people? In England also, folk songs are sung less; likewise in Italy, native folk songs are on the decline, banished from the operas on account of the drive for novelty conducted by charlatans; even in Spain, many songs we are told have disappeared, and nothing of significance is to be found there. Oh, my God, where have the old trees gone under which even yesterday we used to sit, those primeval signs of firm boundaries; what has happened to them, what is happening now? They have been cast into oblivion, even by the people, and we painfully stumble over their roots. Once the summit of those high mountains has been cleared of forest, then the rain will drive the soil downwards, and no tree will ever grow there again. That Germany should not become wasted in this way, that is the reason for our efforts.

> *Arnim and Brentano's main concern is what they call* Fremdartigkeit: *the impact of foreign taste upon German art and literature. But even without such perfidious influences, other more local obstacles exist to the revitalization of true German culture: theatrical entrepreneurs, literary critics and academics, all of whom seek to maintain the divide between high and low art, between the language of the cultivated and that of the people (the* Volk*). As Arnim and Brentano explain:*

It is only because of this linguistic division, in this neglect of the better poetic part of the people that Germany today chiefly lacks a popular poetry [*Volkspoesie*]; it is only in less educated circles, at least where there is little formal education through books, that many a folk song can come into being, which, unpublished and indeed unwritten, flies to us through the air like a white crow. And those, who are tied down by the chains of the world, are also liberated from the cares of the world. With a bitter-sweet joy, reading such poems we are overcome by that old pure feeling of living, about whose origins and mode of existence we are often unclear, but tend to identify with childhood, but which seems to us to come from an earlier period in our lives, and binds everything that lies within us into a unity of joy.

> *Only by rediscovering its indigenous folk culture, whose treasures have lain dormant in the collective unconscious of the nation, can Germany cure itself of this cultural malaise. Participating in its rediscovery is (for author and reader alike) the first step towards the recognition of national identity, and the authors conclude their essay by emphasizing the importance of this national mission, and the role of the artist in it.*

The astral muse is withheld from no one; everyone is an artist who can communicate to others what he finds special in the universe. But conditions are particularly favourable to he who, almost without trying, has been working towards some greater artistic goal, who harvests without labour, and nourishes everything in his blessed life. It is he who touches the emotions of the people, often and deeply; the tried and tested wisdom of centuries lies before him like an open book, put into his hand so that he can make known to all the songs, sagas, the homilies, the stories, prophecies and melodies. He is a fruit tree, which the gentle hand of the gardener has garlanded with white and red roses. Each will find there something that otherwise only a few find by themselves: the power to call deeply into the heart of the world. He brings together his people, otherwise divided by dialect, political prejudice, religious bias, and idle fashion, singing under a single banner. Even if this banner is not bedecked by trophies, but has perhaps only the torn seal of the seafaring argonauts or the cast-off coat of a poor singer, nevertheless, whoever bears it is not looking for any mark of distinction, and who follows it will find therein his duty. For we are all seekers after a higher truth, the Golden Fleece which belongs to all, the riches of our entire people, that which constitutes its inner living art, a weave spun through the ages and by mighty powers, the faith and the wisdom of the people, that which has accompanied it in happiness and in death: songs, sagas, folk lore, sayings, stories, prophecies and melodies. We wish to pass on to everyone that which has proven itself of diamond solid quality through the ages, not truncated, only smoothed so that its colours will shine through all the better. Every joint and every excision is part of the general monument that has been set to the greatest of the modern peoples, the Germans: a monument of the past, for the happy times of the present, and for the future a monument in the competition of life. We want at least to lay the foundations for that which points beyond our powers, firm in the faith that those who come after us will not fail to develop our work to the fullest, adding the crowning glory to our efforts. What lives there, and grows, and draws from life – that is neither from today or yesterday; it was and is and will be; we can never lose it, because it is a part of life; but it can for long periods fall into desuetude, often we most need to urgently conjure it up in our dreams and thoughts. The spirit has both a future and a past, as it has a present – but without a past, who can have a future?

# 17

## 'The nations that act, who suffer for the truth'

### Adam Mickiewicz: The Slavs (1842–4)

*Adam Mickiewicz (1798–1855), author of the Romantic drama* Forefather's Eve *(1823–33), the epic verse novel* Konrad Wallenrod *(1828) and the historical novel* Master Thaddeus *(1834), was the most famous Polish writer of his generation, and its foremost exponent of Romanticism. In 1840, fleeing from the Russian occupancy of his country, Mickiewicz went into exile in Paris, where he became Professor of Slavic Literature at the Sorbonne. Here he wrote a course of lectures,* The Slavs, *introducing contemporary Polish authors to a largely French audience.* The Slavs *is, however, much more than an academic work. In its thirty-nine lectures, it offers a detailed historical exegesis of the world-historical mission of the Polish people, which has, like Christ, Mickiewicz argues, been fated to suffer so that a world of freedom and national self-determination may be born. Written on the eve of the 'bourgeois' revolutions of 1848, Mickiewicz's work combines radical politics and a mystical patriotism with an almost Messianic conviction in the inevitability of the progress of history.*

People are now generally beginning to feel that after a period in which individuals revealed the great truths of the world it is now the nations who have been called to take up such ideas and put them into practice, to make them a reality. It is felt that the nations must now act as individuals have acted in earlier periods. You can guess, after our preceding analysis of political systems, which nations we must build our philosophical hopes upon: those are the nations that act, who suffer for the truth, who make sacrifices for it. And you see why we regard France as a nation that is far more philosophical than Germany, which is full of chairs of philosophy, and produces monstrous piles of philosophical works. You will likewise realise why the Polish nation is nearer to the truth than any other Slavic people, because the revelation of Jesus Christ will always be the measure of those who must follow him, because there is only one path towards the truth: it will always be that of the Cross; and as you know it is the nation that, for a long time now, has been treading that unhappy path. The Slavic peoples should not envy the Polish nation the unhappy glory of

**Source:** Adam Mickiewicz, *Les Slaves: Cours professé au Collège de France (1842–1844)* (Paris: Musée Adam Mickiewicz, 1914), pp. 5 and 12–13. There is no standard translation. **Further reading:** Andrzej Walicki, *Philosophy and Romantic Nationalism: The Case of Poland* (Oxford: Clarendon Press, 1982), esp. pp. 253–67.

having produced and given expression to the highest truths: that nation
has paid for it with cruel sacrifices.

*Mickiewicz begins his lectures proper on Polish literature (Chapter 2) with comments
regarding the institutional context in Poland, where an absence of cultural institutions
has meant that artists have been able to establish closer ties with the people, and hence
deepen their writing.*

The literary sphere is characterized by exactly the same struggle that we
have noted in the political sphere. Just as statutes and laws continually
hamper the development of Christianity, so in the same way schools,
theories, literary criticism [*la rhétorique*] and journals impede and smother
the development of literary genius. All of these work together to prevent
mankind from receiving revelations. That is why great artists hardly ever
come out of schools, and also why they always draw inspiration from that
great sense of life that animates the people. There would not be any other
way of explaining to you how and why great artists can come out of
countries where there are no schools, journals or even publishers.

After all that we have said, we are justified in asserting that the nation
which has most suffered from the reactionary tendencies of the old order,
the nation that has been most oppressed by the established powers, the
Polish nation, has been most open to receive divine revelations.

*To bear out his views on the revelatory nature of Polish poetry, Mickiewicz quotes at
length from the Preface to Zygmunt Krisinski's* The Undivine Comedy *(published in
1835), where the poetic muse is invoked as an ally of the Polish cause. To be effective,
however (as Mickiewicz points out) that muse must divest itself of its ethereal self-image,
and prepare itself for action.*

'Happy is the one in whom you have made your dwelling-place, like God
in the very heart of the world, unobserved, unknown, but magnificent
and radiating in all of its parts, and before which all living creatures
prostrate themselves, saying: He is here. In the same way, [he who is
inspired by the poetic muse] will bear you like a star on his brow, and will
not put between your love and him the gulf of the word. He will love
man, and shine like a hero in the midst of his brothers. And to him who
will not remain faithful, and to him who will soon betray you, and will
deliver you up to the perishable joys of man, you will throw some flowers
upon his head, and turn aside from him; he will pass his life weaving with
those faded flowers a funeral wreath. Woman and he have the same
origin.'

We will look deeper a little later into certain lines of this magnificent
piece, which will allow you to understand the sublime feelings of the
poetry of this Polish author. For him, poetry is not art; it is not a form of
amusement. He is painting for you here the picture of poetic power, the
power of a soul that immerses itself entirely in its imagination, and which

rides thus in its chariot, on that rainbow, across the tempests and the clouds, and which believes it possesses everything, but which loses its way, because it uses its Heaven-sent gifts for its own pleasure.

You will know that several years ago a poetic theory was founded in France which consisted in making similar journeys across time and space, and in imitating by turns the poetry of China, Arabia and so on.

Poetry, for the author whose work we were reading, is of serious inspiration; it is necessary to bear it, as he said, into the depths of one's soul. Words, poetry expressed in mere words, is the source of despair for a soul who feels thus that he has been betrayed. The written word betrays the powerlessness to act. True poetry, even that of the Greeks, means nothing less than action. Greek poetry meant action. And what does the Polish author ask for? It is that those souls who are the best tempered, the most noble, the strongest, those who communicate with Divinity, reserve all their strength for action rather than for words. That is the message of this preface; and pity on those poets who restrict themselves solely to words! It is then that poetry will throw that garland of dead flowers, with which they will be condemned to amuse themselves for the rest of their days.

<br>

18

---

## Reflective and non-reflective modes of artistic creation

Friedrich von Schiller: *On Naive and Sentimental Poetry* (1795–6)

*Although Friedrich von Schiller (1759–1805) was normally classified as a Weimar Classicist, his plays,* The Robbers *(written between 1777 and 1780, first performed 1782), the* Wallenstein *trilogy (1799) and* Maria Stuart *(1800), influenced an entire generation of Romantic writers and playwrights, particularly in France (see, for example, Benjamin Constant's* Reflections on the Tragedy of Wallenstein, *1809). In his essay* On Naive and Sentimental Poetry, *Schiller confronted one of the fundamental paradoxes within the Romantic quest: its desire to merge consciousness with the plenitude of the world (often through dream and fantasy), while at the same time seeking through Romantic theory to put that desire on a theoretical footing. Schiller was aware of the two (exclusive) strands of the*

**Source:** Friedrich von Schiller, *Über naïve und sentimentalische Dichtung,* edited by Johannes Beer (Stuttgart: Reclam, 1952), pp. 40–1 and 84–6. **Standard translation:** *Naive and Sentimental Poetry, and On the Sublime,* translated, with Introduction and notes by Julius A. Elias (New York: F. Ungar, 1967). **Further reading:** John D. Simons, *Friedrich Schiller* (New York: Twayne, 1981), pp. 26–36.

*Romantic mind, and in his essay developed a typology for them: the naïve and the sentimental.*

Because the naïve poet only follows simple nature and his feelings, and restricts himself merely to reproducing the external world, he can only have a single relationship to his subject, and *in this sense* has no choice in the way that he treats his themes. The varied impression that naïve poetry makes depends (leaving to one side its content for the moment, and focusing purely upon the way that content is poetically treated) depends, I say, entirely upon the various degrees of one and the same mode of feeling; even the different external forms of his work have little impact upon the quality of its aesthetic impression. The form may be lyrical or epic, dramatic or narrative: we might indeed be moved to a greater or less extent, but (if we put aside its content) it invariably has the same effect upon us. Our response is uniformly the same, the result of a *single* disposition, so that we cannot differentiate within it. Even differences of language and epoch make no difference here, for it is precisely the pure unity of its origin and its effect that is the characteristic of naive poetry.

With the sentimental poet, however, things are quite different. He *reflects* about the impression that objects make upon him, and the emotion that moves him and us comes solely out of that process of reflection. The object is here related to an idea, and it is only in establishing this relationship that his poetic power exists. The sentimental poet is thus always involved in two conflicting intellectual and emotional states – with actuality as a limit and with his mind as infinitude; and the mixture of feelings that he excites will always bear a trace of these dual origins. Since in this case there is a plurality of principles, it all depends, therefore, on which of the two comes to *predominate* in the sensibility of the poet and in his work, and this consequently allows for a variation in the treatment of the same theme. For now the question arises whether he will tend more towards actuality or towards the ideal – whether he will take the former as an object of aversion, or the latter as an object of attraction. His approach will either be *satirical* (mocking) or it will be (in a broader meaning of the word that will be later explained) *elegiac* (plaintive); every sentimental poet will adhere to one or other of these two approaches.

*Once Schiller has established his typology, he goes into greater detail regarding the respective merits of these two forms of artistic consciousness.*

A few concluding comments need to be made about how these two artistic modes relate to one another and to the ideal of poetry.

Nature has blessed the naïve poet with the gift of always functioning as an undivided unity, of being able at every moment to be an independent and complete totality, able to depict the magnitude of humanity in all its actuality. The sentimental poet has been given the power, or rather has been infused with the strong inclination, to restore from within himself that unity which had been dissolved through abstract thinking, to complete the humanity within himself, and pass over from a restricted state of being into an infinite one. To give human nature its full expression is, however, the common task of both, without which they would not deserve the name of poets. But the naïve poet has always the advantage over the sentimental poet of sensual reality, in that he is able to realize as an actual reality what the latter can only strive to achieve. And that is also what anyone experiences when he thinks about his enjoyment of naïve poetry. At such moments, he feels all the powers of his humanity fully active; he requires nothing more, he is a whole in himself. Without making any differentiation within his feelings, he enjoys at one and the same moment his intellectual activity and his sensual life. The sentimental poet, however, puts him into an entirely different mood. Here he simply feels a strong *inclination*, to produce a sort of internal harmony (which he does actually feel), to make a whole out of himself, and to give complete expression to the humanity within himself. Hence in the latter case, the mind is forever in movement, it is tense, it fluctuates between conflicting feelings; in the former case, it is calm, relaxed, at one with itself, and entirely satisfied.

But if the naïve poet gains over the sentimental poet, on the one hand, a sense of reality, and imparts to his art a real existence that the latter can only nurture an impulse to attain, the latter nevertheless possesses one great advantage over the former, in that he can give that impulse a *greater object* than the former has achieved or is able to achieve. All reality, we know, falls short of the ideal; everything that exists has its limits, but thought has no restrictions. From this limitation, to which everything sensuous is subject, the naïve poet also suffers, whereas the unconditional freedom enjoyed by the powers of the mind is granted to the sentimental poet. The former, therefore, most certainly fulfils his task, but the task itself is somewhat limited; the latter, it is true, only partially fulfils his task, but his task is an infinite one. So much is clear from our own experience. From the naïve poet, one turns with ease and enthusiasm to the living present; the sentimental poet will always for a few moments spoil one's taste for real life. This is because our mind here has been extended by the infinitude of ideas beyond its natural reach, so that nothing in the present can really satisfy it. We prefer to lapse back into our thoughts, where we find nourishment for that inclination stimulated by the world of ideas, instead of seeking outside ourselves for sensuous objects. Sentimental poetry is the offspring of retreat and quiet, and to them it invites us; naïve poetry is the child of life, and it also leads us back into life.

# 19

# Transcendent and universal poetry

## Friedrich von Schlegel: *Aphorisms and Fragments* (1797–1800)

*Friedrich von Schlegel (1771–1829) wrote* On the Study of Greek Poetry *(1797), the novel* Lucinda *(1799) and the* Dialogue on Poetry *(1800), but his main contribution to Romantic theory rests upon the numerous fragments he published in the journal* Athenäum, *which he edited along with his brother August Wilhelm. Cryptic, neologistic and frequently obscure, Schlegel's writing represents the totalizing aspirations of the Romantic mind, its desire to bring as much intellectual and artistic experience as possible under the sway of an aesthetic that was still in the process of being defined. At the centre of Schlegel's own aesthetic lay the notion of irony, which he saw as an intellectual position of self-imposed estrangement that would permit the artist to resolve that impasse that Schiller noted in his* Naive and Sentimental Poetry: *the tension between the spontaneous energies of artistic creation and the theoretically self-reflective elements that often accompanied them. But before elaborating his notion of irony, Schlegel endeavoured to define the key characteristics of Romantic writing.*

### Athenäum fragment

Romantic poetry is a progressive universal poetry. Its mission is not merely to reunite all the different genres of poetry, and to bring them into contact with philosophy and rhetoric. It seeks, and should seek, to mingle and, at times, to entirely fuse poetry and prose, genius and the analytical mind, high-art poetry and folk poetry, to make literature living and social, and life and society poetic, to poetise wit, and to fill and saturate the forms of art with deep cultural values of every kind, animating them with the vibrancy of humour. It embraces all that is poetic, from those great artistic systems which include within them yet further systems, down to the sigh, and the kiss mouthed in artless song by the child creating its own poetry. It can immerse itself so totally in the thing that it is portraying that one might think that its one and only goal was to bring forth poetic individuals; and yet, no form has as yet been designed that is better able to fully express the author's mind: so that many artists, who have just wanted

**Source:** Friedrich von Schlegel, *Kritische Schriften*, edited by Wolfdietrich Rasch (Munich: Hanser, 1971), pp. 38–9, 53, 10–11, 40–1 and 97. **Standard translation:** *Dialogue on Poetry and Literary Aphorisms*, translated, introduced and annotated by Ernst Behler and Roman Struc (University Park: Pennsylvania State University Press, 1968). **Further reading:** Marike Finlay, *The Romantic Irony of Semiotics: Friedrich Schlegel and the Crisis of Representation* (Berlin: Mouton de Gruyter, 1988).

to write a novel, have ended up inadvertently portraying themselves. Only it can, like the epic, become a mirror of the entire world that surrounds it, an image of its age. At the same time, freed from all real and ideal interests, it can also soar on wings of poetic reflection midway between the work and the artist, giving force to this reflection and multiplying it as in an unending series of mirrors. It has the potential for the highest and most comprehensive development, not only in terms of its internal features but also in its external, by organising everything that seeks to become a totality uniformly in all its parts, creating in the process the prospect of a boundlessly developing classicism. Among the arts, Romantic poetry is what wit is to philosophy, and what conviviality, company, friendship and love are to life. Other types of poetry are fully developed, and can now be thoroughly analysed. Romantic poetry is still in the process of becoming; this indeed is its very essence, the fact that it will always be in the process of becoming, that it will never be completed. It cannot be explained away by any theory, and only an inspired criticism would dare to define its ideal. It alone is infinite, as it alone is free, recognising as its fundamental law that the wilfulness of the poet recognises no law. The romantic genre of poetry is the only one that is more than a genre, being, as it were, poetry itself; for, in a certain sense, all poetry is, or should be, romantic.

*Athenäum fragment*
There is a type of poetry whose one and all focus is the relationship of the ideal and the real, and which should thus, following the analogy of the technical language of philosophy, be called transcendental poetry. It begins as satire, with the absolute distinction between the ideal and the real, hovers between the two as elegy, before finally achieving the complete unity of both as idyll. But just as one would give little weight to a transcendental philosophy that was not critical, that did not reflect the act of producing as well as the product, did not contain within its system of transcendental thoughts a characterisation of transcendental thinking; the same is true of that poetry which not infrequently unites in the work of modern poets transcendental materials, and sketches for a poetic theory of the creative act, with aesthetic reflection and noble self-portrayal, such as can be found in Pindar, in the lyric fragments of the Greeks, ancient elegies, and, amongst modern writers, in Goethe; in each of its depictions poetry should depict itself, and always be, at one and the same time, poetry and poetry about poetry.

*Critical fragment*
Philosophy is the natural home of irony, which one might define as logical beauty. Whether it be in oral or written conversations, and not only in the area of systematic philosophy, irony should be practised and

encouraged everywhere; even the Stoics held urbanity for a virtue. To be sure, there is also a rhetorical irony which, if frugally used, can have a superb effect, particularly in a polemical situation; but it runs counter to the elevated urbanity of the Socratic muse, just as the majesty of the most brilliant formal speech contrasts with ancient tragedy performed in the high style. Poetry can also in this regard elevate itself to the heights of philosophy, even though it is not based, like rhetoric, on ironic fundamentals. There are ancient and modern poems which exhale throughout their parts the divine breath of irony. There dwells within them a genuine transcendental buffoonery. Internally, they possess a disposition which offers a perspective on everything, and lifts itself into endless heights over all that is purely conditional, even over its own art, virtue or genius. In its external form, it approximates the mimic manner of the conventional good Italian opera buffo.

### Athenäum fragment

An idea is merely a concept that has been developed into irony, an absolute synthesis of absolute antitheses, the continually self-generating exchange of two conflicting thoughts. An ideal is, at one and the same time, idea and fact. If ideals for today's thinkers have less individuality than the Gods of Antiquity have for artists, then all occupation with ideas would simply be a boring and tiresome game of dice with empty formulas, or, after the fashion of Chinese bigwigs, a meditative contemplation of one's own nose. Nothing is more pathetic and despicable than this cognitive [*sentimental*] speculating without an object. But please don't call this mysticism, since this beautiful old word is so useful and indeed indispensable as a designation for absolute philosophy, from whose position, what appears, from the point of view of other theoretical and practical positions, as purely natural, can be viewed by the spirit as a wonder and a mystery. Detailed speculation is as rare as generalised abstraction, and yet it is these that create the materials of scientific wit, the principles of higher forms of criticism and the upper levels of mental and cultural development [*Bildung*]. The great laws of practical abstraction were precisely what made the Ancients (in whom they were instinctual) the Ancients. It was quite in vain for individuals to give full expression to the ideal of their genre, if these genres themselves also had not been strictly and clearly isolated, and their originality, as it were, freely relinquished. But to put oneself at will, now in this sphere, now in that, as if in another world, not simply with one's reason or imagination but with one's entire soul; to freely give up now this part of the self, now another, and to restrict oneself entirely to yet another aspect of one's being; to seek and to find in an individual his one and all, and to consciously shut out the remaining superfluities: that can only be accomplished by a spirit that, as it were, contains within itself a plethora of spirits and an entire system of personalities, and in whose inner world the universe, which (as one says) germinates in every monad, has fully developed and come to maturity.

*From* Ideas
Irony is a clear recognition of the eternal agility, of the infinite abundance of chaos.

# Part II
# Realism

# INTRODUCTION

As a literary movement, Realism lacked both the theoretical thrust of Romanticism and its metaphysical import. Whereas figures such as Novalis, Coleridge and the French fabulist Gerard de Nerval had (directly or indirectly) drawn inspiration from the philosophical Idealism of Kant, Schleiermacher and Fichte, the writers of the Realist movement kept closer to the pre-theoretical realm of immediate experience; the tangible, the tactile, the solidity of the external world form the defining parameters of their work. It could hardly have been otherwise, for by the mid-nineteenth century, the intellectual climate of Europe had been remade upon the basis of the new 'religion' of the age: scientific positivism (thus named after Auguste Comte's *Course in Positivist Philosophy*, published in six volumes between 1830 and 1842). Where speculation once reigned concerning the transcendental conditions of absolute knowledge and the primary agency of the will, now came the different agenda of the new *sciences humaines*: sociology, psychology and political economy. The focus of these disciplines was upon brute matter in all its physiological, sociobiological and evolutionary forms, the secrets of which they sought to open through methodologies that stressed the quantifiable, the empirical and, above all, the inexorable and all-determining influence of the object(ive) world.

The first victim of the march of positivism and social-scientific rationality was that very notion of the creative potency of the subjective self which, under the guise of 'phantasy' or 'the imagination', had been one of the central unifying tropes within the discourse of European Romanticism. Imagination was now seen as part of an epistemology of pure selfishness; it was exaggeratedly individualistic, and, as such, deemed by many to be both myopically limited, in neglecting non-self-centred areas of experience, and distorting, in its failure to explicate the true relationship between man and his environment. The terms of this critique were memorably articulated in two important essays by George Eliot and John Ruskin (published, and not coincidentally, within a year of one another, in 1856 and 1857). Ruskin's essay on the 'pathetic fallacy' exhibits an almost moral distaste for the 'unhealthy', introverted self-sufficiency of certain types of Romantic sensibility. As Ruskin trenchantly observed, the latter cannot tell 'the difference between the ordinary, proper, and true appearances of things to us; and the extraordinary, or false appearances, when we are under the influence of emotion, or contemplative fancy; false appearances, I say, as being entirely unconnected with any real power or character in the object, and only imputed to it by us' (**Reading 1**). Ruskin's essay constitutes a plea that we recognize not only the integrity of the material world that surrounds us, but also the independence of the viewing subject (the artist), who must show strength of character and firmness of mind in not losing himself in acts of exaggerated empathy.

In her essay on the pre-Romantic poet Edward Young, George Eliot followed Ruskin in refracting her criticisms through a sometimes overt but frequently assumed desideratum of 'wholeness', by which Eliot meant the writer's readiness to respond to the full totality of experience. Eliot's observations, however, form less a critique of Romanticism *per se* (indeed, she explicitly defends 'genuine fancy and bold imaginativeness'), than a condemnation of the abuses perpetrated by a certain inflection within the Romantic mind, which in its straining after the sublime effect only succeeds, as in the poetry of Young, in producing bloated hyperbole and metaphysical abstraction. What the artist must do, Eliot tells us, invoking the nature poetry of the more modest but, for Eliot, more estimable William Cowper, is respect the tangible world, however minutely it might present itself, and reproduce its essential features with sincerity and truthfulness of perception. Only in that way can the essential interconnectedness of life be grasped and the basis laid for 'moral emotion', that ability to empathize with all aspects of human endeavour, however modest their personal or social origins (**Reading 2**).

Realism was, in fact, a practice long before it became a theory. As early as 1815, Walter Scott had penned a short essay on Jane Austen in which he had rightly divined that the English novel had reached an important juncture, where the earlier melodramatic excesses beloved by the practitioners of the Gothic novel and popular Romantic tales were being superseded by a style of writing that was alive to the values and customs practised by those from 'the paths of common life' (by whom the conservative Scott largely meant the lower landed gentry). As Scott explained regarding Austen's novel: 'The narrative of all her novels is composed of such common occurrences as may have fallen under the observation of most folks; and her dramatis personae conduct themselves upon the motives and principles which the readers may recognise as ruling their own and that of most of their acquaintances. The kind of moral, also, which these novels inculcate, applies equally to the paths of common life' (**Reading 3**). The term 'realism' is not used here; nevertheless, Scott's emphasis upon 'copying from nature', the importance of 'credulity' and correct representation, and his preference for the depiction of 'common occurrences', fully anticipate the guiding tropes that informed Realism when it later emerged as a full-blown aesthetic in mid-nineteenth-century France.

The writer who did most in his work to prepare the way for this aesthetic was the great French novelist Honoré de Balzac, author of the epic novel series *The Human Comedy*, published between 1829 and 1848. Balzac saw himself as novelist, historian and sociologist rolled into one, and in the Preface to *The Human Comedy* fully identified himself with the new 'scientific' approach to the social sphere promoted by the *sciences humaines*, an approach that banishes ideals and moral standards in favour of a recognition of the 'facts' of self-interest, personal appetite and *force majeure*. Writing at a time when the theoretical foundations for bourgeois hegemony (political and intellectual) were in the process of being laid in a swiftly industrializing France, Balzac entered into the spirit of this world with characteristic bravura, adopting the taxonomic principles of the new sciences, and most notably the newly founded science of zoology, in order to capture the dynamic interplay of a society where class allegiances, political affiliations and even gender roles were being dramatically challenged. Recording the political, financial and sexual energies that propelled this world forced Balzac to adopt a complexity of perspectives, becoming, in the process, 'more or less patient or perceptive painter of human types, a narrator of the dramas of private life, the archaeologist of social furniture, the cataloguer of professions, the recorder of good and evil', positions that were to be acquitted with such self-effacing realism that the reader might well believe that not Balzac but 'French society would be the real author' of his novels (**Reading 4**).

The type of literature that would result from the expansive energies of the age was welcomed by many, such as the French literary critic and cultural historian Charles-Augustin Sainte-Beuve. In his later essays, Sainte-Beuve would offer a less benign view of Realism, coming to regret its expulsion of ideals and optimism (see, for example, his famous review of *Madame Bovary*, published in 1857); but in an earlier piece, written in the same year as the 'bourgeois' revolution of 1830, he welcomed Realism as the harbinger of a new democratic humanity, viewing the epic sweep of its vision as a correlative of the principle of 'progress' to which French society had, through recent political changes, courageously committed itself. As Sainte-Beuve explained in somewhat triumphalist words (which speak of the optimism of that generation inspired by the impending victory of a liberal revolution), Realism alone possesses the gift to 'reflect and to radiate in a thousand colours the sentiments of a progressive humanity, to rediscover this aspect of humanity, as it has gradually developed, in the depths of the philosophies of the past, to seek it out and follow it through the ages, to integrate it and its passions into a harmonious and living nature' (**Reading 5**).

The German novelist, Theodor Fontane, held to a similar view of the humanizing mission of Realism; but in his case the contact with the cause of radical politics, Republican or proletarian, is explicitly severed. Realism's ultimate goal, Fontane argues in an essay of 1853, was not political, nor did it seek to inculcate a reformist mentality or a desire for social change by confronting the reader with grim depictions of suffering and misery. Works that simply reproduce those realities, Fontane explains (as an early participant in a debate that will last well into the twentieth century), are neglecting to observe the *transforming* capacity that all great art, Realist art included, possesses (**Reading 6**). Fontane embraces Realism, then, but largely for creative and aesthetic–ethical reasons, praising its respect for the apparently insignificant details of life and its capacity for emotional empathy. Realism alone opens up avenues to what is 'true', to the 'actual' (key terms within Realist theory), to that which is grounded in the broadest compassion for ordinary 'flesh and blood'. Realism, in short, is on the side of life.

But what sort of life? Fontane had argued in his essay that the Realist writer must observe a certain propriety in his or her art: no 'naked reproduction of everyday existence'; no blatant propaganda on behalf of the oppressed and dispossessed. And many, even those who were politically engaged, such as the Marxist theoretician, Friedrich Engels (*see* **Reading 18**), were ready to agree. But for others, such as Charles Dickens and George Sand, this was where Realism could fulfil its greatest task: not as propaganda, perhaps, but certainly as a vehicle for the awakening of social conscience. Like his great Russian counterpart, Dostoevsky, Dickens ventured into social realms, and dealt with subclasses of humanity that Fontane would have shunned. And, also like Dostoevsky, Dickens was fully aware of the moral complications of an art-form that necessarily had to engage, if it were to carry out its mission of enlightenment, with what contemporary readerships would have classified as the sordid and the immoral. In his Preface to *Oliver Twist* (**Reading 7**), Dickens justified his depiction of 'the very dregs of life' by both invoking what would become the standard Realist clause of mimetic fidelity (he has simply described the world as it exists), and arguing that the probity of true morality (represented here by the young Oliver) could only be tested in a pervasively immoral milieu. It is only against such backdrops of urban squalor that 'the principle of Good' can be seen as a vital force, surviving still, even in the darkest regions of the soul.

The French novelist and proto-feminist writer, George Sand, was also aware of the tension between the readerly claims of public decency and the writerly requirements of truth-saying. The Preface to her first novel *Indiana* (1832) demonstrates the difficulties for Realist writers in finding a strategic position of speech that would allow them to raise public awareness of social issues without offending against decorum. As Sand observes: 'certain upright figures, certain honourable spirits might be alarmed to see such unpolished virtue, such woeful motivation, and such unjust opinions as are presented here. This gives him deep cause for concern' (**Reading 8**). Her subtly inflected defence of her novel ranges between self-deprecation and a fawning recognition of the superior gifts of discernment possessed by the reader. It also contains a muted moral outrage and the dark hint that the same readers have been complicit (indirectly, at least) in bringing about and maintaining a society that could make such injustices possible. Sand's discourse is even more confounded by the fact that the sentiments uttered by the actual female author in the Preface are at odds with those produced by the assumed male author, creating a tension in her discourse which oscillates between what seems an ostensible defence of patriarchal morality and notions of decency, and an ironic undercutting (through hyperbole and other gestural devices) of the same.

Repression of the instincts that lie within; suppression of the same instincts by the dictates of society. This was to become one of the major themes of Realist fiction, particularly of novels such as Flaubert's *Madame Bovary* (1857), Tolstoy's *Anna Karenina* (1877), Capuana's *Giacinta* (1879), Hardy's *Tess of the D'Urbervilles* (1891) and Fontane's *Effi Briest* (1895), which focused upon the plight of women in patriarchal society. But the malaise was a broad one, infecting all who felt that the ethos of Realism, now understood in its broadest sense to include the decline of religious faith, the rise of ethical nihilism and the collapse of traditional social structures, had closed down for many the avenues to personal happiness and self-realization. Much of the greatest Realist literature, particularly its drama, was written out of this pessimist mind-set, as the plays of Büchner and Hebbel (in Germany), Ibsen and Strindberg (in Norway and Sweden) and Chekhov (in Russia) testify.

In the case of the young Georg Büchner, Realism was coterminous with a vehement historical fatalism, the result of the author's participation in the failed revolutionary activism of the *Vormärz* movement of 1830 to 1840. Observing that failure had left Büchner with a clear recognition of the stark realities of life: the worthlessness of human endeavour and the impotence of personal action seen against the impersonal march of history. As he explained in a letter written to his fiancée in 1834, 'I find in human nature a terrifying uniformity, in human affairs an inexorable force, which is granted to all and to none. The individual is only foam on a wave, greatness a mere accident, the majesty of genius a puppet play, a ludicrous struggle against an iron law, which to recognise is the highest achievement, but to master, impossible' (**Reading 9**). These were sentiments that Büchner would inscribe into his plays, most notably *Danton's Death* (1835), where irony, eroticism and the intoxication of power can do little to still the ennui-inspired death-wish that must come to all who are forced to abandon ideals in the face of *force majeure* and historical necessity.

As the above discussion indicates, Realism was a dominant force in European literature long before the term was coined in the 1830s, and well before it had begun to cohere into a recognizable aesthetic in the mid-1850s. As the rubric for an emerging literary movement, it was first brought to public attention by the minor French novelist and critic Jules Husson (otherwise known as Champfleury). His defence of the painter Gustave Courbet, whose paintings had been shunned by the Academy in 1856 on account of their demotic subject matter, established the terms in which the subsequent debate on Realism would take place. Champfleury's enthusiasm for the new school of painting (somewhat inconsequentially expressed in his book *Le Réalisme*, published in 1857) found a more systematic formulation in the journal of the same name, edited by the critic and novelist Louis-Edmond Duranty, between July 1856 and May 1857. Duranty's articles effectively constitute the first manifestos of the Realist movement, and did much to establish the goals of its aesthetic: its focus upon contemporary rather than historical issues; its grounding in urban experience; its openness to all types of subject matter; and its concern for accuracy and truth (**Reading 10**). It is, above all, the demotic and (latently, at least) politically democratic undertones of these essays, their conviction that 'the masses are as open to pity, to misfortune, to anger etc, as the writer who is addressing them', that imparts to Duranty's manifestos a distinctly radical quality, that sense of being part of an offensive against the cultural and political establishment.

Duranty's writings possess a revolutionary verve that comes from their being at the vanguard of a newly discovered cause; but, in the final analysis, these early attempts to define a Realist aesthetic lack both theoretical focus and coherence. However, that was soon to come, but it would emerge under the guise not of Realism but of a new movement within the literary culture of France and Europe, which would deepen the somewhat naïve tenets of that movement into a systematic but also controversial engagement with reality. It was called Naturalism. One of the earliest attempts to formulate its ethos was made by the Goncourt brothers in their famous Preface to the novel *Germinie Lacerteux* (1864). Here the mimetic desiderata that had dominated Realist writing, from the novels of Dickens and Balzac through to the essays of Champfleury and Duranty, are brought into sharper focus, and imprecise notions such as 'truth' or 'actuality' replaced by the more rigorous rhetoric of 'clinical analysis' and 'social investigation'. The modern writer, argued the Goncourts, is no longer a creative observer of the contemporary scene; he is a 'scientist', quite detached from, indeed indifferent to, his subject matter, delving into the realm of the impure, the debased, the *outré*, because (the Goncourts assure us) that is where his investigations and social conscience have taken him (**Reading 11**).

However, the writer who did most to establish Naturalism as the dominant literary mode was Émile Zola. His prestigious Rougon-Macquart novel series, published in twenty volumes between 1871 and 1893, gave epic shape to his conviction that human destiny was shaped by environmental and hereditary factors. From his early Preface to the second edition of *Thérèse Raquin* (published in 1868) to his lengthy essay, 'The experimental novel' (1880), Zola sought to put that conviction on a scientific basis, attempting to persuade the public of the purely analytical and disinterested nature of his literary project. He did this by aligning his work with that of the physiologist Claude Bernard, who had attempted in his *Introduction to the Study of Experimental Medicine* (1865) to deduce social behaviour from certain physiological 'facts' of human nature, which could then be studied by means of a strictly experimental methodology. Zola elaborated Bernard's findings into a deterministic fatalism, giving fictional shape to a world where, as he noted in his famous Preface to *Thérèse Raquin* (**Reading 12**), 'people [are] completely dominated by their nerves and blood, [and are] without free will, drawn into each action of their lives by the inexorable laws of their physical nature'.

Zola's influence on the course of literature in the late nineteenth century was immense, and immensely controversial. His critics accused him of sensationalism, arguing that his purported 'scientific' techniques were no more than a veneer intended to make his morally repugnant subject matter palatable to a middle-class reading public; while others (and Friedrich Engels was one of them) felt that his documentary perspectivism failed to penetrate beneath the surface of the social problems he was describing (*see* **Reading 18**). But the liberating effect of Zola's influence could not simply be wished away. Not only had he opened up for the novelist entirely new areas of experience, but his style of writing seemed genuinely to fuse the desiderata of art and science.

That Naturalism could function in a rural as well as an urban environment was demonstrated by the writing of the great Italian naturalist Giovanni Verga. As Verga explained in his Preface to *The House by the Medlar Tree* (1881), the world is governed by inexorable laws that determine the course of society, 'that fateful march through life, never-ending, often exhausting and feverish, which humanity follows in order to achieve the conquest of progress' (**Reading 13**). Within the largely peasant world constructed by Verga, where ambition, appetite and the obsessive need for self betterment reigns, the individual has little control over his or her fate or actions: all is predetermined; the actors in this drama participate not out of free choice but from necessity. It is reality stripped to its core, and for the novelist to pass a value judgement upon it, declaring that good, that bad is, Verga argues, a pointless activity: 'already it is much if he manages to stand back from the field of struggle for a moment in order to study it without passion, and to render the scene clearly.'

Some writers and critics attempted to apply Naturalism's concern with laws and scientific determinism to literature itself. This was the approach chosen by the French cultural historian Hippolyte Taine, who argued in his famous Introduction to *A History of English Literature* (4 vols, 1863–4) that literature was subject to three conditioning factors: the racial identity of the author (*la race*), his social, political and geographical environment (*le milieu*) and the historical period in which he wrote (*le moment*). Taine's influence was immense, particularly in Germany where Arno Holz, in his theoretical tract *Art: Its Nature and its Laws* (1891), attempted to find a formula ('Art = Nature minus X', 'X' being the temperament or aesthetic disposition of the individual writer) that would provide a single key to the vagaries of aesthetic development. Many of Holz's contemporaries followed him, believing that in an age dominated by the triumph of scientific positivism, it was inconceivable that art and literature should not be subject to the same laws as natural phenomena. As the critic, Conrad Alberti, supporting the Naturalist cause, argued in his 'The twelve articles of Realism' (1889), 'since all the laws of nature, which regulate mechanical events in the physical world, also determine all intellectual events and phenomena, so art is also subject to exactly the same laws as the mechanical world. Principles such as the struggle for existence, natural selection, heredity and adaptability to the environment are just as eternally valid in art and the history of art as they are in the physiological development of organisms' (**Reading 14**).

The controversial nature of Naturalism's subject matter raised fundamental issues regarding censorship and the right of the state to intervene in literary matters in order to protect public decency. These were issues that plagued the publication of Naturalist fiction wherever it appeared, from France and England (where Zola's works were banned in 1889) to Germany and Russia, where accusations of immorality were levelled against all writers (including the famous Anton Chekhov) who strayed from the safe terrain of predictable melodrama and domestic kitsch. In a letter written in 1887, Chekhov found it necessary to defend himself against such accusations (**Reading 15**). In what was to remain his fullest expression of commitment to the Realist cause, Chekhov avails himself here of a powerful armoury of imperatives: the artist's duty to describe the world as he or she finds it; the unfeasibility of passing absolute judgement on literary texts; the denial of the corrupting influence of literature; and the writer's need to accommodate all moral sensibilities. For, as Chekhov argues, 'to a chemist, nothing on earth is unclean. A writer must be as objective as a chemist: he must abandon the subjective line; he must know that dung-heaps play a very respectable part in a landscape, and that evil passions are as inherent in life as good ones.' The pursuit of truth, Chekhov is sure, must transcend traditional concerns for moral probity and good taste, however much transgressing these may offend some readers.

Implicit in all that Chekhov says is the conviction that Realism and
Naturalism are defensible because the works produced in their name are
an expression of the modern age, and that 'writers are the children of their
age'. A similar defence was launched by the Spanish novelist Benito Pérez
Galdós (author of *Fortunata and Jacinta*, 1887), who enthusiastically
observed in his speech, 'Contemporary society as novelistic material'
(1897), that 'examining the conditions of the social milieu in which we
live' forces the writer to come to terms with new realities, which, in spite
of their 'confusion and nervous disquietude', nevertheless constitute the
experience of modernity. For Pérez Galdós, engaging with this
experience provided both a source of inspiration for the novelist and a
means to the renewal of his art-form. As he noted: 'With the breakdown
of categories masks fall at one blow and faces appear in their true purity.
Types are lost, but man is better revealed to us, and Art is directed solely
to giving to imaginary beings a life that is more human than social'
(**Reading 16**).

The Swedish playwright August Strindberg viewed the same realities
in a less positive light. He too was an observer of emerging mass society,
and depicted in his plays, most notably *The Father* (1887) and *Miss Julie*
(1888), the effects of what happens when traditional culture, where the
strictly demarcated lines between classes allowed for a clear definition of
social and gender roles and, indeed, of personality, gives way to
destabilizing social change. Pérez Galdós had seen the positive side to the
collapse of tradition: the fluency, the energy, the possibilities. Strindberg,
however, driven by his obsession with loosening sexual mores and the
emancipation of women, offers, in the Preface to *Miss Julie* (1888), a
darker and more complex view, one that is nihilistic in the Nietzschean
sense that cultural decline is seen as both destructive and necessary
(**Reading 17**). Strindberg's grim vision not only depicts a world of cruel
struggle, where wife is pitted against husband, gender against gender in a
process of unprincipled and cruel exploitation; it also posits the very
notion of individual character as a 'vacillating, disintegrated' fictive shape,
a conglomeration of 'past and present stages of civilisation, bits from
books and newspapers, scraps of humanity, rags and tatters of fine
clothing, patched together'. With Strindberg, the ethos of Naturalism
reaches a point of no return, where the banishment of ideals and all
humanist values has put into doubt the very continuity of selfhood.

Many reacted against the bleak and cynical world of the Naturalists that
Strindberg shapes in his writing, rejecting it on both moral and aesthetic
grounds. But there was one further ground for not accepting the
Naturalist equation: in spite of its much vaunted 'scientific' methodology,
many argued that it simply did not describe the world with the accuracy
that it claimed for itself. Friedrich Engels was one reader who held to this
view. In a letter written in 1888, Engels argued that Zola had failed to

penetrate beneath the surface of the world he was describing, because he lacked, quite simply, a deeper sense for the greater forces of history, and for the 'typicality' of individuals within their respective social roles and ideological positions. Engels found this deeper sense for the underlying structure of historical change exemplified in the work of Balzac who, in spite of his explicit political affiliations (which were Royalist), was nevertheless capable of writing against his own subjective preferences, and hence was able to capture in his novels the dynamics of that emerging class, the bourgeoisie, which was on the point of gaining the upper hand in French social and political life. As Engels explained: 'That Balzac thus was compelled to go against his own class sympathies and political prejudices, that he *saw* the necessity of the downfall of his favourite nobles, and described them as people deserving no better fate; and that he *saw* the real men of the future where, for the time being, they alone were to be found' allowed him to capture the objective movement of history (**Reading 18**). This was a gift that Balzac possessed, and Zola and his Naturalists (for Engels, at least) lacked.

Engels' concern with typicality introduced into the debate surrounding Naturalism considerations that were ultimately of a historiographical nature, connected to ways of viewing history and to an understanding of the sources of the political agency of historical change. As such, his comments posed fundamental questions regarding the function of literature in society, and its position *vis-à-vis* dominant positions of cultural speech, questions that would remain largely unanswered until later, in the twentieth century. Then, a new debate would emerge, between those, such as the Hungarian Marxist Georg Lukács (*Essays on Realism*, 1948), who saw in Realism the ideal medium for an understanding and articulation of the totality of social action, and those who followed in the wake of Modernist and then Postmodernist deconstructionism, such as Roland Barthes (*Writing Degree Zero*, 1953), who argued that Realism had simply reproduced and consolidated in its themes and its narrative the static, closed world of nineteenth-century bourgeois hegemony, from a world which, ultimately, neither author nor reader can escape. It is a debate that has remained unresolved.

# 1

# 'Of the pathetic fallacy'

## John Ruskin: *Modern Painters* (1856)

*The main works of John Ruskin (1819–1900) were* The Stones of Venice *(3 vols, 1851–3),* Modern Painters, *(5 vols, 1843–60) and the autobiographical* Praeterita *(1885–9). Ruskin was an art critic whose preoccupations were as much socio-ethical as aesthetic (for example, he was a staunch opponent of* laissez-faire *economics). But even when writing about painting, Ruskin's concern for aesthetic integrity, and his insistence that the artist respect the physical and natural integrity of the world, is apparent, as is his distrust of false emotion and Romantic obfuscation. His essay 'Of the pathetic fallacy' (1856) is his major statement on these themes. However, although Ruskin's essay has often been read as a Realist critique of Romanticism, it is important to note that Ruskin's ire is largely directed against neo-classical poets such as Alexander Pope, and against the artificial diction of their nature poetry.*

*Ruskin begins his analysis by arguing that the art critic must learn to discern 'the difference between the ordinary, proper, and true appearances of things to us; and the extraordinary, or false appearances, when we are under the influence of emotion, or contemplative fancy; false appearances, I say, as being entirely unconnected with any real power or character in the object, and only imputed to it by us'. Ruskin calls the construction of these 'false appearances' in art a 'fallacy'.*

It will appear also, on consideration of the matter, that this fallacy is of two principal kinds. Either, as in the case of the crocus [depicted in a poem cited earlier], it is the fallacy of wilful fancy, which involves no real expectation that it will be believed; or else it is a fallacy caused by an excited state of the feelings, making us, for the time, more or less irrational. Of the cheating of the fancy we shall have to speak presently; but, in this chapter, I want to examine the nature of the other error, that which the mind admits when affected strongly by emotion. Thus, for instance, in [Tennyson's poem] 'Alton Locke', –

'They rowed her in across the rolling foam –
The cruel, crawling foam.'

The foam is not cruel, neither does it crawl. The state of mind which attributes to it these characters of a living creature is one in which the

**Source:** John Ruskin, *Modern Painters*, 5 vols (third edition, London: Dent, n.d.), vol. 3, pp. 148, 151–2 and 158. **Further reading:** George P. Landow, *The Aesthetic and Critical Theories of John Ruskin* (Princeton: Princeton University Press, 1971), esp. pp. 378–90.

reason is unhinged by grief. All violent feelings have the same effect. They produce in us a falseness in all our impressions of external things, which I would generally characterize as the 'Pathetic fallacy'.

*Ruskin then turns his attention to the character of poets who are given to the use of the pathetic fallacy, in a tone that is largely critical but not dismissive of the effects of strong emotion upon the artistic temperament. Defining the variants of the pathetic fallacy allows Ruskin to rank the varying strengths of the poetic mind.*

The temperament which admits the pathetic fallacy, is, as I said above, that of a mind and body in some sort too weak to deal fully with what is before them or upon them; borne away, or over-clouded, or over-dazzled by emotion; and it is a more or less noble state, according to the force of the emotion which has induced it. For it is no credit to a man that he is not morbid or inaccurate in his perceptions, when he has no strength of feeling to warp them; and it is in general a sign of higher capacity and stand in the ranks of being, that the emotions should be strong enough to vanquish, partly, the intellect, and make it believe what they choose. But it is still a grander condition when the intellect also rises, till it is strong enough to assert its rule against, or together with, the utmost efforts of the passions; and the whole man stands in an iron glow, white hot, perhaps, but still strong, and in no wise evaporating; even if he melts, losing none of his weight.

So, then, we have the three ranks: the man who perceives rightly, because he does not feel, and to whom the primrose is very accurately the primrose, because he does not love it. Then, secondly, the man who perceives wrongly, because he feels, and to whom the primrose is anything else than a primrose: a star, or a sun, or a fairy's shield, or a forsaken maiden. And, then, lastly, there is the man who perceives rightly in spite of his feelings, and to whom the primrose is for ever nothing else than itself – a little flower, apprehended in the very plain and leafy fact of it, whatever and how many soever the associations and passions may be, that crowd around it. And, in general, these three classes may be rated in comparative order, as the men who are not poets at all, and the poets of the second order, and the poets of the first; only however great a man may be, there are always some subjects which *ought* to throw him off his balance; some, by which his poor human capacity of thought should be conquered, and brought into the inaccurate and vague state of perception, so that the language of the highest inspiration becomes broken, obscure, and wild in metaphor, resembling that of the weaker man, overborne by weaker things.

And thus, in full, there are four classes: the men who feel nothing, and therefore see truly; the men who feel strongly, think weakly, and see untruly (second order of poets); the men who feel strongly, think strongly, and see truly (first order of poets); and the men who, strong as human creatures can be, are yet submitted to influences stronger than they, and see in a sort untruly, because what they see is inconceivably above them. This last is the usual condition of prophetic inspiration.

> *Ruskin reserves his greatest ire for those poets who employ this anthropomorphizing discourse without feeling any of the empathetic emotions that are constituent of the pathetic fallacy. 'There is no greater baseness in literature than the habit of using these metaphorical expressions in cold blood', Ruskin notes, decrying Pope for the 'definite absurdity, rooted in affectation, and coldly asserted in the teeth of nature and fact' of lines which purport to describe a shepherd girl's response to nature. These criticisms lead Ruskin to offer the following damning observation.*

I believe these instances are enough to illustrate the main point I insist upon respecting the pathetic fallacy, – that so far as it *is* a fallacy, it is always the sign of a morbid state of mind, and comparatively of a weak one. Even in the most inspired prophet it is a sign of the incapacity of his human sight or thought to bear what has been revealed to it. In ordinary poetry, if it is found in the thoughts of the poet himself, it is at once a sign of his belonging to the inferior school; if in the thoughts of the characters imagined by him, it is right or wrong according to the genuineness of the emotion from which it springs; always however, implying necessarily *some* degree of weakness of character.

## 2

---

## *'Moral emotion'*

### George Eliot: 'Worldliness and other-worldliness: the poet Young' (1857)

> *In her novels* Adam Bede *(1859),* The Mill on the Floss *(1860),* Felix Holt, the Radical *(1866) and* Middlemarch *(1871–2), George Eliot (1819–80) charted the intellectual and cultural changes that were taking place in mid-nineteenth-century England. She was particularly concerned with the rise of scientific positivism, and the challenges it posed to religion (among her first major publications was a translation of the materialist Ludwig Feuerbach's* The Essence of Christianity, *1853). She also wrote about the emergence of Realism as a cultural paradigm within the arts, which she defended, as in the opening pages of Chapter 17 of her novel*

---

**Source:** George Eliot, *Essays of George Eliot*, edited by Thomas Pinney (New York: Columbia University Press, 1963), pp. 366–7, 381–2 and 385. **Further reading:** Bernard J. Paris, 'George Eliot's religion of humanity', in *George Eliot: A Collection of Essays*, edited by George R. Creeger (Englewood Cliffs, NJ: Prentice-Hall, 1970), pp. 11–36.

*Adam Bede, where she praises the Realist aesthetic for its ability to capture the 'beauty in these commonplace things' that surround us on a daily basis.*

*In her essay on Edward Young, first published in* The Westminster Review *in 1857, she went into greater detail on this theme, unfavourably comparing the pre-Romantic Young (the author of the sentimental, quasi-religious epic* Night Thoughts*) with the rural poet, William Cowper (1731–1800), in whom she divined an autochthonic integrity missing from the former. Eliot argues that Young's work evinces a 'want of genuine emotion', and a personal philosophy whose 'religion exhausts itself in ejaculations and rebukes, and knows no medium between the ecstatic and the sententious'.*

One of the most striking characteristics of Young is his *radical insincerity as a poetic artist*. This, added to the thin and artificial texture of his wit, is the true explanation of the paradox – that a poet who is often inopportunely witty has the opposite vice of bombastic absurdity. The source of all grandiloquence is the want of taking for a criterion the true qualities of the object described, or the emotion expressed. The grandiloquent man is never bent on saying what he feels or what he sees, but on producing a certain effect on his audience; hence he may float away into utter inanity without meeting any criterion to arrest him. Here lies the distinction between grandiloquence and genuine fancy or bold imaginativeness. The fantastic or the boldly imaginative poet may be as sincere as the most realistic: he is true to his own sensibilities or inward vision, and in his wildest flights he never breaks loose from his criterion – the truth of his own mental state. Now, this disruption of language from genuine thought and feeling is what we are constantly detecting in Young, and his insincerity is the more likely to betray him into absurdity, because he habitually treats of abstractions, and not of concrete objects or specific emotions. He descants perpetually on virtue, religion, 'the good man', life, death, immortality, eternity – subjects which are apt to give a factitious grandeur to empty wordiness. When a poet floats in the empyrean, and only takes a bird's-eye view of the earth, some people accept the mere fact of his soaring for sublimity, and mistake his dim vision of earth for proximity to heaven. Thus:

> His hand the good man fixes on the skies,
> And bids earth roll, nor feel his idle whirl, –

may, perhaps, pass for sublime with some readers. But a pause a moment to realize the image, and the monstrous absurdity of a man's grasping the skies, and hanging habitually suspended there, while he contemptuously bids the earth roll, warns you that no genuine feeling could have suggested so unnatural a conception.

*Unlike Young, Cowper possessed the facility to grasp nature in all its vitality, which was an artistic* tour de force *achieved in the face of his own frequently melancholy temperament.*

There was real and deep sadness in Cowper's personal lot; while Young, apart from his ambitious and greedy discontent, seems to have had no great sorrow.

Yet, see how a lovely, sympathetic nature manifests itself in spite of creed and circumstance! Where is the poem that surpasses [Cowper's] 'Task' in the genuine love it breathes, at once towards inanimate and animate existence – in truthfulness of perception and sincerity of presentation – in the calm gladness that springs from a delight in objects for their own sake, without self-reference – in divine sympathy with the lowliest pleasures, with the most short-lived capacity for pain? Here is no railing at the earth's 'melancholy map', but the happiest lingering over her simplest scenes with all the fond minuteness of attention that belongs to love; no pompous rhetoric about the inferiority of the 'brutes', but a warm plea on their behalf against man's inconsiderateness and cruelty, and a sense of enlarged happiness from their companionship in enjoyment; no vague rant about human misery and human virtue, but that close and vivid presentation of particular sorrows and privations, of particular deeds and misdeeds, which is the direct road to the emotions. How Cowper's exquisite mind falls with the mild warmth of morning sunlight on the commonest objects, at once disclosing every detail and investing every detail with beauty! No object is too small to prompt his song – not the sooty film on the bars, or the spoutless teapot holding a bit of mignonette that serves to cheer the dingy town-lodging with a 'hint that Nature lives;' and yet his song is never trivial, for he is alive to small objects, not because his mind is narrow, but because his glance is clear and his heart is large.

*Eliot concludes her essay with words that draw a very clear line between the inflated Romanticism of Young's verse and the Realist breadth of Cowper's.*

The sum of our comparison is this – In Young we have the type of that deficient human sympathy, that impiety towards the present and the visible, which flies for its motives, its sanctities, and its religion, to the remote, the vague, and the unknown: in Cowper we have the type of that genuine love which cherishes things in proportion to their nearness, and feels its reverence grow in proportion to the intimacy of its knowledge.

# 'The art of copying from nature'

## Walter Scott: Review of Jane Austen's *Emma* (1815)

*The extensive fictional output of Sir Walter Scott (1771–1832) (which began with* Waverley *in 1814 and ended, more than thirty novels later, with* Castle Dangerous *in 1831) helped create an apparently insatiable enthusiasm for folk antiquity, chivalry and antiquarian habit throughout Europe. But much of this work (and most notably* Waverley*) shows that Scott fully realized that the values of the Romantic past were being superseded by those of a new, more sober and restrained era – that of Realism. It is precisely that transition which Scott addresses in his review of Jane Austen's* Emma*, published in the* Quarterly Review *in 1815. Scott sees Austen's novel as representing a radical departure from the popular trends of preceding English fiction, which had cultivated a Gothic sensualism that soon wearied the palate of the reading public.*

Here, therefore, we have two essential and important circumstances, in which the earlier novels differed from those now in fashion, and were more nearly assimilated to the old romances. And there can be no doubt that, by the studied involution and extrication of the story, by the combination of incidents new, striking and wonderful beyond the course of ordinary life, the former authors opened that obvious and strong sense of interest which arises from curiosity; as by the pure, elevated, and romantic caste of the sentiment, they conciliated those better propensities of our nature which loves to contemplate the picture of virtue, even when confessedly unable to imitate its excellences.

But strong and powerful as these sources of emotion and interest may be, they are, like all others, capable of being exhausted by habit. The imitators who rushed in crowds upon each path in which the great masters of the art had successively led the way, produced upon the public mind the usual effect of satiety. The first writer of a new class is, as it were, placed on a pinnacle of excellence, to which, at the earliest glance of a surprized admirer, his ascent seems little less than miraculous. Time and imitation speedily diminish the wonder, and each successive attempt establishes a kind of progressive scale of ascent between the lately deified author, and the reader, who had deemed his excellence inaccessible. The stupidity, the mediocrity, the merit of his imitators, are alike fatal to the

**Source:** *Sir Walter Scott: On Novelists and Fiction*, edited by Ioan Williams (London: Routledge, 1968), pp. 229–31. **Further reading:** Robert Ignatius Letellier, *Sir Walter Scott and the Gothic Novel* (Lampeter: Edwin Mellen Press, 1994).

first inventor, by shewing how possible it is to exaggerate his faults and to come within a certain point of his beauties.

Materials also (and the man of genius as well as his wretched imitator must work with the same) become stale and familiar. Social life, in our civilized days, affords few instances capable of being painted in the strong dark colours which excite surprize and horror; and robbers, smugglers, bailiffs, caverns, dungeons, and mad-houses, have been all introduced until they ceased to interest. And thus in the novel, as in every style of composition which appeals to the public taste, the more rich and easily worked mines being exhausted, the adventurous author must, if he is desirous of success, have recourse to those which were disdained by his predecessors as unproductive, or avoided as only capable of being turned to profit by great skill and labour.

Accordingly a style of novel has arisen, within the last fifteen or twenty years, differing from the former in the points upon which the interest hinges; neither alarming our credulity nor amusing our imagination by wild variety of incident, or by those pictures of romantic affection and sensibility, which were formerly as certain attributes of fictitious characters as they are of rare occurrence amongst those who actually live and die. The substitute for these excitements, which had lost much of their poignancy by the repeated and injudicious use of them, was the art of copying from nature as she really exists in the common walks of life, and presenting to the reader, instead of the splendid scenes of an imaginary world, a correct and striking representation of that which is daily taking place around him.

In adventuring upon this task, the author makes obvious sacrifices, and encounters particular difficulty. He who paints from *le beau idéal*, if his scenes and sentiments are striking and interesting, is in a great measure exempted from the difficult task of reconciling them with the ordinary probabilities of life: but he who paints a scene of common occurrence, places his composition within that extensive range of criticism which general experience offers to every reader. The resemblance of a statue of Hercules we must take on the artist's judgment; but every one can criticize that which is presented as the portrait of a friend, or neighbour. Something more than a mere sign-post likeness is also demanded. The portrait must have spirit and character, as well as resemblance; and being deprived of all that, according to Bayes, goes 'to elevate and surprize', it must make amends by displaying depth of knowledge and dexterity of execution. We, therefore, bestow no mean compliment upon the author of *Emma*, when we say that, keeping close to common incidents, and to such characters as occupy the ordinary walks of life, she has produced sketches of such spirit and originality, that we never miss the excitation which depends upon a narrative of uncommon events, arising from the consideration of minds, manners, and sentiments, greatly above our own.

In this class she stands almost alone; for the scenes of Miss Edgeworth are laid in higher life, varied by more romantic incident, and by her remarkable power of embodying and illustrating national character. But the author of *Emma* confines herself chiefly to the middling classes of society; her most distinguished characters do not rise greatly above well-bred country gentlemen and ladies; and those who are sketched with most originality and precision, belong to a class rather below that standard. The narrative of all her novels is composed of such common occurrences as may have fallen under the observation of most folks; and her dramatis personae conduct themselves upon the motives and principles which the readers may recognize as ruling their own and that of most of their acquaintances. The kind of moral, also, which these novels inculcate, applies equally to the paths of common life.

4

## 'French society is the real author'

### Honoré de Balzac: Foreword to *The Human Comedy* (1842)

*Honoré de Balzac (1799–1850) was the author of an epic novel sequence,* The Human Comedy *(published in twenty-four volumes – some comprising several novels or stories – between 1829 and 1848), and was the foremost French novelist of his generation. The most noted novels in the series –* Eugenie Grandet *(1833),* Father Goriot *(1835),* Lost Illusions *(1843) and* Cousin Bette *(1846) – depict a world where moral values and idealism have been replaced by a widespread cynicism that sees the social sphere dominated and propelled by economic self-interest, sexual prowess and political pragmatism. In the Foreword to the series, Balzac sought to put the philosophy that informed his fiction on a scientific basis.*

When the idea of *The Human Comedy* first came to me it initially seemed to be the product of a dream, like one of those impossible projects that one caresses and allows to fly away again; a smiling chimera, who briefly allows us a glimpse of her pretty face, only to spread her wings and return to the heavenly realm of fantasy. But this chimera, like many chimeras,

**Source:** Honoré de Balzac, 'Avant-propos' to *La Comédie Humaine*, edited by Pierre-Georges Catex (Paris: Gallimard, 1976). **Standard translation:** *The Works of Honoré de Balzac*, translated by Ellen Marriage (Philadelphia: Avil Publishing Company, 1901), vol. I, pp. liii–lxix. **Further reading:** E. Preston Dargan, i.a., *Studies in Balzac's Realism* (New York: Russell and Russell [1932], 1967), pp. 1–33.

has become a reality; it has its commandments, and it exercises a tyranny which brooks no dissent.

The idea originated in a comparison between Humanity and Animality.

It would be a mistake to suppose that the great debate which has lately made a stir between Cuvier and Geoffroy Sainte-Hilaire rests upon a scientific innovation. The notion of *organic unity*, formulated in different ways, has occupied the greatest minds for two hundred years. If we re-read those extraordinary works of the mystical authors who studied the sciences in their relation to infinity, writers such as Swedenborg, Saint-Martin, and others, and the works of the most gifted thinkers in Natural History, such as Leibnitz, Buffon, Charles Bonnet etc., one finds in the monads of Leibnitz, in the organic molecules of Buffon, in the vegetative force of Needham, in the encapsulation of similar parts described by Charles Bonnet (who was so bold as to write in 1760: 'Animals vegetate just like plants'); as I say, we find amongst these thinkers the rudiments of that great law of *self for self*, which forms the base for the notion of *organic unity*. There is but one animal. The Creator has made use of one and the same model for every organic being. The animal is a principal that takes its external form, or, to speak more accurately, the differences of its form, from the environment in which it has been compelled to develop. Zoological species are the result of these differences. It will be to the eternal glory of Geoffroy Sainte-Hilaire that he was the first to announce and develop this system, triumphing over Cuvier on this point of high science, whose victory was celebrated by the great Goethe in the final article that he wrote.

Having penetrated this system well before the debates to which it gave rise, I realised that, in this respect, Society resembled Nature. Does not Society make man, according to the environment in which he lives and acts, into as many different men as there are species in zoology? The differences between a soldier, a worker, an administrator, a lawyer, a vagrant, an academic, a statesman, a businessman, a sailor, a poet, a pauper, and a priest are as great, although more difficult to define, than those between the wolf, the lion, the ass, the crow, the shark, the seal, the ewe etc. Thus, there have always existed, and will always exist, social species just as there have always existed zoological species. If Buffon could produce a magnificent work by attempting to represent in a single book the whole realm of zoology, is there not a work in this genre to complete for the social realm? But Nature has imposed limits upon animal species that Society does not need to observe. When Buffon describes the lion, he dismisses the lioness in a few words; but in Society, woman is not always female to the male. Two perfectly dissimilar beings can coexist in one household. The wife of a shopkeeper is sometimes worthy of a prince; and the wife of a prince is often no better than that of an artist. The Social Estate has incongruities which Nature does not permit itself, for the former is nature *plus* society. The description of social species would thus be at least twice that of a description of the animal species, even if we just restricted ourselves to considering the two sexes. We also need to recognise that there is very little drama amongst animals; confusion rarely occurs there; they fight it out amongst themselves, and that's all there is to it. Men also fight between themselves, but their greater or lesser intelligence makes their struggle far more complicated. Although certain thinkers do not as yet admit that the animalistic flows into human nature through that immense tide of life, it is undeniable that grocers become peers, and noblemen sometimes sink to the lowest social rank. As well as that, Buffon found that life was extremely simple amongst animals. Animals have little property, and no arts or sciences; whereas man, by dint of a law that has as yet to be discovered, has a tendency to represent his customs, his thought and his life in all that he uses for his needs. Although Leuwenhoëk, Swammerdam, Spallanzani, Réaumur, Charles Bonnet, Muller, Haller and other patient zoologists have shown us how interesting the habits of animals are, the behaviour of all animal species, to my mind, at least, has remained the same throughout the ages; whereas the dress, the manners, the speech, the residence of a prince, of an artist, of a banker, of a priest, and a pauper are absolutely unlike, and change with every phase of civilisation.

Thus, the work to be written required a three-fold focus: upon men, women and things; in other words, upon people and the material expression that they give to their thinking; in short, upon man and life.

> It is the synoptic coherence of his project, the fact that it embraces all aspects of the behaviour of the human animal in society, that most inspires Balzac, and encourages him to see his novel series as an advance on the work of Walter Scott, whom Balzac (like all his generation) held in artistic awe. In spite of Scott's epic achievements, his novelistic vision lacked (according to the French author) a discernible unity.

In taking note of this lack of unity, which in no way detracts from the Scottish writer's greatness, I saw at once the best system for the realisation of my own project, and the possibility for executing it. Although, so to speak, dazzled by the wondrous fecundity of Walter Scott, who is always himself and always original, I did not despair, for I found the source of his talent in the infinite variety of human nature itself. Chance is the greatest novelist in the world; in order to write productively, we have only to study it. French society will be the real author; I shall only be its secretary. By drawing up an inventory of its vices and virtues, by detailing its major passions, by depicting characters, by focussing upon the major incidents in its social life, by composing types who embody the traits of a number of homogeneous characters, I might perhaps succeed in writing the history overlooked by so many historians: the history of manners. With much patience and fortitude, I might be able to write that book about France in the Nineteenth Century which (as we all regret) we unhappily lack about the civilisations of Rome, Athens, Tyre, Memphis, Persia and India, and, following the Abbé Barthélemy, the brave and patient Monteil has tried to provide for the Middle Ages, but without any real success.

The work is not, as yet, complete. By remaining faithful to the strict lines of a reproduction, a writer might become a more or less accurate, more or less successful, more or less patient or perceptive painter of human types, a narrator of the dramas of private life, the archaeologist of social furniture, the cataloguer of professions, the recorder of good and evil; but, to deserve the praise that every artist strives for, must I not also study the reasons or the cause of these social effects, disclose the hidden meaning of this vast array of figures, passions and events? And finally, after I have sought (I will not say found) this cause, this social motor, must it not be necessary to reflect on natural laws, and identify which societies approximate to, or deviate from, the eternal rules of the true and the good? In spite of the vast scale of these preliminary considerations, which might constitute a study in their own right, the work, to be complete, would need a conclusion. Thus depicted, Society would be seen to bear within itself the reasons for its functioning.

## 5

# 'The mission of art today'

## Charles-Augustin Sainte-Beuve: 'The hopes and wishes of the literary and poetic movement after the Revolution of 1830' (1830)

*Charles-Augustin Sainte-Beuve (1804–69) was the major French literary critic of the period. Although he is largely remembered today for his exhaustively researched and epically conceived literary-historical works such as* Port Royal *(1840–8) and* Chateaubriand and His Literary Group under the Empire *(1861), it was Sainte-Beuve's essayistic and journalistic writing that secured his contemporary fame. Brought together in volumes such as* Literary Criticisms and Portraits *(5 vols, 1832–9),* Monday Chats *(3 vols, 1849–52 and 1861–9) and* New Mondays

**Source:** Charles-Augustin Sainte-Beuve, *Oeuvres*, edited by Maxime Leroy (Paris: Gallimard, 1949), vol. I, pp. 376–7. **Standard translation:** *Paths to the Present: Aspects of European Thought from Romanticism to Existentialism*, edited and translated by Eugen Weber (New York: Dodd, Mead & Co., 1969), pp. 130–4. **Further reading:** Andrew George Lehmann, *Sainte-Beuve: A Portrait of the Critic, 1804–1842* (Oxford: Clarendon Press, 1962).

*(1863–70), these sharply sketched vignettes did much to influence public taste regarding the major literary figures and movements of the day. In 'The Hopes and Wishes of the Literary and Poetic Movement after the Revolution of 1830', Sainte-Beuve attempted to capture an epochal juncture in French literary history: the move from Romanticism to a broader, more socially sympathetic form of literature that would eventually be called Realism. He begins by stressing the positive achievements of early figures such as Madame de Staël, Chateaubriand and a second generation of Romantics such as Hugo; the books that they wrote were of 'a really modern originality, treasures of warmth, of emotion and of life, a scope that was tremendous though sometimes beyond the limits of reality'. These authors also longed (Sainte-Beuve adds) for political harmony, putting their faith in the restored dynasty of Bourbons, in whom they divined a growing liberalism of spirit.*

They were mistaken; but their error, honourable in its principle, did not remain sterile in its results. They locked themselves away in their art, believing that the hour to accomplish their revolution had arrived; they spurred themselves on with that enthusiasm that alone can make for greatness, and they achieved much, believing that they could accomplish even greater things.

Thanks to them, to their theories and to their work, art, which did not as yet involve itself in the general activities of society, at least acquired, during its retreat from the common weal, a deep and distinctive awareness of its identity; it put itself to the test, learnt to recognize its worth, and steeled its tools. I will not attempt to deny that there were many weaknesses in this rather absolute manner of conceiving and practising art, of isolating it from the world, from contemporary political and religious passions, of turning it, above all, into something unattached, amusing, colourful, ingenious. That there was in all of this an extreme preoccupation with the self, an overly amorous predilection for form, I will not attempt to deny, although people have exaggerated many of these weaknesses. People have felt free to jest light-heartedly about the writers of the *Cénacle* group [formed by various French Romantics, including Victor Hugo]; and, certainly, it is best to leave it amongst the memories of life in the Restoration, where it certainly had a right to keep a respectable distance from the political turpitude of that period. But what it would be unjust to dispute is the memorable development of art during these last few years, its liberation from all servitude, the way it established and had recognised its realm of the spirit, its happy conquests in several areas which had not until that point been touched by reality or by life, its intimate interpretation of nature, and its eagle's flight above the highest peaks of history.

However, let us admit it – art has still not become popular. In its development it neither embraces nor reproduces the movement of society, which spreads and advances on a daily basis. Having descended with regret from its medieval heights, it had got too used to looking upon the comfortable terrace of the Restoration as a sort of Royal terrace like the one at Saint-Germain en Laye, a cheerful and sunny plateau where one might dream and sing in the shade, stroll and recline at leisure, without suffering from the dust or heat of the day. It was content to see, from time to time, the people and the mass of society milling confusedly around at its base, on that great common highway where, apart from the beloved name of [Pierre-Jean de] Béranger, no one else retained the name of a true poet.

Today, now that the Restoration has gone, and the terrace so laboriously built has fallen down, and now the people and the poets wish to march together, a new period is opening for poetry; art will henceforth be on a common footing, in the arena with everybody, side by side with an indefatigable humanity. Happily, art possesses both life and youth; it has confidence in itself, it knows what it wants, and knows that there is a place for its kingdom, even in the breast of the Republican nations. Art remembers the past that it loved, that it understood, and from which it has detached itself with tears; but it is towards the future that its wishes and its efforts will henceforth be directed. Sure of itself, aware of the past, it is armed and fully equipped for its distant pilgrimage. The destinies almost infinite of our regenerated society, the torments, religious and obscure, that disturb it, the absolute emancipation towards which it aspires, all invite art to unite with it, so that it may charm it during the voyage, and sustain it in the face of weariness, by acting as the harmonious echo, the prophetic mouthpiece, of its sombre and perplexed thoughts. The mission, the task, of art today, is really to create the human epic; it is to interpret in a thousand ways – in drama, in the ode, in the novel and the *elegy* – yes, even in the elegy turned solemn and primitive once more in the midst of its particular and personal emotions; it is unceasingly to reflect and to radiate in a thousand colours the sentiments of a progressive humanity, to rediscover this aspect of humanity, as it has gradually developed, in the depths of the philosophies of the past, to seek it out and follow it through the ages, to integrate it and its passions into a harmonious and living nature, to give it the canopy of a sovereign sky that is vast and understanding, and out of which the light can always be seen, shining through the periods of darkness.

# 6

# 'The reflection of the entirety of real life'

## Theodor Fontane: 'Our lyric and epic poetry since 1848' (1853)

*With his novels such as* Frau Jenny Treibel *(1893), his masterpiece* Effi Briest *(1895) and* Der Stechlin *(1898), Theodor Fontane (1819–98) was the major German Realist writer of his generation. In an earlier essay, 'Our lyric and epic poetry since 1848', Fontane undertook to analyse the new spirit of pragmatism that had entered the culture of mid-nineteenth-century Germany. For, as Fontane explains in this essay: 'What characterizes every facet of our age is Realism. Doctors have abandoned deductive reasoning and calculations in favour of concrete experience; politicians (of all parties) have now fixed their gaze firmly on the real needs of the people, and have consigned to the bottom drawer their utopian blue prints; and the military shrugs its shoulders over the Prussian military code, and calls for "old Grenadiers" rather than "young recruits".' Fontane's main concern in his essay is to introduce to the public a new generation of German Realists, such as Paul Heyse and Theodor Storm, the premises of whose fiction Fontane admiringly adumbrates in the major part of his essay. Before doing so, however, he outlines what he sees to be the characteristics of the Realist aesthetic, seeking to distance it from certain contemporary materialist theories that saw in it little more than a crude reflection of the external world. True Realism is far more than that, as Fontane explains.*

Above all, what we *don't* understand by the word is that naked reproduction of everyday existence, or, at any rate, of its misery and its shadow side. It is sad enough that we have to confront the existence of these self-evident realities. But it is only recently that people (particularly in the arts) have confused misery with Realism, and by depicting a proletarian on his deathbed, dying surrounded by his starving children, or by producing those so-called *Tendenzbilder* [pictures with a social message] (the plight of Silesian workers, the issue of hunting rights, and similar topics), imagined that they were establishing a brave new direction for the arts. But this direction has about as much in common with genuine Realism as iron ore has with metal: the transfiguration is missing. Certainly, the following acclamation by Goethe might well provide the motto for Realism:

> Just commit yourself to human life in all its richness,
> There where you make contact with it; there is the interest.

---

**Source:** Theodor Fontane, *Sämtliche Werke*, vol. 21, Part I (Munich: Nymphenburger Verlag, 1963), pp. 12–13. There is no standard translation. **Further reading:** A. R. Robinson, *Theodor Fontane: An Introduction to the Man and His Work* (Cardiff: University of Wales Press, 1976).

But the hand that makes that contact must be an artistic one. For in the final analysis, life is at base simply a marble quarry, which provides the raw material for an infinite number of sculptures; they lie dormant, only perceivable to the initiate and only by his hand to be awakened. The block in itself, simply torn out of a larger whole, is not as yet a work of art; nevertheless, we must welcome the recognition, which represents an absolute step forward, that it is above all the material, or, let us rather say, *the real* that is required by all artistic activity. This recognition, which was previously more or less nurtured only by a few individuals, has within a decade risen to an almost universal dominance in the thinking and the work of our writers, and represents a new turning point in our literature. A poem such as the 'Enchanted Rose', which was read in its age with admiration, could hardly be written in the present climate, let alone greeted with accolades by the judges of literary awards; 'Weltschmerz' has, under scorn and ridicule, long been buried; that inanity which 'wished to see no golden corn bloom in the fields/before freedom had come to our land' has been served its sentence, and that floral diction full of empty tinkling which, instead of providing one's mind with flesh and blood, for ten years and more, simply supplied brightly coloured scraps which served to hide the intellectual vacuity that lay within, this has all come to be recognised for what it was. This entire direction in the arts, a mish-mash of deliberate lies, vain narrow-mindedness, and over-blown pathos, has come to its vainglorious end 'in a nothingness of piercing feeling', and Realism has arrived like the spring, fresh, cheerful and full of strength, winning the battle without a struggle.

If we've merely restricted ourselves in the foregoing to negative comments (with the exception of one pithy formulation), and have largely stressed what Realism is not, so now we will in the following give our views (albeit briefly) on what it is: it is the reflection of the entirety of real life, involving all those genuine life forces and interests that are elemental to art; it is, if we may be forgiven this playful formulation, an *Interessenvertretung* [representation of interests or lobby group], of a certain kind. For Realism embraces the plenitude of life, the greatest as well as the smallest: it includes the Columbus, who bestows upon the world yet a new world, and the water fowl, whose entire universe is his pond. Realism draws the noblest thoughts, the deepest feelings into its ambit, and the meditations of a Goethe on the joys and sorrow of his Gretchen are the stuff of which it is made. For all that is *actual*. Realism does not want to focus on the mere world of the senses, and nothing but this; it wants least of all the purely palpable, but it does want the *true*. It excludes nothing, other than lies, the artificial, the nebulous, and the atrophied – four qualities with which we might describe an entire [preceding] literary epoch.

# 7

# 'These melancholy shades of life'

## Charles Dickens: Preface to *Oliver Twist* (1841)

*Charles Dickens (1812–70) was never self-consciously a 'Realist'; but his novels, such as* Oliver Twist *(1838),* Dombey and Son *(1848) and* Hard Times *(1854), engage with some of the major themes of Realist literature: the impact of urbanization upon the poor and disadvantaged; the emergence of a criminal class among the same; the ubiquity of commercialism and the profit motive, and its dissolving effects upon family and friendship. Like the Realists, Dickens felt compelled to defend the probity of his endeavours against accusations of impropriety and salaciousness, arguing, as he does here, in his Preface to* Oliver Twist, *that morality is only effective if it is shown to triumph in the most abject of circumstances.*

The greater part of this Tale was originally published in a magazine [*Bentley's*]. When I completed it, and put it forth in its present form three years ago, I fully expected it would be objected to on some very high moral grounds in some very high moral quarters. The result did not fail to prove the justice of my anticipations.

I embrace the present opportunity of saying a few words in explanation of my aim and object in its production. It is in some sort a duty with me to do so, in gratitude to those who sympathised with me and divined my purpose at the time, and who, perhaps, will not be sorry to have their impression confirmed under my own hand.

It is, it seems, a very coarse and shocking circumstance, that some of the characters in these pages are chosen from the most criminal and degraded of London's population; that Sikes is a thief, and Fagin a receiver of stolen goods; that the boys are pickpockets, and the girl is a prostitute.

I confess I have yet to learn that a lesson of the purest good may not be drawn from the vilest evil. I have always believed this to be a recognised and established truth, laid down by the greatest men the world has ever seen, constantly acted upon by the best and wisest natures, and confirmed by the reason and experience of every thinking mind. I saw no reason, when I wrote this book, why the very dregs of life, so long as their speech did not offend the ear, should not serve the purpose of a moral, at least as well as its froth and cream. Nor did I doubt that there lay festering in

**Source:** Charles Dickens, *Oliver Twist* (Oxford: Clarendon Press, 1966), pp. lxi–lxii and lxiv–lxv. **Further reading:** Alexander Welsh, *The City of Dickens* (Oxford: Clarendon Press, 1971).

Saint Giles's as good materials towards the truth as any flaunting in Saint James's.

In this spirit, when I wished to shew, in little Oliver, the principle of Good surviving through every adverse circumstance, and triumphing at last; and when I considered among what companions I could try him best, having regard to that kind of men into whose hands he would most naturally fall; I bethought myself of those who figure in these volumes. When I came to discuss the matter more maturely with myself, I saw many strong reasons for pursuing the course to which I was inclined. I had read of thieves by scores – seductive fellows (amiable for the most part), faultless in dress, plump in pocket, choice in horseflesh, bold in bearing, fortunate in gallantry, great at a song, a bottle, pack of cards or dice-box, and fit companions for the bravest. But I had never met (except in HOGARTH) with the miserable reality. It appeared to me that to draw a knot of such associates in crime as really do exist; to paint them in all their deformity, in all their wretchedness, in all the squalid poverty of their lives; to shew them as they really are, for ever skulking uneasily through the dirtiest paths of life, with the great, black, ghastly gallows closing up their prospect, turn them where they may; it appeared to me that to do this, would be to attempt a something which was greatly needed, and which would be a service to society. And therefore I did it as I best could.

*In his attempts to depict the less glamorous side of criminal life, Dickens was also aware of the need to observe the requirements of public morality and decency.*

Cervantes laughed Spain's chivalry away, by showing Spain its impossible and wild absurdity. It was my attempt, in my humble and far distant sphere, to dim the false glitter surrounding something which really did exist, by shewing it in its unattractive and repulsive truth. No less consulting my own taste, than the manners of the age, I endeavoured, while I painted it in all its fallen and degraded aspect, to banish from the lips of the lowest character I introduced, any expression that could by possibility offend; and rather to lead to the unavoidable inference that its existence was of the most debased and vicious kind, than to prove it elaborately by words and deeds. In the case of the girl, in particular, I kept this intention constantly in view. Whether it is apparent in the narrative, and how it is executed, I leave my readers to determine.

It has been observed of this girl, that her devotion to the brutal house-breaker does not seem natural, and it has been objected to Sikes in the same breath – with some inconsistency, as I venture to think – that he is surely overdrawn, because in him there would appear to be none of those redeeming traits which are objected to as unnatural in his mistress. Of the latter objection I will merely say, that I fear there are in the world some insensible and callous natures that do become, at last, utterly and irredeemably bad. But whether this be so or not, of one thing I am certain: that there are such men as Sikes, who, being closely followed through the same space of time, and through the same current of circumstances, would not give, by one look or action of a moment, the faintest indication of a better nature. Whether every gentler human feeling is dead within such bosoms, or the proper chord to strike has rusted and is hard to find, I do not know; but that the fact is so, I am sure.

It is useless to discuss whether the conduct and character of the girl seems natural or unnatural, probable or improbable, right or wrong. IT IS TRUE. Every man who has watched these melancholy shades of life knows it to be so. Suggested to my mind long ago – long before I dealt in fiction – by what I often saw and read of, in actual life around me, I have, for years, tracked it through many profligate and noisome ways, and found it still the same. From the first introduction of that poor wretch, to her laying her bloody head upon the robber's breast, there is not one word exaggerated or over-wrought. It is emphatically God's truth, for it is the truth He leaves in such depraved and miserable breasts; the hope yet lingering behind; the last fair drop of water at the bottom of the dried-up weed-choked well. It involves the best and worst shades of our common nature; much of its ugliest hues, and something of its most beautiful; it is a contradiction, an anomaly, an apparent impossibility, but it is a truth. I am glad to have had it doubted, for in that circumstance I find a sufficient assurance that it needed to be told.

Devonshire Terrace
April, 1841.

# 8

# Broken in the 'bitter struggle with the realities of life'

## George Sand: Preface to *Indiana* (1832)

*George Sand was the* nom de plume *of Amandine-Aurore-Lucie Dupin, Baronne Dudevant (1804–76), whose main works include the novels* Indiana *(1832), Valentine (1832),* Lélia *(1833), and the autobiographical* A Winter in Majorca *(1841), in which she described her relationship with her companion, Frederic Chopin. Sand wrote prefaces to most of her novels, but it is the first Preface to* Indiana *(a second edition followed in 1842) which most directly engages with the problems posed by writing Realist fiction. In her Preface, Sand (who writes throughout in the persona of a masculine author) engages in a highly sophisticated, indeed rhetorical, game with the reader, disclaiming any social-critical ambitions (while implying them throughout), and appealing to the refined sensibilities and high moral standards of the reader (while ironically undermining them at the same time), finally absolving herself from any proselytizing intentions by using the imperative of mimetic compliance. As Sand explains, she had no greater goal than to tell a true story.*

Should pages of this book incur the serious reproach that they display an inclination towards new beliefs, should severe judges find their tone imprudent and dangerous, it would be necessary to respond to these critics that they were doing too much honour to a work of little importance; and that to grapple with those serious questions regarding the social order, one would need to feel in possession of an immense spiritual strength or great talent; but such a presumption did not enter at all into the idea of this very simple story, in which this writer has created very little. If, in the course of his task, he has happened to give voice to laments torn from his characters by the social malaise of which they are the victims; if he has not refrained from expressing their aspirations for a better existence, it is society that the reader should blame for its inequalities, and destiny for its injustices. The writer is only a mirror who reflects such circumstances, a machine which traces them, and who has nothing to apologise for if his prints are exact and his image a faithful one.

Bear in mind, then, that the narrator did not take as his subject or his message those cries of pain or anger that are scattered through the drama of human life. He does not have any pretension to conceal a serious moral

**Source:** George Sand, *Indiana* (Paris: Editions Garnier, 1962), pp. 6–7 and 9–12. **Standard translation:** *George Sand in Her Own Words*, translated and edited by Joseph Barry (New York: Anchor Books, 1979), pp. 4–10. **Further reading:** Paul G. Blount, *George Sand and the Victorian World* (Athens, USA: University of Georgia Press, 1979).

inside the form of a story; he has not come as part of some surprise attack upon the edifice that an uncertain future has in store for us, nor does he wish to take a stick to the crumbling edifice of the past. He knows too well that we live in a time of moral ruin, where human reason has need of blinds to soften the harsh daylight that dazzles it. Had he felt enough of a scholar to write a truly useful book, he would have toned down the truth, instead of presenting it in its raw colours and naked effect. Such a book would have had the effect of tinted glasses on tired eyes.

> *Sand continues, justifying the probity of her project (it might seem, to the modern reader, not without a certain tongue-in-cheek regard for the supposedly high moral standards of her readership). The author concludes her introduction by focusing upon the complex nature of her characters: the fraught heroine Indiana, the duplicitous philanderer Raymond, the staid patriarch Sir Ralph.*

Indiana, if you wish to have an explanation for everything in this book, is a type: she is woman herself, that frail being whose task it is to represent all those *passions* repressed, or, if you prefer, suppressed by *social conventions* [*les lois*]; she represents the spirit of self-determination grappling with necessity; love butting her head blindly against all the obstacles placed in her path by civilisation. But the serpent wears and breaks its teeth trying to gnaw through a file, and the powers of the soul exhaust themselves in the bitter struggle with the realities of life. This is what you can conclude from this tale, and it was in this spirit that it was told to him who now passes it on to you.

Despite these protestations, the narrator fully expects reproaches. Certain upright figures, certain honourable spirits might be alarmed to see such unpolished virtue, such woeful motivation, and such unjust opinions as are presented here. This gives him deep cause for concern: for there is nothing that a writer fears more than alienating, by his work, the confidence of men of good will, arousing fatal sympathies in embittered souls, or aggravating the wounds that have already been made too painful by the yoke imposed by society upon the brow of impetuous and rebel minds.

The success that is founded on an illicit appeal to the passions of an epoch is the easiest to achieve, and the least honourable to seek. The author of *Indiana* denies ever having wished to do this; if he believed that this is what he had achieved, he would destroy his work, even if he possessed that naive paternal affection that nurtures its rickety offspring in these days of literary miscarriages.

But he hopes to defend himself by saying that he thought he could better serve his principles with real-life examples rather than with poetic inventions. He believes that his story, with its tone of open sadness, will be able to make an impression upon young and ardent minds. They will hardly distrust an author who fiercely ventures into the world of reality, making contact on the left and on the right with no more regard for one camp than for the other. To depict a cause as odious or ridiculous is simply to persecute it; not to combat it. Perhaps the entire art of the storyteller simply consists in helping the fallen understand their plight, hoping to put them back on the true path, those unhappy ones that he wants to cure.

To try and distance it from every accusation would be to give too much importance to a work that, without doubt, will not make much of a stir. The author thus surrenders himself entirely to his critics. There is just one complaint that seems to him too serious to be accepted: that of having wanted to write a dangerous book. He would greatly prefer to remain for ever a mediocrity than to promote his reputation by ruining his conscience. He will add then just a few more comments in order to counteract the charge that he fears most.

Raymon, you will say, is society; egotism, that is morality and reason. Raymon, the author will reply, is that false rationality, that false morality by which society is governed. He is a man of honour, as the world understands it, because the world never examines things closely enough to see everything. The worthy citizen, he stands by Raymon; and you will not say that he is the enemy of order; for he willingly surrenders his happiness, he sacrifices himself, in the name of social order.

You will then say that you have not been shown in any convincing way how virtue has been rewarded. Alas, others will answer that virtue only triumphs today in boulevard theatres. The author will say that his task was not to depict for you a virtuous society, but a necessary one, and that honour, like heroism, has become difficult in this period of moral decadence. Do you think that this truth disgusts truly honourable men? I believe it is exactly the opposite.

# 9

## 'The individual is no more than foam on the wave'

### Georg Büchner: Letter to Minna Jaegle (1834)

*The plays of Georg Büchner (1813–37), most notably his realization of the French Revolution,* Danton's Death *(1835), and his drama of sexual jealousy and murder,* Woyzeck *(1836), gave expression to a world view that was materialist, deterministic and fatalistic. Büchner briefly sketched the terms of that philosophy (and he applied it as much to history as he did to human nature) in a letter written to his fiancée in 1834 when, following his involvement in the revolutionary activity of the* Vormärz *movement (1830–40), he found himself in exile in Switzerland.*

Gießen, sometime after 10 March, 1834.

There is not a single mountain here that affords a clear view. Hill follows hill, and deep valleys – a vacant mediocrity in everything. I can't get used to this type of nature, and the city is repellent, too. It is Spring here; so I can replace your posy of violets whenever I want to – it is immortal like the lama. Dear girl, what's going on in Strasburg? All sorts of things are happening there, but you don't mention them at all. Je baise les petites mains, en goûtant les souvenirs doux de Strasbourg. [I kiss your delicate hands, tasting the delicious memories of Strasbourg].

'Prouve-moi que tu m'aimes encore beaucoup en me donnant bientôt des nouvelles' [Prove to me that you are still in love with me by sending me some news soon]. And I am supposed to have kept *you* waiting? For several days now I have taken every opportunity to take up my pen, but I have found it impossible to write a single word. I have been studying the history of the French Revolution. I felt as though I were being crushed under the terrible fatalism of history. I find in human nature a terrifying uniformity, in human affairs an inexorable force, which is granted to all and to none. The individual is only foam on a wave, greatness a mere accident, the majesty of genius a puppet play, a ludicrous struggle against an iron law, which to recognise is the highest achievement, but to master, impossible. I no longer deem it necessary to bow down before the prancing show-off horses and bully boys of history. I have grown

**Source:** Georg Büchner, *Werke und Briefe*, edited by Werner R. Lehmann (Munich: DTV, 1981), pp. 256–7. **Standard translation:** Georg Büchner, *Complete Plays, Lenz and Other Writings*, translated with an introduction and notes by John Reddick (Harmondsworth: Penguin Books, 1993), pp. 195–6. **Further reading:** John Reddick, *Georg Büchner: The Shattered Whole* (Oxford: Clarendon Press, 1994), esp. pp. 3–75.

accustomed to the sight of blood. But I am no guillotine blade. *Must* is one of those accursed words which mankind has been baptised with. The saying: 'It must needs be that offences come; but woe to him by whom the offence cometh' is frightening. What is it in us that lies, murders and steals? I don't want to pursue the thought any further. But if only I could lay this cold and tortured heart on your bosom! B. will have put your mind to rest about my whereabouts – I wrote to him. I curse my health. I was burning; the fever covered me with kisses and embraced me like the arms of a lover. Darkness billowed over me, my heart swelled in eternal desire, the stars pierced the darkness, and hands and lips bowed low. And now? What else? I don't even have the sensation of pain and longing. Since I came across the Rhine, I feel as if I have been destroyed within; not a single feeling wells up in me. I am an automat; my soul has been taken from me. Easter is my sole consolation. I have relations near Landau, their invitation and permission to visit them. I've made the journey a thousand times, and never tire of it. – You ask me: do I long for you? Do you call it longing when one can only live in a single point, and then is torn away from that, and leaving one only with a feeling of misery? Give me an answer, please. Are my lips so cold?. . . This letter is a charivari: I will console you with another one.

## 10

## 'Demanding from the artist useful truth'

### Louis-Edmond Duranty: Realist manifesto (1856)

*Louis-Edmond Duranty (1833–80) edited the journal* Le Réalisme, *which ran from July 1856 to May 1857. In its first issue (15 November 1856), Duranty, a colleague of Champfleury and supporter of the painter Gustave Courbet, had promoted Realism as a movement against narrow formalism in art and literature. As Duranty explained, 'Realism, that means the frank and complete expression of individuality; what it attacks is precisely convention, imitation, all types of school. A Realist is entirely independent of his neighbour; he reproduces the sensation that he feels in front of objects according to his nature and his temperament.' In the second edition of the journal, Duranty felt compelled to clarify further what Realism was attempting to achieve.*

**Source:** Louis-Edmond Duranty, *Le Réalisme*, 2 (15 December 1856), p. 1. **Standard translation:** *Realism*, edited by Lilian R. Furst (London: Longman, 1992), p. 31. **Further reading:** Bernard Weinberg, *French Realism: The Critical Reaction, 1830–1870* (London: Oxford University Press, 1937).

# FOR THOSE WHO NEVER UNDERSTAND

## A Summary of the Preceding Issue

Since certain persons who never understand have not understood what was recently written, it is good to draw their attention to what was quite clearly established there:

That Realism proscribes the *historical* in painting, in the novel and in the theatre, so that there should be no lies there, and the artist cannot borrow knowledge from others;

That Realism seeks from artists only the study of their period;

That the best way not to err in this study has always been to cling to the idea of representing the *social* side of man, which is his most visible, the most accessible and most varied side, and to cling likewise to the idea of reproducing the things which affect the life of the greatest number, which occur frequently in the realm of the instincts, desires and passions;

That Realism, consequently, attributes to the artist an aim which arises from a philosophy which is practical and useful, and not simply diverting, thus re-establishing his importance;

That, in demanding from the artist useful *truth*, it is demanding above all sensitivity, an intelligent perspicacity which *sees* a lesson, an emotion in any spectacle irrespective of what it might be, high or low according to convention, and which always extracts this lesson, this emotion from the spectacle, knowing how to represent it in its entirety, and to connect it with its social context, and in such a way that, for example, those isolated, fragmented reproductions of Henry Monnier would be rejected by art and by Realism, although some people might have wanted to have them included;

That the public was the final judge of the worth of the *sentiments* studied in a work of art, because the masses are as open to pity, to misfortune, to anger etc, as the writer who is addressing them; – That any man who has remained *popular* for thirty years has a real value, and any man who has remained *popular* for more than fifty years is a great artist; – That all fame established by the tradition of scholars, professors, and colleges is dubious, and that any intelligent criticism would have to make a serious distinction between them.

It was made clear [in the preceding issue] that we would apply these principles through active criticism of contemporary and older works.

It is possible that some might prefer and find more agreeable those people who say that beauty is the splendour of truth, that the ideal is everywhere, and that one must know how to discover it.

Yes, here are the clear minds whom one must listen to; but those straightforward writers who speak to us of everyday occurrences find themselves roundly disdained on account of the paucity of their imaginations and their claim to draw attention to these beautiful ideas.

When it is said: 'Beauty is the splendour of truth', these are agreeable words which please people, which uplift, and make one at once think of some well-dressed courtesan, of the illuminations on the Champs Elysées, of the Venus of Medici, of the Italian grand masters, of the pictures of Raphael, of English thoroughbreds, of the silken garments of Delisle, and then one immediately understands 'the splendour of truth'. Whereas those vulgar natures of the Realists want to bring people down to things that take place every day. But they come in a thousand variants, and some are very lowly. Every night, one puts on a cotton nightcap before going to sleep, that's a thing that happens often. These Realists are truly idiots or hoaxers, if they think they can interest us in such nonsense.

It is not surprising that such things are said.

We stand virtually alone against a large number of people: some have become our enemies because we won't share their laziness, their unintelligence and their hypocrisy; others are adversaries, because they have accepted without thinking conventional ideas, and no longer want to find the courage to be converted; and finally there are the masses, who are disinterested; but they have been prepared and conditioned by the literary systems that ruled between 1830 and 1848, and are more curious and anxious than sympathetic.

To undertake anything with the faith of a conviction is very rare these days. To express in simple terms things which are simple, but particular, is perhaps, not good enough: people read what one has written, but they do not listen. There are hardly fifty people who will take notice of this journal, let alone agree with it. However, I am not mistaken about the spirit of the times; *people will grow accustomed to it.*

# 11

# The novel has become 'contemporary moral history'

## The Brothers Goncourt: Preface to Germinie Lacerteux (1864)

*Edmond Goncourt (1822–96) and Jules Goncourt (1830–70) jointly wrote some of the most powerful novels of social realism in nineteenth-century French literature, including* Sister Philomène *(1861), set in a Parisian hospital, and* Germinie Lacerteux *(1864), the study of the immoral conduct of a housekeeper. These were novels that looked closely at the lives of previously neglected types of character, whose habits, values and behaviour the Goncourts attempted to reconstruct, often in near documentary exactitude. In the Preface to the latter novel, they defended their practice in the following way.*

We must ask the public to forgive us for presenting it with this book, and to warn it about what it will find therein.

The public loves untrue novels: this novel is a true novel.

It loves those books that pretend to move in polite society: this book comes from the streets.

It loves those smutty little works, the memoirs of girls of pleasure, intimate confessions, erotic filth, and scandals that display themselves in the shop-windows of bookstores. But what it is about to read here is severe and pure. It must not expect the *décolleté* photographs of Pleasure: the study that follows is a clinical analysis of Love.

The public also likes insipid and consoling reading, adventures with a happy ending, fictions which don't disturb its digestion or its serenity: this book, with its sad and violent spectacles, has been written to challenge these habits and upset its health.

Why then have we written it? Was it simply to shock the public and offend its good taste?

No.

Living in the nineteenth century, at a time of universal suffrage, of democracy, of liberalism, we asked ourselves whether what one calls the 'lower orders' did not have the right to a novel; whether this world beneath a world, the people, had to remain under the sway of literary banishment and the disdain of authors who up to now have been silent

**Source:** Edmond and Jules Goncourt, *Germinie Lacerteux* (Paris: Bibliothèque-Charpentier, 1901), pp. v–viii. **Standard translation:** In *Paths to the Present: Aspects of European Thought from Romanticism to Existentialism*, edited and translated by Eugen Weber (New York: Dodd, Mead & Co, 1969), pp. 143–4. **Further reading:** Richard B. Grant, *The Goncourt Brothers* (New York: Twayne, 1972), pp. 13–72.

about whatever heart or soul the people might have. We asked ourselves whether, in this age of equality in which we live, there could be, for writer and reader alike, social classes too unworthy, miseries too deep, dramas too base, catastrophes insufficiently noble in their horror. We became curious to know whether that conventional form of a forgotten literature and a vanished society, Tragedy, was definitively dead; whether, in a country without castes and a legal aristocracy, the misfortunes of humble folk and the poor could still engage the interest, the emotions, the pity as much as the misfortunes of the great and rich; if, in a word, the tears that one weeps amongst the lowly could evoke pity as much as those shed in the better parts of society.

The above considerations caused us to undertake our humble novel, *Sister Philomène* in 1861; they cause us today to publish *Germinie Lacerteux*.

Now, it is of little importance if this book is vilified. These days, now that the novel is expanding and developing and turning into a great serious, passionate, living form of literary study and social enquiry, when it is becoming, through analysis and psychological research, contemporary moral history, now that the novel has assumed the methodology and the duties of science, it can assert its rights to the same liberties and freedoms. Let it seek art and truth; let it show the happy citizens of Paris misery that should not be forgotten; let it open the eyes of the entire world to what the Sisters of Mercy have the courage to witness, what the queens of olden days let their children see in the hospitals: human suffering, immediate and alive, something which teaches charity; let the novel acquire that religion that the previous century called by that vast and grand name: Humanity. It possesses sufficient understanding; it has already found its justification.

# 12

# 'There is a complete absence of soul, I freely admit'

Émile Zola: Preface to second edition of *Thérèse Raquin* (1868)

*Émile Zola (1840–1902) devoted the greater part of his life to writing his epic Rougon-Macquart series, a vast cycle of twenty novels which offer (as the subtitle indicates) 'the Natural and Social History of a Family under the Second Empire'. As an extended narrative, the cycle is structured around the diverse fates of a family that is plagued from its origins by a number of hereditary weaknesses (sexual, mental and alcoholic), which eventually bring the individual members of that family to grief. Zola's novels were informed by a constellation of socio-psychological and quasi-scientific theories (largely drawn from the noted medical pathologist, Claude Bernard), regarding environmental and physiological determinism which, combined with Zola's almost documentary eye for social detail, helped to produce his famous Naturalist method. Zola outlined the terms of this method in great detail in his major essay, 'The experimental novel' (1880); but over a decade earlier he had sketched out its basis in the Preface to his first important novel,* Thérèse Raquin, *where, reacting to the public's outrage over the novel's subject matter (which includes adultery, murder and suicide), he had penned an indignant riposte.*

I had naively believed that this novel could do without a preface. Since I am in the custom of expressing my thoughts as clearly as possible, stressing even the most minute detail of my writing, I had hoped to be understood and judged without a preliminary explanation. It appears that I was wrong.

The critical response to this book was both indignant and extreme. Certain virtuous people, writing in newspapers that were no less virtuous, made a grimace of disgust as they picked it up with the tongs to throw it into the fire. Even the lesser literary reviews, the ones that come out every evening with disclosures of the goings-on in certain bedrooms and private rooms, held their noses and talked of filth and stench. I am not complaining about this reception; on the contrary, I am delighted to find that my colleagues have such maidenly sensitivities. Obviously, my work belongs to my judges, and they can find it nauseating without me having the right to object. But what I do complain about is that not one of these

**Source:** Émile Zola, *Oeuvres Complètes*, edited by Henri Mitterand (Paris: Cercle du Livre Précieux, 1966–70), vol. 1, pp. 519–20 and 522. **Standard translation:** Emile Zola, *Thérèse Raquin*, translated by L. W. Tancock (Harmondsworth: Penguin Books, 1962), pp. 21–3 and 25–6. **Further reading:** F. W. J. Hemmings, *Émile Zola* (Oxford: Clarendon Press, second edition 1968), pp. 20–68.

prim journalists who has dissolved into blushes while reading *Thérèse Raquin* seems to have understood the novel. If they had understood it, they might perhaps have blushed even more, but at least I would be enjoying now the deepest satisfaction of having disgusted them for the right reason. Nothing is more annoying than hearing worthy people shouting about depravity when you know full well that they are shouting about something of which they know nothing.

So now I myself have to introduce my work to my judges. I will do so in a few lines, simply to avoid any future misunderstanding.

What I wanted to do in *Thérèse Raquin* was to study temperaments, not characters. That is the whole point of the book. I have chosen people entirely dominated by their nerves and their blood, who are without free will, and drawn into each action of their lives by the fatal impulses of their flesh. Thérèse and Laurent are human animals, nothing more. I have endeavoured to follow step by step in these animals the mute workings of the passions, the compulsion of their instincts, and the mental dislocations that occur as the result of nervous crises. The love affair between my hero and heroine takes place to satisfy a need; the murder that they commit is the consequence of their adultery, a consequence that they accept just as wolves accept the slaughter of sheep; finally, what I have been obliged to call their remorse is really only a simple organic disorder, a revolt of a nervous system that has been stretched to breaking point. There is a complete absence of soul, I freely admit, because that is how I wanted it.

I hope that by now it is becoming clear that my goal was, above all, a scientific one. When I created my two characters, Thérèse and Laurent, my interest lay in posing and then solving certain problems. I tried to explain the strange attraction that can arise between two different temperaments, and I demonstrated the profound upheavals that can take place when a person with a sanguine nature comes into contact with someone of a nervous disposition. If the novel is read with care, it will be seen that each chapter forms a study of a curious physiological case. In short, I have only had one goal in mind: given a highly sexed man and an unsatisfied woman, to uncover the animal within them, to focus only upon the animal, propel them into a violent drama, and then to observe scrupulously the sensations and the actions of these beings. I have simply applied to two living bodies the analytical procedures that surgeons apply to corpses.

> *Zola goes on to defend himself against accusations of obscenity, taking issue with those critics who castigate him as 'a hysterical wretch who wallows in displays of pornography'. These critics have ignored both the scientific principles upon which the book is based and the right of the modern artist to choose from the broadest array of materials. Zola explains, addressing his ideal reader.*

At the present, there are hardly more than two or three people capable of

The fateful march through life, never-ending, often exhausting and feverish, which humanity follows in order to achieve the conquest of progress, is, seen as a whole from afar, grandiose in its effect. In the glorious light which accompanies it, all anxieties are dispersed, the greed, the egotism, all passions, all the vices are transformed into virtues, all the weaknesses that aid great labour, all the contradictions from which friction the light of truth develops. The humanitarian result conceals how much there is of the petty in the particular interests which produce it; it justifies them almost as the necessary means to stimulate the activity of the cooperating individual who is unaware of the benefit to everybody. Every motive of this universal effort, from the quest for material comfort to the more elevated ambitions, is legitimated only by the fact of its opportunity of achieving the sweep of incessant movement, and when one knows where this immense current of human activity goes, one no longer asks how it got there. Only the observer, overwhelmed himself by the torrent, looking around him, has the right to be interested in the weak who are left in its wake, in the weary who allow themselves to be overtaken by the wave in order to be finished more quickly, in the defeated who raise their desperate arms, and who bow their heads under the brutal foot of those who overrun them, today's winners, having hurried, being keen to arrive, and who will be overtaken tomorrow.

The *Malavoglia, Mastro-don Gesualdo, Duchessa de Leyra, Onorevole Scipioni, Uomo di lusso*, are all likewise the defeated whom the current has deposited on the shore, after having overwhelmed and drowned them, each one bearing the stigmata of its own sin, which should have been the shining example of its own virtue. Each one, from the most humble to the most elevated, has had his part in the struggle for existence, for comfort, for ambition – from the humble fisherman to the nouveau riche – to the woman caught up in social climbing – to the man of intelligence and strong will who feels strength in dominating other men, to remove from himself that part of public opinion which social prejudice denies him for his illegal birth; to make law, though he himself was born outside the law – to the artist who believes he is following his ideal in following another form of ambition. Whoever observes this spectacle does not have the right to judge it; already it is much if he manages to stand back from the field of struggle for a moment in order to study it without passion, and to render the scene clearly, with the appropriate colours, so as to provide a representation of reality as it was, or as it ought to have been.

Milan 19th January 1881.

## 'The supreme of all natural laws'

### Conrad Alberti: 'The twelve articles of Realism' (1889)

*Conrad Alberti (1862–1918) was a writer of novellas (see, for example,* Giants and Dwarfs, *1886) and novels of social conscience such as* Who Is the Strongest? *(1881), but he was equally well known as a literary critic. In this capacity, he wrote frequently for the socially progressive journal,* Society, *particularly on matters relating to the relationship between literature and society. In 1889, he published a 'short systematic synopsis' of the tenets of Naturalism (which he calls Realism), defending it against its critics who accuse it, as Alberti indignantly notes, of 'wallowing in filth, and of cultivating the cult of sensuality'. On the contrary, Alberti counters, Realism is simply following the strictly scientific spirit of the age, which has proven that everything is the product of mechanistic laws.*

**1**

Art is not some celestial thing, which dear God has deposited ready-made into the lap of a mankind that is thirsting after beauty. On the contrary, it has purely human origins. It is a natural and essential product of the organization of the human spirit, as it is a natural fact of the construction of the human brain. Art is the proper and physical sister of politics, technology, science, religion, combined with which it constitutes human culture. It is an essential part of human culture, to which it corresponds as a colour from the solar spectrum corresponds to a pure ray of light. Originally it came into existence simply and exclusively to fulfil practical needs, and as such it has served all peoples in the first stages of their cultural development – helping in the exercise of their religions, in matrimonial matters, in the consolidation of dynastic government, in the practice of magic etc. But even in the highest states of cultural development, in those most famous and immortal works of art, its purely aesthetic goals could never be separated from the real, practical, supra aesthetic qualities that were closely connected with it, from political, social and other qualities that appear, for example, in the Oresteia, the Divine Comedy, Don Quixote, Wilhelm Tell, the Vatican chambers, the tombs of the Medici, and Beethoven's Ninth Symphony.

**Source:** Conrad Alberti, 'Die zwölf Artikel des Realismus: Ein litterarisches Glaubensbekenntnis', in *Die Gesellschaft: Monatsschrift für Litteratur und Kunst* (1889), no. 1, pp. 2–4. There is no standard translation. **Further reading:** Lilian R. Furst and Peter N. Skrine, *Naturalism* (London: Methuen, 1971), esp. pp. 37–41.

## 2

Because it is an essential part of human culture, art is subject to the organic law of progressive development, the supreme of all natural laws. Art is continually engaged in this process of progressive development, both viewed as an entirety and in terms of particular art forms. Only from the point of view of a continual progressive development of circumstances that are grounded in the natural necessity of human arrangements in all their actuality can a factual and positive judgement on artistic periods, artists and works of art be established. Because nationality and race are natural and, we must suppose, foundational (not artificial), or, at the very least, original institutions of mankind, so is the call for a national culture, and with it an art that reflects the character of its people in all the phases of its development, entirely justified. Every national art is, therefore, an organic totality, either complete within itself, or continually developing, born from the actual spirit of the nation, along with which it develops. It is not to be likened to some hastily produced or thrown-together pyramid of good, bad, average collections of books, paintings, statues, etc.

## 3

Since all the laws of nature, which regulate mechanical events in the physical world, also determine all intellectual events and phenomena, so art is also subject to exactly the same laws as the mechanical world. Principles such as the struggle for existence, natural selection, heredity and adaptability to the environment are just as eternally valid in art and the history of art as they are in the physiological development of organisms. For example, it is a constant rule among all works of art, which embody the same motif, that those which assert themselves the longest over all others are those which possess the most powerful organization, in other words, those which can depict this common motif in the most forceful, clearest, and the simplest way, without bringing in foreign or distracting motifs, and thus grab the attention of the viewer and keep it for the longest period of time. So it is that Goethe's Faust outshines all other contemporary Fausts, destroying them as literary works. We can see all the important and eternal laws of nature also acting upon the sphere of art. The law of the preservation of energy is the basic principle of tragedy, particularly of the requirement of catharsis, as well as being a requirement of the organic conclusion to any work of art. The law of the constancy of matter will demonstrate by the same principle that all the poetic motifs of world literature are already present in the oldest of all literatures, in that of the Indian, and, from then on, appear in ever new combinations up to Shakespeare, Goethe, and Dumas, repeating themselves so that only the surface forms, the wording change, while the entirety of the poetic motifs stays, however, the same. The law of minimum energy is the natural principle of the rhyme, as it is, indeed, also the principle of aesthetic practicality, which formerly was wrongly thought to be the highest of all aesthetic principles. For only those treatments of a subject appear to us as practical and hence artistically beautiful which use the minimum of energy necessary for them to achieve their power; anything that is excessive appears to us, as in every situation where we discern excess, as unaesthetic.

### 4

Consequently, any aesthetic law seems only justifiable when it comes across as the application of a general law of nature to the particular conditions of art.

### 15

---

# 'There is no police which we can consider competent in literary matters'

## Anton Chekhov: Letter to M. V. Kiselev (1887)

*Anton Chekhov (1860–1904) was, with plays such as* The Seagull *(1896),* Three Sisters *(1901) and* The Cherry Orchard *(1904), the foremost Russian dramatist in the age of Realism. His early publications largely consisted of short stories, such as 'A Dreary Story' (1889) and 'Ward Number Six' (1892) which, in their factual techniques and depictions of the travails of city life, clearly reflect the influence of French Naturalism. 'On the Road' (1885) and 'Mire' (1886) were two such stories. Both received criticism from many quarters, including from one of Chekhov's friends, Mariya Kiselev. In a letter to the latter written in 1887, Chekhov sought to defend the sometimes sordid nature of his material.*

To M. V. Kiselev,
January 14, 1887

Even your praise of 'On the Road' has not lessened my anger as an author, and I hasten to avenge myself for what you say about 'Mire'.

---

**Source:** Anton Chekhov, *Letters on the Short Story, the Drama, and Other Literary Topics*, selected and edited by Louis S. Friedland (New York: Benjamin Blom Publishers, 1966), pp. 273–7.
**Further reading:** Ronald Hingley, *Chekhov: A Biographical and Critical Study* (London: Allen & Unwin, 1950), esp. pp. 195–218.

Be on your guard, and take firm hold of the back of your chair that you do not faint. Well, here goes.

It is best to meet every critical article with a silent bow, even if it is abusive and unjust – such is the literary etiquette. It is not the correct thing to answer, and all who do so are justly blamed for excessive vanity. But since your criticism is like 'an evening conversation on the steps of the Babinko lodge' . . . and as, without touching on the literary aspects of the story, it raises general questions of principle, I shall not be sinning against the etiquette if I allow myself to continue our conversation.

In the first place, I, like you, do not admire literature of the kind we are discussing. As a reader and a 'private citizen' I am glad to avoid it, but if you ask my honest and sincere opinion about it, I shall say that it is still an open question whether it has a right to exist, – a question that has as yet not been settled. . . . You and I and the critics of all the world have no such firm certainty as would give us the right to disown this literature. I do not know who is right: Homer, Shakespeare, Lope de Vega, the ancients generally who did not fear to grub in the 'dunghill', but who were more stable in their moral relations than we; or the modern writers, fastidious on paper, but coldly cynical in soul and in their manner of life? I do not know who has bad taste: the Greeks, who were not ashamed to sing such love as really is in beautiful Nature, or the readers of Gaboriau, Marlitt, Per Bobo. Like the problems of non-resistance to evil, free-will etc., this question can be settled only in the future. We can only think about it, but to solve it means to go beyond the limits of our competency. Reference to Turgenev and Tolstoy, who avoided this 'dunghill', does not clear up the question. Their aversion does not prove anything; there were writers before them who not only regarded sordidness as 'scoundrelly amongst scoundrels', but held the same view of descriptions of *muzhiks* and clerks and all beneath the titular rank. And a single period, no matter how brilliant, does not give us the right to draw an inference in favour of this or the other tendency. Nor does reference to the corrupting influence of a given literary tendency solve the question. Everything in this world is relative and approximate. There are people who will be corrupted even by juvenile literature, who read, with particular pleasure, the piquant passages in the Psalter and the Proverbs of Solomon, while there are those who become the purer the more they know about the evil side of life. Publicists, lawyers, physicians, initiated into all the secret human sins, are not reputed to be immoral; realist writers are often more moral than archimandrites. And finally, no literature can in its cynicism surpass actual life; a wineglassful will not make drunk the man who has already emptied a whole cask.

2. That the world 'swarms with male and female scum' is perfectly

true. Human nature is imperfect, and it would, therefore, be strange to find only righteous people on this earth. But to think that the task of literature is to gather the pure grain from the muck heap, is to reject literature itself. Artistic literature is called so just because it depicts life as it really is. Its aim is truth, – unconditional and honest. To narrow down its functions to such a specialty as selecting the 'unsullied', is as fatal to it as to have Levitan paint a tree and to forbid him to include the dirty bark and the yellow leaves. I agree with you that the 'cream' is a fine thing, but a littérateur is not a confectioner, not a dealer in cosmetics, not an entertainer; he is a man bound, under compulsion, by the realization of his duty, and by his conscience; having put his hand to the plough he must not plead weakness; and no matter how painful it is to him, he is constrained to overcome his aversion, and soil his imagination with the sordidness of life. He is just like any ordinary reporter. What would you say if a newspaper reporter, because of his fastidiousness or from a wish to give pleasure to his readers, were to describe only honest mayors, high-minded ladies, and virtuous railroad contractors? To a chemist, nothing on earth is unclean. A writer must be as objective as a chemist: he must abandon the subjective line; he must know that dung-heaps play a very respectable part in a landscape, and that evil passions are as inherent in life as good ones.

3. Writers are the children of their age, and therefore, like the rest of the public, ought to surrender to the external conditions of society. Thus, they must be absolutely decent. Only this have we the right to require of the realists. For the rest, you say nothing against the form and execution of 'Mire'. . . . And so, I take it, I have been decent.

4. I admit that I seldom consult my conscience when I write. This is due to habit and the brief, compressed form of my work. Let us say that when I express this or that opinion about literature, I do not take myself into account.

5. You write: 'If I were the editor I would have returned to you this feuilleton for your own good'. Why not go further? Why not go for the editors who print such stories? Why not denounce the Administration of the Press for not suppressing immoral newspapers?

The fate of literature would be woeful (both little and great literature) if you left it to the will of individuals. That's the first thing. In the second place, there is no police which we can consider competent in literary matters. I agree that we must have curbs and whips, for knaves find their way even into literature, but, think what you will, you cannot find a better police for literature than criticism and the author's own conscience. People have been trying to discover such a police since the creation of the world, but nothing better has been found. You would wish me to suffer the loss of one hundred and fifteen roubles and be censured by the editor. Others, among them your father, are delighted with the story. Some send letters of reproach to Souvorin, reviling everything, the newspaper, me, etc. Who, then, is right? Who is the judge?

6. Further, you write: 'leave such writing to spiritless and unfortunate scribblers like Okreits, Pince-nez or Aloe'.

May Allah pardon me if you wrote those lines sincerely! To be condescending toward humble people because of their humbleness does not do honour to the human heart. In literature, the lower ranks are as necessary as in the army, – so says the mind, and the heart ought to confirm this most thoroughly.

16
_____

# 'With the breakdown of categories masks fall at one blow and faces appear in their true purity'

Benito Pérez Galdós: 'Contemporary society as novelistic material' (1897)

*Benito Pérez Galdós (1843–1920) was the author of two epic novel series: the historical* National Episodes, *published in forty-six volumes between 1873 and 1912; and the more topical* Novels of Contemporary Spain, *from which* Fortunata and Jacinta *(1876), the story of an embroiled relationship between four characters, set within the vacillating social mores of Madrid, remains his masterpiece. Pérez Galdós was a sharp observer of the social changes taking place in his swiftly modernizing Spain. The following extract is taken from an essay, first given as a speech to the Spanish Academy in 1897. It is, at the same time, both an analysis and a spirited defence of those changes (and his focus is upon the emergence of mass society), whose disruptive energies the author sees not only as a challenge but as a means of renewal, the source of an energy that can propel Spanish literature into the future.*

This enormous mass without a character of its own, which absorbs and monopolises all of life, subjecting it to endless regulations, legislating frenziedly on everything without leaving out things of the spirit, which are the exclusive domain of the soul, will in the end absorb the

**Source:** Benito Pérez Galdós, 'Contemporary society as novelistic material', translated and reprinted in *Documents of Modern Literary Realism*, edited by George Joseph Becker (Princeton, NJ: Princeton University Press, 1963). **Further reading:** Geoffrey Ribbans, *Reality Plain or Fancy? Some Reflections on Galdós' Concept of Realism* (Liverpool: Liverpool University Press, 1986).

deteriorated remains of the classes at either pole, the traditional depositories of the basic feelings. When this happens, there will be discerned at the centre of this chaotic mass a fermentation from which will issue social forms which we cannot yet guess at, vigorous unities which we cannot succeed in defining in the confusion and bewilderment in which we live.

The result is, from what I have indicated vaguely with my natural laziness of expression, that in the sphere of Art generic types, which symbolised major groupings of the human family, are disappearing and losing life and colour. Even human faces are not what they were, though it would seem ridiculous to say so. You will no longer find those faces which, like masks moulded by the conventionalism of custom, represented the passions, the ridiculous, the vices and the virtues. The little which the people retain of the typical and picturesque is fading and becoming obliterated; even in language we notice the same tendency away from the typical, leading to uniformity of diction and similarity of speech on the part of everybody. At the same time urbanisation is slowly destroying the peculiar physiognomy of each city; and if in the country there is still preserved in people and things a distinctive profile of popular stamp, this will be worn away by the continual progress of the levelling roller which flattens every eminence, and will go on flattening until it produces the longed-for equality of forms in all things spiritual and material.

While this levelling is taking place, Art offers us a strange phenomenon which demonstrates the inconsistency of ideas in the present-day world. In other eras changes of literary opinion manifested themselves over long periods of time with the majestic slowness of all historical process. Even in the generation preceding our own we saw the romantic evolution last long enough to produce a multitude of vigorous works; and to indicate the change in aesthetic ideas, the literary forms which followed romanticism were slow in presenting themselves with vigour and lived for many years, which today seem to us like centuries, when we consider the rapidity with which our tastes are now transformed. We have come to a time when aesthetic opinion, that social rhythm not unlike the ebb and flow of the sea, changes with such capricious speed that if an author lets two or three years pass between imagining and publishing his work, it may well happen that it is out of date the day that it appears. For if in the scientific realm the rapidity with which inventions follow each other, or the applications of physical agencies, makes today's marvels seem commonplace tomorrow and causes every new discovery to be immediately put in the shade by new marvels of mechanics and industry, in the same way in literature, unstable aesthetic opinion seems to be the rule, and we continually see it change before our eyes, fleeting and whimsical, like fashions in clothing. And thus, in the shortest time, we leap from nebulous idealism to the extremes of naturalism; today we love minute details, tomorrow broad and vigorous lines; we are equally ready to see the source of beauty in poorly assimilated philosophical reasoning and in ardent inherited beliefs.

To sum up: the same evolutionary confusion that we note in society, the prime material of novelistic art, is to be found in the latter by the uncertainty of its ideals, by the variability of its forms, by the timidity with which it makes use of profoundly human data; and when society turns into a public, that is, when after having been the inspirer of Art, it looks at it with the eyes of a judge, it betrays the same uncertainty in its opinions, with the result that critics are no less confused than authors.

But do not believe that I have any intention of drawing a pessimistic conclusion from these facts, and asserting that from this social breakdown there must ensue a period of anaemia and death for narrative art. Certainly the lack of unity in social organisation deprives us of generic characters, types that society itself provides in outline, as if they were already the first imprint of artistic handling. But in the measure that the generalised characterisation of persons and things is effaced, their human models appear more clear, and it is in them that the novelist ought to study life in order to achieve the fruits of an Art that is great and lasting. Wise criticism cannot fail to recognise that when the ideas and feelings of a society appear in very clear-cut categories it seems that those characters arrive in the realm of Art already touched with a certain mannerism or conventionalism. With the breakdown of categories masks fall at one blow and faces appear in their true purity. Types are lost, but man is better revealed to us, and Art is directed solely to giving to imaginary beings a life that is more human than social. And no one is unaware that, when we work with purely human materials, the force of genius to express life has to be greater and its effort more profound and difficult, as the plastic representation of the nude is a greater undertaking than the representation of a figure draped with clothes, however scanty they may be. And in proportion to the difficulty, no doubt, the value of the artistic product increases, so that if in periods of powerful principles of unity it shines forth with vivid social meaning, in the unhappy days of transition and evolution it can and ought to be profoundly human.

*Pérez Galdós leaves us on a final note that sees the literature of social dissolution in a positive light.*

[I] conclude by saying that the present-day social situation with all its confusion and nervous disquietude has not been sterile for the novel in Spain, and that perhaps this very confusion and uncertainty have favoured the development of so fine an art. We cannot foresee how far the present disintegration will go. But we may affirm that narrative literature does not have to be lost just because the old social organisms die or are transformed. Perhaps new forms will appear; perhaps works of extraordinary power and beauty which will serve as harbingers of future ideals or as a farewell to those of the past, as the *Quixote* is a farewell to the world of chivalry. Be that as it may, human genius lives in all environments and produces its flowers alike before the happy portals of resplendent monuments and among sad and desolate ruins.

17

---

# 'The Naturalist has abolished guilt with God'

## August Strindberg: Foreword to *Miss Julie* (1888)

*August Strindberg (1849–1912) began his career as a playwright with the historical drama,* Master Olof *(1881), but it was only with his two Naturalist plays,* The Father *(1887) and* Miss Julie *(1888), that he became a major figure in Swedish theatre. Both plays give voice to Strindberg's characteristic philosophy: a blend of simplified Nietzsche and Social Darwinism, fused with a virulent anti-feminism. The result is a dark vision, which sees all social and personal conduct as part of a grim and ineluctable process of conflict and struggle. In the Foreword to* Miss Julie, *he gave his most extensive account of that personal philosophy, and sketched the ways it had affected his dramaturgy.*

I myself find the joy of life in its strong and cruel struggles, and my pleasure in learning, in adding to my knowledge. For this reason I have chosen for this play an unusual situation, but an instructive one – an exception, that is to say, but a great exception, one proving the rule, which will no doubt annoy all lovers of the commonplace. What will offend simple minds is that my plot is not simple, nor its point of view single. In real life an action – this, by the way, is a somewhat new discovery – is generally caused by a whole series of motives, more or less fundamental, but as a rule the spectator chooses just one of these – the one which his mind can most easily grasp or that does most credit to his intelligence. A suicide is committed. Business troubles, says the man of affairs. Unrequited love, say the women. Sickness, says the invalid. Despair, says the down-and-out. But it is possible that the motive lay in

---

**Source:** August Strindberg, 'Naturalism in the theatre', translated by Willis Kingsley Wing, in *Documents of Modern Literary Realism*, edited by George Joseph Becker (Princeton, NJ: Princeton University Press, 1963), pp. 396–8, 398–9 and 401–2. **Further reading:** Martin Lamm, *August Strindberg* (New York: Benjamin Blom, [1948] 1971), pp. 199–233.

all or none of these directions, or that the dead man concealed his actual motive by revealing quite another, likely to reflect more to his glory.

I see Miss Julie's tragic fate to be the result of many circumstances: the mother's character, the father's mistaken upbringing of the girl, her own nature, and the influence of her fiancé on a weak, degenerate mind. Also, more directly, the festive mood of Midsummer Eve, her father's absence, her monthly indisposition, her pre-occupation with animals, the excitement of dancing, the magic of dusk, the strongly aphrodisiac influence of flowers, and finally the chance that drives the couple into a room alone – to which must be added the urgency of the excited man.

My treatment of the theme, moreover, is neither exclusively physiological nor psychological. I have not put the blame wholly on the inheritance from her mother, nor on her physical condition at the time, nor on immorality. I have not even preached a moral sermon; in the absence of the priest I leave this to the cook.

I congratulate myself on this multiplicity of motives as being up-to-date, and if others have done the same thing before me, then I congratulate myself on not being alone in my 'paradoxes', as all innovations are called.

In regard to the drawing of characters, I have made my people somewhat 'characterless' for the following reasons. In the course of time the word character has assumed manifold meanings. It must have originally signified the dominating trait of the soul-complex, and this was confused with temperament. Later it became the middle-class term for the automaton, one whose nature had become fixed or who had adapted himself to a particular role in life. In fact a person who had ceased to grow was called a character, while one continuing to develop – the skilful navigator of life's river, sailing not with sheets set fast, but veering before the wind to luff again – was called characterless, in a derogatory sense, of course, because he was so hard to catch, classify and keep track of. This middle-class conception of the immobility of the soul was transferred to the stage where the middle-class has always ruled.

> Both the ethical and the political self-confidence that underscored that view of character have gone in the age of modernity, destroyed by emerging social forces and theories that make a continued belief in the stability of self untenable. Accordingly, Strindberg expounds a radically different view of character.

I do not believe, therefore, in simple stage characters; and the summary judgement of authors – this man is stupid, that one brutal, this jealous, that stingy, and so forth – should be challenged by the Naturalists who know the richness of the soul-complex and realise that vice has a reverse side very much like virtue.

Because they are modern characters, living in a period of transition more feverishly hysterical than its predecessor at least, I have drawn my figures vacillating, disintegrated, a blend of old and new. Nor does it seem to me unlikely that, through newspapers and conversations, modern ideas may have filtered down to the level of the domestic servant.

My souls (characters) are conglomerations of past and present stages of civilisation, bits from books and newspapers, scraps of humanity, rags and tatters of fine clothing, patched together as is the human soul. And I have added a little evolutionary history by making the weaker steal and repeat the words of the stronger, and by making the characters borrow ideas or 'suggestions' from one another.

Miss Julie is a modern character, not that the half-woman, the man-hater, has not always existed, but because now that she has been discovered she has stepped to the front and begun to make a noise. The half-woman is a type who thrusts herself forward, selling herself nowadays for power, decorations, distinctions, diplomas, as formerly for money. The type implies degeneration; it is not a good type and it does not endure; but it can unfortunately transmit its misery, and degenerate men seem instinctively to choose their mates from among such women, and so they breed, producing off-spring of indeterminate sex to whom life is torture. But fortunately they perish, either because they cannot come to terms with reality, or because their repressed instincts break out uncontrollably, or again because their hopes of catching up with men are shattered. The type is tragic, revealing a desperate fight against nature, tragic too in its Romantic inheritance now dissipated by Naturalism, which wants nothing but happiness – and for happiness strong and sound species are required.

But Miss Julie is also a relic of the old warrior nobility now giving way to the new nobility of nerve and brain. She is a victim of the discord which a mother's 'crime' has produced in a family, a victim too of the day's complaisance, of circumstances, of her own defective constitution, all of which are the equivalent to the Fate or Universal Law of former days. The Naturalist has abolished guilt with God.

*Strindberg then turns his attention to the form of the play.*

In regard to the dialogue, I have departed somewhat from tradition by not making my characters catechists who ask stupid questions in order to elicit a smart reply. I have avoided the symmetrical, mathematical construction of French dialogue, and let people's minds work irregularly, as they do in real life where, during a conversation, no topic is drained to the dregs, and one mind finds in another a chance cog to engage with. So too the dialogue wanders, gathering in the opening scenes material which is later picked up, worked over, repeated, expounded and developed like the theme in a musical composition.

The plot speaks for itself, and as it really only concerns two people, I have concentrated on these, introducing only one minor character, the cook, and keeping the unhappy spirit of the father above and behind the action. I have done this because it seems to me that the psychological process is what interests people most today. Our inquisitive souls are no longer satisfied with seeing a thing happen; we must also know how it happens. We want to see the wires themselves, to watch the machinery, to examine the box with the false bottom, to take hold of the magic ring in order to find the join, and look at the cards to see how they are marked.

In this connection, I have had in view the documentary novels of the brothers de Goncourt, which appeal to me more than any other modern literature.

18

---

# 'The truthful reproduction of typical characters under typical circumstances'

## Friedrich Engels: Letter to Margaret Harkness (1888)

*Friedrich Engels (1820–95) was, with Karl Marx, one of the founding members of the Communist Party, and joint author of* The German Ideology *(1845),* The Communist Manifesto *(1848) and* Capital *(1867–94). But Engels was also (like Marx) a keen analyst of culture, with firm views on how literature, in particular, should engage with political themes and matters. In the following letter, written to Margaret Harkness, the author of several novels on English working-class life, Engels offers his opinion on her most recent novel* A City Girl: A Realistic Story, *which appeared in 1887.*

[Beginning of] April 1888

Dear Miss H[arkness],

I thank you very much for sending me through Messrs. Vizetelly your *City Girl*. I have read it with the greatest pleasure and avidity. It is, indeed, as my friend Eichhoff your translator calls it, *ein kleines Kunstwerk* [a perfect little work of art]; to which he adds, what will be satisfactory to you, that consequently his translation must be all but

---

**Source:** *Marx and Engels on Literature and Art*, edited by Lee Baxandall and Stefan Morawski (St Louis, MO: Telos Press, 1973), pp. 114–16. **Further reading:** Terry Eagleton, *Marxism and Literary Criticism* (London: Methuen, 1976).

literal, as any omission or attempted manipulation could only destroy part of the original's value.

What strikes me most in your tale besides its realist truth is that it exhibits the courage of the true artist. Not only in the way you treat the Salvation Army, in the teeth of supercilious respectability, which respectability will perhaps learn from your tale, for the first time, *why* the Salvation Army has such a hold on the popular masses. But chiefly in the plain unvarnished manner in which you make the old, old story, the proletarian girl seduced by a middle class man, the pivot of the whole book. Mediocrity would have felt bound to hide the, to it, commonplace character of the plot under heaps of artificial complications and adornments, and yet would not have got rid of the fate of being found out. You felt you could afford to tell an old story, because you could make it a new one by simply telling it truly.

Your Mr. Arthur Grant is a masterpiece.

If I have anything to criticise, it would be that perhaps after all, the tale is not quite realistic enough. Realism, to my mind, implies, besides truth of detail, the truthful reproduction of typical characters under typical circumstances. Now your characters are typical enough, as far as they go; but the circumstances which surround them and make them act, are not perhaps equally so. In the *City Girl* the working class figures as a passive mass, unable to help itself and not even making any attempt at striving to help itself. All attempts to drag it out of its torpid misery come from without, from above. Now if this was a correct description about 1800 or 1810, in the days of Saint-Simon and Robert Owen, it cannot appear so in 1887 to a man who for nearly fifty years has had the honour of sharing in most of the fights of the militant proletariat. The rebellious reaction of the working class against the oppressive medium which surrounds them, their attempts – convulsive, half-conscious or conscious – at recovering their status as human beings, belong to history and must therefore lay claim to a place in the domain of realism.

I am far from finding fault with your not having written a point blank socialist novel, a *Tendenzroman* as we Germans call it, to glorify the social and political views of the author. That is not at all what I mean. The more the opinions of the author remain hidden, the better for the work of art. The realism I allude to, may crop out even in spite of the author's opinions. Let me refer to an example. Balzac whom I consider a far greater master of realism than all the Zolas *passés, présents et à venir* in *La Comédie humaine* gives us a most wonderfully realistic history of French 'Society', describing, chronicle-fashion, almost year by year from 1816 to 1848, the progressive inroads of the rising bourgeoisie upon the society of nobles, that reconstituted itself after 1815 and that set up again, as far as it could, the standard of *la vieille politesse française.* He describes how the last remnants of this, to him, model society gradually succumbed before the intrusion of the vulgar moneyed upstart, or were corrupted by him; how the grande dame whose conjugal infidelities were but a mode of asserting herself in perfect accordance with the way she had been disposed of in marriage, gave way to the bourgeoisie, who corned her husband for cash or cashmere; and around this central picture he groups a complete history of French Society from which, even in economical details (for instance the rearrangement of real and personal property after the Revolution) I have learned more than from all the professed historians, economists and statisticians of the period together. Well, Balzac was politically a Legitimist; his great work is a constant elegy on the irretrievable decay of good society; his sympathies are all with the class doomed to extinction. But for all that his satyre is never keener, his irony never bitterer than when he sets in motion the very men and women with whom he sympathises most deeply – the nobles. And the only men of whom he always speaks with undisguised admiration, are his bitterest political antagonists, the republican heroes of the Cloître Saint Merri, the men, who at that time (1830–36) were indeed the representatives of the popular masses. That Balzac thus was compelled to go against his own class sympathies and political prejudices, that he *saw* the necessity of the downfall of his favourite nobles, and described them as people deserving no better fate; and that he *saw* the real men of the future where, for the time being, they alone were to be found – that I consider one of the greatest triumphs of Realism, and one of the grandest features of old Balzac.

I must own, in your defence, that nowhere in the civilised world are the working people less actively resistant, more passively submitting to fate, more *hébétés* than in the East End of London. And how do I know whether you have not had very good reasons for contenting yourself, for once, with a picture of the passive side of working class life, reserving the active side for another work?

# Part III
# Modernism

# INTRODUCTION

Even as the influence of Naturalism was reaching its peak in Europe (and most notably in Germany and Scandinavia), in its homeland, France, the movement was nearing its end as a vital literary force, its self-confidence and strength of direction withering not only under the consistent accusations of moral impropriety made by its foes, but also under the more telling criticisms made by its erstwhile adherents, such as Joris-Karl Huysmans. In his early fiction, novels such as *Martha* (1876) and *The Vatard Sisters* (1879), Huysmans had employed the Naturalist method to uncover the sordid and pathetic life of characters struggling, in vain, against material misery and social prejudice. But by 1884, the year in which he published his novel of aesthetic fabulation, *Against Nature*, Huysmans had come to feel 'a craving to open the windows, to escape from surroundings that were stifling me', desiring in the process 'to shake off preconceived ideas, to break through the limits of the novel'. As he explained in the Preface to the second edition of the same novel, published in 1903 (**Reading 1**), Naturalism was 'marching up a blind alley'; the thrust of its social censor had been blunted, its focus upon poverty, destitution and victimization, and its stock of situations and characters exhausted through over-use. It was a literary form that could not renew itself, because it had (Huysmans concluded) lost that sense for the intangibility and mystery that lies at the heart of personal experience.

Huysmans' *Against Nature*, with its exotic hedonism and almost painful longing for novel sensation, was to become a central text within a new literary movement that was eventually to displace Naturalism as the dominant literary genre within French and European literature: Romantic Decadence. Certainly, the decadent ethos embodied in Huysmans' novel was not new. As early as 1868, the poet Théophile Gautier had written a Preface to Baudelaire's *The Flowers of Evil* (1857), in which he had celebrated a style of writing and a literary self-consciousness that was both enigmatic and disconcerting in its attempts to transfigure a world that oscillated between banality and depravity (**Reading 2**). Gautier called this aesthetic 'decadent' because it reminded him of the work of the Silver Poets of Classical Rome, who likewise wrote about a civilization that had not only lost its natural vigour and sense of purpose in life, but seemed positively to revel in the atrophy and aboulia that such a state entailed. Like these poets, Baudelaire, Gautier argues, has taken upon himself to venture into the darker recesses of the mind in order to fathom (and explicate for the reader) the spiritual malaises of a 'pale, nervous and twisted mankind', subject to the travails of modernity.

Baudelaire had, in fact, anticipated a new generation of French poets, who would come to be regarded as the harbingers of literary modernism in France: *les poètes maudits* [the 'accursed' or 'damned' poets], who were so named after a collection of essays edited by the poet Paul Verlaine in 1884. They included Tristan Corbière, Arthur Rimbaud, Stéphane Mallarmé, Marceline Desbordes-Valmore, Villiers de L'Isle-Adam and Verlaine himself (who appears under the pseudonym 'Pauvre Lelian'). These were 'absolute' poets who had, as Verlaine explained in his Foreword, dispensed with a false romanticism in favour of a new, more self-sufficient type of poetic idiom. Arthur Rimbaud was both the youngest and the most radical among their number. With Rimbaud, art grew out of a lifestyle that pushed both the self (its health and its sanity), and the tolerance of an increasingly prurient society, to an unheard-of extreme. As he wrote in a letter to his friend Georges Izambard in 1871, his goal was no less than to 'arrive at the unknown through a derangement of *all my senses*' (**Reading 3**). Indeed, the motif of self-dissolution that reoccurs throughout the letter, the aggressive amoralism, Rimbaud's artistic absolutism (anything may be permitted in the cause of the exploration of distant realms of experience), all came to fruition in his two collections of poetry, *Illuminations* and *A Season in Hell* (written between 1871 and 1873). They, as with all that Rimbaud wrote, give voice to an amoral sensuality, a wilfully shocking poseurism and an *épater le bourgeois* confrontationalism, which were to remain constants within the decadent self-image, right up to the work of Oscar Wilde and André Gide two decades later.

In spite of its cultivated hedonism and brash insouciance, there resided, nevertheless, at the heart of the decadent imagination a feeling for pure interiority, for the ineffable quality of life grasped as an aesthetically lived experience. That quality resurfaces in its purest form in a movement that was, both in terms of personnel and artistic values, contiguous to Decadence: Symbolism. As the English poet and critic Arthur Symons noted in his contemporary study of the movement, *The Symbolist Movement in Literature* (1899), Symbolism distilled out of the *fin-de-siècle* mind a certain unformulated element of transcendental spirituality, an attachment to inwardness that allowed it to produce a poetry whose formally perfect if hermeneutically challenging valiance could be experienced by writer and reader alike (in the wake of the deterministic quality of Naturalism) as a moment of pure freedom. As Symons eloquently expressed it: 'Here, then, in this revolt against exteriority, against rhetoric, against a materialistic tradition; in this endeavour to disengage the ultimate essence, the soul, of whatever exists and can be realised by the consciousness; in this dutiful waiting upon every symbol by which the soul of things can be made visible; literature, bowed down by so many burdens, may at last attain liberty, and its authentic speech' (**Reading 4**).

The reading public first became apprised of the existence of the Symbolist movement through an aptly timed manifesto, written in 1886 by the minor poet, Jean Moréas. In his manifesto, Moréas sought (in an unconvincing attempt to placate the respectable readership of *Le Figaro*) to counter the 'accusation of obscurity' aimed at the Symbolist movement by giving it a lineage that stretched back to Shakespeare and beyond. The Symbolists were, as Moréas explained, 'enemies of teaching, declamation, false sensibility, and objective description'. Forgoing the simplistic mimetic principles of the Realists, the Symbolist poets 'seek to clothe the Idea in a sensuous form, which, nevertheless, would not be an end in itself, but which would help to express the Idea, whilst remaining subject to it'. It was a process that would, Moréas confidently assured his readers, bring back the French language to the pristine purity that it had long since lost (**Reading 5**).

The greatest exponent of Symbolism and its most persuasive theoretician was, however, the poet Stéphane Mallarmé. In essays such as the 'The book, a spiritual instrument' (1895) and 'The crisis of poetry' (1896), Mallarmé outlined a radically new theory of poetic diction, one which broke not only with the Realists' model of mimetic representation but also with the Romantics' adherence to notions of emotional expressivity. Poetic language, Mallarmé argued, possessed an autotelic status, occupying a realm of pure connotation, qualities that Mallarmé sought to represent in his own poetry, most notably in the ethereal 'The afternoon of a faun' (1876) and 'The virginal, living and beautiful day' (1885). There, meaning and sense may be glimpsed by the interpreting mind but never directly grasped, because the nuances and subtleties of real experience (those nebulous shimmerings of memory, dream and desire) take place at the edge of vision and not at its centre, resisting 'any systems of thought that seek to organise them in any precise way, seeking to retain only the suggestiveness of things' (**Reading 6**).

The inherent perspectivism of Mallarmé's thinking, and its delineation of a world constructed purely through the agency of the creative will, was to establish epistemological relativism as the major assumption of the Modernist mind. Even a writer such as Oscar Wilde, whose tastes, as his novel *The Picture of Dorian Gray* (1891) clearly shows, were for the sensual body culture and refined hedonism of the decadent school, could pen essays such as 'The decay of lying' (1889). Here, Vivian, a Wildean persona, asks of the disbelieving Cyril (and any naive reader who still believes that there is a world beyond art): 'What is nature?' His own reply: 'Nature is no great mother who has borne us. She is our creation.

It is in our brain that she quickens to life. Things are because we see them, and what we see, and how we see it depends on the Arts that have influenced us', provides a succinct formulation of *fin-de-siècle* aestheticism (**Reading 7**). Certainly, 'The decay of lying' may be on one level, in true Wildean fashion, a light-hearted, almost ironic pastiche of art criticism; but it undeniably gave expression to a growing Modernist conviction, one shared by figures as diverse as Marcel Proust, James Joyce and Thomas Mann, that the modern world, with its dissolving intellectual energies, could only be grasped as a meaningful totality when subject to the all-defining activity of the aesthetic will-to-form.

The Symbolist focus upon the translucent nature of the object world (where all is seen as a system of signs pointing to a higher realm) was taken up by Modernist poets throughout Europe, from Gerard Manley Hopkins in England to Rainer Maria Rilke in Germany, both of whom elaborated their own near-mystical metaphysics of presence: Hopkins in his theory of 'Inscape' and Rilke in his 'Thing poems' (the 'Dinggedichte'). What such poets were trying to achieve is well summed up by Ezra Pound in his manifesto for the Anglo-American Imagist school (written in 1913 and extended in 1918) (**Reading 8**). Here, Pound tells us, the goal of the modern poem is to create a single poetic image that will present 'an intellectual and emotional complex in an instant of time'. This image, shorn of superfluous context and distracting qualifications, will be of such a power and exist so completely in the present that the reader will experience 'that sudden sense of liberation; that sense of freedom from time limits and space limits' that are preconditions for the attainment of higher truth.

The Symbolism-Decadence movement represented the first moment within the broader development of literary Modernism in Europe. By the turn of the century it had almost entirely replaced the Realist-Naturalist tradition as the dominant literary paradigm, its tenets and practices taken up by writers as diverse as Gabriele D'Annunzio (in Italy), Stefan George (in Germany) and Alexander Blok (in Russia). All drew inspiration from the intellectually liberating and textually challenging idiom of Symbolism, even if some, such as the Russian Acmeists, believing (as they put it in their manifesto of 1913) in a 'greater balance of powers and a more exact knowledge of the relationships between subject and object than there was in Symbolism', felt that they had to move beyond its distinctive, and inhibiting, other-worldly idiom (**Reading 9**). The Symbolists and Decadents anticipated many of the major themes and tropes that would reappear in the work of the mainstream Modernists: concerns with the fluidity of memory, time and identity; with the artificial boundaries between reason and its Other; a sense for 'deviance', the paranormal and polymorphous sexuality; and a celebration of art and the artist, who now came to replace the Realist focus upon woman and womanhood as symbols for consciousness alienated from the bourgeois realm. But it was the iconoclastic and destabilizing impetus of the Romantic-Decadent movement that made the initial impact on the literary culture of Europe, and upon a series of youthful cultural formations that were collectively known as the Avant-Garde.

The designation was an apt one; for the Avant-Garde were, indeed, an advance guard, the shock troops of literary radicalism in the early years of the twentieth century. When, in his Futurist manifesto of 1909 (one of the earliest formulations of the Avant-Garde spirit), the Italian Filippo Marinetti exhorted his followers to 'take up your pickaxes, your axes and hammers and wreck, wreck the venerable cities, pitilessly!' (**Reading 10**), he was deliberately, and strategically, confusing the boundaries between provocative metaphor and literal reality. From Marinetti's stage-management of fisticuffs at his public lectures in Paris, London and elsewhere, through to the Surrealists' disruption of exhibitions and performances in Paris, where small animals were let loose to the dismay of artists and public alike (whilst megaphones intoned the primacy of the Surrealist agenda), the Avant-Garde introduced into the cultural politics of European art a previously unseen element of material activism.

The exponents of the Avant-Garde sought, above all, to create not only a new artistic medium but a new, more critical attitude to the institutions and practices of traditional high culture. This was most notably the case with the Swiss-based group, the Dadaists. As Tristan Tzara, one of its founding members, explained in his manifesto of 1918 (**Reading 11**), Dada's ire was aimed not at art itself but at those 'literary hacks with a hatred of change', at everyone, including 'grasping academics', who would seek to profit from maintaining arbitrary distinctions between the culture of the salon and that of the market, between the canon and its carnevalistic Other, between that which 'belongs' and that which does not. Together with Hugo Ball, Richard Huelsenbeck, Hans Arp (the co-founding members of Dada), Tzara thought in terms of pure opposition, feeling that he was part of a 'desperate struggle' that would have as its culmination the 'interweaving of contraries and of all contradictions, of the grotesque, of the irrelevant: LIFE'.

That such an intervention into the cultural hegemony of the Establishment would ultimately involve political action is clear from the trajectory followed by the German Expressionists. Their early work moved within a broad ambit between the teasingly subversive satire of Carl Sternheim and Jakob von Hoddis (see, for example, the latter's poem, 'End of the World', 1911), and the gentle trance-like verse of George Trakl, through to the disconcertingly apocalyptic visions of August Stramm and Ernst Stadtler. The Expressionists had as their target the pompous and self-congratulatory culture of Imperial Germany, and, as such, their work contained from the very beginning, at least implicitly, a distinctly oppositional element. But it was not until the First World War (in which Stramm and Trakl among others died) that this anti-bourgeois stance became deepened into a literature of social conscience and political action. Writers such as Ernst Toller (*The Transformation* (1917) and *Mass Man* (1919)), and Georg Kaiser (*The Machine Breakers*, 1922), retained the visionary and elliptical form of the writing of the original Expressionists; but now a greater sense of the social application of the Expressionist vision comes to the fore. As Kasimir Edschmid explained in his manifesto of 1917 (**Reading 12**), it is mankind rather than individual man who now matters, and it is the duty of the Expressionist artist, whose 'eruption of inner life binds him to everything', to lead this baffled and betrayed humanity through its ordeals and sufferings out into a new world of resolution and transfiguration.

If the German Expressionists came increasingly to look beyond purely individual experience to the social impact of their art, and, as the example of Bertolt Brecht showed, with an increasing emphasis upon the political (see, for example, his play, *Drums in the Night*, 1922), yet a further Avant-Garde group of the period, the French Surrealists, chose the path inwards, towards an exploration of the mind and the workings of the unconscious. The latter had begun as acolytes of the Dadaists, and most notably of Tristan Tzara, who moved to Paris in 1919, bringing with him the anarchistic and deflationary tactics of Dada. These were enthusiastically embraced, as was Tzara's irreverent attitude to high culture, by André Breton, Louis Aragon, Paul Eluard and Philippe Soupault as an antidote to the ponderous, unself-critical and overly rationalist spirit that still dominated the French (and European) mind and which, it was deemed, had been largely responsible for bringing about the carnage of the First World War. The Surrealists placed the Dada sense for the random, the ludic and the absurd on a more systematic basis, drawing upon the work of Sigmund Freud to do so. As Breton explained in his first manifesto of 1924 (**Reading 13**), Surrealism could be understood as the artistic equivalent to psychoanalysis: it too sought to open up to scrutiny and creative exploitation 'certain forms of association that have up to now been neglected'. The Surrealists sought access to these realms through the analysis of dreams, 'random' associations, hypnotic outpourings and automatic writing. Their aim was no less than to bring that longing, cherished by the Romantics, to merge the objective and subjective spheres, wish-fulfilment and reality, myth and history, to its final consummation.

The influence of Surrealism upon the direction of European literature in the Modernist period was immense. Its presence can be seen in the early work of W. H. Auden (*Poems*, 1930), in that of the Italian 'hermeticist', Eugenio Montale (*Bones of Cuttlefish*, 1925) and, above all, in that of the great Spanish poet and playwright, Federico García Lorca (*Poet in New York*, 1940). Surrealism allowed such poets to escape from the restraints of traditional metre, allowing the verse line to follow the fragmented and discontinuous modulations of thought, as, at the same time, it freed them from the tyranny of verisimilitude and logical consequentiality in their choice of subject matter. As Lorca noted in his letters (**Reading 14**), 'the absurd, if it's alive is true'; what matters is the degree of intensity with which the phenomenal world can be grasped by the individual vision. As the Spanish poet vividly demonstrated in his own writing, truth and falsehood must be judged against the beauty and violence of elemental experience, and not against those criteria fabricated out of order and 'good sense'.

Surrealism was not a flight from the 'real' world but an attempt to transfigure it, to open it up as text whose inscription would mirror the workings of desire, dream and fantasy. Attempting to find a literary form for phenomena which were, by their very essence, formless produced a body of experimental work that radically transgressed previous literary boundaries and dislodged accepted literary conventions. These included poetry such as Breton and Soupault's *Magnetic Fields* (1920), Eluard's *The Underside of Life or the Human Pyramid* and *Capital of Sorrow* (both 1926), and novels, such as Aragon's *Paris Peasant* (1926), Breton's *Nadja* (1928) and Raymond Queneau's *The Bark Tree* (1933). All these works lead the reader, either through erotic fantasy or metaphysical fabulation, into a unique world in which, as Aragon explains in the Preface to his *Paris Peasant* (**Reading 15**), a new mythology unveils itself among the 'admirable gardens of absurd beliefs, forebodings, obsessions and frenzies' which energize the urban landscape as mediated through the Surrealist optic.

That these obsessions should find concrete form beyond the purely textual was the concern of Antonin Artaud, whose plans for a 'theatre of cruelty' (formulated in a series of essays collected and published as *The Theatre and Its Double* in 1938) provided the most ambitious Surrealist attempt to relocate the aesthetic into the real universe through myth and ceremony. Artaud sought to renew drama by promoting it as a total experience, comprised of light, sound, incantation, dream enactment and ritual. In such an intense environment, actors and audience alike would, as he explained in his famous first manifesto (**Reading 16**), go through a process of 'anarchistic destruction', in which they would make contact with a deeper realm governed by the 'special exorcisms' of minds liberated from all restraint and inhibition. Artaud's own production did not exceed the single effort of *The Cencis* (staged in 1935); but in his desire to free the stage from its dependence on the illusionist heritage of the Realist *pièce bien faite* and the jaded conventions of script and characterization, Artaud opened up an invaluable experimental space that subsequent European theatre would explore more fully.

The Avant-Garde might be regarded as the most radical (some might say the most progressive) moment within the broad development of literary Modernism. Both the content of its work and the radical style with which Avant-Garde artists intervened in the institutions of high culture forced many to rethink the basic assumptions and categories of artistic production, such as the status of art *vis-à-vis* the 'non-artistic', the precarious autonomy of the artist within the market economy of cultural consumption, and the potential for the artistic statement to dislodge social and political prejudice. In spite of these achievements, the impact of the Avant-Garde on the development of mainstream Modernism was mixed. Many, such as the Anglo-American poet, T. S. Eliot, allowed their work to be informed by the vitalizing energies and textual novelties of Avant-Garde writing (in his case most notably by the *vers libre* of the French Symbolists, Tristan Corbière and Jules Laforgue), while seeking, at the same time, to integrate those energies into a sense of the developing totality of tradition. As Eliot argued in his famous essay, 'Tradition and the individual talent' (1919), novelty is a relative, not an absolute value. The writer must judge himself (for others will certainly judge him thus) within the context of previous frameworks of meaning: 'No poet, no artist of any art, has his complete meaning alone. His significance, his appreciation is the appreciation of his relation to the dead poets and artists. You cannot value him alone; you must set him, for contrast and comparison, among the dead.' He added importantly, 'I mean this as a principle of aesthetic, not merely historical, criticism' (**Reading 17**).

A similar awareness of the dissolving energies of Modernism, and a similar desire to find a holistic solution to the challenges posed by those energies, is evident in the work of Virginia Woolf. As is clear from her essay 'Modern fiction' (1919), Woolf was fully aware of the fragmenta-tion of consciousness borne of the modern age, and of the role of art, such as post-Impressionism, in reflecting that fragmentation. Her main concern in this essay (and in her work in general), however, was with finding an aesthetic form that would retain the fluidity and productive tensions of that fragmentation, but (as she showed in her novels *Mrs Dalloway* (1925), *To the Lighthouse* (1927) and, above all, *The Waves* (1931)), within a discourse (for her the narrative discourse of the stream of consciousness technique) that would allow for the structuration of sensibility, and the ordering of time through the perceiving self. As Woolf explains, the modern writer 'has to have the courage to say that what interests him is no longer "this" but "that": out of "that" alone must he construct his work. For the moderns "that", the point of interest, lies very likely in the dark places of psychology. At once, therefore, the accent falls a little differently; the emphasis is upon something hitherto ignored; at once a different outline of form becomes necessary, difficult for us to grasp, incomprehensible to our predecessors' (**Reading 18**).

But even those, such as D. H. Lawrence, who stood to one side of the formal experimentalism that characterizes much of Modernist writing were in little doubt that their generation had reached a point of no return in their approach to (indeed, in their definition of) some of the most fundamental governing ideas of Western culture, such as the notion of character. As Lawrence remarked in a letter written in 1914 (**Reading 19**), in the context of a discussion of Marinetti and the latter's vitalistic views on the formation of selfhood (although the influence of still more powerful figures such as Freud can also be clearly felt here), the traditional 'moral scheme into which all the characters fit' no longer seemed to him a tenable philosophy. To be true to his craft, and to permit it to respond to a radically changed environment which was both material and intellectual, the modern novelist is compelled to strike out into areas where notions of self and the coherence of personality must needs give way to a recognition of those 'allotropic states' that work, 'inhumanly, physiologically, materially', upon the ego, bending it through the force of their more basic instincts. It was the task of fiction to capture those statements as closely as it could in their actual grain. These were sentiments with which all who pursued the project of the Modernist novel, from Woolf and Joyce through to Robert Musil and Italo Svevo, would have concurred.

This widespread concern with issues relating to the (problematic) relationship between language, self and the world was part of the Modernists' break with what they regarded as the naive epistemology inscribed into the Realist aesthetic. In philosophy, these issues were given theoretical formulation by, among others, Fritz Mauthner (*Contributions to a Critique of Language*, 1901), Ferdinand de Saussure (*Course in General Linguistics*, 1916), and Ludwig Wittgenstein (*Tractatus Logico-Philosophicus*, 1921). The psychological consequences of this crisis of language were explored within a more intimate idiom by Hugo von Hofmannsthal, in his fictional letter from Lord Chandos to Francis Bacon (published in 1902) (**Reading 20**). Here the young aristocratic writer, Chandos, explains how he has come to experience a total lack of confidence in the standard communicative faculty of language, 'in the ordinary words that people use, fluently and without even thinking, on a daily basis'. Such words, and the homogenizing patterns of language in which they are embedded, have lost, for Chandos, their semantic credibility, and with that their power to adequately describe either external events or the internal workings of the mind. But Hofmannsthal's hero does survive, by winning through to a higher perspective (in his case, a rediscovery of the sheer tactility of ordinary words cleansed of their abstractions). It was a path chosen by many writers in the Modernist period, who would likewise come to terms with their variously conceived crises of language by choosing solutions formed either from retrospective refashioning (as in the work of Proust), mythic parallelism (as, for example, in Joyce's *Ulysses*), or ironic distantiation (in the case of Thomas Mann), structures that allowed Modernist writers to both analyse and transcend their perceived crises.

Coming to terms with flexible definitions of the self, with new ways of conceptualizing the relationship between language and consciousness, and with new attitudes to the relativity of time and temporality, necessarily involved the writer in a greater awareness of the mechanics and process of writing, and a greater appreciation of the constructivist aspects of linguistic form and literary fictionality: a recognition that language was no longer the passive reflector of the world, but the very medium through which the world is made. T. S. Eliot encapsulated this position well (*see* **Reading 17**) when he spoke of poetry as 'an escape from personality', and the poet's individual self being of secondary importance to the poetic persona, which is created through the 'particular medium' of language. The greatest French poet of the late Modern period, Paul Valéry, would have agreed. Valéry accompanied his own verse, written over a period of thirty years, with a detailed and systematic meditation upon the mechanics of poetic production, and upon the highly wrought and fluid nature of the relationship between the poet and his finished verse, a relationship in which 'the author' figures as simply one moment among many. Here, in essays such as 'Concerning the "Cemetery by the Sea"' (1933), 'Problems of poetry' (1936) and in his 'First lesson from a course in poetics' (1938), Valéry speaks of poetry and the poetic act as the product of 'pure conditions of form, which are more and more thought out, – defined to the point where they propose or almost impose a subject, or, at least, a group of subjects' (**Reading 21**). We are here in a realm of pure textuality, with an aesthetic that seems to be reaching out towards postmodernism, and towards a fundamental revision of the categories of artistic statement, in which the individual author will produce, but never seek to dominate, 'the conditions for precise form' and the free play of signification that constitute the aesthetic freedom of literature.

# 1

## It 'liberated me from a literature that had no future'

Joris-Karl Huysmans: Preface to second edition of *Against Nature*
(1903)

*Joris-Karl Huysmans (1848–1907) began as a Naturalist writer with novels such as*
Martha *(1876) and* The Vatard Sisters *(1879), but by the time he came to write*
*his most important novel* Against Nature *(1884), he had left the quasi-*
*documentary and impersonal style of that idiom far behind. With its world-weary*
*introspection and highly self-conscious cultivation of sensuality,* Against Nature
*provided the Decadent school of writing with its seminal text. In the Preface to the*
*second edition of that novel, Huysmans explained why he felt compelled to revise his*
*early allegiance to Naturalism.*

At the time *Against Nature* appeared, that is to say in 1884, the situation
was the following: Naturalism was exhausting itself by turning the mill
forever in the same circle. The stock of observations that every writer had
stored up, either by taking them from his own experiences or the
experiences of others, was beginning to run out. Zola, who was a gifted
stage-designer, got round this problem by painting tableaux that were
more or less accurate; he was very good at capturing the illusion of the
movement of life; his heroes were devoid of soul, and dominated entirely
by impulse and instinct, which simplified the work of analysis. They
moved around, carrying out a motley assortment of activities, filling out
sleek silhouettes, who were representatives of the various backgrounds
which were the principal characters of his dramas. In this way, he
celebrated the Central Markets, and the big department stores, the
railroads, and the coal mines; and the human beings, lost within these
various environments, had no role to play other than that of utility actors
and extras. But Zola was Zola, in other words, a rather ponderous artist,
but gifted with powerful lungs and massive fists.

As for the rest of us, less robust and concerned with an art form that
was more subtle and truer, we were compelled to ask ourselves whether
Naturalism would not eventually lead to a dead end, and if we were not
soon going to find ourselves running up against a solid wall.

**Source:** Joris-Karl Huysmans, *Oeuvres complètes*, edited by M. Lucien Descaves (Geneva: Slatkine Reprints, 1972), vol. VII, pp. x–xii and xxii–xxiii. **Standard translation:** Huysmans, *Against the Grain*, with an introduction by Havelock Ellis (New York: Dover Publications, 1969 [1931]), pp. xxxiii–xlix. **Further reading:** Robert Baldwick, *The Life of Joris-Karl Huysmans* (Oxford: Clarendon Press, 1955), pp. 78–91.

To tell the truth, these considerations did not occur to me until much later. I was seeking, in a way that I only dimly understood, to escape from an *impasse* in which I was suffocating; but I had no definite plan as such, and *Against Nature*, which, by letting in fresh air, liberated me from a literature that had no future, was a completely unpremeditated work, which formed itself in my mind without any preconceptions, without definite intentions for its future, without any plan at all.

My initial idea was for a brief fantasy, written in the form of an exotic tale. I imagined it a little as a companion piece to *Down Stream* transposed to another world. I pictured to myself a Monsieur Folantin, more cultured, more sophisticated, more wealthy, who has discovered in artificiality a relief from the disgust inspired by the worries of life and the American habits of his time. I pictured him fleeing, on a swift flight into his dreams, seeking refuge in the illusion of extravagant fancies, living, alone, and far from his time, in memories summoned up of more cordial times, of places less vile.

The more I pondered over it, the more the subject grew in stature and seemed to require patient research: all the chapters developed into the distillation of a special field of interest, the sublimates of different art forms, condensing themselves into a melange of precious stones, perfumes, flowers, of literatures religious and lay, of profane music and plain-song.

*Huysmans goes on to outline the premises of his highly eclectic personal philosophy, a combination of rediscovered Catholicism and Schopenhaurian pessimism. He then returns to the subject of Naturalism, and his break with that movement, describing one memorable confrontation with his erstwhile mentor, Zola.*

One thing at any rate is certain, and that is that *Against Nature* represented a definite break with its predecessors, with *The Vatard Sisters*, *En Ménage*, *Down Stream*, and that with it I had set out on a path the end of which I could not see.

More perspicacious than the Catholics, Zola saw this clearly. I remember, after the publication of *Against Nature*, spending a few days with him at Médan. One afternoon, when the two of us were out walking in the country, he suddenly stopped, and with a grim countenance, he reproached me for having written the book, saying that I had dealt a terrible blow to Naturalism, that I was leading the school astray, that I was also burning my boats with such a book, because any subject that could be exhausted by a single book could not provide the basis for a genre of literature, and, in a friendly fashion – for he was a very decent man – he urged me to return to the well-trod path, and knuckle down to a serious study of social customs.

I listened to him, thinking that he was, at one and the same time, both right and wrong – right, because I was indeed undermining Naturalism and barring all avenues back to it for me; wrong, in the sense that the novel, as he conceived it, seemed to me to be moribund, grown stale through useless repetition, and, whether he liked it or not, totally lacking in interest for me.

There were many things that Zola could not understand: first of all, the craving I felt to open the windows, to escape from the surroundings that were suffocating me; then, the desire that had seized me to shake off preconceived ideas, to break through the limits of the novel, to introduce into it art, science, history; in a word, to no longer use this type of literature except as a framework in which to do more serious kinds of work. From my point of view, the thing that seemed the most urgent at that time was to abolish the traditional plot of intrigue, indeed, to eliminate love and women altogether, and focus the ray of light upon a sole character; and, above all, to do something new.

2

---

# The 'fatal idiom' of Decadence

## Théophile Gautier: Preface to Baudelaire's *The Flowers of Evil* (1868)

*Théophile Gautier (1811–72) wrote widely as a poet, drama critic and journalist, but it was his novel* Mademoiselle de Maupin *(1835), in which he argued for the self-sufficient status of the artistic object (an argument encapsulated in the pregnant formula 'l'art pour l'art', or 'art for art's sake'), which secured him his reputation as the leading spokesman for the nascent Decadent-Symbolist movement. Gautier made his most extensive defence of the aesthetic of Decadence, however, in his Preface to Baudelaire's* The Flowers of Evil, *a collection of verse that represented for Gautier the richest and most complex formulation of a culture that had reached a state of terminal decline. Gautier begins his discussion of Baudelaire by clarifying the notion of 'decadence'.*

The poet of *The Flowers of Evil* adored the style that people somewhat inaccurately call decadent, and which is nothing else than art that has arrived at a point of extreme maturity, being the product of those oblique suns that characterize an aged civilization. Its characteristics are an

---

**Source:** Charles Baudelaire, *Les Fleurs du mal*, précédées d'une notice par Théophile Gautier (Paris: Calmann-Lévy, 1868), pp. 16–17 and 19–21. There is no standard translation. **Further reading:** Pierre Emmanuel, *Baudelaire: The Paradox of Redemptive Satanism* (Tuscaloosa: University of Alabama Press, 1972).

ingenious style, which is complex, knowing, full of nuances and refinement, forever pushing back the boundaries of language, borrowing specialist vocabularies from everywhere, and taking colour from every palette, chords from every piano. It strives to capture the most ineffable qualities of thought, and the most fleeting and vague of contours of form, forever alert so that it can communicate the subtle secrets of the neurotic, the confessions of a fading passion, and the depraved and bizarre hallucinations of an obsession that is turning into madness. This decadent style is the last word in a catechism summoned to express everything and pushed to its very limits. In this respect, it reminds one of the language of the late Roman Empire, which was already marbled by the greenness of decomposition, and over-ripe, and of the complicated refinements of the Byzantine school, which was the final form of Greek art, fallen into deliquescence; but such is the necessary and fateful idiom of those peoples and civilizations in which artificial life has replaced natural life, and has brought forth within men obscure desires. It is not, however, without its complexities, this style despised by pedants, for it expresses new ideas in new forms and in a language that one has not heard before. As opposed to Classical style, it makes place for the world of shadows, and in this world of shadows there move, in a confused way, the larvae of superstition, the haggard phantoms of insomnia, nocturnal terrors which creep around and return at the least noise, monstrous dreams which only unconsciousness can put an end to, obscure fantasies which daylight can only marvel at, and all of which the soul, at the bottom of its deepest and final cavern, absorbs from gloom, deformity and the nuances of horror.

> For Gautier, the greatness of Baudelaire lay in his willingness to explore these dark themes, to undertake voyages (and the metaphor was often used by Baudelaire himself) into previously uncharted realms of the mind. But he did so, not because he enjoyed the dubious experiences to which such exotic flights gave rise, but because he was driven by a poetic vocation.

Baudelaire had a perfect hatred for philanthropes, the advocates of progress, utilitarians, humanitarians, utopians and all who sought to change something in unvarying nature and in the fixed constitution of society. He envisaged neither the eradication of hell nor that of the guillotine in order to please thieves and murderers; he did not believe that man was born good, and he recognized that the perverse was something that can always be found in the deepest recesses of the souls of the most pure, the perverse, that bad councillor which compels man to do things that he might otherwise find repugnant. And he does these things precisely because they are repugnant to him, and because he gets pleasure out of contradicting the law, following no motivation other than disobedience, and not for the sake of sensualism, profit or charm. This perversity he found and castigated in other people as well as in himself, just as if he had been a slave caught in the act, but he refrained from all sermonizing, for he regarded it as irremediable beyond damnation. It is, then, wrong for short-sighted critics to accuse Baudelaire of immorality; that is a facile and totally nonsensical subject for jealous mediocrities, which also gives much pleasure to the pharisees and the Monsieur Prudhommes. No one professed a more haughty disdain for intellectual turpitude and base subject matter. He hated evil as if it were a deviation from a mathematical norm, and, gentleman that he was, he held it in contempt as something inconvenient, ridiculous, bourgeois and thoroughly improper. If often he had cause to deal with hideous, repugnant and morbid themes, this was done from the same sort of horror and fascination that might make a bird descend, as if magnetized, into the jaws of the foul serpent, although it is forever able, with a vigorous beating of its wings, to break the spell and soar back into the pure-blue regions of spirituality. He ought to have engraved on his seal as a motto the words: 'spleen and ideal', which provided the title for his first volume of verse. If his bouquet is made up out of exotic flowers, with metallic colours and a vertiginous perfume, the calyx of which, instead of rose water, contains bitter tears or drops of *aqua tofana*, he might reply that hardly anything else will grow out of this compost heap, which is black and saturated with putrefaction just like the soil of the graveyards from those dying civilizations, in which among the noxious miasmas the corpses of preceding centuries are decaying. Without a doubt, forget-me-nots, roses, daisies, and violets are flowers that are more agreeably vernal; but few of these will grow in the black mud that coats the pavements of our cities. Besides, Baudelaire, if he possesses a feeling for those majestic tropical landscapes in which trees, with a bizarre and gigantic elegance, burst forth as in some explosive dream, is only moderately touched by those little rustic beauty spots of the suburbs; and it is not he who would frolic, like those philistine critics of Heinrich Heine, in front of the romantic efflorescence of the new literature, or would be in raptures over the song of the sparrow. He loves to follow pale, nervous and twisted mankind, convulsed by factitious passions and the real modern *ennui*, across the sinuosities of this immense madrepore of Paris, to surprise him in his illnesses, his anguishes, miseries, his protestations and his excitements, his neuroses and his despairs. He observes, as if watching a knot of vipers lying beneath a dung-hill that one has just uncovered, evil instincts crawling towards the light, ignoble habits idly squatting in the mire; and, this spectacle, which attracts and repels him, produces in him an incurable melancholia, for he does not deem himself better than the others, and he suffers seeing the pure canopy of the heavens and the chaste stars obscured by foul vapours.

# 'To arrive at the unknown through a derangement of all my senses'

## Arthur Rimbaud: Letter to Georges Izambard (1871)

*Arthur Rimbaud (1854–91) enjoyed a life lived in studied provocation of the moral and sexual mores of his contemporary France. His 'decadence', however, was not just a matter of lifestyle; it was also part of (indeed, made possible) an aesthetic radicalism which produced poetry of startling originality, such as 'The Drunken Boat' (1871),* Illuminations *and* A Season in Hell *(1872–3), works which combine a delight in the profane empowerments of urban life with an equally deeply felt need for spiritual transfiguration and transcendence. In the following famous letter (written as the events of the Paris Commune were in progress), Rimbaud links, in characteristic fashion, the principle of poetic creativity to explorations beyond the confines of mental stability.*

Charleville, [13] May

1871

Dear Sir,

So, here you are – a teacher, once again! One owes a debt to Society, you tell me; you are a member of the teaching fraternity; your career is going forward. I too follow that principle. I have, quite cynically, chosen the career of the kept man. I dig up old imbeciles from our school; I spin them yarns – the stupidest, dirtiest, nastiest things that I've done in thought and deed; and they repay me with beer and liquor. *Stat mater dolorosa, dum pendet filius* – My duty is to Society, that's true. And I am right. – You too, you are also right – for the moment, anyway. When it comes down to it, all you see in your principle is subjective poetry: your determination to go back to the academic trough – and excuse me for saying this – proves it. But whatever happens you'll end up self-satisfied, someone who has done nothing, and has never wanted to do anything. And that is quite ignoring the fact that your subjective poetry will always be disgustingly tepid. One day, I hope – and many others hope so too – that I will see

**Source:** Arthur Rimbaud, *Oeuvres*, edited by Suzanne Bernard (Paris: Garnier, 1960), pp. 343–4. **Standard translation:** *Rimbaud: Complete Works and Selected Letters*, edited and translated by Wallace Fowlie (Chicago: University of Chicago Press, 1966), pp. 303–4. **Further reading:** Karin J. Dillman, *The Subject in Rimbaud: From Self to 'Je'* (New York: Peter Lang, 1984), esp. pp. 8–44.

an objective poetry in your principle, and I will see it more sincerely than you would be capable of doing! – I will be a worker: that is an idea that holds me in check when mad rage drives me towards the battle that is raging in Paris, – where so many workers are dying even as I write these lines to you! Work now – never, never! I am on strike.

At the moment, I am degrading myself as much as I can. Why? I want to be a poet, and I am working towards making myself a *seer*: you won't understand this at all, and I don't really know how to explain it to you. My goal is to arrive at the unknown through a derangement of *all my senses*. The sufferings are enormous, but one has to be strong, one has to be born a poet, and I know that I am a poet. This is not my fault, at all. It is a mistake to say 'I think': one really ought to say 'I am thought'. Excuse the play on words.

The 'I' is an other. So much the worse for the wood if it finds that it has become a violin, and I feel nothing but contempt for those ignoramuses who argue over things that they know nothing about!

You are not a *teacher* for me. I'm sending you the following: is it satire, as you would say? Is it poetry? It is, quite simply, fantasy. – But I beg you – don't underline it with pencil, nor with too much thought:

'The Tortured Heart'

My sad heart drools at the stern
[. . . . . . . . . .]

This does not mean nothing.

Get back to me: c/o M. Deverriere, for A.R.

With best wishes,

Arth. Rimbaud.

# 4

# 'A literature in which the visible world is no longer a reality, and the unseen world no longer a dream'

## Arthur Symons: *The Symbolist Movement in Literature* (1899)

*Arthur Symons (1865–1945) wrote several volumes of poetry, languorous fin-de-siècle vignettes of urban life such as* Silhouettes *(1892), and* London Nights *(1895); but his contribution to the development of early Modernism was largely as a literary critic and cultural commentator. A friend of W. B. Yeats and Walter Pater, Symons contributed to the 'decadent' journal,* The Yellow Book, *before editing its successor,* The Savoy. *In his* magnum opus, The Symbolist Movement in Literature, *he provided an incisive account of the formation and aesthetic of the Symbolist school of writing. The latter sought to find an idiom in which (in the words that Symons quotes from Thomas Carlyle) 'the Infinite is made to blend itself with the Finite, to stand visible, and as it were, attainable there'.*

It is in such a sense as this that the word Symbolism has been used to describe a movement which, during the last generation, has profoundly influenced the course of French literature. All such words, used of anything so living, variable, and irresponsible as literature, are, as symbols themselves must so often be, mere compromises, mere indications. Symbolism, as seen in the writers of our day, would have no value if it were not seen also, under one disguise or another, in every great imaginative writer. What distinguishes the Symbolism of our day from the Symbolism of the past is that it has now become conscious of itself, in a sense in which it was unconscious even in Gérard de Nerval, to whom I trace the particular origin of the literature which I call Symbolist. The forces which mould the thought of men change, or men's resistance to them slackens; with the change of men's thought comes a change of literature, alike in its inmost essence and in its outward form: after the world has starved its soul long enough in the contemplation and the rearrangement of material things, comes the turn of the soul; and with it comes the literature of which I write in this volume, a literature in which the visible world is no longer a reality, and the unseen world no longer a dream.

The great epoch in French literature which preceded this epoch was

**Source:** Arthur Symons, *The Symbolist Movement in Literature* (London: Heineman, 1980 [1899]), pp. 5–8 and 9–10. **Further reading:** Tom Gibbons, *Rooms in the Darwin Hotel: Studies in English Literary Criticism and Ideas, 1880–1920* (Nedlands: University of Western Australia Press, 1973), pp. 69–97.

that of the offshoot of Romanticism which produced Baudelaire, Flaubert, the Goncourts, Taine, Zola, Leconte de Lisle. Taine was the philosopher both of what had gone before him and of what came immediately after; so that he seems at once to explain Flaubert and Zola. It was the age of Science, the age of material things; and words, with that facile elasticity which there is in them, did miracles in the exact representation of everything that visibly existed, exactly as it existed. Even Baudelaire, in whom the spirit is always an uneasy guest at the orgie of life, had a certain theory of Realism which tortures many of his poems into strange, metallic shapes, and fills them with imitative odours, and disturbs them with a too deliberate rhetoric of the flesh. Flaubert, the one impeccable novelist who has ever lived, was resolute to be the novelist of a world in which art, formal art, was the only escape from the burden of reality, and in which the soul was of use mainly as the agent of fine literature. The Goncourts caught at Impressionism to render the fugitive aspects of a world which existed only as a thing of flat spaces, and angles, and coloured movement, in which sun and shadow were the artists; as moods, no less flitting, were the artists of the merely receptive consciousness of men and women. Zola has tried to build in brick and mortar inside the covers of a book; he is quite sure that the soul is a nervous fluid, which he is quite sure some man of science is about to catch for us, as a man of science has bottled the air, a pretty, blue liquid. Leconte de Lisle turned the world to stone, but saw, beyond the world, only a pause from misery in a Nirvana never subtilised to the Eastern ecstasy. And with all these writers, form aimed above all things at being precise, at saying rather than suggesting, at saying what they had to say so completely that nothing remained over, which it might be the business of the reader to divine. And so they have expressed, finally, a certain aspect of the world; and some of them have carried style to a point beyond which the style that says, rather than suggests, cannot go. The whole of that movement comes to a splendid funeral in M. de Heredia's sonnets, in which the literature of form says its last word, and dies.

*Symons goes on to distance the Symbolists from the writers of its cognate movement, Romantic Decadence, which 'exhibited the thrill of unsatisfied virtue masquerading as uncomprehended vice'. In a book published barely five years after the public ignominy of Oscar Wilde, it had, possibly, to be that way. Perhaps for the same reason, Symons ends his Introduction to his study with words that stress the essentially spiritualizing mission of the Symbolist credo.*

In most of the writers whom I have dealt with [in this study] as summing up in themselves all that is best in Symbolism, it will be noticed that the form is very carefully elaborated, and seems to count for at least as much as in those writers of whose over-possession by form I have complained. Here, however, all this elaboration comes from a very different motive, and leads to other ends. There is such a thing as perfecting form that form may be annihilated. All the art of Verlaine is in bringing verse to a bird's song, the art of Mallarmé in bringing verse to the song of the orchestra. In Villiers de l'Isle-Adam drama becomes an embodiment of spiritual forces, in Maeterlinck not even their embodiment, but the remote sound of their voices. It is all an attempt to spiritualise literature, to evade the old bondage of rhetoric, the old bondage of exteriority. Description is banished that beautiful things may be evoked, magically; the regular beat of verse is broken in order that words may fly, upon subtler wings. Mystery is no longer feared, as the great mystery in whose midst we are islanded was feared by those to whom that unknown sea was only a great void. We are coming closer to nature, as we seem to shrink from it with something of horror, disdaining to catalogue the trees of the forest. And as we brush aside the accidents of daily life, in which men and women imagine that they are alone touching reality, we come closer to humanity, to everything in humanity that may have begun before the world and may outlast it.

Here, then, in this revolt against exteriority, against rhetoric, against a materialistic tradition; in this endeavour to disengage the ultimate essence, the soul, of whatever exists and can be realised by the consciousness; in this dutiful waiting upon every symbol by which the soul of things can be made visible; literature, bowed down by so many burdens, may at last attain liberty, and its authentic speech. In attaining this liberty, it accepts a heavier burden; for in speaking to us so intimately, so solemnly, as only religion had hitherto spoken to us, it becomes itself a kind of religion, with all the duties and responsibilities of the sacred ritual.

# 5

# 'The sumptuous robes of external analogies'

## Jean Moréas: 'Symbolist manifesto' (1886)

*Jean Moréas, the pseudonym of Iannis Papadiamantopoulos (1856–1910), wrote verse which was much influenced by the wistful style of Verlaine (see, for example, Les Syrtes, 1884), before gravitating towards a more exotic post-Romantic idiom originating in his awakened interest in medieval themes and imagery. Moréas's importance lies less, however, in his poetic endeavours than in his proselytizing energies on behalf of the nascent Symbolist movement, for whom he wrote the first major manifesto. The manifesto (published in* Le Figaro *on 18 September 1886) attempts to bring the essentially esoteric and elitist idiom of Symbolism to a wider audience. It is prefaced with a explanatory word from that newspaper's editorial board, who have asked Jean Moréas, as 'one of those most frequently seen amongst these literary revolutionaries', to outline 'the fundamental principles of this new artistic manifestation'. Moréas begins by explaining that all art-forms are subject to a cyclical process.*

The fact is that all art forms are fated to become impoverished and worn out; then, from copy to copy, from imitation to imitation, what was once full of sap and freshness dries out and shrivels up; what was new and spontaneous becomes clichéd and commonplace.

Romanticism, thus, after having vigorously sounded all the bells of revolt, after having its days of glory in battle, lost its vitality and its charm, renounced its audacious heroics, became sedate, sceptical and full of good sense. It attempted some pathetic attempts at a return in the honourable but paltry efforts of the Parnassian poets, before finally, like a monarch experiencing a second childhood, it allowed itself to be deposed by Naturalism, to which one can grant no value other than that of a protest (which was legitimate but ill-advised) against the insipid writing of certain novelists who were then in fashion.

A new art form, then, was overdue, necessary, inevitable. And this art form, which was long in preparation, has now burst forth. And all the anodyne jokes of the wits of the press, all the discomfort of the serious critics, all the bad humour of a public jolted out of its bovine

**Source:** Guy Michaud (ed.), *La Doctrine Symboliste: Documents* (Paris: Librairie Nizet, 1947), pp. 23–6. **Standard translation:** Eugen Weber, *Paths to the Present: Aspects of European Thought from Romanticism to Existentialism* (New York and Toronto: Dodd, Mead & Co, 1969), pp. 202–9. **Further reading:** Kenneth Cornell, *The Symbolist Movement* (New Haven: Yale University Press, 1951).

mindlessness, serve to confirm even more, with each day that passes, the vitality of the present trend in French literature, that trend which hasty judges, through some confusion, call decadent. But note, however, that decadent literatures have normally shown themselves to be hard, mean, timorous and servile: all the tragedies of Voltaire, for example, are marked with the spots of decadence. But can one reproach, with what can one reproach, the new school? Its abuse of pomp, the strangeness of its metaphors, a new vocabulary, where harmonies combine with colours and with words: these are the characteristics of every renaissance.

We have already advanced the title of *Symbolism*, as the only one capable of accurately designating this present tendency of the creative spirit within art. This designation might well find widespread acceptance.

It was said at the beginning of this article that the evolution of art is subject to a cyclic process that is extremely complicated by divergences; thus, to follow the exact affiliation of this new school it would be necessary to return to certain poems of Alfred de Vigny, and go back to Shakespeare, to the mystics, and even further back. These questions would require an entire volume of commentaries. Let us simply say that Baudelaire must be considered as the real precursor of the present movement; that Mr Stéphane Mallarmé provided it with a sense of the mysterious and the ineffable; whilst Mr Paul Verlaine broke, in its honour, the cruel bonds of verse that the worthy fingers of Mr Theodore de Banville had earlier been softening. However, the *Supreme Enchantment* has not as yet been realised: a jealous and stubborn task awaits those who have just arrived on the scene.

Enemies of teaching, declamation, false sensibility, and objective description, the Symbolist poets seek to clothe the Idea in a sensuous form, which, nevertheless, would not be an end in itself, but which would help to express the Idea, whilst remaining subject to it. The Idea, in its turn, must not let itself be deprived of the sumptuous robes of external analogies; for the essential character of Symbolist art consists in never trying to reproduce the Idea in itself. In this art form, therefore, depictions of nature, human actions, indeed all concrete phenomena should not show themselves as such: they are outward forms, whose purpose is to represent their hidden affinities with primordial Ideas.

The accusation of obscurity hurled against this aesthetic by unmethodical readers contains nothing that is surprising. But what can one do about them? The *Pythians* of Pindar, Shakespeare's *Hamlet*, the *Vita Nuova* of Dante, Goethe's *Faust*, Part II, *The Temptation of Saint Anthony* by Flaubert – were they not also accused of being obscure?

For the exact realisation of its synthesis, Symbolism requires an archetypal and complex style: unpolluted words, clear phrasing which will act as a buttress, and alternate with others of undulating faintness, with signifying pleonasms, mysterious ellipses, and the anacoluthon left in suspense, every trope daring and multiform; and finally, good French – restored and modernized – the good and luxuriant and spirited French language of the days before Vaugelas and Boileau, the language of François Rabelais and Philippe de Commines, of Villon, of Rutebeuf, and of so many other writers who were free and ready to hurl their linguistic barbs, just as the Thracian archers did with their sinuous arrows.

*Rhythm*: the old metre revived; a disorder cleverly brought into order; rhyme, incandescent, and hammered like a shield of brass and gold, which will exist beside the rhyme of abstruse fluidity; the alexandrine, with multiple and mobile pauses; and the use of certain prime numbers – seven, nine, eleven, thirteen – which are resolved into the different rhythm combinations of which they are the sum.

6

---

# *To extract the 'pure notion that lies within'*

## Stéphane Mallarmé: 'The crisis of poetry' (1896)

*Stéphane Mallarmé (1842–98) was the leading figure of the French Symbolist movement, the author of poems such as 'The Afternoon of a Faun' (1876) and 'The virginal, living and beautiful day' (1885), whose semantic complexities and subtle modulations of mood have made them among the richest in French literature. But Mallarmé was also an incisive commentator on poetry and poetic writing, which he construed, in true Symbolist fashion, in uncompromisingly absolute terms. In his intriguing, if at times somewhat cryptic essay 'The crisis of poetry', written and published in stages over a period of ten years, the poet adumbrates the revolution (he calls it 'crisis', in the sense of a critical turning point) taking place within contemporary French poetry. Mallarmé begins by describing the changes to prosody made by young poets (the exponents, for example, of* vers libre*).*

The crisis of poetry lies less in the treatment, however interesting, that versification has undergone during this period of interregnum and repose, than in certain new states of the poetic mind.

We must learn to divine those unmistakable rays of light – like arrows

---

**Source:** Stéphane Mallarmé, *Oeuvres complètes*, edited by Henri Mondor and G. Jean-Aubry (Paris: Gallimard, 1945), pp. 365–7 and 368. **Standard translations:** *Selected Prose Poems, Essays and Letters*, translated with an introduction by B. Cook Bradford (Baltimore: Johns Hopkins University Press, 1956), pp. 34–43. **Further reading:** Roger Pearson, *Unfolding Mallarmé: The Development of a Poetic Art* (Oxford: Clarendon Press, 1996).

golden and piercing the meandering of melody: for, since Wagner, music has reunited with verse to form poetry.

Either of these elements could successfully stand apart, and enjoy the triumph of at least partial integrity, in quiet voice in a concert of its own. But the poem: it can speak of their community of interest, re-strengthening them: the instrumentation will be brightened to perfect clarity beneath the veil of sound, whilst the spoken word descends into the twilight of sonority. That modern meteor, the symphony, comes near to thought whether the musician wills it or not. And thought itself no longer simply appeals to the common tongue.

Thus Mystery bursts forth throughout the celestial realms of its own impersonal magnificence; here the orchestra must play a major part in realizing that ancient goal that we have long nurtured as a race, to translate the spoken word into a form of music.

We have two related signs for this —

Decadence and Mysticism (two schools which called themselves thus, or were hastily named so by our press) adopt as a common focus the point of view of an Idealism which (paralleling the nature of fugues and sonatas) shuns purely natural materials and rejects as brutal any systems of thought that seek to organize them in any precise way, seeking to retain only the suggestiveness of things, and to establish a relationship between two exact images, from which will emerge a third aspect, clear and fusible, that can be grasped by the imagination. Abolished is that erroneous aesthetic (although it has produced masterpieces) that would have us enclose within the subtle pages of our book the actual and tangible wood of trees rather than, for example, the fear of the forest, or the silent scattering of thunder throughout the foliage. A few well-chosen sounds trumpeted to the heavens will conjure up the architecture of the palace, the only habitable one, although it is not made of stone, or else the pages of our book would not close.

Monuments, the sea, the human face, in their native plenitude, possess qualities that are alluring in a way that cannot be captured by descriptions, but only by evocation, let us say, *allusion* and *suggestion*. This somewhat arbitrary terminology confirms a possibly decisive development that literature has recently undergone, which both restricts it and sets it free. For what is the charm of literature if it is not, beyond the confines of a fistful of dust or all-encompassing reality, to open the book, and the text itself, to the volatile scattering of the spirit, whose sole purpose for existence lies within the realm of universal musicality?

Speech has only a commercial interest in reality; in literature, allusions are sufficient: their inherent qualities are extracted, and then embodied in an idea.

Song, when it becomes an unburdened joy, soars heavenward.

I call this goal Transposition — Structure is something else.

The pure work of art involves the disappearance of the poet as a speaking subject, who cedes the initiative to the words themselves, which collide with one another once their essential differences are mobilized; they will catch alight in an exchange of gleams like a virtual swath of fire sweeping over precious stones, replacing the audible breathing in the sound of the lyric poetry of old and the personal direction of the enthusiastic phrase.

The structure of a book arises from its inner form and radiates throughout, eliminating all randomness; and for the same reason, it is necessary to dispense with the author. Each theme that occupies its destined place amongst the collective parts of the text will imply a certain harmony within that text, because for every sound there is an echo: motifs of the same kind will establish an equilibrium in space. There will neither be the sublime incoherence of the Romantic text nor that artificial unity that used to be based on the square measurements of the book. Everything will be held as if suspended: the disposition of parts, alternations and contraries, converging on a total rhythm, which will be the very silence of the poem, in its blank spaces, as that silence is translated in its own way by every component of the book, suspended in time and space.

*Mallarmé believed that language had to be cleansed of all contact with the popular mind if it were to succeed in its task of liberating consciousness from the restrictions of the empirical and quotidian world. He ends his essay, accordingly, by emphasizing the need to refashion language as a higher medium of artistic statement.*

One of the undeniable desires of my generation is to separate the different attributions that adhere to the two sides of language: the brutal or the immediate, and the essential.

To narrate, instruct, or even describe: that is necessary (although exchanging human thoughts might be achieved through the silent exchange of money). The elementary use of language ministers to that universal journalistic style which, literature excepted, informs all of our present genres of writing.

What use, however, is the miracle which allows a fact of nature to almost disappear into a shimmering image through the play of language, if it is not to extract from it, distancing that object from the direct and the palpable, the pure notion that lies within?

I say: 'a flower!', and from that oblivion to which my voice has relegated all floral shapes, something different from the familiar petals arises, something of pure music and sweetness, the idea itself, which is absent from all bouquets.

Unlike the mob, which has reduced language to an easy and popular currency, the poet treats language, above all, as dream and song, allowing

its strange blotches of mauve, and its restless violet shadows, is her latest fancy, and, on the whole, Nature reproduces it quite admirably. Where she used to give us Corots and Daubignys, she gives us now exquisite Monets and entrancing Pissaros. Indeed, there are moments, rare, it is true, but still to be observed from time to time, when Nature becomes absolutely modern. Of course, she is not always to be relied upon. The fact is that she is in this unfortunate position: Art creates an incomparable and unique effect, and, having done so, passes on to other things. Nature, upon the other hand, forgetting that imitation can be made the sincerest form of insult, keeps on repeating this effect until we all become absolutely wearied of it.

> *'But have I proved my theory to your satisfaction?' Vivian concludes by asking. Cyril's reply paves the way for a pithy summary of Wilde's philosophy of art, one that he was to repeat in many other contexts.*

*Cyril*: You have proved it to my dissatisfaction, which is better. But even admitting this strange imitative instinct in Life and Nature, surely you would acknowledge that Art expresses the temper of its age, the spirit of its time, the moral and social conditions that surround it, and under whose influence it is produced.

*Vivian*: Certainly not! Art never expresses anything but itself. This is the principle of my new aesthetics; and it is this, more than that vital connection between form and substance, on which Mr. Pater dwells, that makes music the type of all the arts.

8

---

# 'An intellectual and emotional complex in an instant of time'

## Ezra Pound: Imagism 'a retrospect' (1918)

*Ezra Pound (1885–1972) was born in America, but spent almost his entire adult life in Europe, initially, from 1908, in England, where he became part of a wide circle of Modernist writers, which included T. S. Eliot, W. B. Yeats and T. E. Hulme, and then in Italy. Contact with Hulme brought Pound into the ambit of the newly formed Imagist school of poetry, an Anglo-American movement that promoted*

---

**Source:** Ezra Pound, *The Literary Essays of Ezra Pound*, edited by T. S. Eliot (London: Faber and Faber, 1954), pp. 3, 4–5 and 11–12. **Further reading:** Martin A. Kayman, *The Modernism of Ezra Pound* (New York: St. Martin's Press, 1986), esp. pp. 33–65.

*the use of direct and tactile language in place of vague sentiment and subjective effusion. Pound published one of the first manifestos for the Imagists in the journal Poetry in 1913, which acted as the basis for a subsequent, more detailed exposition of its goals.*

There has been so much scribbling about a new fashion in poetry, that I may perhaps be pardoned this brief recapitulation and retrospect.

In the spring or early summer of 1912, 'H. D.', Richard Aldington and myself decided that we were agreed upon the three principles following:

1. Direct treatment of the 'thing' whether subjective or objective.
2. To use absolutely no word that does not contribute to the presentation.
3. As regarding rhythm: to compose in the sequence of the musical phrase, not in sequence of a metronome.

Upon many points of taste and of predilection we differed, but agreeing upon these three positions we thought we had as much right to a group name, at least as much right, as a number of French 'schools' proclaimed by Mr Flint in the August number of Harold Monro's magazine for 1911.

This school has since been 'joined' or 'followed' by numerous people who, whatever their merits, do not show any signs of agreeing with the second specification. Indeed, *vers libre* has become as prolix and as verbose as any of the flaccid varieties that preceded it. It has brought faults of its own. The actual language and phrasing is often as bad as that of our elders without even the excuse that the words are shovelled in to fill a metric pattern or to complete the noise of a rhyme-sound. Whether or no the phrases followed by the followers are musical must be left to the reader's decision. At times I can find a marked metre in 'vers libres', as stale and hackneyed as any pseudo-Swinburnian, at times the writers seem to follow no musical structure whatever. But it is, on the whole, good that the field should be ploughed. Perhaps a few good poems have come from the new method, and if so it is justified.

*After these sobering words, Pound goes on to provide a series of practical guidelines for the would-be poet of* vers libre.

## A FEW DON'TS

An 'Image' is that which presents itself as an intellectual and emotional complex in an instant of time. I use the term 'complex' rather in the technical sense employed by the newer psychologists, such as Hart, though we might not agree absolutely in our application.

It is the presentation of such a 'complex' instantaneously which gives that sense of sudden liberation; that sense of freedom from time limits and space limits; that sense of sudden growth, which we experience in the presence of the greatest works of art.

It is better to present one Image in a lifetime than to produce voluminous works.

All this, however, some may consider open to debate. The immediate necessity is to tabulate A LIST OF DON'TS for those beginning to write verse. I can not put all of them into Mosaic negative.

To begin with, consider the three propositions (demanding direct treatment, economy of words, and the sequence of the musical phrase), not as dogma – never consider anything as dogma – but as the result of long contemplation, which, even if it is some one else's contemplation, may be worth consideration.

Pay no attention to the criticism of men who have never themselves written a notable work. Consider the discrepancies between the actual writing of the Greek poets and dramatists, and the theories of the Graeco-Roman grammarians, concocted to explain their metres.

### LANGUAGE

Use no superfluous word, no adjective which does not reveal something.

Don't use an expression such as 'dim lands *of peace*'. It dulls the image. It mixes an abstraction with the concrete. It comes from the writer's not realizing that the natural object is always the *adequate* symbol.

Go in fear of abstractions. Do not retell in mediocre verse what has already been in good prose. Don't think any intelligent person is going to be deceived when you try to shirk all the difficulties of the unspeakably difficult art of good prose by chopping your composition into line lengths.

What the expert is tired of today the public will be tired of tomorrow.

Don't imagine that the art of poetry is any simpler than the art of music, or that you can please the expert before you have spent at least as much effort on the art of verse as the average piano teacher spends on the art of music.

Be influenced by as many great artists as you can, but have the decency either to acknowledge the debt outright, or to try to conceal it.

Don't allow 'influence' to mean merely that you mop up the particular decorative vocabulary of some one or two poets whom you happen to admire. A Turkish war correspondent was recently caught red-handed babbling in his dispatches of 'dove-grey' hills, or else it was 'pearl-pale', I can not remember.

Use either no ornament or good ornament.

# 9

# 'Here, ethics becomes aesthetics, expanding into the latter's sphere'

## Nikolai Gumilev: 'Acmeism and the legacy of Symbolism' (1913)

*Nikolai Gumilev (1886–1921) began as one of the major poets of the Symbolist movement in Russia (see, for example, Pearls, 1910), before finally breaking with that movement and founding his own school, the Acmeists, in 1913. The Acmeists (who also included Anna Akhmatova and Osip Mandelstam) sought to retain the metaphysical import of Symbolist verse, but rejected what they regarded as the nebulous and affected ethereality of that verse. Gumilev outlined the goals of the Acmeist movement (and its position on Symbolism) in a manifesto of 1913.*

It is clear to the attentive reader that Symbolism has completed its circle of development and is now declining. There is the fact that Symbolist works hardly ever appear anymore, and if any do appear, then ones that are extremely weak, even from the point of view of Symbolism, and that, more and more frequently voices are raised in favour of a reconsideration of values and reputations indisputable not so long ago, and that the Futurists, the Ego-Futurists, and other hyenas that always follow the lion have appeared. To replace Symbolism there is a new movement, which, whatever it is called – Acmeism (from the word 'acme' – the highest degree of something, the flower, the time of flowering), or Adamism (a manfully firm, clear view of life), – demands, in any case, greater balance of powers and a more exact knowledge of the relationships between subject and object than there was in Symbolism. However, for this trend to establish itself fully and be a worthy successor to what preceded it, it must accept the latter's legacy and answer all the questions it posed. The glory of one's forebears carries obligations, and Symbolism was a worthy father.

French Symbolism, the ancestor of all Symbolism as a school, moved purely literary questions into the foreground – free verse, a more original and vacillating style, metaphor elevated above all else, and the notorious 'theory of correspondences'. This last betrays its non-Romance and consequently non-national, alien basis. The Romance spirit is too beloved of the element of light, which separates objects, draws careful,

**Source:** *Nikolai Gumilev on Russian Poetry*, edited and translated by David Lapeza (Ann Arbor, MI: Ardis, 1977), pp. 21–4. **Further reading:** Raoul Eshelman, *Nikolay Gumilev and Neo-Classical Modernism: The Metaphysics of Style* (Frankfurt am Main: Peter Lang, 1993).

clear lines; but this Symbolist merging of all images and objects, the changeability of their appearance, could have arisen only in the misty gloom of Germanic forests. A mystic would say that Symbolism in France is a direct result of Sedan. But at the same time it revealed in French literature an aristocratic craving for the unusual and the difficult to attain and thus saved it from the vulgar Naturalism that threatened it.

We Russians cannot but take French Symbolism into account, if only because the new trend I spoke of above gives a decided preference to the Romance over the Germanic spirit. Just as the French sought a new, freer verse, the Acmeists strive to break the chains of meter by skipping syllables and by freer transposition of stress than ever before; and there are already poems written in a newly devised syllabic system of versification. The giddiness of Symbolist metaphors trained them in bold turns of thought; the instability of vocabulary, to which they became accustomed, prompted them to search in the living national speech for a new one with a more stable content; and a lucid irony, which has not undermined the roots of our faith – an irony which could not but appear if only from time to time in the Romance writers – has now replaced that hopeless German seriousness which our Symbolists so cherished. Finally, while we value the Symbolists highly for having pointed out to us the significance of the symbol in art, we cannot agree to sacrifice to it other methods of poetic influence and we seek the complete coordination of all of them. This is our answer to the question of the comparative 'beautiful difficulty' of the two movements: it is harder to be an Acmeist than a Symbolist, just as it is harder to build a cathedral than a tower. And one of the principles of the new trend is always to take the line of greatest resistance.

German Symbolism, in the persons of its ancestors, Nietzsche and Ibsen, put forth the question of the role of man in the universe, the role of the individual in society, and settled it by finding some sort of objective goal or dogma which he was meant to serve. This showed that German Symbolism did not sense each phenomenon's intrinsic worth, which requires no justification from without. For us, the hierarchy of phenomena in the world is merely the specific weight of each of them, though the weight of the most insignificant is still immeasurably greater than the absence of weight, non-existence, and for that reason, in the face of non-existence, all phenomena are brothers.

We could not bring ourselves to force an atom to bow to God, if this were not in its nature. But feeling ourselves to be phenomena among phenomena, we become part of the world rhythm, accept all the forces acting upon us and ourselves become forces in our turn. Our duty, our freedom, our joy and our tragedy is to guess each hour what the next hour may be for us, for our cause, for the whole world, and to hurry its coming. And for our highest reward, never suspending attention for a moment, we dream of the image of the last hour, which will never arrive.

But to rebel in the name of other conditions of existence, here, where there is death, is as strange as for a prisoner to break down a wall when in front of him there is an open door. Here, ethics becomes aesthetics, expanding into the latter's sphere. Here, individualism in its highest effort creates community. Here, God becomes the Living God, because man felt himself worthy of such a God. Here, death is a curtain, separating us, the actors, from the audience, and in the inspiration of play we disdain the cowardly peeping of 'What will happen next?' As Adamists, we are somewhat like forest animals and in any case will not surrender what is animal in us in exchange for neurasthenia.

*Gumilev proceeds to further distinguish the Acmeist vision from that of the Symbolist, before concluding with a declaration of the Acmeist world view.*

The principle of Acmeism is always to remember the unknowable, but not to insult one's idea of it with more or less likely conjectures. This does not mean that it denies itself the right to portray the soul in those moments when it trembles, approaching another; but then it ought to shudder only. Of course, knowledge of God, the beautiful lady Theology, will remain on her throne, and the Acmeists wish neither to lower her to the level of literature, nor raise literature to her diamond coldness. As for angels, demons, elemental and other spirits, they are part of the artist's material and need not have a specific gravity greater than other images he chooses.

Any movement will experience a passionate love for certain writers and epochs. The loved ones' graves tie people together more closely than anything. In circles familiar to Acmeism, the names most frequently spoken are those of Shakespeare, Rabelais, Villon and Théophile Gautier. The choice of these names is not arbitrary. Each of them is a cornerstone of the edifice of Acmeism, a lofty exercise of one or another of its elements. Shakespeare showed us man's inner world; Rabelais – the body and its joys; Villon told us of a life which has not the slightest doubt in itself, although it knows everything – God, sin, death and immortality; Théophile Gautier found in art worthy garments of irreproachable forms for this life. To unite in oneself these four moments – that is the dream which now unifies the people who so boldly call themselves Acmeists.

# 10

# 'We intend to sing the love of danger, the habit of energy and fearlessness'

## Filippo Tommaso Marinetti: 'The founding and manifesto of Futurism' (1909)

*Filippo Tommaso Marinetti (1876–1944) was the founder and leading member of the Italian Futurists. Although he also wrote poetry (*Destruction, *1904) and plays (*The Feasting King, *1909), his most important publication was the manifesto he wrote for the founding of the Futurist movement in 1909 (published, in fact, in French, in* Le Figaro *on 20 February of that year). Here, the characteristic voice of the Avant-Garde can be heard at its strident best – iconoclastic, provocative, bellicose, and apocalyptic – as it strives to impart a sense of impending cultural conflicts that can only be resolved through a devastation of existing norms and institutions. Marinetti begins his manifesto in the conspiratorial way that was an essential part of the* modus operandi *of many Avant-Garde groups.*

We had stayed up all night, my friends and I, under hanging mosque lamps with domes of filigreed brass, domes starred like our spirits, shining like them with the prisoned radiance of electric hearts. For hours we trampled our atavistic ennui into rich cultural oriental rugs, arguing up to the last confines of logic and blackening many reams of paper with our frenzied scribbling.

An immense pride was buoying us up, because we felt ourselves alone at that hour, alone, awake, and on our feet, like proud beacons or forward sentries against an army of hostile stars glaring down at us from their celestial encampments. Alone with stokers feeding the hellish fires of great ships, alone with the black spectres who grope in the red-hot bellies of locomotives launched down their crazy courses, alone with drunkards reeling like wounded birds along city walls.

Suddenly we jumped, hearing the mighty noise of the huge double-decker trams that rumbled by outside, ablaze with coloured lights, like villages on holiday suddenly struck and uprooted by the flooding Po and dragged over falls and through gorges to the sea.

Then the silence deepened. But, as we listened to the old canal

---

**Source:** Filippo Tommaso Marinetti, in *Marinetti: Selected Writings*, edited by R. W. Flint and translated by R. W. Flint and Arthur A. Coppotelli (London: Secker & Warburg, 1972), pp. 19–20, 21–3. **Further reading:** John J. White, *Literary Futurism: Aspects of the First Avant-Garde* (Oxford: Clarendon Press, 1990).

muttering its feeble prayers and the creaking bones of sickly palaces above their damp green beards, under the windows we suddenly heard the famished roar of automobiles.

'Let's go!' I said. 'Friends, away! Let's go! Mythology and the Mystic Ideal are defeated at last. We're about to see the Centaur's birth and, soon after, the first flight of Angels! . . . We must shake the gates of life, test the bolts and hinges. Let's go! Look there, on the earth, the very first dawn! There's nothing to match the splendour of the sun's red sword, slashing for the first time through our millennial gloom!'

*Marinetti retains this apocalyptic energy when the time comes to delineate the terms of the Futurist manifesto, terms that are the distillation of pure confrontation.*

1. We intend to sing the love of danger, the habit of energy and fearlessness.
2. Courage, audacity, and revolt will be essential elements of our poetry.
3. Up to now literature has exalted a pensive immobility, ecstasy, and sleep. We intend to exalt aggressive action, a feverish insomnia, the racer's stride, the mortal leap, the punch and the slap.
4. We affirm that the world's magnificence has been enriched by a new beauty: the beauty of speed. A racing car whose hood is adorned with great pipes, like serpents of explosive breath – a roaring car that seems to ride on grapeshot is more beautiful than the *Victory of Samothrace*.
5. We want to hymn the man at the wheel, who hurls the lance of his spirit across the Earth, along the circle of its orbit.
6. The poet must spend himself with ardour, splendour, and generosity, to swell the enthusiastic fervour of the primordial elements.
7. Except in struggle, there is no more beauty. No work without an aggressive character can be a masterpiece. Poetry must be conceived as a violent attack on unknown forces, to reduce and prostrate them before man.
8. We stand on the last promontory of the centuries! . . . Why should we look back, when what we want is to break down the mysterious doors of the Impossible? Time and Space died yesterday. We already live in the absolute, because we have created eternal, omnipresent speed.
9. We will glorify war – the world's only hygiene – militarism, patriotism, the destructive gesture of freedom-bringers, beautiful ideas worth dying for, and scorn for woman.
10. We will destroy the museums, libraries, academies of every kind, will fight moralism, feminism, every opportunistic or utilitarian cowardice.
11. We will sing of great crowds excited by work, by pleasure, and by riot; we will sing of the multicoloured, polyphonic tides of

revolution in the modern capitals; we will sing of the vibrant nightly fervour of arsenals and shipyards blazing with violent electric moons; greedy railway stations that devour smoke-plumed serpents; factories hung on clouds by the crooked lines of their smoke; bridges that stride the rivers like giant gymnasts, flashing in the sun with a glitter of knives; adventurous steamers that sniff the horizon; deep-chested locomotives whose wheels paw the tracks like the hooves of enormous steel horses bridled by tubing; and the sleek flight of planes whose propellers chatter in the wind like banners and seem to cheer like an enthusiastic crowd.

*But this is not simply theory. On the contrary, Marinetti exhorts the reader to take literally what some might see simply as shocking metaphors.*

In truth I tell you that daily visits to museums, libraries, and academies (cemeteries of empty exertion, Calvaries of crucified dreams, registries of aborted beginnings!) are, for artists, as damaging as the prolonged supervision by parents of certain young people drunk with their talent and their ambitious wills. When the future is barred to them, the admirable past may be a solace for the ills of the moribund, the sickly, the prisoner. . . . But we want no part of it, the past, we the young and strong *Futurists*!

So let them come, the gay incendiaries with charred fingers! Here they are! Here they are! . . . Come on! set fire to the library shelves! Turn aside the canals to flood the museums! . . . Oh, the joy of seeing the glorious old canvases bobbing adrift on those waters, discoloured and shredded! . . . Take up your pickaxes, your axes and hammers and wreck, wreck the venerable cities, pitilessly!

# 11

# 'Belief in every god that is the immediate product of spontaneity'

## Tristan Tzara: 'Dada manifesto' (1918)

*Tristan Tzara (1896–1963) was one of the founding members of the Dada movement, and among the first to publish Dada-inspired literature (see, for example, his* The First Heavenly Adventure of Mr Antipyrine *(1916) and Twenty-Five Poems (1918)). He was also the most persuasive advocate of its cause, publishing seven manifestos by 1924. The first manifesto, written in 1918, gives exuberant (if, at times, semantically indeterminate) voice to the pet hatreds of the Dadaists: the bourgeois social sphere, and its key self-images of scientific progress, commerce and material achievement, rationalism, morality and propriety; militarism and the conduct of war; and the institutionalization of art, indeed, the very notion of 'high' art itself, and the over-importance that its custodians attach to it. Written against the backdrop of the First World War, Tzara's polemical tract constitutes a call to struggle against those forces which must be removed before culture can be reborn on the basis of a new liberated individualism. Tzara begins, however, in a characteristically self-deflationary way, by questioning the very notion of the artistic manifesto.*

> The magic of a word – DADA
> which has for journalists
> opened the gate to a world
> never before seen has for us
> no importance at all.

To launch a manifesto, you have to want: A.B.C., to rant against 1,2,3, to fly into a rage, and sharpen your wings to conquer, and circulate little and big abc's, to sign things, shout, swear, organise prose into a form of absolute and irrefutable evidence, prove its *ne plus ultra* and maintain that novelty resembles life just as the most recent appearance of someone's fancy woman proves the essence of God. His existence has already been proven by the accordion, the countryside and sweet language. To impose one's ABC is only natural, – but hence regrettable. Everybody does it in the form of the fake crystal Madonna, the monetary system,

**Source:** Tristan Tzara, *Lampisteries: precedées des sept manifestes dada* (Paris: Pauvert, 1963), pp. 19–35. **Standard translation:** Tristan Tzara, *Seven Dada Manifestos and Lampisteries*, translated by Barbara Wright (London: Calder, 1977). **Further reading:** Elmer Peterson, *Tristan Tzara: Dada and Surrealist Theorist* (New Brunswick, NJ: Rutgers University Press, 1971), pp. 3–41.

pharmaceutical products, or a naked leg advertising an ardent but sterile Spring. The love of novelty is a congenial cross, is evidence of a naive I-don't-give-a-damn-ism, a transitory, positive, unmotivated sign. But this need is out of date, too. By giving art the impetus of supreme simplicity – novelty – we are being human and honest in our respect for amusement; impulsive and vibrant in order to crucify boredom. At the lighted crossroads, alert, attentive, lying in wait for years, in the forest.

I am writing a manifesto and there's nothing I want; and yet I'm saying certain things and I am in principle against manifestos, as I am also against principles (measuring jugs for the moral value of phrases – too convenient; approximation was invented by the Impressionists).

I am writing this manifesto in order to show that it is possible to perform quite contradictory actions at the same time, by taking a deep gulp of fresh air; I am against action; but for continual contradiction, and for affirmation also. I am neither for nor against and I will not explain because I hate common sense.

> *And Tzara does not explain; or rather, he offers spoof explanations, 'clarifications' of the origins of the term 'Dada' (it might be baby talk for rocking-horse, an affirmative assertion in a Slavonic language, or the African name for the tail of a holy cow), adumbrating a defiant inconsequentiality that he also celebrates as a motivating energy in other Avant-Garde groups, such as the Futurists and the Cubists. These are the 'new men. Uncouth, bouncing, riding on hiccups [who are leaving] behind them a crippled world and literary quacks with a hatred of change.' Like the Dadaists, these new voices of radical art seek to destroy the hegemony of the cultural custodians of the establishment, in preparation for a sustained campaign of artistic renewal.*

Let each man shout: there is a great negative work of destruction to accomplish. To sweep, to clean. The cleanliness of the individual emerges after the state of madness, the aggressive, total madness of a world left in the hands of bandits who have torn open the centuries and destroyed them. With neither aim nor plan, without organisation: indomitable madness, decomposition. Those who are strong in word or in strength will survive, for they are quick in defence, the agility of their limbs and feelings flames on their faceted flanks.

Morality has given rise to charity and pity, two bowls of fat that have grown like elephants, like planets, and are called good. There is nothing good about them. Goodness is lucid, clear and resolute, and ruthless towards compromise and politics. Morality is the infusion of chocolate into the veins of mankind. That task is not ordained by a supernatural force, but by a trust of ideas merchants and grasping academics. Sentimentality: seeing a group of bored and quarrelling men, they invented the calendar and wisdom as a medication. By sticking labels onto things, the battle of the philosophers was unleashed (mercantilism, scales, meticulous and shabby measures), and one understood once again that pity is a sentiment like diarrhoea in relation to the disgust that undermines health, a foul attempt of carrions to compromise the sun.

I proclaim the opposition of all cosmic faculties to this gonorrhoea of a putrid sun that has emerged from the factories of philosophic thought, a desperate struggle, using every method of

## DADAIST DISGUST

Every product of disgust capable of becoming a negation of the family is DADA; a protest with the fists of one's entire being in destructive action: DADA; knowledge of all the means hitherto rejected by the sexual prudery of easy compromise and good manners: DADA; abolition of logic, dance of those impotent to create: DADA; of every social hierarchy and equation set up as values by our valets: DADA; each object, every object, sentiments, obscurities, apparitions and the precise clash of parallel lines are the means for the struggle: DADA; abolition of memory: DADA; abolition of archaeology: DADA; abolition of prophets: DADA; abolition of the future: DADA; absolute and unquestionable belief in every god that is the immediate product of spontaneity: DADA; elegant and unprejudiced leap from one harmony to another sphere; trajectory of a word, thrown like a screeching disc into the air; to respect all individuals in their folly of the moment: whether serious, fearful, timid, passionate, vigorous, determined, enthusiastic; to strip one's church of every useless and cumbersome accessory; to spit out like a luminous cascade offensive or amorous thoughts, or to cherish them – with the extreme satisfaction that it doesn't matter in the least – with the same intensity in the bush, which is free of insects for blood well born, and gilded with the body of archangels, and with one's soul. Freedom: *DADA DADA DADA*, a howling of contorted pains, interweaving of contraries and of all contradictions, of the grotesque, of the irrelevant: LIFE.

# 12

## 'A really new transfiguration of the artistic world'

### Kasimir Edschmid: 'Expressionism in literature' (1917)

*Kasimir Edschmid (1890–1966) was not one of the major figures in German Expressionism (see his slim novellas* The Raging Life *and* Six Apertures*, both 1916), but his manifesto of 1917 was one of the earliest and most cogent statements of its goals and aesthetic. After briefly outlining his role in the new movement, he goes on to describe the advent of its key representatives in a heightened language that at times takes on missionary connotations.*

Then came the artists of the new movement. They no longer sought the easy effect. They no longer sought the raw fact. For them the moment, the second of Impressionistic creativity was simply an empty husk in the mill of time. They were no longer subject to the ideas, crises and personal tragedies of bourgeois and capitalist thinking.

In them, *feeling* developed in boundless measure.

They did not see.

They perceived.

They did not photograph.

They had eyes.

Instead of rockets, they created continuing agitation.

Instead of the passing moment, the impact upon history. They did not provide the glittering parade of the circus. They aimed for an experience that would last.

Above all, there now arose against the atomistic, fragmented ways of the Impressionists a great all-embracing world feeling.

In it stood the earth, existence as a potent vision. There were feelings in it, and human kind. They called out to be grasped in their essence and in their original nature.

The great music of a poet constitutes his humanity. It only becomes great for him when its environment is great. Not the heroic format (that only leads to decoration); no, great in the sense that its existence, its experience of life partakes of the great existence of the firmament and the earth, that its heart, entwined with all that is happening, beats to the same rhythm as the world.

**Source:** Kasimir Edschmid, *Fruhe Manifeste: Epochen der Expressionismus* (Hamburg: Christian Wegner, 1957), pp. 31–3 and 34–5. There is no standard translation. **Further reading:** *The Era of Expressionism*, edited by Paul Raabe and translated by J. M. Ritchie (London: Calder and Boyars, 1974).

To achieve this requires a really new transfiguration of the artistic world. A new image of the world must be created, one which no longer has anything to do with that world of the Naturalists, which could only be grasped experientially, no longer has anything to do with the fragmented realm of the Impressionists, but rather should be *simple*, actual and, consequently, beautiful.

The earth is an enormous landscape, given by God. It must be so treated that it comes to us unspoilt. No one doubts that what external reality gives us no longer needs to be regarded as the truth.

Reality must be created by us. The meaning of the object world has to be excavated. We can not be satisfied with accepted, conventional, observed facts; an image of the world must be reflected in a pure and unadulterated fashion. That lies, however, only within ourselves.

So the entire realm of the Expressionist artist becomes a vision. He does not see, he perceives. He does not depict, he experiences. He does not describe, he forms. He doesn't take what is in front of him, he searches. Now the chain of facts exists no more: factories, houses, illness, whores, screams and hunger. Now we have the vision of these.

Facts have significance only in so far as that the hand of the artist, reaching through them, grasps what lies behind them.

He sees humanity in the whores, the celestial in the factories. He merges the isolated phenomenon into the greater reality which makes up the world.

He presents the deeper image of the object; the landscape of his art is that of the supreme paradise that God created in the beginning. This is more majestic, more radiant and more eternal than the image which our perception can register in its simple empirical blindness, and which to mirror would provide no inspiration. We seek in the former, depth, the actual and the wonder of the spirit, in which at every moment new fascinations and revelations become apparent.

Everything acquires an affinity to eternity.

*That this new vision of artistic endeavour will require not only a radical break with previous literary traditions, but also a fundamental revision of social and ethical norms, Edschmid has no doubt. It is the 'neuer Mensch' [the new man] who will bring this project to fruition, a mystical-existentialist creature capable of political activism, and in the concluding pages of his essay Edschmid offers a homily to this utopian figure of the Expressionist mind.*

The world is simply there.

It would be pointless to reproduce it. The great task of art is to seek out its final shudder, its basic essence, and to recreate it anew.

Man is no longer an individual bound by duty, morality, society, the family.

In this new art form, he becomes nothing other than the most sublime and the most wretched: *he becomes human.*

It is here that what is new and unprecedented in previous epochs emerges.

It is here that the bourgeois way of thinking is finally no longer thought.

Here those relations that obscure the image of mankind are no more. No love stories, and none of the tragedies which arise out of that collision between convention and the individual's need for liberty, no social dramas, no strict bosses, or jovial officers, no puppets hanging on the strings of psychological philosophies, with laws, points of view, disputes and vices, playing, laughing and suffering in this artificially constructed social existence.

Through all of this surrogate world the brutish hand of the artist can be seen at work. It becomes obvious that these were simply façades. The sham emotions produced by the coulisses and the cross-beams lead to nothing more than the simple man. No blond beast, no wily native, just simple, plain, man himself.

His heart breathes, his lungs burst, he surrenders himself to creation, of which he is not a part, but which sways *within* him, as he reflects it. His life orders itself, without petty logic, without calculation, inhibiting morality and causality, purely according to the vast barometer of his feelings.

With this eruption of his inner life he is bound to everything. He understands the world, the earth resides within him. And he stands upon it, firmly with both legs, his ardour embraces the visible and that which has already been seen.

Now man is even greater, the master of spontaneous emotions. He stands there, his heart so open to understanding, so absolutely to the core saturated by the waves of his blood that it seems as if his heart has been painted onto his breast.

He is no longer just a shape. He is a real man. He is intertwined with the cosmos, but with a cosmic sensibility.

He does not tip-toe through life. He strides through. He does not reflect upon himself, he experiences himself. He does not creep around things, he grasps them at their core. He is not in- or super-human, simply human, cowardly and strong, good and common and majestic, just as God left him at Creation.

All things, whose essence, whose true being he is accustomed to seeing, are thus near to him.

He will not be suppressed; he loves and fights spontaneously.

His powerful emotions alone, not false thought, guide and lead him onward.

It is thus that he moves upwards, towards rapture, allowing intense ecstasies to soar out of his soul.

He arrives at God as the highest summit of a sensibility that is only to be reached through an unsurpassable ecstasy of the spirit.


## 13

## 'This summer the roses are blue; the wood is of glass'

### André Breton: *Manifestos of Surrealism* (1924)

*André Breton (1896–1966) was the founding member of the Surrealist movement in France, who published, in the form of his poetry (*The Mount of Piety, *1919) and his novel (*Nadja, *1928), some of the most memorable works of Surrealist literature. But his main contribution to the development of European Modernism lay in his seminal contribution to the Surrealist school, for which he wrote not one but two manifestos (1924 and 1930). In his first manifesto (an audacious mixture of cultural analysis, autobiographical reverie, automatic writing and sophistical fabulation), he explained how, under the influence of Freud's teachings, he originally arrived at a literary form that would open up a path to the unconscious.*

Completely preoccupied as I still was with Freud in this period, and well versed in his methods of analysis, which I had passing occasion to use on certain patients during the war, I resolved to obtain from myself what we were trying to obtain from them, namely, a monologue spoken as rapidly as possible without any interference by judgements made by the critical faculties. This monologue, therefore, would be without the slightest inhibition, and would come, as close as is possible, to *spoken thought*. It had seemed to me, and it still does – in the manner in which that phrase about the man cut in two had come to me – that the speed of thought is no greater than the speed of speech, and that it does not necessarily defy language, not even the speedy pen. It was in this frame of mind that Philippe Soupault (to whom I had communicated these initial musings) and I undertook to apply ink to some sheets of paper, with a laudable indifference to the literary quality of what might result from this practice. The process itself easily did the rest. By the end of the first day, we were

**Source:** André Breton, *Manifestes du surréalisme* (Paris: Gallimard, 1973), pp. 33–6, 37–8 and 63–4. **Standard translation:** Breton, *Manifestos of Surrealism*, translated from the French by Richard Seaver and Helen R. Lane (Ann Arbor: The University of Michigan Press, 1969), pp. 3–47. **Further reading:** Franklin Rosemount, *André Breton and the First Principles of Surrealism* (London: Pluto, 1978).

able to read to ourselves fifty pages or so obtained in this fashion, and began to compare the results. On the whole, Soupault's pages and mine were remarkably similar: they had the same vices in their construction, similar shortcomings, but also, in both cases, the illusion of an extraordinary verve, an intensity of emotion, a considerable array of images of such a quality that preparing even a single one in longhand would have been previously beyond us, a very special picturesque effect, and, here and there, a distinctive buffoonery. The only differences between our two series of texts seemed to me basically to be the result of our respective personalities, Soupault's being less static than mine, and, if he will permit me this mild criticism, from the fact that he had made the error of putting at the top of certain pages, in a spirit no doubt of mystification, a few words in the form of titles. On the other hand, I must give him credit for continually resisting, with all his might, any inclination to alter, in the slightest way, any passage from these texts that seemed to me to be of a dubious quality. He was without a doubt, in this respect, absolutely right. It is, in fact, extremely difficult to appreciate fully the various features of these texts; one might even say that it is impossible to appreciate them at a first reading. Even to the person who has written them, these features are *as strange as they are to anyone else*, and, naturally, he distrusts them. Poetically speaking, what makes them stand out is, above all, a high degree of *conspicuous absurdity*, the defining feature of this absurdity being, upon closer scrutiny, that it opens up a space for everything that is admissible, everything that is legitimate in the world: the disclosure of a certain number of properties and of facts which are, in the end, no less objective than others.

In homage to Guillaume Apollinaire, who had just died, and who, on several occasions, had (it seemed to us) explored the discipline of this way of writing, without having sacrificed it to mediocre literary purposes, Soupault and I designated this new medium of expression that we now had at our disposal and which we wished to pass on to our friends: SURREALISM.

*But what was Surrealism exactly? Breton answered with a pregnant formulation, penned in the form of a spoof lexical entry in a dictionary.*

Those who contest our right to use the term SURREALISM in the very special sense in which we understand it are being quite hypocritical, for it is undeniable that before us this word had no currency. I will, therefore, define it for once and for all:

SURREALISM (noun, masculine): Psychic automatism in the pure sense of the term, through which one intends to express, be it in a written, spoken or any other form, the actual functioning of thought. Dictated by thought, in the absence of any control exercised by reason, and without any aesthetic or moral considerations.

ENCYCLOPEDIA (Philosophy): Surrealism is based on the belief in the superior reality of certain forms of association that have up to now been neglected: in the supremacy of dreams, in the disinterested play of the mind. Its aim is to ruin for all time all other psychic mechanisms and to substitute itself for them in solving all the major problems of life. Participants in ABSOLUTE SURREALISM are: Messrs. Aragon, Baron, Boiffard, Breton, Carrive, Crevel, Delteil, Desnos, Eluard, Gérard, Limbour, Malkine, Morise, Naville, Noll, Péret, Picon, Soupault, Vitrac.

*What follows this terse adumbration is an extended fantasy upon the Surrealist aesthetic, with examples of its polysemic textuality. The manifesto ends on a note both poetic and cryptic.*

Surrealism, as I envisage it, asserts our absolute non-conformism so vehemently that there can be no question of exploiting it, in the trial of the real world, as a witness for the defence. On the contrary, it could only serve to justify that complete state of distraction which we hope will soon prevail here below. Kant's distraction regarding women, Pasteur's distraction regarding 'grapes', Curie's distraction about vehicles, are, in this regard, profoundly symptomatic. This world is only in a very imperfect way in step with thought, and incidents of this kind are only the most striking episodes so far of a war of independence in which I have the honour to be participating. Surrealism is the 'invisible ray' which will one day secure us victory over our enemies. 'You are no longer trembling, carcass'. This summer the roses are blue; the wood is of glass. The earth, draped in its green mantle, makes as little impression upon me as a ghost. It is to live and to cease to live that are the imaginary solutions. Life is elsewhere.

# 14

## 'My new spiritualist manner, pure disembodied emotion, detached from logical control'

### Federico García Lorca: Letters (1927–28)

*Federico García Lorca (1898–1936) was one of the most original Spanish poets and playwrights of the Modernist period. In plays such as* Blood Wedding *(1933), and in* Songs *(1927),* Gypsy Ballads *(1928) and, above all,* A Poet in New York *(published posthumously in 1940), Lorca forged a unique idiom which conveyed the elemental pressures of life and death in an imagery that was often abrasive and even violent. As his letters indicate, his writing was informed by a feel for the indigenous customs and atmosphere (part-European and, in Lorca's eyes, part-African) of his native Andalusia, whose bright transforming energies pervade his poetry.*

To Sebastian Gasch

[Fragment]                                                    [ca. August, 1927]

In the midst of the Sierra Nevada one is in the *heart of the soul* of Africa. All the eyes are by now perfectly African, with a ferocity and poetry that can hold off the Mediterranean. This tree – the postcard depicts the 'fat chestnut' of Lanjaron – will give you an idea of the vegetation and the rich quality of the water. Here you understand the wounds of St. Roque, the tears of blood, and the taste for the buried knife. Strange and Berberesque Andalusia.

To Sebastian Gasch

[Summer 1927?]

My dear Sebastian,

In effect, you're right in everything you say. But my state is not one of 'perpetual dream'. I've expressed myself badly. Some days I've skirted the dream, but haven't fallen totally into it, possessing, of course, a

**Source:** Federico García Lorca, *Selected Letters*, translated by David Gershator (London and New York: Marion Boyars, 1984), pp. 116, 117, 121, 135, 138 and 139–40. **Further reading:** Rupert C. Allen, *The Symbolist World of Federico García Lorca* (Albuquerque: University of New Mexico Press, 1972).

tether of laughter to hang on to and a secure wooden scaffold. I never venture into territories alien to man, because I beat a fast retreat and almost always rip up the fruits of my voyage. When I do a purely abstract thing, it always has (I believe) a safe conduct pass of smiles and a rather human equilibrium. . . .

My state is always happy, and this dreaming of mine is not dangerous for me, because I have defenses; it is dangerous for one who lets himself be fascinated by the great dark mirrors that poetry and madness wield at the bottom of their chasms. I HAVE AND I FEEL I HAVE MY FEET FIRMLY ON THE GROUND IN ART. I FEAR the abyss and the dreams in the reality of my life, in love, in the daily encounter with others. And that reality is terrible and fantastic.


To Sebastian Gasch

[August or September, 1927]

[Fragments]

But *without torture or dream* (I detest the art of dreams), or complications. These drawings are pure poetry or pure plasticity at the same time. I feel clean, comforted, happy, *a child* when I do them. And I am horrified by the *word* that I have to use to name them. I'm horrified by the painting that they call *direct*, which is nothing but an anguished struggle with forms in which the painter is *always* vanquished and the work is *dead*. In these abstractions I see *created* reality joining itself to the reality that surrounds us like a real clock is attached to the concept the way a barnacle is to a rock. You're right, my dear Gasch, one must connect abstractions. What's more, I would call these drawings you'll be receiving (I'm sending them registered), *Very Human Drawings*. Because almost all of them pierce the heart with their little arrows. . . .

As you probably know, I returned from Lanjaron and I'm once more in the Huerta de San Vicente in bucolic surroundings, eating exquisite fruits and singing on the swing with my brother and sisters all day long and fooling around so much, that at times I'm embarrassed because of my age.

To Sebastian Gasch

[Granada, September, 1928]

My dear Sebastian,

Enclosed are two poems ['Suicide in Alexandria' and 'Swimmer Submerged']. I hope you like them. They answer to my new spiritualist manner, pure disembodied emotion, detached from logical control but – careful! careful! – with a tremendous poetic logic. It is not surrealism – careful! – the clearest self-awareness illuminates them.

They're the first I've done. Naturally, they're in prose because verse is a confinement they can't withstand. But in them you will find, naturally, my true heart's tenderness.

I am always grateful for your praise of my drawings. I must publish a book.

Convince Dali that he should come to Granada.

I feel, as always, a great desire to go to Barcelona to be among you, with you, strolling along the Ramblas, through the marvellous port, through the picnic spots of Montjuit [*sic*], where we had such a good time.

Write me. Keep the drawings you published. My gift to you. And that way you can make a collection of silly trifles.

Adios, Sebastian. Here's an affectionate hug from

Federico

To Sebastian Gasch

[Fragment]                                                    [1928?]

The truth is what's alive and now they try to fill us up with deaths and cork dust. The absurd, if it's alive, is true; the theorem, if it's dead, is a lie. Let the fresh air in! Aren't you bothered by the idea of a sea with all its fish tied by little chains to one place, unknowing? I'm not disputing dogma. But dread the thought of where 'that dogma' leads.

To Jorge Zalamea

[September, 1928]

My dear Jorge:

At last I got your letter. I had already written you one and tore it up.

You must have had a bad summer. Fortunately, autumn, which gives me life, is already coming in. I too have had a bad time. Very bad. One needs to have the amount of happiness God bestowed on me in order not to succumb before the number of conflicts that have assaulted me lately. But God never abandons me. I've worked a lot and I'm working now. After constructing my 'odes', in which I have so much hope, I'm closing this cycle of poetry to do something else. I am fashioning now a sort of VEIN-OPENING poetry, a poetry that has EVADED reality with an emotion reflecting all of my love of things and my mockery of things. Love of death and joking about death. Love. My heart. That's how it is.

All day I turn out poems like a factory. And then I go in for the manly, in the style of a pure Andalusian, to a bacchanal of flesh and laughter. Andalusia is incredible. Orient without poison, Occident without action. Each day I experience new surprises. The beautiful flesh of the South thanks you after you have stepped all over her.

In spite of everything, I'm neither well nor happy. Today is a FIRST CLASS gray day in Granada. From the Huerta de San Vicente (my mother's name is Vicenta) where I live, among magnificent fig trees and corpulent oaks, I behold the panorama of mountains that's the most beautiful (for its atmosphere) in Europe.

As you see, my dear friend, I write to you on *gallo* stationery, because now we have revived the magazine and we're composing the third issue.

I think it will be excellent.

Adios, Jorge. Here's an affectionate embrace from

Federico

Try to be happy! It's necessary to be happy, a *duty* to be happy. Take it from me, I who am passing through one of the saddest and most unpleasant moments of my life.

Write me.

# 15

# 'New myths are born beneath the feet of all of us'

## Louis Aragon: Preface to *Paris Peasant* (1926)

*Louis Aragon (1897–1982) was one of the leading voices of the Surrealist movement in France, a co-founder with André Breton of the journal* Littérature *(1919), and a poet (*Fire of Joy *(1920) and* Perpetual Movement *(1925)).* Paris Peasant *was the only novel he wrote in a Surrealist style. It demonstrates Aragon's concern to balance Breton's fascination with dreams and states of personal consciousness with a broader understanding of the relevance of the Surrealist ethos to our perception of the social realm, here understood in its most concrete sense as the changing cityscape of his native Paris. The novel begins with an important 'Preface to a modern mythology', in which Aragon foregrounds the susceptibility of the external world to the transforming potency of the mind liberated from the conventions of logic and calculation. As Aragon notes, the latter modes, and the 'illusion' of intellectualist supremacy they promote, have dominated Western thinking for too long.*

We are still discovering the full extent of the damage that this illusion has inflicted upon us. Nothing has provided for the progress of the spirit such an almost impossibly insuperable object than this piece of sophistry concerning evidence, which has flattered one of man's most persistent intellectual modes. It can be found at the centre of all forms of logic. It is capable of providing the final proof for all the propositions entertained by man. People invoke its authority in making deductions, and invoking it arrive at their conclusions. And it is in this way that mankind has made for itself a truth that is ever-changing and always self evident, and about which it asks itself in vain why it never seems to be satisfied.

But there is a dark realm that is avoided by the eyes of man because this landscape does not flatter him. This shadow-land, which he imagines he can dispense with in his descriptions of the light, is the face of error with its unknown character, error which, alone, could pay witness to that fugitive reality that light would have wished to retain for itself. But who could fail to understand that the face of error and that of truth could not possibly have different traits? Error travels in the company of certitude. Error asserts itself through evidence. And what one says of truth can also

**Source:** Louis Aragon, *Le Paysan de Paris* (Paris: Gallimard, 1926), pp. 8–11 and 13–14. **Standard translation:** Aragon, *Paris Peasant*, translated by Simon Watson Taylor (London: Picador, 1980), pp. 19–24. **Further reading:** Lucille F. Becker, *Louis Aragon* (New York: Twayne, 1971).

be said of error: the delusion will be no greater. Without the notion of evidence, error would not exist. Without evidence, one would not even pause to think about error.

I had just reached this point in my thoughts when, without anything having announced its approach, spring suddenly arrived.

It was evening, towards five o'clock, on a Saturday: all of a sudden, it happened – everything was bathed in a different light, and yet it was as cold as ever; it was impossible to say what was happening. What was clear was that the direction of my thoughts would never be the same again; they are in full flight, pursuing an imperious preoccupation. The lid of the box has just been opened. I experience my liberty with such intensity that I am no longer master of myself. It is useless to try and understand anything. I will be unable to get any new projects beyond their starting points as long as this heavenly climate lasts. I am the genie of my senses and of chance. I am like a gambler seated at the roulette table; try to persuade him to invest his money wisely, and he will laugh in your face. My body is a roulette wheel, and I am betting on red. Everything is a permanent distraction, except distraction itself. A noble feeling prompts me to surrender to this abandon, and I can no longer hear the reproaches that you aim at me. Instead of worrying about the behaviour of men, look instead at the women passing by. They are great patches of radiance, flashes of light that have not yet been stripped of their furs, of their brilliant and restless mystery. I would not like to die without having approached each of them, without having at least touched their hands, without having felt her weaken under this pressure, giving up all resistance, and then the conquest!

It sometimes happens that one returns home late at night, after having encountered I don't know how many of these desirable jewels, but without having attempted to take possession of a single one of these lives left rashly within my reach. Then, whilst undressing, I ask myself with disgust what the point of my existence is. What a way to live! Would it not be better to go out again, to track down my prey, for me myself to be the prey of something that is lurking in the darkness? The senses have at least established their dominion on earth. What is reason going to do from now on? Reason, reason, Oh, abstract phantom of the wakeful state! I had already banished you from my dreams; and now that I have reached that point where those dreams are about to merge with external reality, there is no room here for anything except myself. In vain, reason speaks to me, denouncing the dictatorship of sensuality; in vain, it warns me against error, which reigns there. Madame, please enter, this is my body, this is your throne. I caress my delirium like a handsome pony. False duality of man, let me dream a little about your delusions.

*Aragon elaborates upon his critique of 'humanity's stupid rationalism', arguing for a synthesis that will allow reason to be informed by darker but more productive mental states. The Preface concludes with the following eulogy to these creative and all-transforming energies of the mind.*

I no longer wish to hold back from the errors of my fingers, the errors of my eyes. I know now that they are not only crude traps, but strange paths towards a goal that they alone can reveal to me. There corresponds to every error of the senses a strange flower of reason. Glorious gardens of absurd beliefs, of presentiments, obsessions and frenzies. Unknown and ever-changing gods take shape there. I will gaze upon their leaden countenances, those hemp-seeds of the imagination. How beautiful you are in your castles of sand, you columns of smoke! New myths are born beneath the feet of all of us. Legend begins there where man has lived, there where he lives. I want my thoughts to occupy themselves from now on only with those despised transformations. Every day the modern awareness of existence subtly changes. A mythology ravels and unravels itself. It is a science of life that belongs only to those who have no experience of it. It is a living science that begets and then terminates its life. Is it still possible for me (I am twenty-six years old) to take part in this miracle? How long will I have this feeling for the marvellous quality of everyday life? I see it fade away in everybody, who advances in his own life as if on a road that is becoming increasingly smoother, who advances into the habits of the world with an increasing ease, and who rids himself increasingly of a taste for and perception of the unusual. It is with the greatest sorrow that I will never know this world.

## 16

# 'The theatre is as bloody and as inhuman as dreams'

## Antonin Artaud: 'The theatre of cruelty: first manifesto' (1933)

*Antonin Artaud (1896–1948) played a central role in the French Surrealist movement, writing two volumes of poetry,* Umbilical Limbo *and* Nerve Scales *(both 1925), in which he transfigured the mundane through his own heightened, almost mystical, sense for the grain of unreality. Such sentiments were carried over into his later writings on the theatre, where he attempted to elaborate an aesthetic for*

**Source:** Antonin Artaud, *Le Théâtre et son double* (Paris: Gallimard, 1966), pp. 135–41. **Standard translation:** *The Theatre and Its Double*, translated by Victor Corti (London: Calder & Boyers, 1970). **Further reading:** Eric Sellin, *The Dramatic Concepts of Antonin Artaud* (Chicago: University of Chicago Press, 1975), esp. pp. 81–106.

*a dramatic medium that would liberate mankind's deeper self through actions that drew upon mythic, primitive and magical ritual. Artaud collected his thoughts on this new dramaturgy in a series of essays published in 1938 under the title* The Theatre and Its Double. *The essay 'The theatre of cruelty' constitutes the first manifesto of this new ritualistic dramaturgy. It begins:*

We cannot continue to prostitute the idea of theatre, whose sole value lies in its magic and violent relationship with reality and with danger.

Posed in this fashion, the problem of the theatre must surely arouse universal attention, since it will be surely understood that the theatre, on account of its obvious physicality, and because it requires *the utilisation of space* (and it is the only real medium to offer this), allows the magic methods of art and language to develop organically and in their entirety, like revived forms of exorcism. From all of this, it will be evident that the theatre will never recover its unique powers of action until it has recovered its own language.

That is to say, that instead of going back to texts considered as definitive and sacred, it is essential, above all, to break the theatre's subjugation to the text, and to rediscover the notion of a unique language that exists somewhere between gesture and thought.

We can only define this language through the possibilities of dynamic expression, locating it in a space opposed to the possibilities of expression defined through dialogistic language. And what theatre can still seize from language is the possibility of an expansion beyond words, of a development in space, of action which is dissociative and acts upon sensibility. It is here that intonation, the particular pronunciation of a word, comes into play, as well as (beyond the audible language of sounds) the visual language of objects, of movements, attitudes, gestures, provided that their meanings, their physiognomy, their combinations are extended into signs, and those signs made to form a sort of alphabet. Once it has recognised this language of space, this language of sounds, cries, lights and onomatopoeia, the theatre must organise them by creating true hieroglyphs out of characters and objects, making use of their symbolism and of their interaction in all facets and at all levels of the theatrical experience.

For the theatre, it is a question, then, of creating a metaphysics of the word, of gesture, of expression, in order to rescue it from the dominance of psychology and the human. But all of this is no use unless there is behind this effort a kind of real metaphysical impulse, which draws upon certain unusual ideas, whose very essence lies in the fact that they cannot be contained, nor even formally designated. These ideas touch upon Creation, Growth and Chaos, and are all of a cosmic order, providing us with a first glimpse into a domain of which the theatre, up until now, has been totally ignorant. These ideas can create a kind of exhilarating equation between Mankind, Society, Nature and Objects.

However, there is no question of putting metaphysical ideas directly on stage; rather, the goal is to create temptations, vacuums, around these ideas. Humour with its anarchy, poetry with its symbolism and imagery, give us a sort of initial inkling of how to channel the impulse within these ideas.

It is necessary now to talk about the purely material side of this language; that is to say, about the ways and means that it has of acting upon our sensibilities.

It would be spurious to say that it calls on music, dancing, mime, or mimicry. It is obvious that it uses movement, harmonies, rhythms, but it does so only up to a point where they combine to produce a unified expressive effect, which does not benefit any particular art form. This is not to say that it does not employ ordinary facts, ordinary passions, but rather that it uses them as a springboard, in the same way that HUMOUR as DESTRUCTION can serve to reconcile laughter with the practices of reason.

But by using a truly oriental concept of expression, this concrete and objective language of the theatre succeeds in captivating and commanding our senses. It runs through our sensibility. Abandoning Western ways of using speech, it turns words into incantations. It empowers the voice. It uses the vibrations and the qualities of the voice. It tramples it wildly underfoot with its rhythms. It beats out sounds. It aims to exalt, to benumb, to bewitch, to arrest our sensibilities. It releases a new lyricism of gestures which, because it is distilled or amplified through the air, ends up by surpassing the lyricism of words. Finally, it breaks the intellectual subjugation of language, by conveying the sense of a new more profound intellectualism that is hidden under gestures and signs, and which are now elevated to the dignity of special exorcisms.

For, all this magnetism, all this poetry, and these effective methods of enchantment would come to nothing if they did not physically put the mind on a direct path to something, if true theatre proved unable to give us the sense of a creation of which we possess at the moment only one side, but whose completion will be achieved on other levels.

And it makes little difference that the other levels are really conquered by the mind, that is to say by our intellect, for this reduces them, and that has neither meaning nor sense. What is important is that, by sure means, our sensibilities are put into a deeper and subtler state of perception; that is the object of magic and ritual, of which the theatre is only a reflection.

## Technique

It is a matter of giving to the theatre a function, understood in the proper sense of the word; something that is as localised and as fixed as the circulation of blood in our arteries, or the apparently chaotic development of dream images in our minds, and we must do this by effective concatenation, a true enslavement of our waking selves.

Theatre will never be itself again, that is to say it will never be a true means of illusionism, unless it provides the audience with truthful distillations of dreams, where the public's taste for crime, its erotic obsessions, its savagery, its fantasies, its utopian sense of life and things, and even its cannibalism can dramatically emerge on a level that is not fictional or illusionary, but a part of the self.

In other words, the theatre must overhaul itself with all means available, for the sake not only of all the aspects of the objective, external world, but also for the internal world, that is, man considered metaphysically. It is only thus, we believe, that we will be able to talk again in the theatre of the rights of the imagination. Neither Humour, nor Poetry, nor the Imagination mean anything unless they systematically examine man (his ideas on reality and his poetic place in reality) by means of a process of anarchistic destruction, which will produce a prodigious array of forms that will constitute the spectacle.

But to view the theatre as a second-hand psychological or moral operation, and to believe that dreams themselves are only a substitute for something else, is to diminish the profound poetic span of dreams as well as that of the theatre. If the theatre is as bloody and as inhuman as dreams, that is because it manifests, and irretrievably anchors in us, the idea of perpetual conflict and violence, where life is lacerated every minute, where everything in creation rises up and attacks our condition as created beings. It is also to perpetuate, in a relevant and concrete manner, certain metaphysical ideas contained in the Fables, in which atrocity and energy suffice to prove the origin and the purport of the basic principles of life.

This being so, one can see that, through its proximity to those principles which it poetically transfuses with its energy, this naked language of the theatre, which is a non-virtual but real language, must allow, through the use of the nervous magnetism of man, the ordinary limits of art and words to be transgressed. Only that way can it actively, or, in other words, magically, *in true terms*, realise a sort of total creation, where nothing else will remain for man other than to take his place between dream and the active world.

# 17

# 'An escape from personality'

## T. S. Eliot: 'Tradition and the individual talent' (1919)

*Thomas Stearns Eliot (1888–1965) was one of the seminal poetic voices of the Modernist period (his career begins with* Prufrock and Other Observations, *published in 1917), but he was also a sophisticated and original theoretician of his art, publishing a number of works of literary criticism, including* The Sacred Wood *(1920), in which the essay 'Tradition and the individual talent' first appeared. It is Eliot's most important essay, for here he enunciates what is clearly a conservative defence of the essentially anti-Romantic impulse within Modernism. The notion of tradition that he celebrates in the first part of the essay is not simply invoked as a means of justifying the canon; for Eliot, it provides the sole framework in which literary statement can acquire hermeneutic intelligibility: without the context of the already-said, the individual text is doomed to the amorphous articulation of pure interiority. For that reason, Eliot advocates (in the concluding part of his essay) not self-expression as the guiding medium of the poetic utterance, as it had been, for example, with the Romantics, and most notably in Wordsworth, but the impersonal mastery of technique and poetic memory, which allows the poet both to work with the materials of modernity, however shoddy they may be, and at the same time to transcend them (as Eliot was to do in his epic poem,* The Waste Land, *1922) through cultural juxtaposition and mythic distantiation.*

No poet, no artist of any art, has his complete meaning alone. His significance, his appreciation is the appreciation of his relation to the dead poets and artists. You cannot value him alone; you must set him, for contrast and comparison, among the dead. I mean this as a principle of aesthetic, not merely historical, criticism. The necessity that he shall conform, that he shall cohere, is not one-sided; what happens when a new work of art is created is something that happens simultaneously to all the works of art which preceded it. The existing monuments form an ideal order among themselves, which is modified by the introduction of the new (the really new) work of art among them. The existing order is complete before the new work arrives; for order to persist after the supervention of novelty, the *whole* existing order must be, if ever so slightly, altered; and so the relations, proportions, values of each work of art toward the whole are readjusted; and this is conformity between the

**Source:** *Selected Prose of T. S. Eliot*, edited by Frank Kermode (London: Faber and Faber, 1975), pp. 38–9, 42 and 43. **Further reading:** Mowbray Allan, *T. S. Eliot's Impersonal Theory of Poetry* (Lewisburg, PA: Bucknell University Press, 1974).

old and the new. Whoever has approved this idea of order, of the form of European, of English literature will not find it preposterous that the past should be altered by the present as much as the present is directed by the past. And the poet who is aware of this will be aware of great difficulties and responsibilities.

*As Eliot explains, in an analysis that foreshadows (and possibly in a language of greater clarity) the critique of 'the subject' that was to find prominence among post-Structuralists, such as Jacques Derrida, later in the century, 'the progress of an artist is a continual self-sacrifice, a continual extinction of personality'.*

The point of view which I am struggling to attack is perhaps related to the metaphysical theory of the substantial unity of the soul: for my meaning is, that the poet has, not a 'personality' to express, but a particular medium, which is only a medium and not a personality, in which impressions and experiences combine in peculiar and unexpected ways. Impressions and experiences which are important for the man may take no place in the poetry, and those which become important in the poetry may play quite a negligible part in the man, the personality.

*Eliot then quotes several lines from Tourneur's* The Revenger's Tragedy *(1607) to demonstrate the impersonality of literary expression, before continuing with his general thesis.*

It is not in his personal emotions, the emotions provoked by particular events in his life, that the poet is in any way remarkable or interesting. His particular emotions may be simple, or crude, or flat. The emotion in his poetry will be a very complex thing, but not with the complexity of the emotions of people who have very complex or unusual emotions in life. One error, in fact, of eccentricity in poetry is to seek for new human emotions to express; and in this search for novelty in the wrong place it discovers the perverse. The business of the poet is not to find new emotions, but to use the ordinary ones and, in working them up into poetry, to express feelings which are not in actual emotions at all. And emotions which he has never experienced will serve his turn as well as those familiar to him. Consequently, we must believe that 'emotion recollected in tranquillity' is an inexact formula. For it is neither emotion, nor recollection, nor, without distortion of meaning, tranquillity. It is a concentration, and a new thing resulting from the concentration, of a very great number of experiences which to the practical and active person would not seem to be experiences at all; it is a concentration which does not happen consciously or of deliberation. These experiences are not 'recollected', and they finally unite in an atmosphere which is 'tranquil' only in that it is a passive attending upon the event. Of course this is not quite the whole story. There is a great deal, in the writing of poetry, which must be conscious and deliberate. In fact, the bad poet is usually unconscious where he ought to be conscious, and conscious where he ought to be unconscious. Both errors tend to make him 'personal'. Poetry is not a turning loose of emotion, but an escape from emotion; it is not the expression of personality, but an escape from personality. But, of course, only those who have personality and emotions know what it means to want to escape from these things.

18

---

# *'From the beginning of consciousness to the end'*

## Virginia Woolf: 'Modern fiction' (1919)

*In the pages of her essays (collected as* The Common Reader *in two volumes, 1925 and 1932), Virginia Woolf (1882–1941) laid the basis for her theory of the modern novel. She did so (see, for example, 'Mr Bennett and Mrs Brown', published in 1924) largely within a critique of the late Realist tradition, which she saw represented in the work of H. G. Wells, Arnold Bennett and John Galsworthy. In her essay 'Modern fiction', she argued that their work, and the realist novel in general, no longer possessed the capacity to capture the fragmented and subjectively troubled grain of the experience of modernity. Her own major novels were* Mrs Dalloway *(1925),* To the Lighthouse *(1927) and* The Waves *(1931).*

Whether we call it life or spirit, truth or reality, this, the essential thing, has moved off, or on, and refuses to be contained any longer in such ill-fitting vestments as we provide. Nevertheless, we go on perseveringly, conscientiously, constructing our two and thirty chapters after a design which more and more ceases to resemble the vision in our minds. So much of the enormous labour of proving the solidity, the likeness to life, of the story is not merely labour thrown away but labour misplaced to the extent of obscuring and blotting out the light of the conception. The writer seems constrained, not by his own free will but by some powerful and unscrupulous tyrant who has him in thrall, to provide a plot, to provide comedy, tragedy, love interest, and an air of probability embalming the whole so impeccable that if all his figures were to come to life they would find themselves dressed down to the last button of their coats in the fashion of the hour. The tyrant is obeyed; the novel is done to a turn. But sometimes, more and more often as time goes by, we suspect a

---

**Source:** Virginia Woolf, *Collected Essays*, 4 vols (London: The Hogarth Press, 1966), vol. 2, pp. 105–8. **Further reading:** Michael Rosenthal, *Virginia Woolf* (London: Routledge, 1979), esp. pp. 35–48.

momentary doubt, a spasm of rebellion, as the pages fill themselves in the customary way. Is life like this? Must novels be like this?

Look within and life, it seems, is very far from being 'like this'. Examine for a moment an ordinary mind on an ordinary day. The mind receives a myriad impressions – trivial, fantastic, evanescent, or engraved with the sharpness of steel. From all sides they come, an incessant shower of innumerable atoms; and as they fall, as they shape themselves into the life of Monday or Tuesday, the accent falls differently from of old; the moment of importance came not here but there; so that, if a writer were a free man and not a slave, if he could write what he chose, not what he must, if he could base his work upon his own feeling and not upon convention, there would be no plot, no comedy, no tragedy, no love interest or catastrophe in the accepted style, and perhaps not a single button sewn on as the Bond Street tailors would have it. Life is not a series of gig–lamps symmetrically arranged; life is a luminous halo, a semi-transparent envelope surrounding us from the beginning of consciousness to the end. Is it not the task of the novelist to convey this varying, this unknown and uncircumscribed spirit, whatever aberration or complexity it may display, with as little mixture of the alien and external as possible? We are not pleading merely for courage and sincerity; we are suggesting that the proper stuff of fiction is a little other than custom would have us believe it.

It is, at any rate, in some such fashion as this that we seek to define the quality which distinguishes the work of several young writers, among whom Mr. James Joyce is the most notable, from that of their predecessors. They attempt to come closer to life, and to preserve more sincerely and exactly what interests and moves them, even if to do so they must discard most of the conventions which are commonly observed by the novelist. Let us record the atoms as they fall upon the mind in the order in which they fall, let us trace the pattern, however disconnected and incoherent in appearance, which each sight or incident scores upon the consciousness. Let us not take it for granted that life exists more fully in what is commonly thought big than in what is commonly thought small. Anyone who has read *The Portrait of the Artist as a Young Man* or, what promises to be a far more interesting work, *Ulysses*, now appearing in the *Little Review*, will have hazarded some theory of this nature as to Mr. Joyce's intention. On our part, with such a fragment before us, it is hazarded rather than affirmed; but whatever the intention of the whole, there can be no question but that it is of the utmost sincerity and that the result, difficult or unpleasant as we may judge it, is undeniably important. In contrast with those whom we have called materialists, Mr. Joyce is spiritual; he is concerned at all costs to reveal the flickerings of that innermost flame which flashes its message through the brain, and in order to preserve it he disregards with complete courage whatever seems to him adventitious, whether it be probability, or coherence, or any other of these signposts which for generations have served to support the imagination of a reader when called upon to imagine what he can neither touch nor see. The scene in the cemetery, for example, with its brilliancy, its sordidity, its incoherence, its sudden lightning flashes of significance, does undoubtedly come so close to the quick of the mind that, on a first reading at any rate, it is difficult not to acclaim a masterpiece. If we want life itself, here surely we have it. Indeed, we find ourselves fumbling rather awkwardly if we try to say what else we wish, and for what reason a work of such originality yet fails to compare, for we must take high examples, with *Youth* or *The Mayor of Casterbridge*. It fails because of the comparative poverty of the writer's mind, we might say simply and have done with it. But it is possible to press a little further and wonder whether we may not refer our sense of being in a bright yet narrow room, confined and shut in, rather than enlarged and set free, to some limitation imposed by the method as well as by the mind. Is it the method that inhibits the creative power? Is it due to the method that we feel neither jovial nor magnanimous, but centred in a self which, in spite of its tremor of susceptibility, never embraces or creates what is outside itself and beyond? Does the emphasis laid, perhaps didactically, upon indecency contribute to the effect of something angular and isolated? Or is it merely that in any effort of such originality it is much easier, for contemporaries especially, to feel what it lacks than to name what it gives? In any case it is a mistake to stand outside examining 'methods'. Any method is right, every method is right, that expresses what we wish to express, if we are writers; that brings us closer to the novelist's intention if we are readers. This method has the merit of bringing us closer to what we were prepared to call life itself; did not the reading of *Ulysses* suggest how much of life is excluded or ignored, and did it not come with a shock to open *Tristram Shandy* or even *Pendennis* and be by them convinced that there are not only other aspects of life, but more important ones into the bargain.

However this may be, the problem before the novelist at present, as we suppose it to have been in the past, is to contrive means of being free to set down what he chooses. He has to have the courage to say that what interests him is no longer 'this' but 'that': out of 'that' alone must he construct his work. For the moderns 'that', the point of interest, lies very likely in the dark places of psychology. At once, therefore, the accent falls a little differently; the emphasis is upon something hitherto ignored; at once a different outline of form becomes necessary, difficult for us to grasp, incomprehensible to our predecessors.

# 'The old stable ego' is no more

## D. H. Lawrence: Letter to Edward Garnett (1914)

*The works of David Herbert Lawrence (1885–1930) include not only the novels* Sons and Lovers *(1913),* The Rainbow *(1915) and* Women in Love *(1920) and* Love Poems and Others *(1913), but also more discursive tracts, such as* Fantasia of the Unconscious *(1923), which focus upon the workings of the mind and the unconscious. Lawrence will inevitably be remembered as a frank explorer of sexuality and the complex energies that feed into male–female relationships, explorations that produced the controversial novel* Lady Chatterley's Lover *(1928), whose reprint in 1961 led to claims of pornography and a protracted legal case. But Lawrence's modernism inflected itself through diverse channels, one of which lay in his notion of the flexibility of character and personal identity. In the letter reprinted here, he adumbrates (albeit at times with some grammatical obscurity) the outlines of a theory of the self that owes much to Freud, Nietzsche and other exponents of vitalistic models of selfhood, such as Henri Bergson.*

*Lerici*, per Fiascherino, Golfo della Spezia, Italia

5 junio 1914

Dear Garnett,

First let me remember to thank you for letting the two books be sent to the Consul in Spezia.

About Pinker, I will do as you say, and tell him that the matter of the novel is not settled, and I will call on him in some fifteen or twenty days.

I don't agree with you about the Wedding Ring. You will find that in a while you will like the book as a whole. I don't think the psychology is wrong: it is only that I have a different attitude to my characters, and that necessitates a different attitude in you, which you are not as yet prepared to give. As for it being my *cleverness* which would pull the thing through – that sounds odd to me, for I don't think I am so very clever, in that way. I think the book is a bit

**Source:** *The Letters of D. H. Lawrence*, edited by George J. Zytaruk and James T. Boulton, 7 vols (Cambridge: Cambridge University Press, 1981), vol. 2, pp. 182–3. **Further reading:** Daniel J. Schneider, *D. H. Lawrence: The Artist as Psychologist* (Lawrence: University of Kansas Press, 1984), esp. pp. 59–81.

futuristic – quite unconsciously so. But when I read Marinetti – 'the profound intuitions of life added one to the other, word by word, according to their illogical conception, will give us the general lines of an intuitive physiology of matter' I see something of what I am after. I translate him clumsily, and his Italian is obfuscated – and I don't care about physiology of matter – but somehow – that which is physic – non-human, in humanity, is more interesting to me than the old-fashioned human element – which causes one to conceive a character in a certain moral scheme and make him consistent. The certain moral scheme is what I object to. In Turgenev, and in Tolstoi, and in Dostoyevsky, the moral scheme into which all the characters fit – and it is nearly the same scheme – is, whatever the extraordinariness of the characters themselves, dull, old, dead. When Marinetti writes: 'it is the solidity of a blade of steel that is interesting by itself, that is, the incomprehending and inhuman alliance of its molecules in resistance to, let us say, a bullet. The heat of a piece of wood or iron is in fact more passionate, for us, than the laughter or tears of a woman' – then I know what he means. He is stupid, as an artist, for contrasting the heat of the iron and the laugh of the woman. But what is interesting in the laugh of the woman is the same as the binding of the molecules of steel or their action in heat: it is the inhuman will, call it physiology, or like Marinetti – physiology of matter, that fascinates me. I don't care so much about what the woman *feels* – in the ordinary usage of the word. That presumes an *ego* to feel with. I only care about what the woman *is* – what she *is* – inhumanly, physiologically, materially – according to the use of the word: but for me, what she *is* as a phenomenon (or as representing some greater, inhuman will), instead of what she feels according to the human conception. That is where the futurists are stupid. Instead of looking for the new human phenomenon, they will only look for the phenomena of the science of physics to be found in human beings. They are crassly stupid. But if anyone would give them eyes, they would pull the right apples off the tree, for their stomachs are true in appetite. You mustn't look in my novel for the old stable ego of the character. There is another ego, according to whose action the individual is unrecognisable, and passes through, as it were, allotropic states which it needs a deeper sense than any we've been used to exercise, to discover are states of the same single radically-unchanged element. (Like as diamond and coal are the same pure single element of carbon. The ordinary novel would trace the history of the diamond – but I say 'diamond, what! This is carbon'. And my diamond might be coal or soot, and my theme is carbon.)

You must not say my novel is shaky – It is not perfect, because I am not expert in what I want to do. But it is the real thing, say what you like. And I shall get my reception, if not now, then before long. Again

I say, don't look for the development of the novel to follow the lines of certain characters: the characters fall into the form of some other rhythmic form, like when one draws a fiddle-bow across a fine tray delicately sanded, the sand takes lines unknown.

I hope this won't bore you. We leave here on Monday, the 8th. Frieda will stay in Baden-Baden some 10–14 days. I am not going by sea, because of the filthy weather. I am walking across Switzerland into France with Lewis, one of the skilled engineers of Vickers Maxim works here. I shall let you know my whereabouts.

Don't get chilly and disagreeable to me.

Au revoir D. H. Lawrence

Please keep this letter, because I want to write on futurism and it will help me. – I will come and see Duckworth. Give *Bunny* my novel – I want *him* to understand it.

I shall be *awfully* glad to see Bunny again – and Mrs Garnett and you.

20
_____

## 'Beyond the void of language'

Hugo von Hofmannsthal: 'Letter [from Lord Chandos]' (1902)

*The Austrian Hugo von Hofmannsthal (1874–1929) was a poet, dramatist (*The Fool and Death *(1893) and* The Problem Man *(1918)), and librettist (*The Rosenkavalier, *1910), whose works reveal an early Modernist fascination with social identity, role-playing and language. These interests received a more sustained theoretical elaboration in his 'Letter [from Lord Chandos]', a complex and highly subtle meditation upon the psychological effects of what happens to the perceiving self when consciousness and language become dislocated from one another. Lord Chandos (an invention of Hofmannsthal's) is writing to Lord Bacon to explain why he is no longer able to continue with his literary activities. He has, he confesses, lost that sense of the 'unity of being' that he once divined in the universe, that happy bond between nature and civilization which allowed him to work (naïvely, in the Schillerian sense)*

**Source:** Hugo von Hofmannsthal, *Gesammelte Werke*, 10 vols (Frankfurt am Main: Fischer, 1980), vol. 8, pp. 465–6, 467 and 469–70. **Standard translation:** *Selected Prose*, translated by Mary Hottinger and Tania and James Stern (New York: Pantheon Books, 1952), pp. 129–41. **Further reading:** Steven P. Sondrup, *Hofmannsthal and the French Symbolist Tradition* (Bern and Frankfurt am Main: Herbert Lang, 1976), esp. pp. 37–56.

*within accepted literary genres and conventions. Above all, Chandos no longer has confidence in the ability of language to describe the world.*

My problem, in short, is this: I have entirely lost the facility to think or talk about anything in a coherent fashion. It began as a growing realisation that I was no longer finding it possible to discuss a lofty or general topic in the ordinary words that people use, fluently and without even thinking, on a daily basis. I experienced an inexplicable discomfort even pronouncing terms such as 'spirit', 'soul' or 'body'. I found it mentally impossible to express an opinion on what was happening at court, on the events taking place in parliament, or on anything else for that matter. And this was not motivated out of a consideration for others (for you are fully familiar with my frankness that at times borders on irresponsibility). It was, rather, that those abstract words, of which the tongue must avail itself as a matter of course if it is to pronounce judgement on any matter at all, fell apart in my mouth like mouldy fungi. It happened one day that, whilst reprimanding my four-year-old daughter, Katherina Pompilia, for a childish lie which she had just been guilty of committing, whilst seeking to convince her of the necessity of always being truthful, the concepts that were forming themselves in my mouth suddenly took on such a scintillating hue and so flowed into one another that it was all I could do to bring the sentence to a spluttering end. It was as if I had been overcome by an attack of nausea; and indeed I went white in the face, and, with a violent pressure on my forehead, I left the child to herself, slamming the door behind me, and did not get a grip on myself until I had mounted my horse and galloped out onto the lonely heath.

Gradually, however, this malaise spread within me like a corrosive rust. Even in familiar and everyday conversations, all the opinions which are normally expressed with ease and somnambulistic assurance became so doubtful that I had to stop participating in such conversations. It filled me with an almost irrational anger (which I was only able to conceal with the greatest effort) to hear things such as this affair had turned out well or badly for this or that person; Sheriff N. was an evil man, the Parson T. a good one; farmer M. was to be pitied; his sons were wastrels; yet another was to be envied because his daughter was such a good housekeeper; one family was improving its lot, whilst another is going to the dogs. All of this seemed to me to be totally spurious, mendacious, and hollow. I felt intellectually compelled to subject everything that surfaced in such conversations to intense scrutiny. Just as I had once inspected with a magnifying glass a piece of the skin of my little finger, which looked like a field full of furrows and holes, in a similar vein I now looked at men and their behaviour. I was no longer able to make sense of them through the simplifying perspective of habit. Everything disintegrated for me into pieces, the pieces into further pieces, and nothing allowed itself any more to be comprehended by a single concept. Isolated words floated around me; they formed into eyes, which stared at me and into which I, in turn, was forced to stare. They were whirlpools, which merely to look into made me dizzy, which circled incessantly, and through which I was led into the void.

*The young Chandos tries to flee his anxiety by immersing himself in the Classics; but his attempts are in vain, and they leave him with a feeling of isolation that is even more intense than before. And yet it is precisely in this heightened state of mind that he is able to reach a deeper insight into ordinary existence.*

Since that time, I lead an existence that you, I fear, will hardly be able to comprehend, so spiritless, and so mentally vacuous is its course. It is an existence, it is true, which hardly differs from that of my neighbours, my relations and most of the land-owning nobility of this realm, and is not entirely without its pleasant and lively moments. I can't really explain what these good moments consist in; words desert me, once again. For it is indeed something that is entirely without a name and even barely nameable which, at such moments, reveals itself to me, filling like a vessel some aspect or other of my everyday environment with an overflowing flood of higher life. I cannot expect you to understand me without providing you with examples, but I must ask you to forgive their incongruity: a watering-can, a harrow abandoned in a field, a dog lying in the sun, a neglected cemetery, a cripple, a modest cottage – all these can become the vessels of my revelations. Each of these objects and a thousand others like them, over which the eye is wont to glide with an understandable indifference, can suddenly at any moment (which I am utterly powerless to evoke) assume a sublime and deeply moving quality, which words seem to me too poor to describe. Indeed, even the distinct image of an absent object, which has been mysteriously selected in this fashion, can find itself filled to the brim with this soft but suddenly rising flood of divine presence.

*Chandos proceeds to evoke further examples of this transfiguration of the quotidian world, before arriving at a passage where he describes, in almost rhapsodic prose, the near trance-like state that is required for this higher realm to be entered.*

These dumb and, sometimes, inanimate things of nature rise up towards me with such a plenitude, such a presence of love that my blessed vision can find nothing in sight devoid of life. Everything, everything that exists, everything that enters my mind, everything which touches my most abject thoughts appears to me to be important. Even my own ponderous self, and the general torpor of my brain, seem of value. I feel an exhilarating and never-ceasing play of forces in and around me, and amongst these diverse forces there is not one into which I cannot submerge myself. When that happens, I feel as if my body consists of clear signs which open up the entire universe for me; or that we might enter into a new and momentous relationship to the entire cosmos, if only we could think with the heart. As soon as this strange enchantment departs from me, however, I find myself in a state of total confusion; I could then just as little explain in rational language the inner nature of this harmony that interweaves through me and the entire world, and how it came to make itself felt upon me, than I could say anything precise about the inner workings of my intestines or a congestion in my blood.

21

# *'I did not* want to say, *but* wanted to make'

## Paul Valéry: 'Concerning "Le Cimetière marin"' (1933)

*Paul Valéry (1871–1945) represents that moment of neo-classicism within the Modernist movement. His major poems, 'The Young Fate' (1917) and the volume Charms (1922), reveal a mind that is analytical, self-aware and, above all, intent upon the formal organization of experience through a poetic idiom that is both highly crafted yet fully tuned to the nuances of the external world. Valéry also wrote extensively about the nature of poetic creation, where he sought to displace Romantic notions of authorial expressivity with a stress upon the dynamic (if sometimes indeterminate) workings of language and textuality. The following extract explains how one of his most important poems, 'The Coastal Cemetery', published in 1920, came into being.*

It is necessary to say, right from the beginning, that 'Cimetière marin', *as it has turned out*, is *for me* the result of the *intersection* of inner effort and an external chance event. One afternoon in 1920, our dear departed friend, Jacques Rivière, who was paying a visit, found me at a certain 'stage' in my 'Cimetière marin', considering whether to revise, suppress, substitute, to alter it, here and there. . . .

He did not rest until he was allowed to read the poem, and, having read it, until he could carry it off with him.

It was thus *by accident* that the shape of that work was fixed. It was none of my doing. Moreover, in general I cannot go back over anything that I

**Source:** Paul Valéry, *Oeuvres* (Paris: Gallimard, 1969), pp. 1500, 1503–4. **Standard translation:** Valéry, *The Art of Poetry*, translated by Denis Folliot (London: Routledge & Kegan Paul, 1958), pp. 140–52. **Further reading:** Walter Newcombe, *The Poetic Theory of Paul Valéry: Inspiration and Technique* (Leicester: Leicester University Press, 1970).

have written without thinking that I should now make something different out of it, if some outside intervention or some circumstance or other had not already broken the temptation of going on with it forever. I love only work for work's sake: beginnings bore me, and I suspect that everything that comes at the first attempt is capable of improvement. Spontaneity, even of the highest quality, even when seductive, never really seems to belong *to me*. I am not saying that 'I am right': I am saying that is how I am. . . . The notion of a Me [*Moi*] is no simpler than the notion of Author: a further degree of consciousness opposes a new *Self* [*Même*] to a new *Author*.

Literature, then, only interests me *profoundly* in so far as it propels the mind to certain transformations, – those in which the stimulating properties of language are of paramount importance. I can, it is true, take a liking to a certain book, read and re-read it with pleasure; but it never possesses me entirely unless I can find there evidence of a process of thought that is as powerful as that of language itself. The strength to bend the common word to unexpected ends without violating 'time-honoured forms'; the capturing and distilling of things that are difficult to say; and, above all, the simultaneous management of syntax, harmony and ideas (which is the problem faced by the purest poetry), are, in my eyes, the supreme goals of our art form.

> *Valéry then elaborates upon the distinction between prose fiction, which is firmly embedded in the external world, and the quite different universe of poetry, which is formed through the internal and less definable workings of suggestion and connotation. These manifest themselves in a language that is set in motion by the poet, although, as Valéry explains, the latter is rarely in total control of these textual processes.*

If, then, anyone asks me, if I am questioned (as I often am, and sometimes rather brusquely), about what I *wanted to say* in a certain poem, I reply that I did not *want to say*, but *wanted to make*, and that it was the intention of *making* which *wanted* what I said. . . .

As far as 'Cimetière marin' is concerned, this intention manifested itself initially only as a rhythmic figure, empty, or filled with indeterminate syllables, but one that had come for quite a while to obsess me. I registered the decasyllabic form of the figure, and I reflected on how little this form was used in modern poetry; it seemed to me poor and monotonous. It was of little worth compared to the alexandrine, which three or four generations of great poets before me had so prodigiously cultivated. The demon of generalisation encouraged me to try and extend this *Ten* to the power of *Twelve*. It suggested a certain stanza of six lines, and the idea of a composition built upon the number of these stanzas, and secured by the diversity of tones and functions assigned to them. Between the stanzas, contrasts and correspondences could be set up. This last condition soon required that the poem in the making would become a monologue of 'me', into which the most simple and the most permanent themes of my emotional and intellectual life, such as had imposed themselves upon my adolescence, and which were associated with the sea and the light of certain Mediterranean shores, would be evoked, woven together, juxtaposed. . . .

All this was leading to the theme of death, and coming within the realm of pure thought. (The chosen line of ten syllables has a certain relation to the verse form of Dante.)

It was necessary for my poetic line to be dense and strongly rhythmical. I knew that I was moving towards a monologue that would be as personal but also as universal as I could make it. The type of line chosen, and the form adopted for the stanzas, set me conditions that favoured certain 'movements', made possible certain changes of tone, called forth a certain style. . .the 'Cimetière marin' was conceived. And then a somewhat lengthy process of labour ensued.

Whenever I think about the art of writing (in poetry or in prose), the same 'ideal' presents itself to my mind. The myth of 'creation' seduces us into wanting to make something from nothing. I dream, thus, that I am progressively discovering the origins of my work in pure conditions of form, which are more and more thought out, – defined to the point where they propose or almost impose a subject, or, at least, a group of subjects.

Let us note that the conditions for precise form are nothing less than the expression of intelligence and of the consciousness we have of the means at hand, of their range as well as their limits and defects. That is how it occurred to me to define the writer as a correlation between a particular 'mind' and Language.

But I know the illusionary quality of my 'Ideal'. The nature of language is the last thing in the world that lends itself to coherent combinations; and, besides, the formation and the habits of the modern reader, who has been rendered oblivious to all concerns of structure through a perpetual diet consisting of incoherence and instantaneous effect, hardly encourage one to drift off into regions that are too distant from him. . . .

Nevertheless, simply thinking about constructions of this kind remains for me the most poetic of ideas: the idea of composition.

# Part IV
# The Literature of Political Engagement

# INTRODUCTION

In 1926, Pierre Naville, a lesser-known figure within the French Surrealist movement, published a tract entitled *The Revolution and the Intellectuals* (**Reading 1**). In it, Naville argued that the Surrealist assault upon conventional society was doomed to remain largely ineffectual, because it had failed to deepen its *épater le bourgeois* stance into a coherent and effective political activism. The shocking antics and playful provocations of the Surrealists, Naville contended, had been quickly absorbed by a public that had not only become tolerant of such behaviour, but ironically was beginning to enjoy it. To think that the world could be changed through the promotion (however provocative) of automatic writing and dream symbolism was both naive and arrogant, and ultimately achieved nothing more than 'keeping the illusion of freedom alive'. Protest was not the same as revolution; to achieve the latter, Naville concluded, artists had to actively participate in the political struggles of the proletariat, and align themselves with its most organized and progressive wing: the Communist Party.

Naville was not alone in this act of distantiation from his erstwhile Avant-Garde colleagues. As the 1910s turned into the 1920s, voices of dissent could be clearly heard throughout the Modernist movement, qualifying, withdrawing, repudiating the early energies and youthful iconoclasm that had brought it into existence a decade or more earlier, in favour of a more pragmatic type of writing that would be responsive to historical and political change. These voices were particularly strident in Germany, where erstwhile Expressionists such as J. S. Becher, Kurt Hiller and Hanns Johst moved away from the intense subjective inwardness of their earlier work to embrace an ethos that possessed a greater focus upon the political, social and (in Johst's case) national realms. Writers elsewhere in Europe followed a similar trajectory. In England, for example, Michael Roberts, in his famous Preface to the *New Signatures* anthology (1932), condemned those poets who in the Modernist period had 'held themselves aloof from ordinary affairs and produced esoteric work which was frivolously decorative or elaborately erudite'; while the young Louis MacNeice fulminated in his study, *Modern Poetry* (1938), against the 'ennui and ironical self-pity' that characterized much Modernist verse (and he was thinking here particularly of T. S. Eliot), seeking to put in its place a poetry that would articulate a clearer set of beliefs, and would be alive to the needs of 'Man Functioning' as part of a 'system of individuals determined by their circumstances, a concrete, therefore, of sensuous fact' (**Reading 2**). Even mainstream Modernists such as Thomas Mann and D. H. Lawrence had, however reluctantly, arrived at a similar recognition, registering, in works such as Lawrence's *Kangaroo* (1922), and Mann's *Mario and the Magician* (1930), the apparently inexorable encroachment of the values and politics of mass society upon contemporary culture.

Many of the initiatives of this generation had, in fact, already been anticipated by a French novelist who was to become for many the iconic embodiment of the committed writer: Émile Zola. The latter's intervention into the Dreyfus affair in 1898 (by means of an open letter to the French President, later to be known as 'I accuse!') brought to the surface the hypocrisy and double standards that existed underneath the French Republic's ostensible defence of democratic rights and personal liberty. Far from being motivated by such high-minded principles, political life in France was dominated (Zola argued in his famous missive) by 'passions of reaction and intolerance', its institutions under the control of powerful cliques and self-serving interest groups who sought 'to exploit patriotism for works of hatred'. Zola was to travel a bitter road, incurring both public ignominy and exile for his labours; but in the end, by mobilizing popular opinion in the direction of natural justice, he succeeded in bringing about the freedom of Dreyfus, himself becoming, in the process, a symbol around which progressive forces in French politics could rally. As many of his contemporaries, such as the German novelist, Heinrich Mann, recognized, Zola had broken with the tradition of the apolitical writer in a way that was both dramatic and effective (**Reading 3**). Believing in 'the steady march towards the truth', Mann contended that Zola had, through his writings and through his actions, deliberately moved out of the relatively safe terrain of *belles-lettres* into the cold light of judicial and political day, where he had risked all – reputation, livelihood and liberty – for the sake of political justice.

Zola had certainly not been the first to bridge the gap between art and politics. In the late eighteenth and early nineteenth centuries, Romantic and pre-Romantic writers such as Shelley in England, the 'Storm and Stress' dramatists in Germany and Rousseau in France had penned at least part of their work with a critical eye to its greater effect upon the public weal. But these were the exceptions to a rule that was, at least, tacitly followed by artists and non-artists alike, particularly during the nineteenth century, a rule constituted from a set of aesthetic conventions and accepted practices which stipulated the absolute independence of the artistic realm from the social, and, most decidedly, from the functional, utilitarian, pragmatic priorities that seemed increasingly to characterize the values and *mores* of an ascendant bourgeois class. The political commitment demonstrated by Zola in the Dreyfus case, and in novels of social conscience, such as *Nana* (1880) and *Germinal* (1885), broke with this tradition of artistic self-sufficiency to establish a counter-paradigm, in which the divide between the personal and the civic, the aesthetic and the ethical might be crossed. This counter-paradigm came to form one of the most dominant movements in late nineteenth- and early twentieth-century writing: the literature of political engagement. From the plays of social conscience of George Bernard Shaw (*Major Barbara*, 1905, *John Bull's Other Island*, 1907) and Maxim Gorky (*Lower Depths*, 1902), and the committed literature of Bertolt Brecht, W. H. Auden and André Malraux in the 1930s, a body of work grew up to parallel the great Modernist writing of Joyce, Proust, Svevo and Thomas Mann. There were certainly points of agreement and convergence between the Modernists and this new generation of committed writers, shared strategies of opposition and confrontation that emerged most clearly in the work of the Avant-Garde. But the differences between the two groups were ultimately of greater significance, with the committed writers largely eschewing the linguistic and epistemological concerns of the Modernist perspective, retaining a modified form of Realism in the place of the Modernist's formal experimentation, and, above all, evincing a greater preparedness to engage directly with the brute facticity of history and historical crisis.

The committed writers of this generation looked to one source, above all, for guidance and inspiration in their tasks: the newly created Soviet Union. The victorious Bolshevik Revolution of 1916 had taken place in the midst of a world war that had been conducted on all sides by myopic politicians and arrogant military establishments, by nations driven by the needs of nationalistic self-aggrandizement, and by capitalistic classes determined to secure or expand their economic supremacy in the world's markets. The First World War and its aftermath, the shoddy morality of the victors, and the rapacious treatment of the defeated, had brought about a widespread loss of faith in the values of liberal-humanism and the institutions of Western democracy. In contrast, revolutionary Russia seemed to embody a moral idealism and a youthful vitality that held open, both politically and culturally, a new future for a Europe that seemed to many to have entered into a state of terminal decline (a mood that was given epic shape and legitimation in Oswald Spengler's *The Decline of the West*, 1918–20). The transforming, almost utopian spirit which informed the cultural expectations that accompanied the Russian Revolution received seminal expression in Trotsky's *Literature and Revolution* (1924), where, in almost visionary tones, Trotsky conjures up a classless society which is still in the making, in which political 'self-government' will combine with a new universal culture to allow man, for the first time, to 'raise his instincts to the heights of consciousness' (**Reading 4**).

That achieving such absolute goals would require practical organiza-tion and mass agitation Trotsky well knew, as did the other key players in the Bolshevik cultural hierarchy, such as Alexander Bogdanov, the leading theoretician of the 'Proletcult' (the 'Movement for Proletarian Culture and Education'), founded in 1918. Bogdanov sought to reach a mass audience by the most direct means possible, by bringing culture into the factories, workshops and streets of Russia's cities. These initiatives were given an even greater momentum by the 'On Guard' movement, and by RAPP (the 'Russian Association of Proletarian Writers'), cultural formations that emerged as the major representatives of official literary policy after 1923. In an attempt to effect a complete break with the inherited norms of 'bourgeois' culture, which both groups saw as persisting in the literature of 'fellow travellers', radicals such as the Futurist Vladimir Mayakovsky (the leading voice of yet another organization, known as LEF, the 'Left Front of Art'), and individualists such as Esenin and Zamyatin, these groups espoused a proletarian militancy that was intended to turn literature into an ideological wing of the New Economic Plan being pursued by Stalin and his aparachiks. As On Guard exhorted in its manifesto of 1923 (**Reading 5**), contemporary literature must be encouraged to engage with the only two themes that were regarded as consistent with the further development of the new workers' state: 'labour and struggle'. All else belonged to a pre-revolutionary era, and as such had to be rejected.

The initiatives of RAPP and the On Guard were failures, however; their simplistic proletarian radicalism and repetitive 'reportage' focus upon factories and collectivized farms had failed (even for the true believers) to produce a worthwhile corpus of revolutionary writing. Now that the first five-year plan had been brought to fruition, the call was for a literature that could reflect the values of 'restoration' and 'reconstruction', a literature that would incorporate the varied energies of socialism, without breeding party factionalism. The name given to this new form of literature was Socialist Realism. As its name indicates, Socialist Realism distanced itself from both the experimental initiatives of the Modernist movement and the propagandistic priorities of RAPP. As Andrey Zhdanov energetically exhorted at the first congress of the new Union of Soviet Writers in 1934, Socialist Realism alone was able to produce 'great works of art' capable of transmitting the enthusiasm and 'heroic endeavour' that permeated the new Soviet Union stabilized under Stalin's rule (**Reading 6**). The literature of Socialist Realism would certainly be tendentious; after all, it had as its goal the creation of a true communist society; but it would anchor that tendentiousness in the experiences of representative individuals, whose struggles and conflicts, trials and tribulations, tragedies and triumphs would serve as living proof of the elemental energies and inviolable optimism that informed the historic mission of the Soviet people.

In the Soviet Union, the claims made on behalf of Socialist realism were regarded as *ex cathedra*, directives to be automatically followed by the writer in fulfilment of his or her place within the cultural life of the nation. Elsewhere in Europe debate was possible, and no more so than in Germany. Here a number of theorists emerged both to deepen and to refine the conceptual terrain occupied by Soviet theory. They included Walter Benjamin (*The Work of Art in the Age of Mechanical Reproduction*, 1936), Ernst Bloch (*Heritage of Our Times*, 1934) and Georg Lukács ('It is a question of Realism', 1938). As the famous debate between Lukács and Bloch, carried out in the pages of the émigré journal *Das Wort* [The Word] between 1938 and 1939 demonstrated, the points of contestation within this group were sharp, and revealed a fundamental dichotomy within Marxist aesthetics and its epistemological underpinning. The specific cause for disagreement between the two lay in diverging assessments of the political heritage of German Expressionism. As Lukács argued in his essay, 'It is a question of Realism', all politically 'progressive' literature (and under this rubric he included the great Realist novels of the nineteenth century, most notably those of Walter Scott and Balzac) 'seeks to uncover those deeper, hidden, mediated, not immediately perceptible relationships that constitute social reality', which for Lukács were those of class identity and ideology. 'It is this', Lukács added, 'that constitutes *the artistic dialectic of essence and appearance*' (**Reading 7**). Works of literature, such as those produced by the Expressionists, which obscure such laws by focusing upon the deformed or irrational surface of society, those 'subjective, twisted and unintelligible resonances' favoured by James Joyce and others, necessarily obscure that deeper logic, and hence, *nolens volens*, must help fascism in its cause, because this is an ideology that thrives upon mystification and irrationalism.

But, as Ernst Bloch pointed out in his reply, 'Lukács works with a notion of reality as something that is fully closed and integrated, a notion which, certainly, has no place for the subjective factor evident in Idealism, but which nevertheless retains that assumption of a closed "Totality"' (**Reading 8**). In fact, far from presenting us with objective paradigms in which we can study society, Lukács' 'laws' impart to the social realm a cohesion and solidity that, in an era experiencing the dramatic demise of bourgeois hegemony, it simply does not possess. On the contrary, Bloch argues, the Expressionists were advancing the progressive political cause by giving graphic depiction to the 'confusion, immaturity and incomprehension' that were the emotive traits of the 'sick bed of capitalism' in its years of crisis, between the First World War and the advent of fascist dictatorship. For Bloch, it was precisely the cultural surface of irrationalism that needed to be depicted.

The impact of Soviet literary policy upon creative writers in Russia and elsewhere did not, however, always take such a theoretically sophisticated direction. For those who espoused an open adherence to the party line of the Comintern, such as the German 'proletarian-revolutionary' authors Willi Bredel (*Machine Factory N & K*, 1930) and Ernst Ottwalt (*Law and Order*, 1929), it was a straightforward matter of adapting individual preference to whatever desiderata were current in Moscow. But for others (to remain within the German context), such as Hermann Broch, Kurt Tucholsky and Heinrich Mann, matters were more complex, and influenced by the requirements of local practice and individual need. Nevertheless, the tenor of much Soviet theory (if not the detail) was taken over by many of the major European voices of this generation, such as the French novelist Henri Barbusse. He had been among the first to identify those nefarious wellsprings of nationalistic self-empowerment and aggrandizement that propelled the European nations into war in 1914, his *Under Fire* (1917) becoming one of the most noted pacifist war novels of the period. By 1932 (the year of the publication of his study of Zola), that pacifism had sharpened into a fervent espousal of radical socialism, in whose populist energies he saw the last chance for a society caught within 'definite crises, the crises of liquidation'. Purely personal solutions are a thing of the past, Barbusse argued here; active struggle necessarily compels the writer to choose which side he or she is on, and to actively align with the political forces of progress (**Reading 9**).

Similar sentiments were expressed by writers elsewhere in Europe, by, for example, the English novelist Ralph Fox. Fox was, perhaps, a minor figure in comparison with Barbusse, but the sentiments expressed in his study, *The Novel and the People* (published in 1937, a year after his death in the Spanish Civil War), reflect a desire that was widespread among many Western European socialists: to merge the Soviet drive for a classless society and universal political emancipation with the liberal–humanist concern for the individual and personal liberty, and, in literature, to find a form of Socialist Realism that would allow the novel to mediate between anarchistic individualism and the proselytizing requirements of revolutionary politics. Only such a synthesis would, Fox contends (endowing literature with a unique potential for social change), allow the contemporary writer 'to fight against the objective, external horrors accompanying the collapse of our social system, against Fascism, against war, unemployment, the decay of agriculture, against the domination of the machine, [but also] against the subjective reflection of all these things in his own mind' (**Reading 10**).

In the final analysis, the influence of the Soviet experience pushed committed writing into one of two directions: in the novel, it encouraged a politicization of the Realist tradition, a practice that frequently produced, particularly among Russian writers, simplistic and crudely executed accounts of the Communist mission (see, for example, Fyodor Gladkov's *Cement* (1925), or Nikolai Ostrovosky's *The Making of a Hero* (1934)). But it also gave rise to works of politically sophisticated and consummate humanist breadth, such as Ignazio Silone's novels *Fontamara* (1933) and *Bread and Wine* (1937), and André Malraux's *Man's Estate* (1933) and *Days of Hope* (1937), in which the formation and articulation of political consciousness and ideology are framed against larger issues, which are personal and even metaphysical in nature.

The second direction went towards a politicization of Modernism, towards a type of literature that would enable writers to graft the energies of revolutionary politics on to the dynamic textual forms and strategies favoured by Avant-Garde (or erstwhile Avant-Garde) authors. This was most notably the case in poetry and drama (although Avant-Garde innovations clearly inform novels such as Hermann Broch's *The Sleepwalkers* (1930–2), and Alfred Döblin's *Berlin Alexanderplatz* (1929), which are memorable for their use of the shifting perspectives and narrative complexities). Such a direction was supremely evident in the work of the Spanish poets of this generation, such as Federico García Lorca and Rafael Alberti, who inflected their literature of protest through a Surrealist optic that was alive to the tragedy and irrational violence that those who exist on the wrong side of political power must suffer, as it was in the work of W. H. Auden, whose early verse is provocatively obscure and angular in its conspiratorial confrontation of the social realm.

What many of the writers of politicized Modernism had in common was a desire to demystify notions such as authorial inspiration and artistic creativity, and replace them with a perspective that would give greater credit to the conventions, procedures and practices of an artistic process that is (or would be, in the optimal circumstances of a social-democratic society) open to all. In this view, politics was regarded as part of, not an adjunct to, the formal structure of the text. As the Russian Futurist and leader of the LEF movement Vladimir Mayakovsky argued in his *How Are Verses Made?* (1926), the poetic process should be seen as a form of 'manufacture', a quite specific set of techniques and forms of knowledge that the poet masters through use and practice. As he dryly observes, seeking to reverse the wisdom of several generations regarding poetic 'inspiration': 'A good notebook and an understanding of how to make use of it are more important than knowing how to write faultlessly in worn-out meters' (**Reading 11**).

As in all his writing, Mayakovsky's tone in *How Are Verses Made?* is largely satirical, debunking, playful and naturally anti-authoritarian. These were oppositional values that also permeated the work of the erstwhile German Expressionist playwright Bertolt Brecht, author of the irreverent, scatological *Baal* (1918). Brecht, however, took Mayakovsky's suggestive *aperçus* much further, elaborating upon their basis a sophisticated dramaturgy, which brought into theoretical alignment not only deliberations regarding the formal pre-conditions of political statement, but also issues relating to the ownership of the productive apparatus itself, and the place of that apparatus within the commercial nexus of the entertainment industry. As the legal case around his *Threepenny Opera* shows, Brecht attempted to intervene in the latter terrain whenever he found it possible to do so. But his greatest success lay in devising a pedagogy of the stage that would (as he explained in his *A Brief Organum for the Theatre*, 1949) disrupt within the audience (through strategically deployed 'alienation devices') the unreflective consumerism that it had been encouraged to adopt, and replace it with an analytical, confrontational perspective capable of registering the political and historical import of the actions depicted on the stage, adopting a 'method [which] treats social situations as processes, and traces out all their inconsistencies' (**Reading 12**).

The assault upon 'capitalist-bourgeois' society, the utopian blueprints for the future, and the energies put into the service of a historical mission, came not only from the Left during this period. Politicians, ideologues and writers of quite a different political persuasion were also organizing themselves in anticipation of the collapse of Western democracy. They were called fascists. The goal of the fascists (who came to power in Italy in 1922, and Germany in 1933) was not a classless society, to be achieved under the auspices of a workers' state, but the nation, which was to be revitalized and set on a heroic footing through the cleansing of its undesirable constituent parts: socialists, liberals, the intellectually decadent, the physically unfit and Jews. But these were, perhaps, the crudest terms in which fascism won support for itself. For underwriting its explicit politics lay a set of assumptions about the world that at first sight look as if they belong to a realm beyond the political, but in fact constitute the essential premises of its political ethos. It was a 'philosophy' that involved an anti-Enlightenment belief in the supremacy of irrational motives in human behaviour, and a corresponding valorization of the animalistic and the biological as defining traits of the self; a celebration of the charismatic personality and the virtues of firm leadership; and finally a conviction that nations and races were locked into a neo-Darwinistic struggle for survival, from which only the fittest and most determined would emerge.

Precisely because the fascist world view claimed a vantage point beyond the internecine factionalism of traditional party politics, it frequently drew into its ambit writers who regarded themselves as apolitical, and who had little interest in the institutional terrain of politics. D. H. Lawrence was one such writer. Like many of the literary fellow-travellers of fascism, Lawrence held himself aloof from concrete political realities and certainly from involvement in political parties or movements. Yet as his *Fantasia of the Unconscious* (1923) reveals (**Reading 13**), Lawrence's world view was permeated by many of the key tropes of the fascist mind-set: a vitalistic belief in the deeper forces that work within the individual, and which remain inaccessible to 'shallow', 'mechanistic' scientific enquiry; and a residual atavism that sees all authentic life as belonging to a distant, primitive past, whose energies can only be revitalized through myth, ritual and ceremony. These were values that Lawrence hoped to mobilize here and in other writings, such as the novel *Kangaroo* (1923), against 'our mistaken democracy' and the debased culture of 'the masses', celebrating a process of renewal that would see the 'grey and opaque' intellectual traditions of the West replaced by a new and powerful vitalism.

The energy, the restlessness, the impatience, the continual commitment to movement that attracted so many intellectuals to fascism also informed the political philosophy of the erstwhile Italian Futurist, Filippo Marinetti. In his essay 'Beyond communism', written in 1920, Marinetti drew upon all the breathless rhetoric and provocative iconoclasm of Italian Futurism to construct an image of a fascist-inspired Italy forging into a future, where the cultural and political goals of the Italian fatherland would finally be realized. For, as Marinetti explained, 'the fatherland represents the greatest expansion of individual generosity, overflowing in every direction on all similar human beings who sympathise or are sympathetic'. Above all, this new nation will be founded on pure energy, in a new state that will be mobilized (as Marinetti explains in a rhetoric that fuses, or confuses, fascist aggrandizement with sporting prowess) through 'heroism, fantasy, enthusiasm, gaiety, variety, novelty, speed, [and] record-setting' (**Reading 14**).

Metaphors of energy and renewal, of rebirth and regeneration, were key tropes within the discourse of fascism, particularly when, as in the case of the French writer Drieu la Rochelle, the fascist mind endeavoured to contrast the dynamic, youthful energies that allegedly propelled that 'movement' with the moribund and discredited 'system' of parliamentary democracy that it had come to replace in many European countries. As Drieu's piece (**Reading 15**), written in 1941, at the height of the Nazi invasion of Europe, makes clear, the attraction of fascism lay not so much in its ideology or formulated policies, but in the way it valorized the masculine body, and the force field of the body: physical prowess, strength, virility, direct action, the unpremeditated and machismo assertiveness, qualities that were supremely evident in sport and military combat. As Drieu explained (having in view the 'achievements' of the Hitler Youth on the battlefields of Europe), 'this is a type of man who rejects culture, who grows strong even in the midst of sexual and alcoholic depravation, and who dreams about giving to the world a physical discipline that will have a radical effect. This is a man who does not believe in ideas, and therefore not in doctrines. This is a man who believes only in action, and who links his actions to the most direct of myths.'

The ethos of naked instrumentality extolled by the fascists relegated all other values: rational enquiry, moral scruple, respect for the weak, conscience; all belonged, it was confidently asserted, to a superannuated past: they had been made redundant by the march of history. And, as the German poet Gottfried Benn made clear in his essay 'The new state and the intellectuals' (1933), 'where history speaks, individuals should fall silent'. For, as Benn further explains: 'History proceeds not in a democratic but in an elemental way; at its turning points, it is always elemental. It does not care for elections, but sends forward the new biological breed. It has no other method: it says: this breed has arrived: now act and suffer, incorporate the spirit of your generation and your species into the march of time; do not deviate: act and suffer, as the law of life demands' (**Reading 16**). History has moved on, leaving those who still have misgivings about the triumph of totalitarianism behind, but opening up for others, such as Benn and the other literary fellow-travellers of the Right, paths into a new future, where the demoralizing and perplexing tensions within modernity would be finally undone, expunged by a new state dedicated to the dynamic virtues of mass mobilization and firm leadership.

That so many writers of this generation had been prepared willingly to sacrifice in their political affairs both critical acumen and intellectual honesty was a cause for concern to those, such as the French cultural critic Julien Benda, who had kept faith with the tradition of liberal–humanism. In his *The Great Betrayal* [*Le Trahison des clercs*] (1927), Benda castigated not only the mistaken idealism and intellectual myopia of this generation of politicized writers; he also condemned the less noble factors that lay behind their embrace of radical politics: a worship of force and the need to identify with power and the powerful; the desire to be on the right side of history, however barbaric its moral trajectory might be; and finally, common or garden careerism. Nevertheless, many still held faith with the traditions and values of liberal–humanism, believing that it alone offered a positive point of resistance to rising totalitarianism. Thomas Mann was one. The most famous German novelist of this period, the author of the epic *Buddenbrooks* (1901), *Death in Venice* (1912) and *The Magic Mountain* (1924), Mann had largely held himself aloof from party politics until 1930. But, in September of that year, Hitler's National Socialists dramatically increased their vote at the general election. The time for equivocation and polite commentary was past. Mann entered the fray with his speech 'German address: A call to reason' (1930), unambiguously denouncing Nazism (**Reading 17**). His speech was both a sophisticated analysis of the false redeemerism of the Nazi cause and an exhortation to his largely middle–class audience that they should resist the false panaceas of resurgent nationalism and (against their natural inclinations) align themselves with the Social Democrats. But although Mann's intervention was part of a strategy that was clearly political, the content of his speech was not. For what Mann invokes here to counter the growing threat of the Nazi menace are values that belong to a realm that might best be described as transpolitical, and which included, as he explained, common standards of decency and 'bourgeois ideals and goals, such as freedom, intellectual attainment, culture, in general'. The 'political' (Mann implies here) must be redefined, so that it moves away from intolerance and dogmatism and towards a humanism that will respect the basic rights of individuals and nations alike.

Mann's sentiments were shared by many, particularly by those compelled to witness the extremes of both communism and fascism, such as George Orwell. Orwell's involvement in the Spanish Civil War (documented in his *Homage to Catalonia*, 1938) taught him that, in spite of the progressive long-term objectives pursued by the communists, they had been too willing to sacrifice in the immediate present truth, objectivity, honesty, personal liberties, and even individual lives, to make pursuing such goals humanly defensible. As Orwell later explained in his 1946 essay, 'Why I write', the writer cannot avoid the political: events force him to take a stand. But in making a political statement through the medium of literature, he should not give up those qualities that are essentially human: those complex and possibly contradictory energies and values of individual selfhood, those 'ingrained likes and dislikes' which should not, Orwell argues, be sacrificed to the 'essentially public, non-individual activities that this age forces on all of us' (**Reading 18**).

In the final analysis (as Orwell's experience demonstrates), the private history of the writer, his or her firsthand contact with political dogma, may well militate against the acceptance of impersonal ideologies. This was certainly the experience of many who found that their earlier allegiance to communism could not be sustained in the face of the overwhelmingly deleterious practical consequences of that ideology. The winning of faith, and its subsequent loss, forms a recurrent theme in much of the writing of this period, works such as Arthur Koestler's novel *Darkness at Noon* (1938). Both the depths of this generation's commitment to communism and its subsequent disillusion were later described by Koestler, within the context of his own pained political journey, which began (as he explained in his contribution to the anthology *The God That Failed*, published in 1950) with 'emotional fervour and intellectual bliss', and ended with disillusion, apostasy and self-loathing (**Reading 19**). This was the death of one self: but out of it a new one emerged, one alive to the more expansive emotions of 'fear and pity', and convinced that notions such as charity are not 'bourgeois abstractions', but the very 'gravitational force that keeps civilization in orbit'.

That many writers of this generation felt that a position was needed which could retain the experience of the mission of politics, but within a world view that had a greater respect for a spiritual component to human experience and a greater commitment to certain inalienable rights that might best be described as trans- or post-political, is clear from Koestler's retrospective account of his own 'trahison des clercs' recorded in *The God that Failed*. In the immediate postwar period, the one philosophy that seemed to offer the greatest hope for a theoretical position which might reconcile that recognition of humankind's necessary being in the world with an insistence upon the unnegotiable right to personal freedom was Existentialism. Its tenets were variously defined by its two most noted French practitioners: Albert Camus and Jean-Paul Sartre. Camus' concern was with justice, which he conceived of as a metaphysical prerequisite that had to be met before humanity could reach its true sense of selfhood. As he argued in his two major theoretical works *The Myth of Sisyphus* (1942) and *The Rebel* (1951), political forces of history have sought throughout history to relativize the modest terrain in which personal freedom can move. Those false absolutes, those doctrinaire philosophies (whether of the Left or the Right) which, as Camus noted in *The Rebel*, 'disregard individual death, and give the name of immortality to the prodigious agony of the collective', must be abandoned in favour of the less absolute but immeasurably more serviceable priorities that underscore and sustain the claims of the individual to dignity and freedom (**Reading 20**).

Camus's position, however, involved neither a retreat from history nor a refusal to act in the defence of human values, whenever historical circumstances made that necessary. Indeed, as Sartre consistently argued in his works (and most notably in his epic *Critique of Dialectical Reason*, 1960), individual freedom is impossible without collective freedom (irrespective of whether that is conceived of in terms of class or ethnicity), even for those who are not directly involved in the latter. As Sartre explained in his most extended statement on the issue *What is Literature?* (1946), every writer is, simply through his or her membership of the social weal, politically committed in one way or another. The notion of an uncommitted writer is, Sartre argues, a contradiction in terms; by the very act of making public their ideas, all writers act upon a readership, which correspondingly acts upon a world. Even 'to speak is to act'. In Sartre's model of the 'engaged' writer, politics finally abandons its affinities with the totalizing and monolithic ideologies of the 1920s and 1930s, re-emerging as a medium that must be controlled by (rather than control) the individual, so that effective social action should not lose awareness of its origins in the domain of ethical choice. In such a world, Sartre passionately argues, 'literature would finally become aware of itself; it would finally understand that form and content, public and private, are identical, that the formal liberty of expression, and the material freedom to act' are the same (**Reading 21**).

# 1

# 'The moral scandals provoked by the Surrealists do not necessarily presuppose the overthrow of intellectual and social *values*'

### Pierre Naville: *The Revolution and the Intellectuals* (1926)

*Pierre Naville (b. 1903) participated in the French Surrealist movement from 1924, making sporadic contributions to the journal* Surrealist Review. *His main importance, however, lies in the fact that he was the first to identify a theoretical impasse within the Surrealist position: namely that it wanted to help in the political revolution of French society, but was unwilling to abandon its highly individualistic aesthetic founded on dreams and the primacy of the unconscious. In his extended essay,* The Revolution and the Intellectuals, *Naville analysed their predicament in some detail, focusing upon the different, and what he regarded as irreconcilable, conceptual frameworks that divided the 'dialectical' Marxists from the 'metaphysical' Surrealists.*

Broadly speaking, it is necessary to understand the general articulation of their response in terms of that double movement of which we spoke above, which is at one and the same time both dialectical (involving the progress of the mind fully shaped in terms of its own self-awareness), and metaphysical (which consists in a theoretical speculation on the data of internal experience and of certain experiences of external objects and events). It is beyond this kind of perpetual activity at the limits of the self, aided by a notion that is becoming increasingly clearer of the needs of the revolution, that they have, thanks to certain recent events, been driven into the Marxist camp.

But, considering the origins and the exercise of Surrealism as a movement of intellectual spontaneity, we are forced to recognize that from now on it can only take up one of two options:

1. It can either persevere with its negative anarchic disposition, which is *a priori* a mistaken attitude, because it provides no justification for the idea of a revolution that it claims to believe in, an attitude dictated by its refusal to compromise its own existence and the sacred character of the individual in the struggle that would lead to the disciplined action of class struggle.

**Source:** Pierre Naville, *La Révolution et les intellectuels* (Paris: Gallimard, 1975), pp. 76–7, 83–5 and 88–9. There is no standard translation. **Further reading:** Maurice Nadeau, *History of Surrealism*, translated from the French by Richard Howard, with an Introduction by Roger Shattuck (Harmondsworth: Penguin, 1973), pp. 139–44.

2. Or it can resolutely commit itself to revolutionary activity, the only true revolutionary activity: Marxism. This would involve it recognizing that spiritual force, a substance that resides entirely within the individual, is deeply connected to a social reality, which it, in fact, presupposes. That reality manifests itself for us in the organization of class action. In this case, struggle is aimed directly against the bourgeoisie, and part of a profound proletarian struggle, which is governed by the movements of the masses, and supported by intellectuals who are resolutely determined to recognize freedom only on that terrain where the bourgeoisie has been destroyed.

*But for Naville, the Surrealists have not reached sufficient political maturity to take the second option; as he explains, their ideas have not progressed beyond the radical but purely individualistic categories in which they were first formed. The Surrealists are, without doubt, subjecting themselves to a process of self-scrutiny (and Naville is here thinking of recent essays by André Breton, committing the Surrealists to the revolutionary cause), but, as a group, they still refuse to recognize the authority of the Communist Party line, the acceptance of which would (according to Naville) make their torturous theorizing unnecessary.*

At this moment, a number of considerations are emerging, sentimental, poetic, dialectical (rarely theoretical), all of which are detrimental to the consolidation of revolutionary truth. Men are examining problems in a new light, that of a revolutionary truth that is evident but not rigid. A new bout of intellectual enlightenment seems to them to justify a critique that will start all over again from the basics. They see themselves in front of a truth that is purer, more open; they yield to the desire to test it out. They become anxious about the restricting nature of directives upon them, upon their metaphysical projections, and about the force that appears, in spite of their efforts, to be detached from them. This force has become foreign to them, an enemy. That obsession with mystery that lies at the heart of Surrealism is not satisfied with external mystery, which is contiguous to the real world, a mystery that can only be discovered through a methodical process; they must have access to the inner world, that internal spiritual source and its dialectical development.

They do not understand the displacement of the individual that takes place when the latter is submitted to a process that transcends him. Their need for truth only requires a certain free development of the personal proclivities of the individual. It is here that they can keep the illusion of freedom alive. That the individual does not exist, that his reality is derived from realities that are vaster and even far more mysterious than his own, does not enter into their deliberations. We have seen how Surrealism is involved in a movement whose methodology was originally idealist. The Surrealists asserted that they had, through adherence to that movement, contact with revolutionary reality. But the life of dream, of love, and the different artistic, literary and pseudo-philosophical occupations to which the Surrealists devoted themselves, and which they deemed, on their own confession, to be primordial, possessing a revolutionary demeanour and freed from any bourgeois contact, continue to retain certain mystical recesses and corners, points of connection that are too easily assimilated into the bourgeois world. 'Your ideas,' said Marx, 'are they not also the product of the bourgeois conditions of production and ownership?'

The question can be succinctly put: do the Surrealists believe in a liberation of the spirit prior to the abolition of the bourgeois conditions of material life, or do they recognize that a revolutionary spirit can only be created as the result of a successful revolution? The question is all the more important since, as we well know, the West, and particularly France, continues to live in an atmosphere of bourgeois intellectualism, in face of which the diversions of the Surrealists, for example, offer a very meagre form of escape.

*Naville moves on to discuss a statement by André Breton in which the latter aligns the Surrealists with the masses and against the bourgeoisie. But Naville remains sceptical about what can be achieved by the Surrealists in their assault upon dominant culture.*

The moral scandals provoked by the Surrealists do not necessarily presuppose the overthrow of intellectual and *social* values; the bourgeoisie does not fear them. It absorbs them easily. Even the violent attacks of the Surrealists against patriotism have come to look like a purely moral scandal. These sorts of scandal do not prevent the preservation of the intellectual hierarchy within the bourgeois republic.

The bourgeoisie does not fear intellectuals who proclaim themselves moderate or even extreme left wing. In reality, it does not prohibit them from making contact with it. The masses, being the most common bearers of revolutionary force, do not seek out the support of the intellectuals, which is frequently suspect.

Certainly, intellectuals are often rebels. Rebellion makes possible for them an individual satisfaction that can be perpetually renewed, but constantly shattered, also. The goals that they have in view are swift, immediate and fragile; with the Surrealists, these goals end by merging with their intellectual horizon. They disappear into the distance.

In the final analysis, and in spite of what they have said on this subject, it is possible to assert that the Surrealists portend a liberation of the spirit prior to the abolition of the bourgeois conditions of material life, and, up to a certain point, independent of it. One sees thus what sort of assistance they might bring to the revolutionary struggle. Auxiliaries, certainly, but *temporary* ones, as long as the forceful movement of opposition to the bourgeoisie coincides with the progressive determination of the struggle for the dictatorship of the proletariat.

# 2

# 'The productive neurotics will include the political reformers'

## Louis MacNeice: *Modern Poetry* (1938)

*Louis MacNeice (1907–63) was one of the foremost representatives of the 'Auden generation' of the 1930s (see his Poems, 1935), a generation that also included Stephen Spender, Christopher Isherwood and Cecil Day-Lewis (and which had made its first collective appearance in the journal New Signatures in 1932). In his study, Modern Poetry, MacNeice defended the iconoclastic work of the Auden group, seeing in it an epochal break with the dominant Modernist idiom in poetry, which for MacNeice was represented, above all, by T. S. Eliot and W. B. Yeats. Unlike these poets, the Auden group wrote in order to make contact with the real world, although their personal philosophies were (as MacNeice's pen sketch of Auden indicates) every bit as complex as those of the Modernists.*

The poets of *New Signatures*, unlike Yeats and Eliot, are emotionally partisan. Yeats proposed to turn his back on desire and hatred; Eliot sat back and watched other peoples' emotions with ennui and an ironical self-pity:

> I keep my countenance,
> I remain self-possessed
> Except when a street piano mechanical and tired
> Reiterates some worn-out common song
> With the smell of hyacinths across the garden
> *Recalling things that other people have desired* [italics in original]

The whole poetry, on the other hand, of Auden, Spender, and Day-Lewis implies that they have desires and hatreds of their own and, further, that they think some things *ought* to be desired and others hated.

This does not mean, however, that their world is a crude world of black and white, of sheep and goats. Auden, for example, has the advantage of seeing the world both in terms of psycho-analysis and of a Marxian doctrine of progress [see above]. Thereby nearly all the detail in the world becomes significant for him. For Auden *qua* psychologist anything, almost, will become (a) an example or symbol of a neurosis

**Source:** Louis MacNeice, *Modern Poetry: A Personal Essay*, second edition (Oxford: Clarendon Press, 1968), pp. 25–6 and 28–30. **Further reading:** Peter McDonald, *Louis MacNeice, the Poet in His Contexts* (Oxford: Clarendon Press, 1991), esp. pp. 10–36.

demanding cure, or (b) an example or symbol of how a neurosis produces good (for Auden believes that all progress is due to neurotic restlessness). For Auden *qua* Marxist, on the other hand, nearly everything will be either (a) a product of the enemy, of reaction, bad and to be fought against, or (b) a relic of an obsolete past, once perhaps good but now bad and to be deplored, though often with reverence and affection, or (c) an earnest of better things, a pioneer of the future – or else a symbol of one of these three types. It will be seen that the neurotic who needs curing will often be identifiable with the political enemy, while the productive neurotics will include the political reformers. Auden, therefore, cannot, like many politicians, be accused of having crude animosities. The issues are simplified but the people remain complex. And Auden shows great sympathy with people.

> *MacNeice continues his critique of the 'ugly and sordid, morbid and cynical' nature of modern poetry, which he sees embodied, in particular, by Eliot's 'Sweeney Among the Nightingales' (1920). MacNeice also takes issue with Wyndham Lewis, whose theory of satire construes human beings as 'doomed animals or determinist machines'. As MacNeice explains, the Auden generation of poets are also interested in the concrete circumstances of life, but seek to conserve their human core.*

Wyndham Lewis maintains that it is the artist's or writer's business to depict the Without of people and not their Within. This principle leads to the presentation of much that is sordid or trivial. The presentation of the Without without reference to the values of the Within will (as Mass Observation tends to) give results which are only quantitatively true. Thus the half-hour a man spends in the lavatory will be given more prominence than the ten minutes he spends arranging flowers.

Nearly all poets, however, have selected surface details with reference to inner, or spiritual, criteria. The heroic moods were given more prominence than the everyday moods of boredom or irritation because in the latter man did not seem to be exercising such a specifically human faculty, and most poets, following the Greeks, have been more interested in man functioning as man than in man as an animal or a machine or a visual mass based on the cube and the cylinder. Baudelaire wrote about ennui but his ennuis were heroic. The truthful representation of ennui can be valuable as a foil, not a foil to a fancy world, but a patch of drab in the real world which also has its lights and colours.

The poets of *New Signatures* are interested in Man Functioning. They select their detail (for they still, like the Imagists but not for the same reason, believe in particulars) in order to illustrate the workings of vital principles. Original Sin is for them more cardinal than Original Inertia.

The poet is once again to make his response as a whole. On the one side is concrete living – not just a conglomeration of animals or machines, mere flux, a dissolving hail of data, but a system of individuals determined by their circumstances, a concrete, therefore, of sensuous fact and what we may call 'universals'; on the other side is a concrete poet – not just an eye or a heart or a brain or a solar plexus, but the whole man reacting with both intelligence and emotion (which is how we react to anything in ordinary life) to experiences, and on this basis presenting something which is (a) communication, a record, but is also (b) a creation – having a new unity of its own, something in its shape which makes it poetry.

3

---

## 'And so the political can be intellectual, and the intellect can act!'

### Heinrich Mann: 'Zola' (1917)

*The early novels of Heinrich Mann (1871–1950), such as the trilogy* The Goddesses *(1903), were written within the* fin-de-siècle *idiom of refined aestheticism, but from his novel* The Man of Straw *(1918), Mann's writing revealed a growing political radicalism that had its origins in the author's abhorrence of the First World War and the political ideologies that had brought it about. In his essay on Zola, written at the height of the war, Mann lauded the French writer's transition from aloof artistic self-sufficiency to civic-minded responsibility that culminated in the latter's intervention in the Dreyfus case. In doing so, Zola had broken with the ivory tower Olympianism of Flaubert, and the other precursors of the Symbolist tradition, to take up the political and ethical challenges of his time.*

From work emerges the idea; from work also the struggle. That's not, however, what [Zola's] predecessor, Flaubert, thought. Flaubert had held himself distant from the fray, in a spirit of derision; and his inspiration came to him not from work but from form. He did not portray the working man, only the stupidity of people. He felt no love for his century or for those around him; despite his unique revolutionary impact 'he was never prepared to admit that everything interacts with everything else, and that the popular press was the younger if perhaps seedier sister of Madame Bovary'. Too deeply committed to the self-indulgences of romantic sensibility, he had won through to an insight into reality, but only through self-sacrifice and complaint. He would gladly have

---

**Source:** Heinrich Mann, *Geist und Tat: Franzosen von 1780–1930* (Frankfurt am Main: S. Fischer Verlag GmbH, 1931), pp. 24–5, 31 and 40–2. There is no standard translation. **Further reading:** David Gross, *The Writer and Society: Heinrich Mann and Literary Politics in Germany, 1890–1940* (Atlantic Highlands, NJ: Humanities Press, 1980), esp. pp. 103–22 and 153–61.

abandoned reality; and he did abandon it, when it became too gross. Having outgrown that old unfruitful spiritualism, he managed to survive through scepticism, arriving, amidst it all, at the most penetrating of insights into the void. Reality never meant much to him, but he, nevertheless, mastered it so well that he was able to encourage it to produce new ideals.

But it was precisely out of this reality that Zola created. Flaubert wrote for the sake of writing. What else could he do? He lived under the Second Empire. Having survived this period, he did not, unlike a younger generation, attempt to depict it in writing; it weighed upon him too much, had become a part of him. Aestheticism is a product of periods that are without hope, of political states that destroy hope. Flaubert was famous, but was never pompous and always supportive of others; a good man, and yet created around him neither followers nor conviviality. Even in old age, he did not appear venerable. For the aesthete has no regard for age. Authority, public respect, indeed all elevated sentiments are regarded by the moralist as. . . .

Will Zola rise as high? Even ten years after his first appearance as a Naturalist, he remained basically unknown to the public. He continued his struggle during all this time without a cease-fire. He subsidized, as is often the way, the meagre income that he got from his books with his journalism, but this provided a good schooling for Zola: for he had committed himself to producing two books a year. He got married, at that most difficult moment, just before the [Franco-Prussian] war; lived after that in a solid middle-class fashion; in country retreats, with ample opportunity for exercise. And with work, struggle, disappointment the years go by, amidst pressing worries, the bankruptcy of his publishers, under renewed struggles, the years go by. What ever-increasing vicissitudes he had to endure, and that embittered waiting in front of a door that seemed to be permanently locked. Fame was long overdue! It was not only he, but the age itself, life, in fact, that demanded fame for him, its prophet!

> *Zola did eventually win through to fame, and to something greater: the recognition that the writer must be fully committed to political and ethical ideals, and prepared to defend these ideals against the exigencies of* Realpolitik.

Much has been achieved, for we [i.e. Zola] have been working and have written twenty novels, and have secured a number of at least partial victories for the truth. Early in his career, Zola once remarked in a period of uncertainty: 'I don't deny the greatness of the exertions that are today being made; I don't deny that we are more or less getting closer to freedom and justice. But it is my conviction that mankind will always remain mankind, creatures of the earth, sometimes good, sometimes bad, according to circumstances. If my characters fail to win through to goodness that is because we are still standing at the threshold of our potential for perfection.' Zola himself was also standing at this threshold, and the exertions that he would have to make might well have lasted for ever. Freedom, justice? 'I believe rather in the steady march towards the truth. Only by recognizing truth can better social conditions be brought about.' For this was his own personal path. At the beginning, the prospects did not look good. Early Naturalism had such an effect because it appeared to despair of the impenetrable materiality of the world. He depicted suffering in order to agitate his readers; but he became more consoling the more his intellectual sympathy developed. It was through work that Zola and his writing gained in intellectual depth, as he worked on reality with a will to reach true actuality. His work rehearsed, as it developed, the flux of life itself: initially, its material side, but out of this, through work and energy, there grew an image of the spirit and the majesty of mankind. Our lives are spent in struggle, therefore nothing is impossible. Emotionally moving and great: at the moment of its very inception there begins the potential for perfection. And mankind cannot be left behind, now that it is standing upon the summit of a hill. *L'Assommoir* is nothing else than a sermon in praise of facts. In *Germinal*, however, there resounds the Gospel of a future humanity; it can be heard in the very earth itself, out of this slow and indifferent earth it echoes with the hammer blows of the miners, finally seeking to erupt and become a reality.

*Zola's contention that the writer must adopt a conscious stance towards the political issues and injustices of the day was tested out by the Dreyfus case.*

He had developed to a point where he was ready to step out from his work and commit himself to action, and precisely at that moment when matters concerning Captain Dreyfus had reached a stage where they required an active spirit. It should have surprised no one that Zola took action here: it was the result of everything that was well known about him. This was the act that brought together the various strands of his work to a conclusion. And it was to his good fortune, he who had been sent a mission by his epoch, that he should find his way to events in this way. He went to meet them, long before they had become apparent. In 1891, while he was working on *La Débâcle*, an observer wondered at the determined energy that exuded from Zola's actions and speech; it was as if he felt himself to be on the eve of a battle. That year, he made it known that he wished to express his opinions and be more active. There followed silence, and then the complaint that he lacked ability: he needed more time to prepare himself, and he was reluctant to make uninformed pronouncements. But his passionate hope that it might be different could be clearly seen, a hope that he might crown his happy career by adding to his success as a writer the public achievements of a politician. But, Oh, frustrated ambition! For when have people paid any consideration to anything but the cheapest of political pronouncements? It was just at this time that he declined to become a Member of Parliament. The mandate imposed a too onerous duty upon him – he still had his life's work to complete. And he had never aspired to easy victories: how could cheap ovations and triumphs, which have only an external effect, ever have satisfied him? If he were to join the political fray, then there had to be important issues and a struggle for ideas at stake in an arena that for too long had been dominated by the activities of mediocre minds.

But his main worry was whether this mediocrity could be overcome. Perhaps it was a necessary feature of political life? Experience seemed to suggest that this was the case; men of intellectual accomplishment, famous for achievements in other fields, had not succeeded here. They were simply not wanted, and they were not given the time to impress their intellectual calibre upon any undertaking. Perhaps they would not have been able to do it anyway, lacking what the politician needs above all: an indifference to larger concerns and the ultimate consequence of his activity, and an accommodation to the tricky survival from one day to the next, living in hope of an outcome that will never materialize. We others [Zola] were used to completing a task, and to signing our name to it. The action for which we were created had to be as perfect as a work of art, and had to possess the same symbolic value. But where was such an action to be found? Zola asked himself this question in vain; the question of how this divide, which seemed to be growing bigger and bigger, might be crossed between the intellectual cream of the nation and its political leaders. In his early days, he had, like all writers, despised political activity. But now he had come to realize what politics in reality was: 'the most passionately animated area in which the lives of the nations struggle, and where history is sown for future generations with truth and justice.' Literature and politics focus on the same themes, have the same goals, and must mutually inspire each other, if they are not to degenerate. The intellect is action, and it acts for the sake of people. And so the political can be intellectual, and the intellect can act!

# 4

## 'This new art is incompatible with pessimism, with skepticism, and with all other forms of spiritual collapse'

### Leon Trotsky: *Literature and Revolution* (1924)

*Leon Trotsky, the pseudonym of Lev Davidovich Bronstein (1879–1940), was, along with Lenin, one of the guiding spirits behind the Bolshevik Revolution of 1917. His official position within the new Soviet government was Commissar of Foreign Affairs and of War, but Trotsky was also a highly cultured intellectual, who believed that the arts had a central role to play in the formation of the new state, views to which he gave detailed formulation in his* Literature and Revolution. *Trotsky was undeniably a believer in the cause of Soviet Communism; but in this book, written at a time when his own position of power within the hierarchy was under challenge from the emerging Stalin, Trotsky is careful to emphasize the provisional nature of what has been achieved so far, in both political and cultural terms, discussing the Revolution in the present tense throughout, not as an event of the past but as an ongoing reality, and a set of tasks to be achieved for the future.*

It is silly, absurd, stupid to the highest degree, to pretend that art will remain indifferent to the convulsions of our epoch. The events are prepared by people, they are made by people, they fall upon people and change these people. Art, directly or indirectly, affects the lives of the people who make or experience the events. This refers to all art, to the grandest, as well as to the most intimate. If nature, love or friendship had no connection with the social spirit of an epoch, lyric poetry would long ago have ceased to exist. A profound break in history, that is, a rearrangement of classes in society, shakes up individuality, establishes the perception of the fundamental problems of lyric poetry from a new angle, and so saves art from eternal repetition.

But does not the 'spirit' of an epoch work imperceptibly and independently of the subjective will? Of course in the final analysis, this spirit is reflected in everybody, in those who accept it and who embody it, as well as in those who hopelessly struggle against it, and in those who passively try to hide from it. But those who hide themselves passively are imperceptibly dying off. Those who resist are able to revive the old art with one kind of antiquated flame or another. But the new art, which will

**Source:** Leon Trotsky, *Literature and Revolution* (Ann Arbor: University of Michigan Press, 1960), pp. 12, 14–15 and 229–30. **Further reading:** *Leon Trotsky: On Literature and Art*, edited by Paul N. Siegel (New York: Pathfinder Press, 1970).

lay out new landmarks, and which will expand the channel of creative art, can be created only by those who are at one with their epoch. If a line were extended from present art to the Socialist art of the future, one would say that we have hardly now passed through the stage of even preparing for its preparation.

*Trotsky briefly reviews 'non-revolutionary' literature, before turning his attention to the transitional nature of existent proletarian writing.*

However significant the achievements of individual proletarian poets may be in general, their socalled 'proletarian art' is only passing through an apprenticeship. It sows the elements of artistic culture widely, it helps a new class to assimilate the old achievements, even though in a very thin veneer, and in this way it is one of the currents of the Socialist art of the future.

It is fundamentally incorrect to contrast bourgeois culture and bourgeois art with proletarian culture and proletarian art. The latter will never exist, because the proletarian regime is temporary and transient. The historic significance and the moral grandeur of the proletarian revolution consist in the fact that it is laying the foundations of a culture which is above classes and which will be the first culture that is truly human.

Our policy in art, during a transitional period, can and must be to help the various groups and schools of art which have come over to the Revolution to grasp correctly the historic meaning of the Revolution, and to allow them complete freedom of self-determination in the field of art, after putting before them the categorical standard of being for or against the Revolution.

The Revolution is reflected in art, for the time being only partially so, to the extent to which the artist ceases to regard it as an external catastrophe, and to the extent to which the guild of new and old poets and artists becomes a part of the living tissue of the Revolution and learns to see it from within and not from without.

The social whirlpool will not calm down so soon. There are decades of struggle ahead of us, in Europe and in America. Not only the men and women of our generation, but of the coming one, will be its participants, its heroes and its victims. The art of this epoch will be entirely under the influence of revolution. This art needs a new self-consciousness. It is, above all, incompatible with mysticism, whether it be frank, or whether it masquerades as romanticism, because the Revolution starts from the central idea that collective man must become sole master, and that the limits of his power are determined by his knowledge of natural forces and by his capacity to use them. This new art is incompatible with pessimism, with skepticism, and with all other forms of spiritual collapse. It is realistic, active, vitally collectivist, and filled with a limitless creative faith in the Future.

> *The goal of all true literature [Trotsky contends] is the creation of a socialist society, which alone can provide mankind with the means for political and cultural self-realization.*

There is no revolutionary art as yet. There are the elements of this art, there are hints and attempts at it, and, what is most important, there is the revolutionary man, who is forming the new generation in his own image and who is more and more in need of this art. How long will it take for such art to reveal itself clearly? It is difficult even to guess, because the process is intangible and incalculable, and we are limited to guesswork even when we try to time more tangible social processes. But why should not this art, at least its first big wave, come soon as the expression of the art of the young generation which was born in the Revolution and which carries it on?

Revolutionary art which inevitably reflects all the contradictions of a revolutionary social system, should not be confused with Socialist art for which no basis has as yet been made. On the other hand, one must not forget that Socialist art will grow out of the art of this transition period.

In insisting on such a distinction, we are not at all guided by a pedantic consideration of an abstract program. Not for nothing did Engels speak of the Socialist Revolution as a leap from the kingdom of necessity to the kingdom of freedom. On the contrary, it is developing the features of 'necessity' to the greatest degree. Socialism will abolish class antagonisms, as well as classes, but the Revolution carries the class struggle to its highest tension. During the period of revolution, only that literature which promotes the consolidation of the workers in their struggle against the exploiters is necessary and progressive. Revolutionary literature cannot but be imbued with a spirit of social hatred, which is a creative historic factor in an epoch of proletarian dictatorship. Under Socialism, solidarity will be the basis of society. Literature and art will be tuned to a different key. All the emotions which we revolutionists, at the present time, feel apprehensive of naming – so much have they been worn thin by hypocrites and vulgarians – such as disinterested friendship, love for one's neighbour, sympathy, will be the mighty ringing chords of Socialist poetry.

# 5

# 'All ideological doubts are absolutely inadmissible'

## Manifesto of the 'On Guard' group (1923)

*The 'On Guard' group, founded in 1923 by Semyon Rodov and G. Lelevich, replaced the* Proletcult *as the principal vehicle for the dissemination of official Soviet policy on literature. It launched a number of manifestos in its journals,* On Guard *and* October, *displaying its uncompromising militancy towards the 'old writers' (and most notably the so-called 'fellow-travellers'), and energetically emphasizing its rejection of inherited literary forms and genres. The new Soviet literature was to use only contemporary material, and be written exclusively by authors from proletarian or peasant backgrounds. The following extract is taken from the 'On Guard' manifesto of 1923. It begins with a caustic dismissal of competing, non-political trends and figures in Russian literature, before delineating its own goals.*

For a year already, ever since the appearance of N. Ossinsky's 'notorious' articles, a literary-critical leap-frog has been going on in the U.S.S.R. Everybody who has, or imagines he has, some concern in artistic literature has been making his voice heard as the voice of the ten. One Communist takes a liking for the nun-like Achmatova, another for the pornographically-slavophil Pilnyak, a third for the Serapion Brotherhood, with its 'emancipation from ideology', and so geniuses are at hand, the Revolution is saved, and the Vikings, who are called upon to manage our revolutionary literature, are found. The most inexcusable muddle reigns in our ranks upon all questions of literature. The old battle flags must be once more proudly and unconquerably raised before the face of reviving bourgeois literature and the wavering Fellow-Travellers.

Art has always served and serves now as a mighty instrument of immediate influence upon the emotive impressionability of the masses. In the meanwhile, the Proletariat has achieved very little, almost nothing, in the sphere of art.

Proletarian literature is the one sphere in which the working-class has succeeded in notably strengthening its position and in creating something of value. Proletarian writers have produced a whole series of works, which express the new interpretations and conceptions of the working-class, and which have given rise to a considerable literary movement.

**Source:** *Soviet Literature: An Anthology*, edited and translated by George Reavey and Marc Slonim (Westport, CT: Greenwood Press, 1934), pp. 403–6. **Further reading:** Hermann Ermolaev, *Soviet Literary Theories, 1917–1934: The Genesis of Socialist Realism* (New York: Octagon Books, 1977), pp. 27–38.

Nobody would undertake now to deny the existence of a Proletarian literature. Proletarian literature has acquired a definite social significance which was particularly manifest in the years of civil war, when the old writers either escaped abroad or entrenched themselves in pure art or middle-class niceties, while the younger bourgeois attempted various formal subtleties.

Through these years the voice of our Proletarian literature ran in unison with the Revolution and made itself heard even amid its thunders.

Given, however, the new conditions of revolutionary development, Proletarian literature ought to dig deeper and find new outlets. First of all, Proletarian literature must finally free itself from the influence of the past in the sphere of ideology as well as in that of form. The cultural backwardness of the Russian Proletariat, the century yoke of bourgeois ideology, the defeatist streak in Russian literature in the last years and in the decade before the Revolution – all this taken together inevitably influences, and makes possible further influence upon, Proletarian literature.

The framework of the content of Proletarian literature, which has had, until our days, two fundamental themes – labour and struggle – must be widened. To labour, it is necessary to add Proletarian construction, and to make a comprehensive use, in the artistic reflection of the struggle, of our heroically rich contemporaneity and of our great epoch. Nearer to living, concrete contemporaneity.

We must, at the same time, make use of the Proletarian past, so rich in struggles, defeats and victories, and of the perspectives of its future conquests for the creation of a revolutionary Proletarian romanticism.

These important problems of the content of Proletarian literature demand of the Proletarian writer, besides the lyrical approach which has predominated in the last five years, an epic approach, which will alone permit us to create the monumental work adequate to the epoch. These problems of content, too, compel the Proletarian writer to search for a corresponding form, which can only be synthetical.

Standing *On Guard* over our fundamental problem – the widening and deepening of the content, and the working out of a new synthetic form of Proletarian literature – we shall engage in merciless battle against both the stagnation and self-repetition of *several groups of Proletarian writers and the excessive pursuit of form* and its various elements.

While engaged on this work we shall stand firmly *on guard over a firm and clear Communist ideology* in Proletarian literature. In view of the revival, ever since the beginning of NEP, of the activity of bourgeois literary groups, all *ideological doubts* are absolutely *inadmissible*, and we shall make a point of bringing them to light.

We shall stand *on guard over the organizational structure* of the All-Russian Association of Proletarian writers, and we shall fight for its consolidation.

We shall fight those Manilovs, who distort and slander our revolution by the attention they pay to the rotten fabric of the Fellow-Travellers' literary creation, in their *attempt to build* an aesthetic *bridge between the past and present.*

We *shall fight* those *diehards* who have, without sufficient criteria, congealed in ecstatic pose in front of the granite monument of *old bourgeois-gentry literature*, and who do not wish to emancipate the working-class of its oppressive *ideological burden.*

We *shall fight* those *desperate* people who, in search of the new, support all the acrobatics of literary juggling and propound theories of 'the future', forgetting the present and sinking into the slime of flowery phrases.

And finally, as a public group in Proletarian literature, *we count it our duty to fight not only against manifest white-guard and finally discredited literary tendencies, but also against those writers' groups which disguise themselves with the false mask of the revolution, but which are, in reality, reactionary and counter-revolutionary.*

*A clear, firm, and severely consistent Communist policy in art and literature will be the leading principle of our review.*

We have in our hands the battle-tried weapon of the proletariat – its Marxist method and the growing will of the working-class for knowledge and creation – and we shall therefore be able to fulfil the task we have assumed.

The editors of *On Guard* will count principally upon the attention and the sympathetic interest of the wide mass of the Communist Party and of the working-class, of the Communist youth and proletarian students.

We count upon the support and active collaboration of all proletarian writers, of all comrade Communists and workers, working in the sphere of the artistic word or interested in it, and *we call upon them to join in a communal and united effort to build up proletarian literature and Communist solidarity, and to wage an unflagging struggle upon the ideological front.*

# 6

# 'Comrade Stalin has called our writers engineers of human souls'

## Andrey Alexandrovich Zhdanov: 'On Socialist Realism' (1934)

*Andrey Alexandrovich Zhdanov (1896–1948) was the government spokesman for the Union of Soviet Writers, an organization that emerged in the early 1930s to replace an earlier cultural grouping known as RAAP (the Russian Association of Proletarian Writers). The latter's attempts to impose a rigid doctrine upon the development of Soviet literature had found acceptance among neither writers nor the reading public. Unlike RAAP, the new organization favoured a broader approach to literary production, one that sought (perhaps following the theoretical initiatives of Georg Lukács) to mobilize the traditions of the Realist novel in the direction of Soviet ideology. At the first meeting of the Union, in August 1934, Zhdanov outlined the basis of this new literary aesthetic, which he called 'Socialist Realism'.*

The key to the success of Soviet literature is to be sought for in the success of socialist construction. Its growth is an expression of the successes and the achievements of our socialist system. Our literature is the youngest of all literatures of all peoples and countries. And at the same time it is the richest in ideas, the most advanced and the most revolutionary literature. Never before has there been a literature which has organized the toilers and oppressed for the struggle to abolish once and for all every kind of exploitation and the yoke of wage slavery. Never before has there been a literature which has based the subject matter of its works on the life of the working class and peasantry and their fight for socialism. Nowhere, in no country in the world, has there been a literature which has defended and upheld the principle of equal rights for the toilers of all nations, the principle of equal rights for women. There is not, there cannot be in bourgeois countries a literature which consistently smashes every kind of obscurantism, every kind of mysticism, priesthood and superstition, as our literature is doing.

Only Soviet literature, which is of one flesh and blood with socialist construction, could become, and has indeed become, such a literature – so rich in ideas, so advanced and revolutionary.

Soviet authors have already created not a few outstanding works,

**Source:** *Problems of Soviet Literature: Reports and Speeches at the First Soviet Writers' Congress*, by A. Zhdanov, Maxim Gorky, N. Bukharin, K. Radek and A. Stetsky (Moscow: Co-operative Publishing Society of Foreign Workers in the USSR, 1935), pp. 17–19 and 20–2. **Further reading:** C. V. James, *Soviet Socialist Realism: Origins and Theory* (London: Macmillan, 1973).

which correctly and truthfully depict the life of our Soviet country. Already there are several names of which we can be justly proud. Under the leadership of the Party, with the thoughtful and daily guidance of the Central Committee and the untiring support and help of Comrade Stalin, a whole army of Soviet writers has rallied around our Soviet power and the Party. And in the light of our Soviet literature's successes, we see standing out in yet sharper relief the full contrast between our system – the system of victorious socialism – and the system of dying, mouldering capitalism.

Of what can the bourgeois author write, of what can he dream, what source of inspiration can he find, whence can he borrow this inspiration, if the worker in capitalist countries is uncertain of the morrow, if he does not know whether he will have work the next day, if the peasant does not know whether he will work on his plot of ground tomorrow or whether his life will be ruined by the capitalist crisis, if the brain worker has no work today and does not know whether he will receive any tomorrow?

What can the bourgeois author write about, what source of inspiration can there be for him, when the world is being precipitated once more – if not today, then tomorrow – into the abyss of a new imperialist war?

The present state of bourgeois literature is such that it is no longer able to create great works of art. The decadence and disintegration of bourgeois literature, resulting from the collapse and decay of the capitalist system, represent a characteristic trait, a characteristic peculiarity of the state of bourgeois culture and bourgeois literature at the present time. Gone never to return are the times when bourgeois literature, reflecting the victory of the bourgeois system over feudalism, was able to create great works of the period when capitalism was flourishing. Everything now is growing stunted – themes, talents, authors, heroes.

*Zhdanov then proceeds to outline the content and style of the new socialist literature that will come to replace 'bourgeois' writing. He calls it 'socialist realism', because, avoiding the confusing experimentation of the Modernists, it will unite the solid feel of the nineteenth-century realist novel with inspiration drawn from the 'heroic' facts of socialist life.*

In our country the main heroes of works of literature are the active builders of a new life – working men and women, men and women collective farmers, Party members, business managers, engineers, members of the Young Communist League, Pioneers. Such are the chief types and the chief heroes of our Soviet literature. Our literature is impregnated with enthusiasm and the spirit of heroic deeds. It is optimistic, but not optimistic in accordance with any 'inward', animal instinct. It is optimistic in essence, because it is the literature of the rising class of the proletariat, the only progressive and advanced class. Our

Soviet literature is strong by virtue of the fact that it is serving a new cause – the cause of socialist construction.

Comrade Stalin has called our writers engineers of human souls. What does this mean? What duties does the title confer upon you?

In the first place, it means knowing life so as to be able to depict it truthfully in works of art, not to depict it in a dead, scholastic way, not simply as 'objective reality', but to depict reality in its revolutionary development.

In addition to this, the truthfulness and historical concreteness of the artistic portrayal should be combined with the ideological remoulding and education of the toiling people in the spirit of socialism. This method in *belles-lettres* and literary criticism is what we call the method of socialist realism.

Our Soviet literature is not afraid of the charge of being 'tendentious'. Yes, Soviet literature is tendentious, for in an epoch of class struggle there is not and cannot be a literature which is not class literature, not tendentious, allegedly non-political.

And I think that every one of our Soviet writers can say to any dull-witted bourgeois, to any philistine, to any bourgeois writer who may talk about our literature being tendentious: 'Yes, our Soviet literature is tendentious, and we are proud of this fact, because the aim of our tendency is to liberate the toilers, to free all mankind from the yoke of capitalist slavery.'

To be an engineer of human souls means standing with both feet firmly planted on the basis of real life. And this in its turn denotes a rupture with romanticism of the old type, which depicted a non-existent life and non-existent heroes, leading the reader away from the antagonisms and oppression of real life into a world of the impossible, into a world of utopian dreams. Our literature, which stands with both feet firmly planted on a materialist basis, cannot be hostile to romanticism, but it must be a romanticism of a new type, revolutionary romanticism. We say that socialist realism is the basic method of Soviet *belles-lettres* and literary criticism, and this presupposes that revolutionary romanticism should enter into literary creation as a component part, for the whole life of our Party, the whole life of the working class and its struggle consist in a combination of the most stern and sober practical work with a supreme spirit of heroic deeds and magnificent future prospects.

# 7

## 'The artistic dialectic of essence and appearance'

### Georg Lukács: 'It is a question of Realism' (1938)

*Georg Lukács (1885–1971) was, along with Walter Benjamin, Theodor Adorno and Ernst Bloch, one of the foremost theoreticians of Marxist aesthetics in the inter-war period. Lukács attributed to literature (and, more specifically, to the nineteenth-century Realist novel) a unique ability to penetrate the surface of society and to reconstruct the deeper laws that govern it, an ability he defended against both the functional-didactic school within the Marxist camp (which sought to see explicit politics promoted in the novel), and Modernist writers, who favoured a more fractured or impressionistic engagement with the social world. It was in furtherance of this latter debate that Lukács launched, in 1938, a critique upon certain Expressionist writers in the pages of the émigré journal* The Word (Das Wort). *It provided him with the occasion to formulate, once again, his support for the Realist aesthetic.*

It is, of course, self-evident that without abstraction there can be no art; for otherwise, how could art ever produce generalizations? But the process of abstraction must, like any activity, have a sense of direction; and that is precisely what is at issue in this debate. Every major Realist writer works through his experiences (even making use of the process of abstraction), in order to get right down to the laws governing objective reality, seeking to uncover those deeper, hidden, mediated, not immediately perceptible relationships that constitute social reality. Since these relationships do not lie on the surface, and since those deeper laws only manifest themselves in complex and irregular ways, as trends, the major Realist writers are faced with an enormous task that is both artistic and ideological in nature. Firstly, they must intellectually uncover and then artistically shape these relationships; and, secondly, and this is inseparable from the first task, they must conceal in their art the relationships that they have just discovered, in the process going beyond pure abstraction. Out of this *two-fold* labour arises a new artistically formed insight into the realm of pure immediacy, into the shaped surface of reality which, although it permits the essence of life to *shine through* (something that does not happen in real life), it nevertheless comes across

**Source:** *Das Wort*, 6 (1938), pp. 121–2, 129–30 and 136–7. **Standard translation:** 'Realism in the balance', translated by Rodney Livingstone, in *Aesthetics and Politics*, Afterword by Fredric Jameson; translation editor Ronald Taylor (London: Verso, 1977), pp. 28–59. **Further reading:** Eugene Lunn, *Marxism and Modernism: An Historical Study of Lukács, Brecht, Benjamin, and Adorno* (Berkeley: University of California Press, 1982), pp. 75–90.

with a sense of immediacy, as life as it really is. And the resulting image is of the entirety of the surface of life, with all its social determinants, which is not simply a subjectively perceived and exaggerated moment, abstracted from the complex of social totality.

It is this that constitutes *the artistic dialectic of essence and appearance*. The richer, the more diverse, and the more 'cunning' (as Lenin pointed out) this dialectic is, the more firmly is it able to grasp the vital contradictions of life and society, and the greater and more penetrating will its Realism be.

In contrast to this, what does it mean to talk of 'abstracting from life'? If the surface of life is experienced only in an unmediated way, then it is bound to appear opaque, fragmented, chaotic and incomprehensible, and must remain *fixed as such*, if the writer consciously or otherwise excludes and ignores those objective mediations which alone permit an intellectual penetration of reality. Reality never ceases moving. Intellectual and artistic activity must move either *towards* or *away* from it.

> *Lukács then spells out the defining features of the great Realist novel, emphasizing its superiority over other, more experimental forms of narrative. Writers who work within the former mode represent a genuine Avant-Garde, which is far more valuable than the superficial 'Avant-Garde' of the Modernists.*

Since Realist writers, from the creators of Don Quixote and Oblomov through to the Realists of our days, start from the creation of types, they must strive to seek out those features of people, and their relationships, and the situations in which people act, which are *permanent*, and which determine over long periods the objective tendencies of society, indeed the tendencies of humanity as a whole.

*Such writers form a genuine ideological Avant-Garde*, for they are able to capture those vital but not immediately obvious tendencies hidden within objective reality, and in such a deep and true fashion that their depictions are often later confirmed by subsequent events. And this doesn't happen in the simple way that a successful photograph mirrors the original; it takes place more as the expression of a complex and rich understanding of reality, as a reflection of those tendencies that had remained hidden, and had only fully emerged at a later point in their development, where they could be grasped by all. Great Realism, therefore, does not depict those aspects of social reality which are evident to the senses, but those more permanent and hence objectively more significant aspects, i.e. those that deal with mankind in its very complex relations with reality, and indeed with the *permanent* aspects within this great complexity. Over and above this, it recognises and depicts tendencies which at the time of their formation only existed in embryonic form, and were unable to develop in all of their objective and subjective human and social potential. *To grasp and give form to such tendencies is precisely the great historical mission of a real*

*Avant-Garde.* Whether a writer really belongs to the Avant-Garde is something that only history can reveal, by confirming that he was able to *correctly* recognise the *essential* aspects of his time, the historical trends, the social relevance of certain people, and to portray them in an effective and lasting fashion. Hopefully, after what has already been said, no further argument is required to prove that a real Avant-Garde can only be made up out of *major Realist writers.*

It is, then not a question of how sincerely someone subjectively feels that he belongs to the Avant-Garde, or how eager one is to march at the forefront of artistic development, or even being the first to discover some brilliant formal technique. What matters is the social and human content of Avant-Garde work, of the breadth, depth and truth of the ideas that have been 'prophetically' anticipated.

> *It is, above all, the universality of the Realist novel, the fact that, unlike 'Avant-Garde' writing (and Lukács targets James Joyce here), it responds to the needs of a broad readership, that constitutes its politically and socially civilizing mission. Precisely because its appeal is so broad, Realist literature alone is capable of mobilizing the 'political humanism' that is required if the Popular Front (a broad-based grouping of communist and other left-wing groups founded in a number of European countries after 1933) is to be successful in its struggle against fascism.*

Only when one views the great past and present masterpieces of Realism *as a whole*, and learns from them, and takes pains to make them accessible and comprehensible to a reading public, will the topical, cultural and political value of the great Realist tradition become evident: its inexhaustible diversity, which stands in contrast to the – at very best – tiny single track of the Avant-Garde. Cervantes and Shakespeare, Balzac and Tolstoy, Grimmelshausen and Gottfried Keller, Gorky, Thomas and Heinrich Mann are read by readers from the broad mass of the people, who, in a multitude of ways, bring to bear their own personal experiences in reading this literature. The broad and lasting popularity of great Realist literature rests precisely on this fact: the possibility of access is open – one might say – through an infinite number of doors. The wealth of its subject matter, its profound and accurate portrayal of those permanent, essential features of human life, is what produces the great progressive influence of these master works. In reading this literature, people clarify in the process their own experiences and knowledge of life, expand their human and social horizons, and through a living form of humanism are prepared to embrace the political battle-cry of the Popular Front, and to comprehend its political humanism. Through that understanding for the great progressive and democratic stages in human history, which is transmitted through Realist art, fertile ground is laid in the soul of the broad masses for the revolutionary democracy that is represented by the Popular Front. The deeper anti-fascist agitational literature is rooted in this soil, the more deeply grounded will be the values to admire and those to hate – and the greater will be its resonance amongst the people.

It is a very narrow doorway that leads to Joyce and the other representatives of the 'Avant-Garde': one must have a certain 'knack' to understand at all what they are up to. And whilst with the great Realists even a partial access produces a rich yield in human terms, from 'Avant-Garde' literature the broad masses of the people are capable of learning absolutely nothing. Precisely because reality and life are missing in this literature, it imposes upon its readers a narrow and subjective concept of life (just as, in political circles, secretarians do). Realism, by contrast, due to the wealth of its created life, answers the questions that readers themselves have always asked – answers to life, and the questions that life itself has posed! Understanding the art of the 'Avant-Garde' is such an arduous and difficult experience, however, and produces such subjective, twisted and unintelligible resonances that the ordinary person finds it impossible to translate them back into the language of his own experiences.

Living contact with the life of the people, the progressive development of the masses' own experience – this is the great social mission of literature.

8

---

# 'To analyse the disjunctions within the surface structure of the world'

## Ernst Bloch: 'Discussing Expressionism' (1938)

*Ernst Bloch (1885–1977) was one of the foremost Marxist critics of the age, analysing in his major work,* Heritage of These Times *(1934), the methods by which fascism sought to shore up the crisis within late capitalism by exploiting popular sentiment for the culture of the past. Bloch's Marxism was, like that of his friend and colleague Walter Benjamin, informed by a certain spiritual redeemerism (part of Bloch's Jewish heritage), and by an appreciation of the aesthetically liberating moment within the European Avant-Garde. This appreciation formed the basis of*

**Source:** Ernst Bloch, 'Diskussionen über Expressionismus', in *Vom Hasard zur Katastrophe: Politische Aufsätze aus den Jahren 1934–1939* (Frankfurt am Main: Suhrkamp, 1972), pp. 366–77. **Standard translation:** 'Discussing Expressionism', translated by Rodney Livingstone, in *Aesthetics and Politics*, Afterword by Fredric Jameson; translation editor Ronald Taylor (London: Verso, 1977), pp. 16–27. **Further reading:** Wayne Hudson, *The Marxist Philosophy of Ernst Bloch* (London: Macmillan, 1982).

*his defence of German Expressionism against Georg Lukács (and other Party critics, such as Bernhard Ziegler), who could see in Expressionist art and literature only fragmentation and decadence. But these were, as Bloch argues in the following extract from an important essay of 1938, precisely those features of a decaying capitalist society that needed to be brought to the surface, and not displaced by desiderata drawn from the norms of 'classical' art.*

This is not the place to analyse this issue in detail: it is exactly because it is so important that it requires the most thorough investigation; but this would involve a full discussion of the dialectical-materialist theory of reflection. But this much we can say here: Lukács works with a notion of reality as something that is fully closed and integrated, a notion which, certainly, has no place for the subjective factor evident in Idealism, but which nevertheless retains that assumption of a closed 'Totality'. This is a concept that has always thrived best in Idealist systems, and most notably in classical German philosophy. Whether reality is like this is precisely the question: if it is then Expressionist experiments with disruptive and interpolative techniques, as well as recent work with montage and other fragmenting devices, must certainly be judged as trivial games. But perhaps Lukács's reality, that cohesively mediated system of total relationships, is not so objective at all. Perhaps Lukács's reality possesses in itself features of those systems of classical philosophy. Perhaps genuine reality does include disruption. Because Lukács works with a concept of reality as objective and closed, he denounces any artistic attempt, in this case Expressionism, to burst asunder any image of the world, even that of capitalism. For that reason, he sees in those artistic works that seek to analyse the disjunctions within the surface structure of the world, and to discover anything new in its rifts, purely subjective dislocation. He thereby equates these experiments with fragmentation with the condition of decadence.

At this point in his analysis, Lukács's critical insight leaves him entirely. Certainly, the Expressionists took advantage of the fact that advanced bourgeois society was in a state of decline, and sought even to advance this decline. Lukács disparages them because 'they colluded in the ideological decline of the imperialist bourgeoisie, without offering either criticism or opposition, indeed, were at times their engineers'. But, in the first place, this crude notion of 'collusion' contains little truth; Lukács himself recognized that Expressionism was 'ideologically a not inconsiderable component of the anti-war movement'. Moreover, concerning 'collusion' in a productive sense, the actual encouragement of *cultural* decadence: is there not a dialectical relationship between growth and decay? Are not confusion, immaturity and incomprehension always, and at all times, an essential part of bourgeois decadence? Might they not – contrary to Lukács's simplistic and certainly unrevolutionary interpretation – belong to the transition from the old world to the new? Or at least be a part of the struggle involved in this transition? These questions can only be answered by a detailed examination of specific works, and not by voicing opinionated judgements made in advance. The Expressionists were indeed the 'engineers' of cultural decline: would it have been better had they been doctors ministering at the sickbed of capitalism? Should they have sought to put together again the surface structure of the world (somewhat as the exponents of the New Objectivity [*Neue Sachlichkeit*] and Neo-Classicism have tried to do), instead of continuing with their attempts at demolition? Ziegler even reproached the Expressionists with 'subversion of subversion', a double fault, then, without realizing in his hatred that a plus results from this equation. He entirely fails to understand the importance of the demise of Neo-Classicism. He is even less able to understand those strange phenomena that emerged when the superficial world collapsed, to say nothing of the issue of montage. To him this is all 'junk hastily stuck together', and something for which he cannot forgive the fascists, although they also don't want any of it, and share his opinion entirely. Expressionism has its importance in exactly that area that Ziegler condemns; it has destroyed pedantry and academicism, to which artistic values had been reduced. Instead of those never-ending 'formal analyses' of *objets d'art*, it has moved mankind and its concerns into the centre of the picture, and provided it with the greatest degree of genuine self-expression.

> In defence of his case, Bloch goes into greater detail regarding the achievements of Expressionism, whose vitality and energetic protection of the human sphere is contrasted with the tired and hackneyed aesthetic of a regurgitated neo-Classicism, a term that Bloch almost certainly uses as synonymous with Socialist Realism.

The most important thing is this: that Expressionism, for all the pleasure that it took in 'barbaric art', had as its goal the humane; it embraced everything human, and the forms of expression of its unknown centre. Quite apart from their pacifism, proofs of that are provided by the caricatures the Expressionists produced and their use of industrial imagery. The word 'mankind' [*Mensch*] was used in that period as frequently as its opposite [*Unmensch*, or racial inferior] is used today by the Nazis. It was also misused: the concept 'resolute humanity' could be heard everywhere, in anthologies with titles like *The Dawning of Mankind* and *Friends of Mankind*: clichéd categories, but certainly not pre-fascist ones. Sincerely revolutionary, lucidly humanist materialism has a good reason to reject this empty terminology; no one expects it to take Expressionism as a role model or to accept it as its 'precursor'. But there is also no reason to drum up interest again in Neo-Classicism by renewing an outmoded fight with an Expressionism that has long since lost its legitimacy. Even if an artistic movement is not a precursor of anything, it might still – in its power of expression and its subsequent development – have more to offer young artists than Classicism. For although Classicism is certainly a cultural form, it is one that has become distant from life, distilled to abstraction: culture formed without temperament.

9

---

## *'Reality is social'*

### Henri Barbusse: *Zola* (1932)

*Henri Barbusse (1873–1935) wrote the intriguing existential-erotic novel* Hell *(1908), but he did not come to prominence until the publication of the pacifist war novel,* Under Fire *(1916). Barbusse was one of the founding members of the 'Clarté' socialist movement in 1919, but he soon went his own way into a brand of militant socialism after that time. His study of Zola, written in that crucial year of 1932 (when fascism was on the point of triumph in Germany and elsewhere), is both a passionate study of the great committed Naturalist novelist, and a plea to fellow-writers to countenance radical solutions to the crisis of capitalism.*

Zola's life sends out a clear message to us, in a period in which we are witnessing the degeneration of a society, the death-throes of an international empire.

Reality is social. Social phenomena occupy the entire stage. Just as during the war, the backdrop entirely dominates the characters. Harsh reality is here, the war is here: definitive crises, economic crises, which have been seen coming for ages by men of genius, seen coming for years by men of good sense who have tried, as best as they could, to shout the news from the rooftops.

What drama could so demand our attention other than this total drama that is also a personal one. It affects us, the 'intellectual workers', who are at the same time both actors in, and photographers of the age, and whose trade it is to talk aloud. What, from now on, can survive for us of those theories of the divine right of the poet, of the dictatorship of beauty, or even of art as a means of aristocratic or common distraction, as a means of escape and flight?

---

**Source:** Henri Barbusse, *Zola* (Paris: Gallimard, 1932), pp. 284–5, 289–90 and 291–3. **Standard translation:** Henri Barbusse, *Zola*, translated from the French by Mary Balairdie Green (London: Dent & Sons, 1932). **Further reading:** Frank Field, *Three French Writers and the Great War: Studies in the Rise of Communism and Fascism* (Cambridge: Cambridge University Press, 1975), pp. 19–78.

The worth of a person, irrespective of whom he might be, lies entirely in his social utility. The only question we can ask these days of the man in the street is: 'What use is he?' In the same way, this is the first question that prompts itself when we stand in front of a work of art: what use is it? What relevance does it have to the misfortunes and hopes of this age?

But that smug old dogma of art for art's sake is not dead. Indeed, it would be more accurate to say that it is being revived. It continues to befuddle the minds of writers, for, like all antiquated dogmas, it has assumed attenuated and refined forms, which appear honourable. It continues to exist in its entirety when it limits itself by excluding the political as an element of contemporary life, that is to say by rejecting the most effective and vital component in universal action. (The economic fact at the base, and the political fact at the end – such is historical reality.)

To serve something, to be useful to the community of mankind, other than by blessing it with beauty or by wasting its time in games, this is the first duty, which, in the present artistic chaos, will distinguish the new men.

Moreover, that is a task that has been set for us by that great reality, throbbing like a machine, in front of which we now find ourselves. We are not free to avoid it.

We are confronted by the problem that Zola, by dint of his entire strength, finally came to overcome, and we are in the presence of precisely the same body of opposition, but our situation is far more tragic. The new men have less leisure, more immediate exigencies, and obligations that require all their strength.

*As Barbusse argues, writers have come to learn through hard experience that they are a part of history. But it is also important that they recognize that it is social classes which make history, not individuals.*

Individual dramas are like playthings in the collective drama. It is necessary to repeat this: even when one is considering a particular fact, one must, in order to substantiate its truth, situate it within the collective reality, the collective reality which transforms the face of things and in which the very destiny of the human species is played out.

The system of individual enrichment that has run the world until now has only succeeded in encompassing every country with an abyss. War, in all its forms, is gathering on every frontier. Tariffs, armaments, money speculation, fascism (the terrorist and police phase of imperialism in crisis), a propaganda of parodies and lies to obfuscate and throw into confusion the social question through big words, and an illusionary reformism: all maintain the exploitation of man by man. Capitalism = egotism, nationalism, anarchy, war, self-destruction.

Is it possible to write without describing and explaining, even partially, contemporary society (describe and explain, those are the same things for the honest artist), without showing the degeneration of bourgeois society, the decadence of bourgeois government, the barbarous and devastating use it has made of civilization, its powerlessness to resist the waves of economic catastrophes, and the sort of deluge towards which we are being driven? And without showing that all the possibilities for rectification and regeneration lie with the great human masses, who up to now have been held in check? Zola wrote in his notebook (and this was more than thirty years ago): 'Our only hope lies with the people.' Let us take our place in that great positive and materialist tradition by repeating, more emphatically and more clearly, the words of the last of our grand masters: 'Hope lies only with the international proletariat and its organization.'

All around us, literature is seeking a true direction. It will find it only by joining the path taken by the man that we have been coming closer to, and moving beyond that point where he stopped when he died, and according to the fine curve he traced by making literature a thing of the earth. From a partial realism to a partial realism, we will arrive at a comprehensive realism, which we must make our responsibility. The art built upon these immense foundations, which logically belong to it, will be truly social, and truly revolutionary.

*As Barbusse contends, the era of 'fashionable literature', of 'Kodak-like, stenographic super-impressionism, acrostics and irony', is gone. The tasks of the future require a more decisive mentality.*

The time for approximation is past. What we now need is a clear goal that will accord with the ultimatum of the universal future. The primitive efforts of the Realists and the Naturalists had been to make the novel an ally of science, and independent of bourgeois morality (at that time, this emancipation involved a struggle). The task now is to make the novel an ally of a scientific morality as rigorous as the metrical system.

I am speaking here purely from the point of view of literature, and in my role as a writer within that literature. I am not trying to make our artistic credo dependent upon a political one. But penetrating to the very depths of reality, in whatever aspect it manifests itself, necessarily leads to the same conclusions. And all who produce works of positive truth work along parallel lines.

We cannot but work along parallel lines to the revolutionary political parties, not because we obey some preordained dogma, but because we are depicting the same precise and luminous image of reality. Not dependence, but parallelism. It is exactly the same in politics as it is in science. The thinker obeys only himself. He is not our servant, and we are not his. But, because of the focus, the illumination of his method, his steady penetration of nature, and his struggle against superstition and idolatry, he works exactly in the same sense as we do, and this makes him, like us, a revolutionary. It is the thinker who speaks as a thinker through the mouth of Dr Veressaiev, when he exclaims, seeing the heroic proletarian nailed to his cross: 'There does not exist a bandage that can mend the wounds as long as the nails are there!'

Yes, literature must remain literature. We agree. The artist must live his life. He must attain and express human nature and emotion. We are certainly compelled to admit that his temperament and his talent bring to his living construction of the world supra-technical qualities that are difficult to fathom. But through his acute awareness of the contemporary society that he depicts, either in its entirety or in part, he serves and must serve the same cause as those political movements of emancipation. The true thinker, the writer of perception, and the true socialist are separated only by the law of the division of labour.

## 10

# 'To break down the old division within bourgeois realism'

### Ralph Fox: *The Novel and the People* (1937)

*Ralph Fox (1900–36), an active member of the British Communist Party in the 1920s and 1930s, voiced in his novels (*Storming Heaven, *1928), and in various essays, a political line that was significantly further to the left than that pursued by his contemporaries among the Auden movement. His experiences in Russia, in the early days of the new government (and remembered in his autobiography,* People of the Steppes, *1925), reveal a desire for active involvement in politics that was eventually to lead to his death, fighting for the Republican cause in Spain, in 1936. Before this involvement, however, he penned his only full-length work of literary criticism,* The Novel and the People, *in which he elaborated his own humanistically informed English version of Socialist Realism.*

Man today is compelled to fight against the objective, external horrors accompanying the collapse of our social system, against Fascism, against war, unemployment, the decay of agriculture, against the domination of the machine, but he has to fight also against the subjective reflection of all these things in his own mind. He must fight to change the world, to

**Source:** Ralph Fox, *The Novel and the People* (London: Lawrence & Wishart, 1979), pp. 104–6 and 109–11. **Further reading:** Valentine Cunningham, *British Writers of the Thirties* (Oxford: Oxford University Press, 1988).

rescue civilisation, and he must fight also against the anarchy of capitalism in the human spirit.

It is in this dual struggle, each side of which in turn influences and is influenced by the other, that the end of the old and artificial division between subjective and objective realism will come. We shall no longer have the old naturalistic realism, no longer the novel of endless analysis and intuition, but a new realism in which the two find their proper relationship to one another. Certainly, the modern realists, the heirs of Zola and of Maupassant, have felt the inadequacy of the method of their masters. But lack of dialectic, of a philosophy which enables them really to understand and to perceive the world, has led them along the false trail of supplementing that naturalism by a creaking, artificial symbolism. This is the gravest fault of those endless, powerful, but unsatisfactory works of Jules Romains and Céline.

How is it possible to make this combination, to break down the old division within bourgeois realism? First of all by restoring the historical view which was the basis of the classical English novel. Here let me emphasise that this does not imply merely the need for plot and narrative, for it is living man with whom we are concerned, and not merely the external circumstances in which man has his being. This is the mistake made by many Socialist novelists who have used all their talent and energy to depict a strike, a social movement, the construction of Socialism, a revolution or a civil war, without considering that what is supremely important is not the social background, but man himself in his full development against that background. Epic man is man in whom no division any longer occurs between himself and his sphere of practical activity. He lives and changes life. Man creates himself.

It is only the fairest self-criticism to acknowledge that neither the Soviet novel nor the novels of Western revolutionary writers have yet succeeded in fully expressing this, with a few rare exceptions. There is the best of excuses. The events themselves, the Russian civil war, the construction of socialist industry, the revolution in the life of the peasant, the fight against exploitation and the defence of the working class against Fascism, all these things appear so heroic, so impressive, that the writer feels that by merely writing them down the effect must be overwhelming. Indeed, it is often of the greatest emotional significance, but an emotional significance which, nevertheless, is only that of first-class journalism. The writers do not add thereby to our knowledge of man, or really extend our consciousness and sensibility.

*Drawing upon the appreciative comments made by Marx and Engels regarding the great works of world literature and the (at least, implicitly) progressive values they embody, Fox makes a plea that the committed writer should seek to represent in his or her work a broader humanistic understanding of people and society.*

It is not the author's business to preach, but to give a real, historical picture of life. It is only too easy to substitute lay figures for men and women, sets of opinions for flesh and blood, 'heroes' and 'villains' in the abstract for real people tortured by doubts, old allegiances, traditions and loyalties, but to do this is not to write a novel. Speeches mean nothing if one cannot understand all the processes of life behind any speech. Certainly, characters may have, and should have, political opinions, provided they are their own and not the author's. Even though in some cases a character's opinions coincide with those of the author, they should be expressed with the voice of the character, and this in turn implies that the character must possess his own individual voice, his personal history.

A revolutionary writer is a party writer, his outlook is that of the class which is struggling to create a new social order, all the more reason therefore to demand from him the widest sweep of imagination, the utmost creative power. He fulfils his party mission by his work in creating a new literature, free from the anarchist individualism of the bourgeoisie in its period of decay, and not by substituting slogans of the party on this or that question of the day for the real picture of the world his outlook demands from him. He will be unable to make that picture a true one unless he is truly a Marxist, a dialectician with a finished philosophical outlook. Or, as Fielding would have put it, unless he has made a real effort to master the learning of his time.

Such a view of the artist implies that he excludes nothing from his perception of life. Proletarian literature is still very young, less than ten years old outside of the Soviet Union, and the reproach has often been made that, at least in capitalist countries, it has tended to deal only with certain men and with limited aspects of these men. The strike-leader, the capitalist 'boss', the intellectual seeking a new faith, beyond these, it is suggested, the new writers have not ventured far, and they have succeeded only to a slight extent in showing us even these characters as men of flesh and blood. The reproach is to some extent justified, though it ignores the epic stories of Malraux, the two novels of Ralph Bates, the work of John Dos Passos and Erskine Caldwell. Yet there is no human character, no emotion, no conflict of personalities outside the scope of the revolutionary novelist. Indeed, he alone is able to create the hero of our times, the complete picture of modern life, because only he is able to perceive the truth of that life. Yes, there have been few novels by revolutionaries free of those faults criticised by Marx and Engels. Much has yet to be done before the new literature is able to fulfil its tasks, and it will always remain true that you must have great novelists before you get great novels. On the other hand, the sceptic would do well to remember that in the grim battle of ideas in the world of to-day, the majority of the best of the writers of the bourgeoisie have begun to move sharply to the Left and that this movement has brought them into contact with declaredly revolutionary writers. From this contact we may be justified in hoping there will come the fertilisation of genius which we are seeking, for it should have been sufficiently clear in this essay that the revolutionary both accepts all that is vital and hopeful in the heritage of the past, and rejects nothing in the present which can be used to build the future.

11

## 'Poetry is a manufacture'

### Vladimir Mayakovsky: *How Are Verses Made?* (1926)

*Vladimir Mayakovsky (1883–1930) was the supreme poet, dramatist and theoretician of Russian Futurism, a movement that politicized itself after the Revolution in the form of the creation of the Left Front. In all he did (from working as a painter and cartoonist in the Russian Telegraph Agency through to his agitational theatre), Mayakovsky sought to demystify the high-cultural aura that surrounded art and literature, seeking to open up these areas to popular access by making visible common artistic techniques and skills that could be learned by all. Applying this service to poetry, Mayakovsky wrote his most extended treatise,* How Are Verses Made? *In the concluding pages to this work, he drew up a practical guide for the would-be poet.*

A man who has just got hold of a pen for the first time, and wants to write poetry after a week, won't find my book much use.

My book will be useful to a man who, despite all the obstacles, wants to be a poet; a man who, knowing that poetry is one of the most difficult things to manufacture, wants to master and to pass on some of what seem the most mysterious techniques of this productive process.

Some conclusions:

1 Poetry is a manufacture. A very difficult, very complex kind, but a manufacture.
2 Instruction in poetical work doesn't consist of the study of already fixed and delimited models of poetical works, but a study of the procedures of manufacture, a study that helps us to make new things.

**Source:** Vladimir Mayakovsky, *How Are Verses Made?* translated from the Russian by G. M. Hyde (London: Jonathan Cape, 1970), pp. 55–8. **Further reading:** Victor Terras, *Vladimir Mayakovsky* (Boston: Twayne, 1983).

3 Innovation, innovation in materials and methods, is obligatory for every poetical composition.

4 The work of the verse-maker must be carried on daily, to perfect his craft, and to lay in poetical supplies.

5 A good notebook and an understanding of how to make use of it are more important than knowing how to write faultlessly in worn-out metres.

6 Don't set in motion a huge poetry factory just to make poetic cigarette lighters. You must renounce the uneconomical production of poetical trifles. Reach for your pen only when there is no other way of saying something except verse. You must work up things you've prepared only when you feel a clear social command.

7 To understand the social command accurately, a poet must be in the middle of things and events. A knowledge of theoretical economics, a knowledge of the realities of everyday life, an immersion in the scientific study of history are for the poet, in the very fundamentals of his work, more important than scholarly textbooks by idealist professors who worship the past.

8 To fulfil the social command as well as possible you must be in the vanguard of your class, and carry on the struggle, along with your class, on all fronts. You must smash to smithereens the myth of an apolitical art. This old myth is appearing again now in a new form under cover of twaddle about 'broad epic canvases' (first epic, then objective, and in the end politically uncommitted), or about the 'grand style' (first grand, then elevated, and in the end celestial) and so on and so forth.

9 Only by approaching art as a manufacture can you eliminate chance, arbitrariness of taste and subjectivity of values. Only by regarding it as a manufacture can you get the different aspects of literary works in perspective: poems, and reports by workers' and peasants' journalists. Instead of mystically pondering a poetic theme you will have the power to tackle a pressing problem with accuracy, by means of poetic tariffs and standards.

10 You mustn't make the manufacturing, the socalled technical process, an end in itself. But it *is* this process of manufacture that makes the poetic work fit for use. It's the difference just in these methods of production that marks the difference between poets, and only a knowledge, a mastery, an accumulation of the widest possible range of varied literary devices makes a man a professional writer.

11 The everyday circumstances of poetry have as much influence on the composition of a real work of art as other factors do. The word 'Bohemian' has become a term of opprobrium describing every artistic-Philistine way of life. Unfortunately war has often been waged on the word 'Bohemian', and only on the word. But what remains

actively with us is the individualist and careerist atmosphere of the old literary world, the petty interests of malevolent coteries, mutual back-scratching; and the word 'poetical' has come to mean 'lax', 'a bit drunk', 'debauched' and so on. Even the way a poet dresses and the way he talks to his wife at home has to be different, and entirely dictated by the kind of poetry he writes.

12  We, the poets of the Left Front, never claim that we alone possess the secrets of poetical creativity. But we are the only ones who want to lay these secrets open, the only ones who don't want to surround the creative process with a catchpenny religio–artistic aura of sanctity.

My undertaking here is the feeble undertaking of just one man, making use of the theoretical work of my fellow students of literature.

These students of literature must bring their work to bear on contemporary material and give their help freely to the poetry of the future.

But that is not enough.

The organs of mass education must shake the teaching of the old aesthetics to its very foundation.

12

---

# 'The theatre must alienate everything that it depicts'

## Bertolt Brecht, *A Short Organum for the Theatre* (1949)

*Bertolt Brecht (1898–1956) was not only one of the foremost writers of political drama in the inter-war years (see, for example,* The Measures Taken *(1930) and* St Joan of the Stockyards *(1932)); he was also its most sophisticated theoretician. Brecht wished to create an 'epic theatre', a theatre that would remain alive to the political dynamics of history and historical change. For this to be a success, a break had to be effected with traditional drama (Brecht called it 'Aristotelian'), which tended to promote a static view of human character with which the audience was encouraged, in an unthinking way, to empathize. As Brecht explained in his* Organum *(a work that extends the insights of his earlier notes to the music drama,* Rise and Fall of the City of Mahagonny, *1930), his goal was to develop a new*

---

**Source:** *Brecht on Theatre: The Development of an Aesthetic*, edited and translated by John Willett (New York: Hill & Wang, 1964), pp. 179–80, 191–3. **Further reading:** Keith A. Dickson, *Towards Utopia: A Study of Brecht* (Oxford: Clarendon Press, 1978), pp. 225–53.

*dramaturgy for the stage, one founded on specific techniques that would 'alienate' the audience from such easy identifications, and break up their passive positions as simple consumers of the theatrical experience.*

The following sets out to define an aesthetic drawn from a particular kind of theatrical performance which has been worked out in practice over the past few decades. In the theoretical statements, excursions, technical indications occasionally published in the form of notes to the writer's plays, aesthetics have only been touched on casually and with comparative lack of interest. There you saw a particular species of theatre extending or contracting its social functions, perfecting or sifting its artistic methods and establishing or maintaining its aesthetics – if the question arose – by rejecting or converting to its own use the dominant conventions of morality or taste according to its tactical needs. This theatre justified its inclination to social commitment by pointing to the social commitment in universally accepted works of art, which only fail to strike the eye because it was the accepted commitment. As for the products of our own time, it held that their lack of any worthwhile content was a sign of decadence: it accused these entertainment emporiums of having degenerated into branches of the bourgeois narcotics business. The stage's inaccurate representations of our social life, including those classed as so-called Naturalism, led it to call for scientifically exact representations; the tasteless rehashing of empty visual or spiritual palliatives, for the noble logic of the multiplication table. The cult of beauty, conducted with hostility towards learning and contempt for the useful, was dismissed by it as itself contemptible, especially as nothing beautiful resulted. The battle was for a theatre fit for the scientific age, and where its planners found it too hard to borrow or steal from the armoury of aesthetic concepts enough weapons to defend themselves against the aesthetics of the Press they simply threatened 'to transform the means of enjoyment into an instrument of instruction, and to convert certain amusement establishments into organs of mass communication' ('Notes to the opera *Mahagonny*'): i.e. to emigrate from the realm of the merely enjoyable. Aesthetics, that heirloom of a by now depraved and parasitic class, was in such a lamentable state that a theatre would certainly have gained both in reputation and in elbowroom if it had rechristened itself thaëter. And yet what we achieved in the way of theatre for a scientific age was not science but theatre, and the accumulated innovations worked out during the Nazi period and the war – when practical demonstration was impossible – compel some attempt to set this species of theatre in its aesthetic background, or anyhow to sketch for it the outlines of a conceivable aesthetic. To explain the theory of theatrical alienation except within an aesthetic framework would be impossibly awkward.

*Brecht goes on to outline the premises of this new 'scientific' dramaturgy, which will combine entertainment and didacticism. The emotive must not be ignored but be put into the service of rational (read political) aims. As Brecht explains, 'We need a type of theatre that not only evokes those feelings, insights and impulses that are possible within any given historical field of human relations in which the action takes place, but employs and gives rise to those thoughts and feelings which themselves play a role in the changing of this field.' One device, in particular, will make these changes possible: the famous alienation device, which distances the audience from the events depicted, thus forcing a cognitive instead of a purely emotive response. Brecht goes on (in sections 42 through to 46 of the* Organum*) to explain what this device is, and how it came into existence.*

The kind of acting which was tried out at the Schiffbauerdamm Theater in Berlin between the First and Second World Wars, with the object of producing such images, is based on the 'alienation effect' (A-effect). A representation that alienates is one which allows us to recognize its subject, but at the same time makes it seem unfamiliar. The classical and medieval theatre alienated its characters by making them wear human or animal masks; the Asiatic theatre even today uses musical and pantomimic A-effects. Such devices were certainly a barrier to empathy, and yet this technique owed more, not less, to hypnotic suggestion than do those by which empathy is achieved. The social aims of these old devices were entirely different from our own.

The old A-effects quite remove the object represented from the spectator's grasp, turning it into something that cannot be altered; the new are not odd in themselves, though the unscientific eye stamps anything strange as odd. The new alienations are only designed to free socially-conditioned phenomena from that stamp of familiarity which protects them against our grasp today.

For it seems impossible to alter what has long not been altered. We are always coming on things that are too obvious for us to bother to understand them. What men experience among themselves they think of as 'the' human experience. A child, living in a world of old men, learns how things work there. He knows the run of things before he can walk. If anyone is bold enough to want something further, he only wants to have it as an exception. Even if he realizes that the arrangements made for him by 'Providence' are only what has been provided by society he is bound to see society, that vast collection of beings like himself, as a whole that is greater than the sum of its parts and therefore not in any way to be influenced. Moreover, he would be used to things that could not be influenced; and who mistrusts what he is used to? To transform himself from general passive acceptance to a corresponding state of suspicious inquiry he would need to develop that detached eye with which the great Galileo observed a swinging chandelier. He was amazed by this pendulum motion, as if he had not expected it and could not understand its occurring, and this enabled him to come on the rules by which it was governed. Here is the outlook, disconcerting but fruitful, which the theatre must provoke with its representations of human social life. It must amaze its public, and this can be achieved by a technique of alienating the familiar.

This technique allows the theatre to make use in its representations of the new social scientific method known as dialectical materialism. In order to unearth society's laws of motion this method treats social situations as processes, and traces out all their inconsistencies. It regards nothing as existing except in so far as it changes, in other words is in disharmony with itself. This also goes for those human feelings, opinions and attitudes through which at any time the form of men's life together finds its expression.

Our own period, which is transforming nature in so many and different ways, takes pleasure in understanding things so that we can interfere. There is a great deal to man, we say; so a great deal can be made out of him. He does not have to stay the way he is now, nor does he have to be seen only as he is now, but also as he might become. We must not start with him; we must start on him. This means, however, that I must not simply set myself in his place, but must set myself facing him, to represent us all. That is why the theatre must alienate what it shows.

13

---

# 'We live in an age of mistaken democracy'

## D. H. Lawrence: Foreword to *Fantasia of the Unconscious* (1923)

*David Herbert Lawrence (1885–1930) broke with taboos, social and sexual, in important novels such as* Sons and Lovers *(1913),* Women in Love *(1920) and, most notably,* Lady Chatterley's Lover *(1928). But Lawrence's politics, although not so publicly expressed, were equally iconoclastic, merging as they did (see, for example,* Kangaroo, *1923) with that growing movement of reaction against parliamentary government, indeed against the entire mass democratic tradition, which set in after the First World War, a war that had caused many to be cynical about the liberal-humanistic values which were supposed to underpin that tradition. Lawrence's quest for an alternative source of intellectual and moral legitimacy took him to diverse*

---

**Source:** D. H. Lawrence, *Fantasia of the Unconscious* and *Psychoanalysis and the Unconscious* (London: Heinemann, 1961), pp. 11–12, 14 and 15–16. **Further reading:** John R. Harrison, *The Reactionaries: A Study of the Anti-Democratic Intelligentsia* (New York: Schocken Books, 1967), pp. 163–89.

*atavistic and mythological sources, which, on the surface, do not appear to possess any*
*political significance. But informing them all is Lawrence's sense of the redundancy of*
*the Western rational-scientific heritage, and the political culture that it has spawned.*
*This constellation of alternative values – vitalistic, impatiently individualistic,*
*irrationalist and uncompromisingly elitist – finds characteristically polemical*
*expression in the Foreword to his* Fantasia of the Unconscious.

The present book is a continuation from *Psychoanalysis and the Unconscious.*
The generality of readers had better just leave it alone. The generality of
critics likewise. I really don't want to convince anybody. It is quite in
opposition to my whole nature. I don't intend my books for the
generality of readers. I count it a mistake of our mistaken democracy that
every man who can read print is allowed to believe that he can read all
that is printed. I count it a misfortune that serious books are exposed in
the public market, like slaves exposed naked for sale. But there we are,
since we live in an age of mistaken democracy, we must go through with
it.

I warn the generality of readers, that this present book will seem to
them only a rather more revolting mass of wordy nonsense than the last. I
would warn the generality of critics to throw it in the waste paper basket
without more ado.

As for the limited few, in whom one must perforce find an answerer, I
may as well say straight off that I stick to the solar plexus. That statement
alone, I hope, will thin their numbers considerably.

Finally, to the remnants of a remainder, in order to apologise for the
sudden lurch into cosmology, or cosmogony, in this book, I wish to say
that the whole thing hangs inevitably together. I am not a scientist. I am
an amateur of amateurs. As one of my critics said, you either believe or
you don't.

I am not a proper archaeologist nor an anthropologist nor an
ethnologist. I am no 'scholar' of any sort. But I am very grateful to
scholars for their sound work. I have found hints, suggestions for what I
say here in all kinds of scholarly books, from the Yoga and Plato and St
John the Evangel and the early Greek philosophers like Herakleitos down
to Frazer and his 'Golden Bough', and even Freud and Frobenius. Even
then I only remember hints – and I proceed by intuition. This leaves you
quite free to dismiss the whole wordy mass of revolting nonsense,
without a qualm.

Only let me say, that to my mind there is a great field of science which
is as yet quite closed to us. I refer to the science which proceeds in terms
of life and is established on data of living experience and of sure intuition.
Call it subjective science if you like. Our objective science of modern
knowledge concerns itself only with phenomena, and with phenomena as
regarded in their cause-and-effect relationship. I have nothing to say

against our science. It is perfect as far as it goes. But to regard it as exhausting the whole scope of human possibility in knowledge seems to me just puerile. Our science is a science of the dead world. Even biology never considers life, but only mechanistic functioning and apparatus of life.

> *In the place of this 'mechanistic' scientific orthodoxy, Lawrence wishes to see the return of an earlier primitive world view, one that will define itself through the 'intense potency of symbols', and will manifest itself in 'ritual, gesture and myth-story'. Although Lawrence is aware that his vitalistic, pagan philosophy will not find favour among all readers, his conviction in its rejuvenating potency remains unshaken.*

If my reader finds this bosh and abracadabra, all right for him. Only I have no more regard for his little crowings on his own little dunghill. Myself, I am not so sure that I am one of the one-and-onlies. I like the wide world of centuries and vast ages – mammoth worlds beyond our day, and mankind so wonderful in his distances, his history that has no beginning yet always the pomp and the magnificence of human splendour unfolding through the earth's changing periods. Floods and fire and convulsions and ice-arrest intervene between the great glamorous civilisations of mankind. But nothing will ever quench humanity and the human potentiality to evolve something magnificent out of a renewed chaos.

I do not believe in evolution, but in the strangeness and rainbow-change of ever-renewed creative civilisations.

So much, then, for my claim to remarkable discoveries. I believe I am only trying to stammer out the first terms of a forgotten knowledge. But I have no desire to revive dead kings, or dead sages. It is not for me to arrange fossils, and decipher hieroglyphic phrases. I couldn't do it if I wanted to. But then I can do something else. The soul must take the hint from the relics our scientists have so marvellously gathered out of the forgotten past, and from the hint develop a new living utterance. The spark is from dead wisdom, but the fire is life.

> *Lawrence concludes his Foreword by stressing the connection between his personal philosophy (a cross between mythic revivalism and psychoanalysis) and his creative writing.*

One last weary little word. This pseudo-philosophy of mine – 'pollyanalytics', as one of my respected critics might say – is deduced from the novels and poems, not the reverse. The novels and poems come unwatched out of one's pen. And then the absolute need which one has for some sort of satisfactory mental attitude towards oneself and things in general makes one try to abstract some definite conclusions from one's experience as a writer and as a man. The novels and poems are pure passionate experience. These 'pollyanalytics' are inferences made after-wards, from the experience.

And finally, it seems to me that even art is utterly dependent on philosophy: or if you prefer it, on a metaphysic. The metaphysic or philosophy may not be anywhere very accurately stated and may be quite unconscious, in the artist, yet it is a metaphysic that governs men at the time, and is by all men more or less comprehended, and lived. Men live and see according to some gradually developing and gradually withering vision. This vision exists also as a dynamic idea or metaphysics – exists first as such. Then it is unfolded into life and art. Our vision, our belief, our metaphysic is wearing woefully thin, and the art is wearing absolutely threadbare. We have no future; neither for our hopes nor our aims nor our art. It has all gone grey and opaque.

We've got to rip the old veil of a vision across, and find what the heart really believes in after all; and what the heart really wants, for the next future. And we've got to put it down in terms of belief and of knowledge. And then go forward again, to the fulfilment in life and art.

## 14

## 'The idea of the fatherland is generous, heroic, dynamic, Futurist.'

### Filippo Tommaso Marinetti, 'Beyond Communism' (1920)

*In his famous Futurist manifesto of 1909, Filippo Tommaso Marinetti (1876–1944) had exhorted his readers to demolish the values and institutions of 'bourgeois' society. That assault had largely been framed in cultural terms, but underwriting it lay an aggressively held philosophy that was, at its base, elitist, pugilistic and misogynistic. Marinetti's decision to join the Italian Fascist Party in 1919 (which, led by the charismatic Mussolini, promoted itself as the party of masculine vitality and determined nationalism) was not a surprising one. But as the following extract from an essay of 1920 indicates, Marinetti's Avant-Garde exuberance threatened, at times, just as much to disrupt as to facilitate the party-political agenda of the Fascists.*

We Italian Futurists have amputated all the ideologies and everywhere imposed our new conception of life, our formulas for spiritual health, our aesthetic and social dynamism, the sincere expression of our creative and revolutionary Italian temperaments.

---

**Source:** *Marinetti: Selected Writings*, edited and translated by R. W. Flint and Arthur A. Coppotelli (London: Secker & Warburg, 1972), pp. 142–3 and 147–9. **Further reading:** James Joll, *Intellectuals in Politics: Three Biographical Essays* (London: Weidenfeld & Nicolson, 1960), pp. 131–78.

After having struggled for ten years to rejuvenate Italy, after having dismantled the ultrapasséist Austria-Hungarian Empire at Vittorio Veneto, we were put in jail, accused of criminal assault on the security of the state, in reality of the guilt of being Italian Futurists.

We are more inflamed than ever, tireless and rich in ideas. We have been prodigal of ideas and will continue to be so. We are therefore in no mood to take directions from anyone, nor, as creative Italians, to copy the Russian Lenin, disciple of the German Marx.

Humanity is marching toward anarchic individualism, the dream and vocation of every powerful nature. Communism, on the other hand, is an old mediocritist formula, currently being refurbished by war-weariness and fear and transmuted into an intellectual fashion.

Communism is the exasperation of the bureaucratic cancer that has always wasted humanity. A German cancer, a product of the characteristic German preparationism. Every pedantic preparation is antihuman and wearies fortune. History, life, and the earth belong to the improvisers. We hate military barracks as much as we hate Communist barracks. The anarchistic genius derides and bursts the Communist prison. For us, the fatherland represents the greatest expansion of individual generosity, overflowing in every direction on all similar human beings who sympathize or are sympathetic. It represents the broadest concrete solidarity of spiritual, agricultural, fluvial, commercial, and industrial interests tied together by a single geographical configuration, by the same mixture of climates and the same coloration of horizons.

In its circular expansion, the heart of man bursts the little suffocating family circle and finally reaches the extreme limits of the fatherland, where it feels the heartbeats of its fellow nationals as if they were the outermost nerves of its body. The idea of the fatherland cancels the idea of the family. The idea of the fatherland is generous, heroic, dynamic, Futurist, while the idea of the family is stingy, fearful, static, conservative, passéist. For the first time a strong idea of *patria* springs today from our Futurist conception. Up to now it has been a confused mish-mash of small-townishness, Greco-Roman rhetoric, commemorative rhetoric, unconscious heroic instinct, praise for dead heroes, distrust of the living, and fear of war.

But Futurist patriotism is an eager passion, for the becoming-progress-revolution of the race.

As the greatest affective force of the individual, Futurist patriotism, while remaining disinterested, becomes the most favorable atmosphere for the continuity and development of the race.

The affective circle of our Italian heart expands and embraces the fatherland, that is, the greatest maneuverable mass of ideals, interests, and private and common needs fraternally linked together.

The fatherland is the greatest extension of the individual, or better: the largest individual capable of living at length, of directing, mastering, and defending every part of its body.

The fatherland is the psychic and geographical awareness of the power for individual betterment.

*Marinetti goes on to further explain why Communism is irrelevant to the new Fascist Italy, contesting, in the process, rigid categories such as 'proletarian' and 'bourgeois'. He then progresses to an assertive promulgation of his distinctive political philosophy, outlining the shape of this Futurist-Fascist state and its cultural desiderata.*

We want to free Italy from the Papacy, the Monarchy, the Senate, marriage, Parliament. We want a technical government without Parliament, vivified by a council or exciter [*eccitatorio*] of very young men. We want to abolish standing armies, courts, police, and prisons, so that our race of gifted men may be able to develop the greatest number of free, strong, hard-working, innovating, swift men.

All that, in the great affectionate solidarity of our race on our peninsula within the firm circle of boundaries conquered and deserved by our great victory.

We are not only more revolutionary than you, Socialist officials, but we are beyond your revolution.

To your immense system of levelled and intercommunicating stomachs, to your tedious national refectory, we oppose our marvellous anarchic paradise of absolute freedom, art, talent, progress, heroism, fantasy, enthusiasm, gaiety, variety, novelty, speed, record-setting.

Our optimism is great.

The Italian blood shed at Tripoli was better than that shed at Abba Garima. That shed on Corso, better; that shed on the Piave and at Vittorio Veneto, better.

By means of the schools of physical courage that we propose, we want to increase this vigour of the Italian blood, predisposing it for every audacity and an ever-greater creative artistic capacity, to invent and enjoy spiritually.

One must cure all cowardices and all languors and develop the spiritual elegance of the race, so that the best thing to be found in a tumultuous crowd is the sum of its spiritual elegances: heroic, and generous.

One must increase human capacity to live the ideal life of lines, forms, colours, rhythms, sounds, and noises combined by genius.

If they could relieve the hunger of every stomach, there would always be those who can overcome their lust for refined, privileged dinners.

One must stimulate spiritual hunger and satiate it with great, joyous, astonishing art.

Art is revolution, improvisation, impetus, enthusiasm, record-setting, elasticity, elegance, generosity, superabundance of goodness, drowning in the Absolute, struggle against every hindrance, an aerial dance on the burning summits of passion, destruction of ruins in the face of holy speed, enclosures to open, hunger and thirst for the sky . . . joyous, airplanes gluttonous for infinity. . . .

There are shadowy, flaccid human masses, blind and without light or hope or willpower.

We will tow them after us.

There are souls who struggle without generosity to win a pedestal, a halo, or a position.

These base souls we will convert to a higher spiritual elegance.

Everyone must be given the will to think, create, waken, renovate, and to destroy in themselves the will to submit, conserve, copy.

When the last religions are in their death throes, Art should be the ideal nutrient that will console and reanimate the most restless races, unsatisfied and deluded by the successive collapse of so many unsatisfying ideal banquets.

15

---

# 'Reinstating in his spirit and in his body the values of force'

## Pierre Drieu la Rochelle: 'The renaissance of European man' (1941)

*As for so many of his generation, the seminal experience for Pierre Drieu la Rochelle (1893–1945) was the First World War. The callous way in which it had been conducted, the absence of heroism and ideals, and the shoddy peace which followed, served to convince the young French writer that European society was ripe for radical change. Drieu's major works, the story 'The Comedy of Charleroi' (1934) and the novel Gilles (1939), provide further analysis of this moral malaise, and give unmistakable indications of a growing attachment to fascism, an attachment that led to his collaboration with the Vichy government after the German invasion in 1940. In 1945, after the Allied victory in France, Drieu committed suicide. His major theoretical treatise is* Notes Towards an Understanding of This Century *(1941), written at a time of his greatest faith in the fascist mission to 'rejuvenate' Europe.*

---

**Source:** Pierre Drieu la Rochelle, *Notes pour comprendre le siècle* (Paris: Gallimard, 1941), pp. 149–51, 152–5 and 159–61. There is no standard translation. **Further reading:** Robert Soucy, *Fascist Intellectual: Drieu la Rochelle* (Berkeley: University of California Press, 1979), esp. pp. 175–210.

Certain ideas which first appeared towards the end of the nineteenth and the beginning of the twentieth century have provided European mankind with the means for a renaissance, the like of which has not been seen for centuries – a revolution that seeks to reverse everything.

At one fell swoop, new customs have definitively caught up with the ideas that called them into existence.

In reaction against the city, a new man has been born, who rides by horse in town and country, reinstating in his spirit and in his body the values of force, of courage, of affirmation, keen to embrace experience and the test of valour, to establish a rapport, direct and constant, between feeling, thought and action. This application of reason, beyond the diverging excesses of rationalism and romanticism, had inevitably to enter into the political order and find there its consummation.

Somewhere between Russia, Italy and Germany, this new man appeared, no longer preoccupied with those weighty and dense doctrines of the nineteenth century, or, if choosing to live by them, had quickly decided to dismantle them, and only to keep their practical elements. This man walked again in the footsteps of Nietzsche. Abandoning the most recent excesses of intellectualism, after a vertiginous plunge into books that might have been fatal (but which, not being so, hardened him for living), he became a nihilist confronting a *tabula rasa* on which all the categories and the decrepit restrictions of a rationality converted into rationalism, and a morality converted into hypocrisy, had been abolished. In an age where the old norms have entirely exhausted their vigour, the most immoral men are the most moral.

There is more morality and reason in a man who gets rid of a clock that is not working than there is in someone who persists in repairing it, even when he is certain that it will forever fail to keep time either by the moon or the sun.

The men of this new age, living in Eastern, Central or Meridian Europe, realize that they have been abandoned by reason and morality. They hasten into the jungle that has grown up among the ruins of the world in which they were born, acknowledging nothing other than the myth of Life, knowing well that passion continually re-creates reason, and that they must never stop to organize themselves around a dominant direction, subjecting their many desires to the principal single one, graduating both its means and its effect. Re-creating reason, the man of action re-creates morality, which is only one aspect of reason.

*Drieu solemnizes the 'new man' in a secular liturgy that celebrates the latter's virtues and strengths, which most notably emanate from a newfound confidence in the body and physical prowess.*

The new man has appeared, with a timely impetus, in Italy and Germany. He appeared at first in a compromised and mutilated form in Russia, for the 'barbarians' there were 'primitives', influenced and undermined by the decadence of their neighbours; and, as dogs without a master scavenge for food in dustbins, they were forced to consume the most rotten fare.

The new man reinstates to its position of dominance the values of the body. He takes his cue from the requirements and the potential of the body.

This is the great revolution of the twentieth century, which has been grasped by one section of the French mind, but without it being able to crystallize that understanding and make it accessible to the nation: the Revolution of the Body, the Restoration of the Body.

The new man takes his cue from the body; he knows that the body is the articulation of the soul, and that the soul can only express itself, unfold, and be certain of itself through the body. There is nothing more spiritual than this recognition of the body. It is the soul that calls out, which welcomes the greeting, which finds its liberation in its rediscovery of the body.

There is nothing less materialist than this movement. The lamentable error of our latest rationalists (in which they have fully given evidence of the decline, the degeneration of their pseudo-humanism) has been to appeal to materialism in the face of a revolution that is saving and restoring the sources and the supports of the spirit.

No, European youth, which has, going through the often narrow and strained commercial spectacles of sport, rediscovered the elementary rhythms of human respiration, the elementary rhythms of human activity, was not materialist. Within its ranks, there emerged the most bitter enemies of materialism, enemies of the old capitalist materialism as well as yesterday's socialist materialism.

My dear members of the stock exchange and parliament, this youth was not materialist, these boy scouts, these *Wandervögel*, who rediscovered the joys of walking through sun and rain, and the vigil under the starry skies, and trees, streams, sport, and simple fare.

They transcend the city, the factory, the laboratory; their bodies are spiritual vases in which an anger against the bondage to science and to industry, which are belated in recognizing their major social duties, is being prepared.

Within this restored body, the values of the soul can flow generously. Valour, the spirit of decision-making and of creation are at work here. No thought without action. One thinks only to the point where thinking acts; one puts it to the test, adapts it, and thereby assures it a solid base for it to climb even higher.

European youth, which had no longer been able to form its thoughts in any proper way (because it had been deprived of the better portion of its thought) remade its mind-set, remade itself.

An irresistible force was in the making, the sole force that has ever been, or ever will be, found its way to health again, the true force of the audacious spirit dwelling within the courageous body; this force would be entirely in the right, in a world that is made up of debris and rubbish.

*But it is not all idealism, or harmless enjoyment of youth culture. This physically empowered, self-conscious 'new man' possesses more ominous qualities.*

This is a type of man who rejects culture, who grows strong even in the midst of sexual and alcoholic depravation, and who dreams about giving to the world a physical discipline that will have a radical effect. This is a man who does not believe in ideas, and therefore not in doctrines. This is a man who believes only in action, and who links his actions to the most direct of myths.

This man bears a singular resemblance to that warrior class which springs up during all periods of upheaval. He is the descendant of the crusader, of the mercenaries of the Hundred Years War, of those who have sold their swords in any magnificent or religious war, the descendant of the Spanish Conquistador, of the Puritan pioneer, of the Jacobin volunteer, of Napoleon's Old Guard. And beyond that, he looks back to the soldiers of Alexander and Caesar, who like him experienced a brutal reaction against over-refinement.

This man here endeavours intensely and obsessively to free himself from the restraints of urban life. In order to flee from them, he goes into the labour camps or joins the army. He has fear of himself. But his son does not fear himself; in his son, there is no internal conflict; here the revolution has taken place and prospers.

This new child, this child of our continent, this child of the twentieth century, asserts his new faith, his new values, his new desires, his new spirit of action, in the face of the debris of the ideologies of the nineteenth century, which he carries with him as he moves forward into the future. He talks of socialism and nationalism. But in bringing the two things together, he has changed and transformed them utterly; in modifying the one with the other, he has gone beyond them both.

# 16

# 'Where history speaks, individuals should fall silent'

Gottfried Benn: 'The new state and the intellectuals' (1933)

*Gottfried Benn (1886–1956) was one of the major German poets of the Modernist period, the author of iconoclastic and often esoteric poems, published in volumes such as* Morgue *(1912),* Flesh *(1917) and* Narcosis *(1925). In the early 1930s, however, Benn came within the sway of Hitler and his Nazi Party, impressed by the seeming vitality and élan of that movement. Abandoning his previous apolitical stance, Benn wrote, after the Nazi seizure of power in 1933, a number of works in support of the new regime, attempting to justify the new state to his erstwhile Modernist friends and colleagues, whose liberal and democratic convictions he dismissed as relics of the march of history.*

I read a short time ago in a newspaper, that in the waiting room of one of the new Prussian ministries there is a notice containing the following message: 'Where a new state is being built, personal concerns must take second place.' Quite right! That means: where history speaks, individuals should fall silent. It is the concrete formula of the new concept of the state. If one applies this formula to our topic, one could with full justification ask: just why are intellectuals today demonstrating against the new state? It arose in opposition to them. The new state arose in opposition to the intellectuals. The emergence of this new state constitutes a struggle against everything that might be attributed to the intellectuals over the past decade. The latter, who greeted every revolutionary thrust from the side of the Marxists with enthusiasm, who accredited that movement with a new revelatory potential, and were prepared to grant it all sorts of inner credit, these same people saw it as a matter of intellectual honour to characterize the national revolution as immoral, destructive, an affront against the direction of history. What a strange direction, and what a strange view of history, to view negotiations about wages as the content of all human struggle! And one might add in the same context, what an intellectual shortcoming, what a moral deficiency not to be able to see the great cultural achievements of one's opponents, not to see in their vast feeling for self-sacrifice and surrender of the self to the totality, to the state, to their race, the immanent, in their

**Source:** Gottfried Benn, *Gesammelte Werke in vier Bänden*, edited by Dieter Wellershoff (Wiesbaden: Limes Verlag, 1961), vol. 4, pp. 440–1, 443–4 and 448–9. There is no standard translation. **Further reading:** Reinhard Alter, *Gottfried Benn: The Artist and Politics, 1910–1934* (Bern: Peter Lang, 1976), pp. 57–144.

turning away from the economic to the mythical collective, *not* to see in all of this the anthropologically deeper sense of life! About these intellectuals and who they are, I will remain silent.

I will, however, speak in the name of the spirit of the times, and all who bow to it. How does this spirit of the times view our current situation? I don't mean that wretched spirit, which has for too long been ambling around in our historical inheritance as a support to our sense of nationhood, and which viewed heroism as weak and self-sacrifice as base. What I am describing is that spirit of necessity, that most super-human of all forces in the world, stronger than iron, more powerful than light, which remains for ever within call of the great and within a wing-stroke of the transcendental deed. How does it view contemporary history? Can it make sense of it at all?

Yes! For just as there have certainly been historical moments in which the essentially meditative spirit has remained unmoved even by the political passions of the day, has been unable to recognize the true features of the age, unable to identify the essence of its time, in which the hour of a new dawn has really begun, and the shadowy image of things, only to see from a distance the outline of the past disappearing, so it is equally certain, it seems to me, that the present possesses such a clear historical shape that the spirit can freely project its vision and its calculations beyond the present into the future, partaking of a form of knowledge that is drawn from the laws of nature.

*Benn goes on to argue that the historical import of the Nazi revolution forms a higher standard against which the moral and political criticisms made against the new state by its liberal enemies must be regarded as insignificant.*

The intellectuals say now that this represents the victory of the base: the more noble spirits are always on the side of Schiller [and his ideals of human rationality and freedom]. But from where do we get our standards of 'noble' and 'base'? For the thinking person, there has been since Nietzsche only one standard for judging the historically authentic: its appearance as the new genetic type, as the really new change within the constitution of the human, as, in brief, the new breed; and that, one must say, is already here. Who can doubt that the majority of this new breed is at hand, and is on the side of the new state? It is positively and negatively present, both in what it struggles against and in what it constructs. A genuine new historical movement has arrived, its expression, its language, its legitimacy is beginning to develop. As a breed, it is neither good nor bad: its life has just begun. It is just beginning its life, and its life is already being invaded by defamation from the side of all of those declining generations, who argue that culture is being threatened, ideals, law, and mankind threatened – it sounds like an echo from the past: from Lombardy, from Hungary, from Versailles, when the Gauls attacked, and the Goths, and the Sansculottes: these were the complaints that were heard then. And so it is starting out on its life, but all those who are distinguished, composed, successful throw themselves against it; but it is history itself that will nullify these attacks, for in its essence it does not proceed in a composed and democratic way. History proceeds not in a democratic but in an elemental way; at its turning points, it is always elemental. It does not care for elections, but sends forward the new biological breed. It has no other method. It says: this breed has arrived: now act and suffer, incorporate the spirit of your generation and your species into the march of time; do not deviate: act and suffer, as the law of life demands. And, consequently, this new biological breed does act, and naturally certain social relations are adjusted in the process, certain privileged ranks swept away, certain cultural commodities devalued. But they too, these groups, did they not also direct themselves against a society that could no longer create any standards, could set up no transcendental values. Does such a society deserve anything more than the yoke and a new rule of law?

> *It is, above all, youth which will benefit from the arrival of the new state, and Benn concludes his essay with a panegyric upon their energy, their selfless commitment to the community and their ability to combine in a single form idealism and pragmatism.*

Great, spiritually motivated youth, the spirit of the times, the spirit of necessity, that most super-human of all forces in the world, stronger than iron, more powerful than light, sanctions you: the intelligentsia, which seeks to disparage you, was at its end. What could it bequeath to you? Its members lived, after all, only from fragments and sickening self-revelations. Burnt-out entities, over-refined forms, and everywhere this miserable, bourgeois-capitalist appendage. Acquiring a villa was the culmination of their visionary pretensions, owning a Mercedes satisfied their yearning for the high moral ground. Do not waste your time on argumentation and words: forgo the spirit of reconciliation, close the doors, and build the state!

---

# 17

# 'A wave of anomalous barbarism'

## Thomas Mann: 'An appeal to reason' (1930)

*As the author of novels such as* Buddenbrooks *(1901) and* The Magic
Mountain *(1924), and the aesthetic-erotic novella* Death in Venice *(1912),
Thomas Mann (1875–1955) regarded himself as an essentially apolitical writer (see
his* Observations of a Non-Political Man, *1918). But matters changed in 1924
when a close friend, the German Foreign Minister Walter Rathenau, was
assassinated by right-wing extremists, a brutal event that convinced Mann that the
newly founded Weimar Republic needed to be actively defended. Mann's political
commitment was further tested in 1930, when the Nazi Party won substantial
support in the General Election of that year. His response to that ominous event took
the form of the speech, a 'German address', in which Mann sought to draw the
attention of the electorate (and, most notably, its educated middle-class sections) to the
inherently nihilistic consequences of Hitler's policies.*

I do not hold with the remorselessly social point of view which looks
upon art – the beautiful and useless – as a private pastime of the
individual, which in times like these may almost be relegated to the
category of the reprehensible. There was a time – the epoch of æsthetic
idealism – when Schiller could extol 'pure play' as the highest state of
man. But even though that day be past, yet we need not quite subscribe
to the school of action which would put idealism on the level of frivolity.
For form, be it never so playful, is akin to the spirit, to that which leads
one on to social betterment; and art is the sphere wherein is resolved the
conflict between the social and the ideal.

And yet there are hours, there are moments of our common life, when
art fails to justify itself in practice; when the inner urgency of the artist
fails him; when the more immediate necessities of our existence choke
back his own thought, when the general distress and crisis shake him too,
in such a way that what we call art, the happy and impassioned
preoccupation with eternally human values, comes to seem idle,
ephemeral, a superfluous thing, a mental impossibility.

*For Mann, it is precisely this juncture that art has reached in the wake of Hitler's
ominous success at the recent General Election. 'I am a child of the German*

---

**Source:** Thomas Mann, *Order of the Day*, translated by H. T. Lowe-Porter (New York: Alfred
A. Knopf, 1942), pp. 46–7, 53–8. **Further reading:** T. J. Reed, *The Uses of Tradition* (Oxford:
Clarendon Press, 1974), pp. 275–316.

*bourgeoisie', Mann tells his audience, but even he must abandon his previously apolitical stance, and lend active support to those who can best resist Hitler. Mann then provides a remarkably insightful analysis of the origins of Hitler's National Socialism and the reasons for its popular success.*

One need not be a great psychologist to recognize in these trials, in both the foreign and the domestic field, the causes which, together with the bad economic situation, conditioned the sensational election results. The German people took advantage of a garish election poster, the so-called National-Socialist, to give vent to its feelings. But National-Socialism could never have attained the strength or scope it has shown as a manifestation of popular feeling had it not, unknown to the mass of its supporters, drawn from spiritual sources an element which, like everything born of the time-spirit, possesses a pragmatic truth, legitimacy, and logical necessity, and by virtue of them lends reality to the popular movement. The economic decline of the middle classes was accompanied – or even preceded – by a feeling which amounted to an intellectual prophecy and a critique of the age: the sense that here was a crisis which heralded the end of the bourgeois epoch that came in with the French Revolution and the notions appertaining to it. There was proclaimed a new mental attitude for all mankind, which should have nothing to do with bourgeois principles such as freedom, justice, culture, optimism, faith in progress. As art, it gave vent to expressionistic soul-shrieks; as philosophy, it repudiated the reason and the at once mechanistic and ideological conceptions of bygone decades; it expressed itself as an irrationalistic throwback, placing the conception *life* at the centre of thought, and raised on its standard the powers of the unconscious, the dynamic, the darkly creative, which alone were life-giving. Mind, quite simply the intellectual, it put under a taboo as destructive of life, while it set up for homage as the true inwardness of life the Mother-Chthonic, the darkness of the soul, the holy procreative underworld. Much of this nature-religion, by its very essence inclining to the orgiastic and to bacchic excess, has gone into the nationalism of our day, making of it something quite different from the nationalism of the nineteenth century with its bourgeois, strongly cosmopolitan and humanitarian cast. It is distinguished in its character as a nature-cult precisely by its absolute unrestraint, its orgiastic, radically anti-humane, frenziedly dynamic character. But when one thinks what it has cost humanity, through the ages, to rise from orgiastic nature-cults, from the service of Moloch, Baal, and Astarte, with the barbaric refinements of its gnosticism and the sexual excesses of its divinities, to the plane of a more spiritual worship, one stands amazed at the light-hearted way in which today we repudiate our gains and our liberations – while at the same time one realizes how fluctuating and ephemeral, in a general sense how really meaningless, such a philosophical reaction must be.

It may seem daring to associate the radical nationalism of our day with these conceptions from a romanticizing philosophy. Yet the association is there, and it must be recognized by those concerned to get an insight into the relations of things. And there is even more: there are other intellectual elements come to strengthen this National-Social political movement – a certain ideology, a Nordic creed, a Germanistic romanticism, from philological, academic, professorial spheres. It addresses the Germany of 1930 in a high-flown, wishy-washy jargon, full of mystical good feeling, with hyphenated prefixes like race- and folk- and fellowship-, and lends to the movement a concomitant of fanatical cult-barbarism, more dangerous and estranging, with more power to clog and stupefy the brain, than even the lack of contact and the political romanticism which led us into the war.

Fed, then, by such intellectual and pseudo-intellectual currents as these, the movement which we sum up under the name of National-Socialism and which has displayed such a power of enlisting recruits to its banner, mingles with the mighty wave – a wave of anomalous barbarism, of primitive popular vulgarity – that sweeps over the world today, assailing the nerves of mankind with wild, bewildering, stimulating, intoxicating sensations. The fantastic development, the triumphs and catastrophes of our technical progress, our sensational sports records, the frantic overpayment and adoration bestowed upon 'stars,' the prize-fights with million-mark purses and hordes of spectators – all these make up the composite picture of the time, together with the decline and disappearance of stern and civilizing conceptions such as culture, mind, art, ideas. Humanity seems to have run like boys let out of school away from the humanitarian, idealistic nineteenth century, from whose morality – if we can speak at all of morality in this connection – our time represents a wide and wild reaction. Everything is possible, everything permitted as a weapon against human decency; if we have got rid of the idea of human freedom as a relic of the bourgeois state of mind – as though an idea so bound up with all European feeling, upon which Europe has been founded, for which she has made such sacrifices, could ever be utterly lost – it comes back again, this cast-off conception, in a guise suited to the time: as demoralization, as a mockery of all human authority, as a free rein to instincts, as the emancipation of brutality, the dictatorship of force.

# 18

# 'Acting politically without sacrificing one's aesthetic and intellectual integrity'

## George Orwell: 'Why I write' (1946)

*In his major works (*Homage to Catalonia *(1938),* Animal Farm *(1945) and* Nineteen Eighty-four *(1949)), George Orwell, pseudonym of Eric Arthur Blair (1903–50), traced a trajectory that was to become an increasingly familiar one for the writers of the committed generation of the 1930s and 1940s: a line away from an initial sympathy with the communist cause (and an affiliation with those British parties that supported that cause) and, following the experience of the Spanish Civil War, towards a fundamental abhorrence of all types of totalitarian ideology. Although, as he explains in the following extract, Orwell never abandoned the recognition that politics was a constituent part of the writer's response to the world, he became increasingly aware of the problems involved in accommodating a political statement within a literary form that could be true to personal experience.*

Every line of serious work that I have written since 1936 has been written, directly or indirectly, *against* totalitarianism and *for* democratic Socialism, as I understand it. It seems to me nonsense, in a period like our own, to think that one can avoid writing of such subjects. Everyone writes of them in one guise or another. It is simply a question of which side one takes and what approach one follows. And the more one is conscious of one's political bias, the more chance one has of acting politically without sacrificing one's aesthetic and intellectual integrity.

What I have most wanted to do throughout the past ten years is to make political writing into an art. My starting point is always a feeling of partisanship, a sense of injustice. When I sit down to write a book, I do not say to myself, 'I am going to produce a work of art'. I write it because there is some lie that I want to expose, some fact to which I want to draw attention, and my initial concern is to get a hearing. But I could not do the work of writing a book, or even a long magazine article, if it were not also an aesthetic experience. Anyone who cares to examine my work will see that even when it is downright propaganda it contains much that a full-time politician would consider irrelevant. I am not able, and I do not want, completely to abandon the world-view that I acquired in

**Source:** George Orwell, *Such, Such Were the Joys* (New York: Harcourt, Brace and Company, 1953), pp. 9–11. **Further reading:** David L. Kubal, *Outside the Whale: George Orwell's Art and Politics* (Notre Dame, IN: University of Notre Dame, 1972).

childhood. So long as I remain alive and well I shall continue to feel strongly about prose style, to love the surface of the earth, and to take pleasure in solid objects and scraps of useless information. It is no use trying to suppress that side of myself. The job is to reconcile my ingrained likes and dislikes with the essentially public, non-individual activities that this age forces on all of us.

It is not easy. It raises problems of construction and of language, and it raises in a new way the problem of truthfulness. Let me give just one example of the cruder kind of difficulty that arises. My book about the Spanish Civil War, *Homage to Catalonia*, is, of course, a frankly political book, but in the main it is written with a certain detachment and regard for form. I did try very hard in it to tell the whole truth without violating my literary instincts. But among other things it contains a long chapter, full of newspaper quotations and the like, defending Trotskyists who were accused of plotting with Franco. Clearly such a chapter, which after a year or two would lose its interest for any ordinary reader, must ruin the book. A critic whom I respect read me a lecture about it. 'Why did you put in all that stuff?', he said. 'You've turned what might have been a good book into journalism.' What he said was true, but I could not have done otherwise. I happened to know, what very few people in England had been allowed to know, that innocent men were being falsely accused. If I had not been angry about that I should never have written the book.

In one form or another this problem comes up again. The problem of language is subtler and would take too long to discuss. I will only say that of later years I have tried to write less picturesquely and more exactly. In any case I find that by the time you have perfected any style of writing, you have always outgrown it. *Animal Farm* was the first book in which I tried, with full consciousness of what I was doing, to fuse political purpose and artistic purpose into one whole. I have not written a novel for seven years, but I hope to write another fairly soon. It is bound to be a failure, every book is a failure, but I know with some clarity what kind of book I want to write.

Looking back through the last page or two, I see that I have made it appear that my motives in writing were wholly public-spirited. I don't want to leave that as the final impression. All writers are vain, selfish and lazy, and at the very bottom of their motives there lies a mystery. Writing a book is a horrible, exhausting struggle, like a long bout of some painful illness. One would never undertake such a thing if one were not driven on by some demon whom one can neither resist nor understand. For all one knows that demon is simply the same instinct that makes a baby squall for attention. And yet it is also true that one can write nothing readable unless one constantly struggles to efface one's own personality. Good prose is like a window pane. I cannot say with certainty which of my motives are the strongest, but I know which of them deserve to be followed. And looking back through my work, I see that it is invariably where I lacked a *political* purpose that I wrote lifeless books and was betrayed into purple passages, sentences without meaning, decorative adjectives and humbug generally.

19

---

## 'The intoxicating effect of a sudden liberation'

### Arthur Koestler: 'The initiates' (1949)

*Arthur Koestler (1905–83), a noted writer and journalist of Hungarian descent, found his way to Communism when he was in his mid-twenties, working as a journalist in Berlin. His experiences of the intrigues within the Party, of its uncompromising policies and, above all, of the cynical philosophy that underscored its politics, formed the basis for much of his subsequent writing, most notably his famous novel* Darkness at Noon *(1940). In his contribution to the anthology* The God That Failed, *published in 1949 (which included testimonies from other ex-Communists such as Ignazio Silone and Stephen Spender), Koestler left one of the most vivid firsthand accounts of the emotional and intellectual attractions that Communism, as an all-embracing and all-explaining conceptual framework, had exerted upon him and others of his generation.*

As part of a closed system which made social philosophy fall into a lucid and comprehensive pattern, the demonstration of the historical relativity of institutions and ideals – of family, class, patriotism, bourgeois morality, sexual taboos – had the intoxicating effect of a sudden liberation from the rusty chains with which a pre-1914 middle class childhood had cluttered one's mind. Today, when Marxist philosophy has degenerated into a Byzantine cult and virtually every single tenet of the Marxist programme has become twisted round into its opposite, it is difficult to recapture that mood of emotional fervour and intellectual bliss.

I was ripe to be converted, as a result of my personal case-history; thousands of other members of the intelligentsia and the middle-classes of my generation were ripe for it, by virtue of other personal case-histories; but, however much these differed from case to case, they had a common denominator: the rapid disintegration of moral values, of the pre-1914

---

**Source:** Arthur Koestler, *The God That Failed*, edited by Richard Crossman (London: Hamish Hamilton, 1950), pp. 29–30, 32 and 75–6. **Further reading:** Iain Hamilton, *Koestler: A Biography* (London: Secker and Warburg, 1982), esp. pp. 15–47.

pattern of life in postwar Europe, and the simultaneous lure of the new revelation which had come from the East.

I joined the Party (which to this day has remained 'the' Party for all of us who once belonged to it) in 1931, at the beginning of that short-lived period of optimism, of that abortive spiritual renaissance, later known as the Pink Decade. The stars of that treacherous dawn were Barbusse, Romain Rolland, Gide and Malraux in France; Piscator, Becher, Renn, Brecht, Eisler, Seghers in Germany; Auden, Isherwood, Spender in England; Dos Passos, Upton Sinclair, Steinbeck in the United States. (Of course, not all of them were members of the Communist Party.) The cultural atmosphere was saturated with Progressive Writers' congresses, experimental theatres, committees for peace and against Fascism, societies for cultural relations with the U.S.S.R., Russian films and *avant-garde* magazines. It looked indeed as if the Western world, convulsed by the aftermath of war, scourged by inflation, depression, unemployment and the absence of a faith to live for, was at last going to 'clear from the head the masses of impressive rubbish; – Rally the lost and trembling forces of the will – Gather them up and let them loose upon the earth – Till they construct at last a human justice' (Auden).

*It was, above all, the emotionally and intellectually resolving impact that the communist creed exerted upon the acolyte that proved decisive.*

Even by a process of pure elimination, the Communists, with the mighty Soviet Union behind them, seemed the only force capable of resisting the onrush of the primitive horde with its swastika totem. But it was not by a process of elimination that I became a Communist. Tired of [studying] electrons and wave-mechanics, I began for the first time to read Marx, Engels and Lenin in earnest. By the time I had finished with *Feuerbach* and *State and Revolution*, something had clicked in my brain which shook me like a mental explosion. To say that one had 'seen the light' is a poor description of the mental rapture which only the convert knows (regardless of what faith he has been converted to). The new light seems to pour from all directions across the skull; the whole universe falls into pattern like the stray pieces of a jigsaw puzzle assembled by magic at one stroke. There is now an answer to every question, doubts and conflicts are a matter of the tortured past – a past already remote, when one had lived in dismal ignorance in the tasteless, colourless world of those who *don't know*. Nothing henceforth can disturb the convert's inner peace and serenity – except the occasional fear of losing faith again, losing thereby what alone makes life worth living, and falling back into outer darkness, where there is wailing and gnashing of teeth.

*Such euphoria, however, could not outlast the day-to-day reality of being part of a movement that systematically promoted the 'necessary lie, the necessary slander; the necessary intimidation of the masses to preserve them from short-sighted errors; the necessary liquidation of oppositional groups' as a part of its political philosophy. In 1937, matters came to a crisis for Koestler, who rediscovered through his experience of incarceration in the Spanish Civil War (where he fought on the Republican side) the basis for a new humanism beyond political dogma.*

I spent four months in Spanish prisons, in Malaga and Seville, most of the time in solitary confinement and most of the time convinced that I was going to be shot. When, in June 1937, thanks to the intervention of the British Government, I was unexpectedly set free, my hair had not greyed and my features had not changed and I had not developed religious mania; but I had made the acquaintance of a different kind of reality, which had altered my outlook and values; and altered them so profoundly and unconsciously that during the first days of freedom I was not even aware of it. The experiences responsible for this change were fear, pity, and a third one, more difficult to describe. Fear, not of death, but of torture and humiliation and the more unpleasant forms of dying – my companion of patio-exercises, Garcia Atadell, was garrotted shortly after my liberation. Pity for the little Andalusian and Catalan peasants whom I heard crying and calling for their *madres* when they were led out at night to face the firing squad; and finally, a condition of the mind usually referred to in terms borrowed from the vocabulary of mysticism, which would present itself at unexpected moments and induce a state of inner peace which I have known neither before nor since.

The lesson taught by this type of experience, when put into words, always appears under the dowdy guise of perennial commonplaces: that man is a reality, mankind an abstraction; that men cannot be treated as units in operations of political arithmetic because they behave like the symbols for zero and the infinite, which dislocates all mathematical operations; that the end justifies the means only within very narrow limits; that ethics is not a function of social utility, and charity not a petit-bourgeois sentiment but the gravitational force that keeps civilization in orbit. Nothing can sound more flatfooted than such verbalizations of a knowledge which is not of a verbal nature; yet every single one of these trivial statements was incompatible with the Communist faith which I held.

# 20

# 'Beyond nihilism'

## Albert Camus: *The Rebel* (1951)

*Albert Camus (1913–60) was the author of the novels* The Outsider *(1942) and* The Plague *(1947), and of plays such as* Caligula *(1944) and* The Just *(1950), in which he explored the response of individuals, acting in a variety of extreme situations, to a world that is bereft of the comfort of transcendental values. At the centre of Camus's thinking is a preoccupation with death: that which the individual must suffer (or choose to suffer in the form of suicide), but also that fate which individuals, often working in the guise of historical agents, impose upon others. It was with this configuration of problems that Camus engaged in his two major theoretical works* The Myth of Sisyphus *(1942) and* The Rebel. *Here he attempted to locate a residual existential position from which the individual can assert his or her dignity and right to freedom in the face of larger historical forces that seem to make that assertion irredeemably absurd.*

Undoubtedly, there is an evil that men accumulate in their desperate desire for unity. But there is yet a further evil that lies at the root of this confused movement. Confronted with this evil, confronted by death, man from his very depths cries out for justice. Christianity has historically responded to this protestation against evil simply by proclaiming its Kingdom and offering Eternal Life, and then demanding faith. But suffering consumes hope and faith; after which it alone remains, as something that cannot be explained. The toiling masses, exhausted through suffering and death, are masses which live without God. Our place is, henceforth, by their side, far from those learned scribes, old and new. Christianity has historically postponed to a point beyond history the cure of evil and of murder; but these experiences are, nevertheless, endured as a part of history. Contemporary materialism also believes that it has the answer to all questions. But, as a slave to history, it increases the domain of historical murder, whilst leaving it, at the same time, without any justification, except a future one, which, once again, demands faith. In both cases, one must go on waiting; but while this is happening the innocent continue to die. For twenty centuries, the sum total of evil has

**Source:** Albert Camus, *L'homme revolté* (Paris: Gallimard, 1951), pp. 363–6. **Standard translation:** *The Rebel*, translated from the French by Anthony Bowen (Harmondsworth: Penguin Books, 1971), pp. 267–9. **Further reading:** Lev Braun, *Witness of Decline: Albert Camus: Moralist of the Absurd* (Rutherford, NJ: Fairleigh Dickinson University Press, 1974), particularly pp. 107–82.

remained undiminished in the world. No paradise, neither a divine nor a revolutionary one, has come about. Injustice remains bound to all suffering, even that which in the eyes of mankind seems warranted. The long silence of Prometheus, who remains overwhelmed by the forces that surround him, continues to cry out. But Prometheus has seen, during this time, men turn against, and mock him. Wedged in between human evil and destiny, between terror and arbitrary fate, all that remains to him is his power to rebel, in order to save from murder him who might become a murderer, and to do this without surrendering to the arrogance of blasphemy.

One will understand, then, that rebellion involves a strange kind of love. Those who can find no solace either in God or History are condemned to live for those who, like them, cannot live: for those who are dejected. The purest form of rebellion, then, is crowned with the heart-rending cry of Karamazov: if all are not saved, what good is the salvation of just one? Thus, condemned Catholic prisoners, shut away in the dungeons of Spain, refuse to take communion today because the priests of the regime have made it compulsory in certain prisons. These also, these solitary witnesses of crucified innocence, refuse salvation if it must be bought with injustice and oppression. This insane generosity is the generosity of rebellion, which unhesitatingly makes available the force of its love, and pits itself against injustice without a moment's delay. Its honour lies in its refusal to make calculations, distributing everything that it has to life and living men. In this way it is prodigal in what it bequeaths to future men. Real generosity towards the future consists in giving everything to the present.

Rebellion proves, thus, that it is the very movement of life itself, and that one cannot deny it without renouncing life. Each time its pure cry is heard something is brought into existence. It is love and fecundity; or it is nothing. Revolution without honour, the calculated revolution, which in preferring man as an abstraction to man of flesh and blood, denying reality whenever it deems it necessary, puts resentment in the place of love. As soon as rebellion, forgetful of its expansive origins, allows itself to be contaminated by resentment, it negates life, courts destruction and brings to prominence those sneering cohorts of petty rebels, slaves in the making, who end up by offering themselves for sale today in all the markets of Europe, to all types of servitude. It is no longer true rebellion or revolution, but rancour and tyranny. Then, when revolution, in the name of power and history, turns into that immoderate and mechanical system of murder, a new rebellion is consecrated in the name of moderation and life. We are at that extremity now. In the depth of the darkness, however, a light, which we can already discern, is starting to shine, for which we have only to struggle for it to shine forth. Amidst the ruins, all of us are working for a renascence, beyond the limits of nihilism, but few know of this.

Already, in effect, rebellion, without pretending that it can solve everything, can at least begin its tasks. From this moment on, the high sun will shine down on the very movement of history. Around the devouring flames, shadowy combatants act for a moment and then disappear, and the blind, touching their eyelids, cry out that this is history. But the men of Europe, abandoned to the shadows, have turned their backs upon that fixed and radiant point. They forget the present for the future, the plenitude of life for the chimera of power, the misery of the slums for a vision of the Radiant City, simple justice for an empty Promised Land. They despair of personal liberty and dream of a strange universal freedom; disregard individual death, and give the name of immortality to the prodigious agony of the collective. They no longer believe in things that really exist in the world, or in living man; the secret about Europe is that it no longer loves life. Its blind men hold the puerile belief that to love life, even for a day, is tantamount to providing a justification for the many centuries of oppression. That is why they want to efface joy from the face of the world, and postpone it to a later date. Impatience with limits, the rejection of their double being, and the despair of being a man have finally driven them to inhuman excesses. Denying the true grandeur of life, they have had to stake all on their own excellence. Unable to do anything better, they have deified themselves, and then their troubles began: the gods put out their eyes. Kaliayev, and his brothers throughout the world, refuse, on the contrary, to be deified, because they reject that unlimited power to inflict death. They choose instead, to give example, the only original rule of life today: to learn how to live and how to die, and, in order to be a man, refuse to be a god.

# 21

# To 'transcend the antinomy between word and action'

## Jean-Paul Sartre: *What Is Literature?* (1946)

*In his novel trilogy* The Roads to Freedom *(1945–49), Jean-Paul Sartre (1905–80) sought to combine his early Existentialism (as expressed, for example, in his novel* Nausea, *1938) with a deeper appreciation of the necessity of historical action. Sartre's major theoretical works set themselves the task of reconciling these two axes of his work: the concern with achieving personal authenticity within the reflective sphere of self-consciousness (see* Being and Nothingness, *1943), and the insistence that such a realm of inner freedom must take its place 'in the world', as part of a more general process of liberation for others (his* Critique of Dialectical Reason *(1960) was his most ambitious attempt to grapple with this issue within a neo-Marxist framework). In* What Is Literature? *Sartre outlined the role that literature (understood in the broadest sense of the term as an active reconfiguration of the world through language) might play in this process.*

To speak is to act: once you have named a thing it can no longer remain quite the same; it has lost its innocence. By describing the behaviour of an individual you reveal it to him: he sees himself. And, as you are, at the same time, naming it for everyone else, he knows that he is *seen*, at the same moment that he *sees* himself; his furtive gesture, which he forgot while making it, begins to take on a significant existence, assumes an existence for us, it becomes a part of the objective spirit, it takes on new dimensions, it is recuperated. After that, how can you expect him to act in the same manner? Either he will persist in his behaviour out of obstinacy and in recognition of his cause, or he will abandon it. Thus, by speaking, I reveal the situation by my very intention of changing it; I reveal it to myself and to others *in order* to change it; I strike at its very heart; I transfix it, and bring it into full view; in the present, I dispose of it, with each word that I utter, I engage myself a little more with the world, and at the same time, I emerge from it a little more, since I am passing beyond it, into the future.

Thus, the writer of prose is a man who has chosen a certain mode of secondary action that one could designate as the action of disclosure. One

**Source:** Jean-Paul Sartre, *Qu'est-ce que la littérature?* (Paris: Gallimard, 1948), pp. 29–30 and 194–6. **Standard translation:** *What Is Literature?*, translated from the French by Bernard Frechtmann (London: Methuen, 1950), pp. 12–14 and 118–19. **Further reading:** John Halpern, *Critical Fictions: The Literary Criticism of Jean-Paul Sartre* (New Haven, CT: Yale University Press, 1976), pp. 41–52.

is, then, justified in asking this second question: what aspect of the world do you seek to disclose, what changes do you wish to bring about in the world through this process of disclosing? The 'committed' [*engagé*] writer knows that language is action: he knows that to reveal is to change, and that one can only reveal by planning changes. He has abandoned the impossible dream of providing an impartial picture of society and the human condition. Man is the being towards which one cannot retain an impartiality, not even God. For God, if he existed, would be, as certain mystics have seen Him, in a *situation* vis-à-vis mankind. And he is also a being who cannot even see a situation without changing it, for his gaze congeals, destroys, or sculpts, or, as does eternity, changes the object in itself. It is in love, hatred, anger, fear, joy, indignation, admiration, hope and despair that mankind and the world reveal themselves *in their truth*. Without a doubt, the committed writer might be mediocre, he might even be aware of being so, but as one cannot write without the intention of succeeding perfectly, the modesty with which he views his work ought not divert him from constructing it *as if* it were going to exert the greatest influence.

*The ultimate goal of this process is freedom, which Sartre characteristically construes as a merging of the political and the personal, because self-liberation in the latter realm is not possible without universal liberation in the former.*

Spiritualization, that is to say *renewal*. And there is nothing else to spiritualize, nothing else to renew other than this multicoloured concrete world, with its ponderousness, its opaqueness, its zones of generality, and its swarm of anecdotes, and that invincible Evil which eats away at it without ever being able to destroy it. The writer will renew it as it is, the raw, sweaty, stinking, banal world, in order to lay before it freedoms on the basis of a freedom. Literature, in a classless society, would be then the world conscious of itself, suspended in a free act and offering itself to the free judgement of all men, the self-reflexive presence of a society without classes; it is through the book that the members of this society could at any time assess their state, recognize themselves and their situation. But just as the portrait comprises the model, and simple presentation already the catalyst of change, just as the work of art, taken as the sum of its exigencies, is not a simple description of the present but a judgement upon that present in the name of the future, and, finally, as every book contains an appeal, so is this presence of self already a transcendence of self. The universe is not contested in the name of simple consummation, but in the name of the hopes and sufferings of those who inhabit it. Thus concrete literature will be the synthesis of negativity, like the power of uprooting from the given, from the plan, like the sketch of a future order; it will be a celebration, the mirror of a flame that burns all that is reflected in it, and the generosity, that is to say free invention, the gift. But if it is going to be able to unite those two complementary aspects of freedom, it is not enough simply to grant the writer the freedom to say anything: he must write for a public that has the freedom to change everything, which means beyond the suppression of classes, the abolition of all dictatorships, the constant renewal of the ranks, the continual overthrow of order once it has become ossified. In a word, literature is in essence the subjectivity of a society in a state of permanent revolution. In such a society, it would transcend the antinomy between word and action. Certainly, under no circumstances could it be classed as an act; it would be false to say that the author *acts* upon his readers; he only appeals to their freedom, and in order for his work to have any effect, it is necessary for the public freely to choose to accept it on its own merits. But in a collectivity that is constantly correcting, judging and transforming itself, the written work can provide an essential condition for action, for, in other words, the moment of reflective consciousness.

Thus, in a society without classes, without repressive authority, and without stability, literature would finally become aware of itself; it would finally understand that form and content, public and private, are identical, that the formal liberty of expression, and the material freedom to act, complete one another, and that one must use the former to lay claim to the latter, that it best manifests the subjectivity of the person when it translates most deeply the needs of the collective, and vice versa; that its function is to express the concrete universal to the concrete universal, and that its end is to appeal to the freedom of men so that they can put into effect and maintain the reign of human freedom.

# Part V
# Postmodernism

# INTRODUCTION

In spite of the fluidity of its conceptual contours and its at times (over-) determining presence in recent cultural discourses, 'Postmodernism' nevertheless provides the most productive paradigm for our under-standing of the theoretical and aesthetic practices that characterize recent European literature. As a specific term of literary analysis, Postmodernism first emerged in America to describe the positive, energetic and ludic qualities of certain emerging North and South American writers, such as John Barthes, Ken Kesey and Richard Brautigan (to which was soon added the magisterial figure of the Argentine Juan Luis Borges). Their work both broke with the weighty and unself-reflective ideologizing of the literature produced in the politicized 1930s and 1940s, as it distanced itself from the monumentalist and mytho-poeticizing procedures pursued by many of the mainstream Modernists. In spite of obvious differences (most notably in their attitude to politics and their divergent self-positionings within the public sphere), both traditions had in their own way, it was argued, aimed for a literature of depth, articulating their discrete projects within metanarratives that were deemed by many to be both anonymously (and dangerously) utopian in the first case, and elitist and triumphalist in the second. The Postmodernists, by contrast, as the early commentators of that movement noted – critics such as Irwin Howe ('Mass society and post-modern fiction', 1959), Susan Sonntag (*Against Interpretation*, 1966), Lesley Fiedler ('Cross the border – close the gap: Post-Modernism', 1971) – moved within a more accessible and modest realm, their way into the future propelled by an energy that had as its source an enthusiastic exploration of new rules and games. In place of the ponderous pretensions of earlier forms of twentieth-century writing, Postmodernism followed an aesthetic line which chose surfaces against relationships, texture rather than depth, believing in those unique forms of liberation with which play, wit and the erotic invest life.

But that Postmodernist literature could move within a darker ambit was also observed, most notably by the American critic Ihab Hassan, who, in his *The Dismemberment of Orpheus* (1971), stressed the negative echoes of its discourse which he saw pervading the near-misanthropic visions of, among others, Jean Genet and Samuel Beckett. For Hassan, the ludic spirit which provided that point of energy around which the Postmodern aesthetic resolved served to obscure (or perhaps transfigure) that Other of the Postmodern imagination, that ethos of self-deprecation whose gravitational pull was towards waste, exhaustion and silence. For the European mind, emerging out of a decade of war, civil unrest and genocide, these were appropriate tropes. The admonition made in 1955 by the German cultural theorist Theodor Adorno, that writing poetry after Auschwitz could only be deemed a barbaric act, foregrounded both the minimalist and ethically introspective parameters within which Postmodernism would necessarily have to move in early postwar Europe. This was a literature of the *tabula rasa*, beginning from a *Nullpunkt* of expectations and of hope, written from a position of absolute zero. Particularly in Germany, Italy and England, writers turned to a 'new realism' to construct what Heinrich Böll called a 'rubble literature', seeking to portray a landscape that had been devastated not only in material but also in spiritual terms (**Reading 1**).

Böll's position was minimalist, cautious, defensive, but it was by no means defeatist. On the contrary, much of the literature written in immediate postwar Europe possessed a residual vitalism that lifted it above the poverty of its devastated environment. This was true of the 'kitchen sink' realism practised in England, most notably in plays such as John Osborne's *Look Back in Anger* (1956) and Arnold Wesker's *Chips with Everything* (1962), and novels such as John Braine's *Room at the Top* (1957), Alan Sillitoe's *The Loneliness of the Long Distance Runner* (1959) and David Storey's *This Sporting Life* (1960), which reveal a native vigour and a caustic vitality that finds an outlet in the common passions of everyday life and a healthy disrespect for authority and the status quo. The same was true for Italian writers, particularly those such as Cesar Pavese, Paolo Volponi and Elio Vittorini, who belonged to the emerging school of neo-Realism (*neo-verismo*). As the later fabulist and writer of metafictions, Italo Calvino, noted in his Preface to his own neo-Realist novel, *The Path to the Nest of Spiders* (1964), the writers of this generation felt 'a sense of life as something that can begin again from scratch, a general concern with problems, even a capacity within us to survive torment and abandonment' (**Reading 2**). It was precisely because all – author, reader and public alike – were subject to the same material deprivation, had gone through the same experiences of war and civil war, Calvino tells us (stressing the positive dimension of the collapse of pre-war Italian society), that a community of communication could open up for this new younger generation of Italian writers.

That the minimalism evident in so much of the literature published after the Second World War would lead writers to dispense with the grandiose metaphysical projections and political ideologies of the past, indeed, with all larger frameworks of meaning that seek to position the individual within enclosed hermeneutic systems, was clear from the writing of the French existentialist Albert Camus. In his *The Myth of*

*Sisyphus* (1942) and *The Rebel* (1951), Camus elaborated a theory of the absurd around what he perceived to be mankind's residual need to find absolute meaning in a world which resists meaning to all except those who are (like the condemned or the suicidal) prepared to accept hopelessness as an inextricable part of the human condition. But as Camus affirmed in his famous reconstruction of the legend of Sisyphus, recognizing this fact is the first step to its overcoming; 'even the very struggle to reach the summit is enough to fill the heart of man': it is precisely in the embrace of absurdity that man asserts his human identity (**Reading 3**).

A similar metaphysical scepticism characterized the work of the playwrights of the 'Theatre of the Absurd', who included Samuel Beckett, Eugene Ionesco, Jean Genet and Harold Pinter. Their work differs at points that are both political and dramaturgical; but what links them is a common desire, as Ionesco noted regarding his own work, to liberate the spectator 'from our banal existences, from habit, and from mental sluggishness, which conceal from us the strangeness of the world' (**Reading 4**). In place of the *pièce bien faite*, the Absurdists developed, in their different ways, through farce, black humour, mime, mock realism, and a combination of all these genres, an affective dramatic strategy that sought to uncover, as in the plays of Harold Pinter, the 'violent, sly, anguished' dispositions that reside beneath, but are rarely communicated, through language (*see* **Reading 15**).

Camus's levelling of absolute ethical norms, the Absurdists' abandonment of the defining potency of social roles and behavioural norms, and their radical mistrust of essentialist notions of self and human agency, paralleled a number of theoretical initiatives launched during this period in the philosophy of language, discourse theory and literary criticism, initiatives that formulated most clearly around the movement of Structuralism (and later Post-Structuralism). The Structuralists moved the axis of hermeneutic explication away from authorial intentionality and, following the linguist Ferdinand de Saussure, on to those impersonal grammars and taxonomies that provide for the generation of meaning within texts. This displacement of humanist notions of self and individual creativity found its most forceful statement in the writing of Roland Barthes, particularly in iconoclastic works such as *Writing Degree Zero* (1953), *On Racine* (1960) and, most trenchantly, in the polemical essay of 1968, 'The death of the author'. Here, in one of the seminal texts of the Structuralist movement, Barthes sought, with an almost Avant-Garde bravado, to dismantle an established literary anthropology that had become an institution in Western philology. For Barthes's target here is not only author-centred criticism but all closed systems of interpretation that seek to impose a definitive coherence on what is, for Barthes, an unstoppable process of semantic production. Construing literature through the latter optic allows us to see its greater cultural importance, not as a form of isolated self-expression but as an 'activity that one might designate as counter-theological, an activity that is truly revolutionary, for by refusing to arrest the production of meaning, one is ultimately refusing God and his hypostases: reason, science and the law' (**Reading 5**).

As is also clear from Barthes's essay, by disengaging the sign from its referent, the Structuralists (like Postmodernist writers) sought to hold open the free play of signification to allow those dynamic and, at times, aleatory workings within texts to stress themselves against stabilized and canonized models of meaning. The move that was being charted here might best be described (using Barthes's later words) as a move from 'work to text'. It was taken further by Post-Structuralist critics such as Julia Kristeva (whose notion of 'intertextuality' precisely identified the diverging and sometimes conflicting levels of writing within texts) and most systematically, perhaps, by Jacques Derrida, through his concept of 'différance'. In doing so, the Post-Structuralists broke both with the logocentric metaphysical systems of the past and with the taxonomic models of the Structuralists, whose formal systems of binary oppositions and generative grammars had the effect, it was argued, of closing down meaning even in the very process of its formation. As Derrida explained in his *Writing and Difference* (1967), writing is essentially a restless movement, a process of infinite equivocality which allows the signified no resting place; far from involving a fixing of semantic sense, 'writing is, on the contrary, the reawakening of the meaning of the will to will: it is freedom, a break with the realm of empirical history', a process that continually defers, because ultimately it has only itself as its true subject (**Reading 6**).

Linguistic self-consciousness, a determined disavowal of the easy complicity between author, text and reader, and a willingness to allow the polysemic and the connotative agency of language to assert itself against the safely denotative, formed the premises of the emerging Postmodern project in Europe, most notably in the novel. As John Fowles noted in one startling moment of self-reflection in his *The French Lieutenant's Woman* (1969), the contemporary novelist had, in the wake of the Structuralist critique of the subject, been forced to surrender not only the poetic licence of verisimilitude but also the myth of absolute notions of control and authority. Now, Fowles tells us, in the age of the Structuralist and Postmodern reconfiguration of the relationship between author and text, a new freedom has emerged for authors and characters alike. Certainly, the author may remain a privileged figure within the creative act, but 'what has changed is that we are no longer the gods of the Victorian image, omniscient and decreeing; but [are recast] in the new theological image, with freedom our first principle, not authority' (**Reading 7**).

The most systematic attempt to devise a new poetics of fiction in the early Postmodern period was made by a group of writers who worked within a framework known as 'The new French novel' (the *'nouveau roman'*). They included Alain Robbe-Grillet (*Jealousy*, 1957), Nathalie Sarraute (*The Planetarium*, 1959), Michel Butor (*Passing Time*, 1956) and Claude Simon (*The Flanders Road*, 1960). What they sought to undo, as Robbe-Grillet explained in his collection of essays, *Towards a New Novel* (1965), was the literary hegemony of the great Realist novel, whose unself-reflective anthropocentric conceptual grid, it was argued, tended to produce an image of a stable, coherent universe open to clear and full explication. The novels themselves (and Balzac is the target here) exuded a simplistic self-confidence that could no longer be sustained in a new environment, where the comfortable rapport between human sentience and the object–world has been both materially and theoretically shattered. The new novel, in an act of redress, set itself the task of reclaiming the world *as it is*, devoid of illusions, bereft of ready–made signification and without 'essentialist conceptions of man'. As Robbe-Grillet explained in a seminal essay written in 1963, once the myth of depth is abolished, 'objects will simply be *there*, before becoming *something*; and they will be there afterwards, hard, unalterable, present for always, as if mocking their own meaning, this meaning that seeks in vain to reduce them to the precarious role of tools, of transitory and unworthy materials' (**Reading 8**).

Once the world has been freed of preconceived meaning, the contours of the self become both more fluid and more impersonal, but, paradoxically, perhaps, more in tune with those deeper mental states that resist rational categorization and analysis. This was certainly an argument that underscored the work of Nathalie Sarraute. In novels such as *Tropisms* (1939), *Portrait of a Stranger* (1948) and *The Planetarium* (1959), Sarraute sought to complete (at least part) of the Modernist project: its attempt to find a linguistic form for essentially pre-linguistic modulations of consciousness (what Sarraute calls 'the unnamed'). In the distinctive narrative techniques of her novels, Sarraute attempted to find a solution to this problem, whilst at the same time, on a thematic level, showing characters (as she explained in an essay in 1971) struggling to find words for those evasive mental states that are in 'perpetual transformation', and resistant to the easy demarcations of conventional language (**Reading 9**).

After the *nouveau roman*, the Postmodern novel in Europe largely developed in one of two directions: towards the metafiction of writers such as Georges Perec (*Life, A User's Manual*, 1978) and Italo Calvino (*If on a Winter's Night a Traveller*, 1979), on the one hand, and towards the Magic Realism of Günter Grass (*The Tin Drum*, 1959), Michel Tournier (*The Erl-King*, 1970), Salman Rushdie (*Midnight's Children*, 1981) and, within a genre closer to science fiction, J. G. Ballard (*Crash*, 1974) on the other. Perec's work, in particular, with its use of linguistic games, diversions and puzzles, reflects the ludic, open (inter-) textuality of the Postmodern aesthetic. But it possesses something else: a desire to reach out to broader forms and modes of textual statement, to non–high-cultural artefacts, and to the enthusiastic profusions of popular media, such as television and the cinema. The ubiquitous presence of these media of popular culture constitutes both a challenge and an opportunity for writers intent on finding, as Perec explained in 1967, 'a new structure for the contemporary "imaginaire" '. As he argued in an essay from that year, the mass media (with its multi-textualities) can help the writer achieve an emancipatory role, and Perec points here to the healthy influence of the contemporary American Avant-Garde, whose eclecticism and aesthetic crossovers have opened up possibilities for 'implication, simultaneity and discontinuity' that may well provide a new rhetoric for the writer in the Postmodern period (**Reading 10**).

Forms of inter-textual play were not absent from the work of the magic Realists, but they found employment in ways that supported a broader historical and (sometimes) political reading of the contemporary world. In its attempts to grasp the fluid contours of the Postmodern experience, the magic Realist novel collapsed traditional distinctions between the fantastic and the normal, the supernatural and the natural, the objective and the subjective in order to demonstrate, using myths and recurrent symbols, how these spheres interact to determine private lives and national destinies. The image of Postmodernity that emerges from these texts is sometimes liberating, but at other times it is rooted in a vision of the contemporary world that sees the latter as the site of violent and irrational forces. For those writers who hold to such a vision, such as J. G. Ballard, Postmodernity moves not within the ambit of dream but of nightmare, and the energies unleashed are not the product of liberation but of a pathology of the self. In this culture of dark excess, as Ballard noted in the 1974 Introduction to his novel *Crash*, even interiority has been externalized. In this Baudriallardian dystopia, the individual is impelled by a manufactured optimism, the product of 'the iconography of mass merchandising, naivety and guilt-free enjoyment of all the mind's possibilities', including the freedom to destroy and be destroyed (**Reading 11**).

The deconstructive work that Structuralism and Post-Structuralism performed for the novel, liberating that genre from simplistic notions of authorial intentionality and textual referentiality, also found its place among poets writing in the Postmodern period, most notably in France and Italy. Many, such as Francis Ponge (*The Making of the Pre*, 1971) and Yves Bonnefoy (*In the Lure of the Threshold*, 1975), welcomed the importance placed by Barthes, Derrida and others upon (in Bonnefoy's words) 'the activity of the signifier', because it helped bring about 'the denunciation of certain illusory aspects of our consciousness of ourselves'. As Bonnefoy further explained in his inaugural address to the French Academy in 1983: 'we have learned to better perceive a web without beginning or end of transitory representations, of fictions without any authority.' Yet, as the poet also affirms, there is pushing against this recognition of the self-generating nature of textuality a need to retain the personal grain of the poetic utterance, to establish a bond between subjectivities that emerge both at the point of origin and at the reading of the text. The saying of 'I' continues to be *felt* as a personal significance, as does the need to register the metaphysical import of poetic perception, which (*pace* Derrida) seeks its grounding precisely in the presence of the object-world that surrounds us (**Reading 12**).

Other European poets have attempted to resolve such issues by looking to nature or myth to provide idioms that are not frozen by the self-referential hypertrophies of theory. Eastern and South-eastern European writers, in particular, such as the Polish poets Tadeusz Rózewicz (*Faces of Anxiety*, 1969), Czeslaw Milosz (*Hymn of the Pearl*, 1981) and Zbigniew Herbert (*A Study of the Object*, 1961), have been forced away from clear statement and close verisimilitude, not by epistemological considerations, but by political constraints that compel the poet to circumvent the easy identification of the signified. The process has given rise to languages that are often cryptic, encoded, frequently surreal, but also at times (as, for example, in the writing of the Serbian Vasko Popa), universal and mythic. As Ted Hughes (himself a poet who, in *Crow* (1970), elaborated his own private mythology) points out in his Introduction to Popa's work (whose main titles include *The Unrest Field* (1956) and *Earth Erect* (1972)), 'his poems turn the most grisly confrontations into something deadpan playful: a spell, a riddle, a game, a story'. This is a poetry of mythic encoding that leaves us with 'solid hieroglyphic objects and events, meaningful in a direct way, simultaneously earthen and spiritual, plain-statement and visionary' (**Reading 13**).

Finding a new idiom for the interaction between poetry and the public sphere was a task pursued by many poets in the Postmodern period, from Hans Magnus Enzensberger (*Disappearing Furies*, 1980) in Germany, through to Italian poets such as Pier Paolo Pasolini (*Gramsci's Ashes*, 1957), and Alfredo Giuliani and Nanni Balestrini (founding members of the 1960 'Novissimi' group). The Novissimi group, in particular, sought to articulate a form that would, through dissociative imagery, heightened ellipsis and irregular grammar, dislocate the reader from conventional notions of the poetic. But as Giuliani made clear in his famous Introduction to the Novissimi anthology of 1961, the renewal of the idiom of poetry is not simply a matter of personal creative volition; it requires poet and reader alike to confront such broader issues as the politics of the literary market, the control of publishing and distribution means, and the commodification of language in late capitalist society. The poet must engage with such realities, particularly as they manifest themselves in popular culture, for the latter constitutes a potency, a 'heteronomous semanticity' that can be mobilized against dominant trends within inherited high culture. As Giuliani explains: 'the techniques of mass culture entail a mental decomposition which we must take into consideration when we wish to produce a recomposition of meanings' (**Reading 14**).

Postmodernist writers viewed literature not as a closed system of canonic texts, but as a broader cultural activity, a form of practice that aimed to redraw the boundaries between the private and public spheres, seeking to undermine that easy subject–object relationship between producer and consumer that has often contributed to the consolidation of traditional power structures. Dramatists, in particular, could follow the important precedents set here by Bertolt Brecht, whose epic theatre (drawing upon the radical dramaturgy of producers such as Erwin Piscator) sought to provoke the audience into a critical engagement with the stage and its productions. The proselytizing momentum of Brecht's work was, however, largely rejected by Postmodern writers in favour of texts that looked for the political, not in the impingement of global ideologies, but in its exercise as a form of power at the local level of interpersonal relationships and in the contestations of power that they entail. In this respect, Harold Pinter spoke for many when he rejected the 'warnings, sermons, admonitions, ideological exhortations, moral judge-ments [and] defined problems with built-in solutions' that surfaced in the plays of the 1920s and 1930s (**Reading 15**). His further insistence that we interrogate not only the content of power but, above all, the linguistic forms that support it, seeing language as a form of repression, as covert violence even, parallels the enquiries made by Michel Foucault among others (see, for example, his *Discipline and Punish*, 1975) into how power relations are articulated on a micro-level through bodily gesture and the manipulation of space.

That this configuration of power as an exercise of the personal, and politics as the domain of the public, might have a tangible historical identity, might in fact constitute (as, for example, in the case of fascism) a recurring norm, was also recognized by playwrights in the era of Postmodernity, such as the East German Heiner Müller. Explicitly rejecting the Naturalist naivety that was the heritage of Socialist Realism, Müller characterized his plays, such as *Death in Berlin* (1971), *Battle* (1975) and the *Hamletmachine* (1979), as 'laboratories of social fantasy', seeing in them spaces where alternative readings of the political realm could be constructed and deconstructed (**Reading 16**). Significantly, drawing just as much upon the 'new wave' cinema of Jean-Luc Godard and the American performance art of Robert Wilson as upon the epic theatre of

Brecht, Müller's work demonstrates, as does Perec's, the transnational flow of textual paradigms in the age of Postmodernism.

Fantasy is also a part of the dramaturgy of the Italian satirist Dario Fo, but here the popular contact is established through pantomime, slapstick, clownery and the burlesque, forms that deliberately subvert the high-cultural pretensions of conventional theatre. Underwriting Fo's work is a commitment to the principle of the carnevalistic, which is intended to deflate the trappings and pompous exercise of institutional hegemony in all its guises (and most noticeably as it emanates from establishment institutions such as the police, the Church and the media). Fo's plays target those ceremonial forms that seek to bestow upon the often arbitrary exercise of power the aura and legitimacy of authority. In the theatre these areas of governmentality are subject to ridicule and satire, reduced to absurdity and hence deprived of their mystique through 'an explosion of liberation' that comes from the ironic perspective (**Reading 17**).

In the 'vocal pieces' ('*Sprechstücke*') of Peter Handke, confrontation is stripped down to its most affective level in a consciously anti-didactic dramaturgy that clearly departs from the *Lehrstücke* of Bertolt Brecht. In 'plays' such as *Offending the Audience* (1965) and *Cries for Help* (1967), language no longer functions as a referential medium (there is no world beyond the text and its performance), but as a series of perlocutionary speech acts: as insults, interrogations, accusations and exhortations, aimed at the audience actually present at the performance. The latter find themselves interpolated, not as in traditional drama, as an anonymous group of cultural connoisseurs, but as a quite specific group of individuals, participants in a dramatic event whose ultimate purpose is to position them as representatives of political reaction. In Handke's minimalist stage, the politics of Postmodernity resists its displacement into the relatively harmless realm of literary symbolism. Once removed from the comforting aura of its fictional status, drama assumes a gestural potency whose aim is not (as Handke explains in the Preface to *Offending the Audience*) to revolutionize, in the naïvely didactic sense of the word, but 'to raise people's consciousness' about the conditions under which political action can occur and be effective (**Reading 18**).

Abolishing the conventions that secure the divisions between the public and private spheres, fictional and non-fictional forms of textuality, and the division between producer and consumer opened up a space of writing for individuals and groups that had traditionally been marginalized from dominant literary discourses. Women were such a group. In the period of Postmodernity, many feminist writers took advantage of the aporia that had resulted from the decentring of conventional notions of selfhood and artistic agency to find a voice over and beyond that provided by a largely male-centred literary canon. As Simone de Beauvoir argued in her epochal *The Second Sex* (1949), female identity had hitherto appeared in male discourse as the 'privileged Other, through whom the subject fulfils himself'. Woman had been the shadow side of masculine sexuality, invoked as something beyond the legitimate and interpolated solely to delineate the (positive) contours of male selfhood (**Reading 19**).

Feminist writers contested this status, but nevertheless, many sought to retain the distinctive grain of female subjectivity and the corporeal and emotional experiences associated with its often strained assertion in the world. Finding a voice for that subjectivity (particularly as it defined itself as a moment of personal/political struggle) was the task of a generation of women writers in Europe, from Doris Lessing and Angela Carter through to Marguerite Duras, Christa Wolf and Elsa Morante, all of whom, in their different ways, give voice to the pain of becoming a knowing subject in their search for a form of writing ('*écriture féminine*') which might stand against that centring around the Logos which had hitherto excluded them from the canon of male writing.

Perhaps the most persuasive attempts to theorize this initiative came from the work of three French Feminists: Luce Irigary (*Speculum of the Other Woman* (1974) and *This Sex Which Is Not One* (1977)), Julia Kristeva (*About Chinese Women* (1974) and *Polylogue* (1977)) and Hélène Cixous (*The Third Body* (1970) and 'Laugh of the Medusa' (1976)). All attempted to elucidate positions of speech that engage with, but position themselves beyond, the dominating (and defining) gaze of male discourse. Mystical in certain cases (as in Kristeva's cultivation of an extreme interiority), Lacanian-analytically inflected in others (Cixous), the project was nevertheless a common one: to facilitate the voice that speaks from the margin, which preserves its integrity through subversion and dissidence. As with the broader strategy followed by the Postmodernists, this was also a process of liberation and self-liberation, in which the external world opened itself to change through the empowerment of certain types of subjectivity that cross masculinity and femininity, as conventionally defined. Here, the giving of the self is not equated with self-surrender, but forms, as Cixous explains in her *The Newly Born Woman* (1975), a new 'way of thinking through the non-identical' (**Reading 20**). Within this context, of a subjectivity freed from the constraints of a crude 'masculine/feminine' binary opposition, the anima, as Cixous lyrically describes it, finds its ultimate voice, allowing herself to speak 'the tongue of a thousand tongues, sound without obstruction or death. To life, she refuses nothing. Her language is beyond capacity, it transports; it does not retain, it makes possible'.

# 1

# 'A literature of war, of homecoming and of rubble'

## Heinrich Böll: 'In defense of rubble literature' (1952)

*Heinrich Böll (1917–85) was the first writer in postwar Germany to gain international recognition, winning the Nobel Prize in 1972 for novels such as* Adam Where Art Thou? *(1951),* Billiards at Half-past Nine *(1959) and* The Clown *(1963). Böll's earliest novels are minimalist both in form and content, describing characters living between the false ideals of the past and an absence of ideals in the present, members of a society that has unselfcritically given itself over to economic prosperity and material reconstruction. In an essay written in 1952, Böll sought to explain why such a minimalism seemed the only choice for writers confronted with the material and moral devastation of postwar Germany.*

The first literary attempts of our generation after 1945 were called, in an attempt to belittle them, 'Rubble Literature'. We did not resist this classification, because it was, in fact, accurate: the people about whom we wrote did indeed live amongst rubble; they had just returned from the war, and the men, the women and even the children had been equally scarred. But they were sharp-eyed; they could see. In no way did they live in a condition of peace; neither their environment nor their behaviour, nor anything within or beyond them could have been called idyllic. And we writers felt so close to them that we could identify with them entirely, as we could with the black-marketeers and the victims of the black-marketeers, with refugees and with all the others who had lost their homes in different ways. Above all, we identified, of course, with the generation to which we ourselves belonged, and which, to a large extent, found itself in a strange and problematic situation – it had survived the war, and had come home. This was the return from a war, for whose end none had dared to hope.

So we wrote about the war, about people returning from the war, and about what we had seen in the war, and about what we had found on our return: rubble. This writing came to be known through three catch phrases: it was a literature of war, of homecoming, and of rubble.

These designations were not unjustified: it had been a war which had lasted six long years, and we had returned from it to find only devastation,

**Source:** Heinrich Böll, *Essayistische Schriften und Reden, 1952–1963,* edited by Bernd Balzer (Cologne: Kiepenheuer & Witsch, 1979), pp. 31–5. **Standard translation:** *Missing Persons and Other Essays,* translated by Leila Vennwitz (New York: McGraw-Hill, 1977), pp. 126–31. **Further reading:** J. H. Reid, *Heinrich Böll: A German for His Times* (Oxford: Berg, 1988).

and this is what we had written about. What was strange, suspicious, even, was the reproachful, almost offended tone with which these labels were used. People didn't exactly make us responsible for the fact that there had been a war, and that everything lay in ruins; but they clearly resented the fact that we had seen and continued to see those things. But we were not wearing blindfolds, and could see clearly: a good eye belongs to a writer's tools of trade.

To have offered our contemporaries some escape into an idyllic world would have been an anathema to us; their awakening too appalling. Or should all of us have played blind-man's buff instead?

> *The past is one horror; the present-in-the-making yet another. As Böll goes on to explain, in the soullessness of a reconstructing Germany, the individual must once more give way again, not to war this time, but to the demands of an increasingly bureaucratic and impersonal society.*

He who has eyes to see, let him see! And in our beautiful mother language 'seeing' has a meaning that goes well beyond purely optical definitions; who has eyes to see, for him things will become totally clear, and it must be possible to see through things, by means of language, to see into the very depth of things. The eye of the writer should be humane and incorruptible: there is really no need to play blind-man's buff; here are rose-tinted glasses, and glasses tinted blue or black – they will colour reality according to need. Pink is well rewarded today, and is generally very popular – and the possibilities for corruption are manifold. But black also comes into fashion now and then, and when it becomes popular, it is also well paid. But we would see things as they are, and with a humane gaze, which at most times will be not quite dry and not quite wet, but damp; and it is worth remembering that the Latin word for dampness is *humor*. But we shouldn't forget that our eyes can become dry and wet, that there are things which do not give occasion for humour. Each day our eyes see many things: they see the baker, who bakes our bread; they see the girl working in the factory – and our eyes remember the graveyards. Our eyes see the rubble: the cities that have been destroyed, the cities that have become cemeteries, and our eyes see buildings arising around us, which look like stage settings, buildings, in which people do not live but, rather, are administered, treated as insurance customers, as citizens, as members of a municipality, as people who either wish to invest their money, or withdraw it. There exist numerous reasons for bureaucratizing individuals.

It is our task to remind people that mankind does not exist simply to be administered, and that the destruction in our world is not simply of an external nature, or so negligible that we can presume to deal with it within a few years.

# 2

# Making 'literature out of our condition of poverty'

## Italo Calvino: Preface to *The Path to the Nest of Spiders* (1964)

*Italo Calvino (1923–85) entered the canon of Postmodernism with works of pure
fabulation such as the trilogy* The Cloven Viscount *(1952),* The Baron in the
Trees *(1957) and* The Non-existent Knight *(1959). But Calvino had begun as
a writer of neo-Realism with his novel of the Italian Resistance,* The Path to the
Nest of Spiders. *In the second edition of that novel, Calvino explained how the lost
war had created a* tabula rasa *for himself and other writers, forcing the abandonment
of previous cultural models while opening up new, more popular ones that galvanized
Calvino and other young exponents of the 'neo-Realist' school.*

This was my first novel; I can almost say it was my first piece of writing,
apart from a few stories. What impression does it make on me now, when
I pick it up again? I read it not so much as something of mine but rather as
a book born anonymously from the general atmosphere of a period; from
a moral tension, a literary taste in which our generation recognised itself,
at the end of World War II.

Italy's literary explosion in those years was less an artistic event than a
psychological, existential, collective event. We had experienced the war,
and we younger people – who had been barely old enough to join the
partisans – did not feel crushed, defeated, 'beat'. On the contrary, we
were victors, driven by the propulsive charge of the just-ended battle, the
exclusive possessors of its heritage. Ours was not easy optimism, however,
or gratuitous euphoria. Quite the opposite. What we felt we possessed
was a sense of life as something that can begin again from scratch, a
general concern with problems, even a capacity within us to survive
torment and abandonment; but we added also an accent of bold gaiety.
Many things grew out of that atmosphere, including the attitude of my
first stories and my first novel.

This is what especially touches us today; the anonymous voice of that
time, stronger than our still-uncertain individual inflections. Having
emerged from an experience, a war and a civil war that had spared no
one, made communication between the writer and his audience
immediate. We were face to face, equals, filled with stories to tell; each
had his own; each had lived an irregular, dramatic, adventurous life; we

**Source:** Italo Calvino, *The Path to the Nest of Spiders*, translated by Archibald Colquhoun (New
York: The Ecco Press, 1976), pp. v–vii and xxii–xxiii. **Further reading:** Martin McLaughlin,
*Italo Calvino* (Edinburgh: Edinburgh University Press, 1998).

snatched the words from each other's mouths. With our renewed freedom of speech, all at first felt a rage to narrate: in the trains that were beginning to run again, crammed with people and sacks of flour and drums of olive oil, everybody told his vicissitudes to strangers, and so did every customer at the tables of the cheap restaurants, every woman waiting in line outside a shop. The grayness of daily life seemed to belong to other periods; we moved in a varicoloured universe of stories.

So anyone who started writing then found himself handling the same material as the nameless oral narrator. The stories we had personally enacted or had witnessed mingled with those we had already heard as tales, with a voice, an accent, a mimed expression. During the partisan war, stories just experienced were transformed and transfigured into tales told around the fire at night; they had already gained a style, a language, a sense of bravado, a search for anguished or grim effects. Some of my stories, some pages of this novel originated in that new-born oral tradition, in those events, in that language.

But . . . but the secret of how one wrote then did not lie only in this elementary universality of content; that was not its mainspring (perhaps having begun this preface by recalling a collective mood has made me forget I am speaking of a book, something written down, lines of words on the white page). On the contrary, it had never been so clear that the stories were raw material: the explosive charge of freedom that animated the young writer was not so much his wish to document or to inform as it was his desire to *express*. Express what? Ourselves, the harsh flavour of life we had just learned, so many things we thought we knew or were, and perhaps really knew or were at that moment. Characters, landscapes, shooting, political slogans, jargon, curses, lyric flights, weapons, and love-making were only colours on the palette, notes of the scale; we knew all too well that what counted was the music and not the libretto. Though we were supposed to be concerned with content, there were never more dogged formalists than we; and never were lyric poets as effusive as those objective reporters we were supposed to be.

For us who began there, 'neorealism' was this; and of its virtues and defects this book is a representative catalogue, born as it was from that green desire to make literature, a desire characteristic of the 'school'.

*As Calvino explains, neo-Realism had little in common with the provincial Realism favoured by some nineteenth-century Italian writers; on the contrary, neo-Realism looked outwards to the example of contemporary American fiction (that of Ernest Hemingway, for example), whose 'language, style [and] pace had so much importance for us'. Looking back from the 1960s, the neo-Realist school had, with most of its early exponents either dead or writing in a different style, clearly run its course; but its achievements were undeniable.*

When I say that we then made literature out of our condition of poverty,

I am not speaking so much of an ideological program as of something deeper in each of us.

Nowadays, when writing is a regular profession, when the novel is a 'product' with its 'market', its 'demand' and its 'supply', with its advertising campaigns, its successes, and its routine, now that Italian novels are all 'of a good average level' and are among the superfluous goods of a too quickly satisfied society, it is hard to recall the spirit in which we tried to imitate a kind of fiction that still had to be built entirely with our own hands.

I continue to use the plural, but I have already explained that I am speaking of something dispersed, not agreed upon, something that emerged from the scattered corners of the provinces, without explicit common reasons, unless they were partial and temporary. More than anything else it was, you could say, a widespread potential, something in the air. And soon extinct.

By the 1950s the picture had changed, starting with the masters: Pavese dead, Vittorini sealed off in a silence of opposition, Albert Moravia in a different context, taking on a different meaning (no longer existential but naturalistic); and the Italian novel assumed its elegiac-moderate socio-logical course. We all finally dug ourselves niches, more or less comfortable (or found our own avenues of escape).

But there were some who continued along the path of that first fragmentary epic. For the most part, they were the more isolated, the outsiders, who retained that strength.


3

_____


## *'The feeling of absurdity'*

### Albert Camus: *The Myth of Sisyphus* (1942)

*Albert Camus (1913–60) was, together with Jean-Paul Sartre, one of the leading exponents of Existentialism in postwar France. Both in his fictional work (most notably in his novel* The Outsider, *1942) and in his theoretical writing such as* The Myth of Sisyphus *(1942), Camus sought to explicate the notion of the Absurd, a term he used to typify that disjunction between the essential lack of*

**Source:** Albert Camus, *Le Mythe de Sisyphe: Essai sur l'absurde* (Paris: Gallimard, 1942), pp. 82–4 and 165–6. **Standard translation:** Albert Camus, *The Myth of Sisyphus and Other Essays*, translated by Justin O'Brien (New York: Vintage Books, 1955). **Further reading:** David Sprintzen, *Camus: A Critical Examination* (Philadelphia: Temple University Press, 1988), pp. 41–64.

*immanent meaning in the world and the human need for sense and purpose. As he explained in the early pages of* The Myth of Sisyphus*: 'A world that one can explain even with faulty reasoning is a familiar world. On the other hand, in a world suddenly divested of illusions and light man feels himself a stranger. His exile is without relief, because he has been deprived both of memories of his lost homeland and of hope for a promised land. This divorce between man and his life, the actor and his surroundings is exactly what constitutes the feeling of absurdity.' Recognizing this existential fact leads for some into the final exit of suicide; but for others it is, as Camus argues, a precondition for self-liberation and freedom, although this can only be reached not through mystical self-absorption but by confronting death, as Absurdist man tries to do.*

The Absurd enlightens me on one point: there is no tomorrow. From now on, this will be the reason for my inner freedom. I shall draw here two comparisons. Mystics, to begin with, find freedom in self-surrender. By losing themselves in their god, by consenting to his rules, they become secretly free. By spontaneously consenting to this subservience, they regain their inner independence. But what does this freedom really mean? The only thing that might be said is that they *feel* free within themselves, and not so much free as liberated. Similarly, the Absurdist man, his gaze totally fixed on death (seen here as the clearest of Absurd experiences), feels released from everything beyond that intense focus that is crystallizing in him. He enjoys a freedom with regard to everyday rules. One sees here that the original premises of existential philosophy retain all their relevance. The return to self-consciousness, the escape from the slumber of everyday life, mark the first steps of Absurdist freedom. But it is the Existential exhortation that is here addressed, and with it that spiritual leap that basically escapes consciousness. In the same way (and this is my second comparison), the slaves of Antiquity were not their own masters. But they knew that freedom which consists in not feeling responsible (as footnote; it is a matter here of a comparison of fact, not an apology of humility. Absurdist man is the opposite of the reconciled man). Death too has patrician hands, which crush but also liberate.

To lose oneself in that bottomless certainty, to feel, from that point on, so distant from one's own life that one can add to it and go through it without the myopic vision of the lover – this constitutes the principle of liberation. This new independence has a limit, like any freedom of action. It does not write a check on eternity. But it does replace those illusions of *freedom*, which all stopped with death. The divine openness of the condemned man in front of whom the prison doors open in a certain early dawn, his unbelievable indifference to everything, other than the pure flame of life; one clearly feels here that death and absurdity are the principles of the only true freedom: that which a human heart can experience and live. This is the second consequence. Absurdist man glimpses thus a universe that is burning but icy, transparent and limited, where nothing is possible but all is given, and beyond which all is destruction and nothingness. He might then decide to agree to live in such a universe and draw from it his strength, his refusal to hope, and his incontrovertible evidence of a life that has no consolations.

*Like Nietzsche before him, Camus used parable, myth and allegory to illustrate his philosophy, drawing in this particular work upon the legend of Sisyphus, the King of Corinth, whom the gods have condemned to roll the same rock up a hill, day after day, knowing that it will simply roll back down. Camus' existential humanism, however, allows him to glimpse a positive dimension to Sisyphus' hopeless task.*

One does not discover the Absurd without first trying to write a manual of happiness. 'What! To go through such a narrow gate . . . ?' But there is only one world. Happiness and the Absurd are two sons sprung from the same soil. They cannot be separated. The mistake would be to say that happiness is necessarily born from a discovery of the Absurd. It would be just as accurate to say that the feeling for the Absurd is born from happiness. 'It is my belief that all is good', said Oedipus, and his words are sacred. They echo across the savage and limited universe of man. They teach that all is not, and has never been, exhausted. They banish from this world a god who had arrived dissatisfied and with a taste for futile suffering. They make of fate a human matter that must be decided amongst men.

All of Sisyphus's silent joy is captured in these words. His destiny is evident to him. The rock is his fate. Likewise, the Absurd man, when he contemplates his torment, reduces the idols to silence. In a universe suddenly restored to its silence, a multitude of little voices cries out from the earth in wonder. Calls, secret and insensible, invitations from every countenance, they are the necessary reverse and the price of victory. There is never sun without shade, and it is necessary to know the night. Absurdist man says yes, and his effort is unceasing. If there is a personal fate, there is no higher destiny; or, at least there is, but one which he regards as fated and hence despicable. For the rest, he knows that he is master of his days. At that subtle moment where man looks back over his life, Sisyphus, returning to his rock, ponders upon that train of unrelated events that became his fate, were created by him, united by the gaze of his memory and soon sealed by his death. Thus, convinced of the wholly human origin of all that is human, a blind man eager to see, and knowing that night is not yet over for him, he continues his movements. The rock is still rolling.

I leave Sisyphus at the bottom of the mountain! One will always find one's burden. But Sisyphus teaches us the higher fidelity that denies the gods and lifts up rocks. He also decides that all is good. This universe, henceforth without master, does not appear to him sterile or futile. Each of the grains of this rock, each piece of stone on this mountain covered by darkness, represents for him a world in itself. Even the very struggle to reach the summit is enough to fill the heart of man. It is necessary to imagine Sisyphus happy.

4

---

## *To be 'bludgeoned into detachment from our banal existences, from habit'*

### Eugene Ionesco: *Notes and Counter-Notes* (1962)

*Eugene Ionesco (1912–94) was one of the founding figures of the Theatre of the Absurd, a genre that also included Ferdinand Arrabal, Jean Genet and, from the English-speaking world, Samuel Beckett and Harold Pinter. Like these dramatists, Ionesco sought, in plays such as* The Bald Prima-Donna *(1950),* The Chairs (1952), Victims of Duty *(1953) and, perhaps most notably, the critical allegory on fascism,* Rhinoceros *(1960), to demonstrate how cruelty and violence are inscribed into the commonplace rituals and practices that govern 'normal' life. In order to be able to recognize the existence of the irrational at the centre of the apparently rational, we must, Ionesco argued in his essay 'Experience of the theatre' (1962), be forcibly distanced from the enervating and stultifying regime of habit, a process that drama is well placed to advance. Ionesco explains this in his distinctive paratactic style.*

To push theatre out of that zone where it is neither theatre nor literature is to restore it to its proper place, to its natural boundaries. What was important was not obscuring the devices of the theatre but, on the contrary, making them more visible, clearly evident, and to get right down to the essence of the grotesque, of caricature, beyond the insipid irony of witty drawing-room comedies. Not drawing-room comedies but farce, with the force of extreme parody. Humour, certainly, but delivered with all the techniques of burlesque. A hard comedy, without finesse, excessive. Not dramatic comedies, either. But back to the unbearable. To push everything towards a paroxysm, to where tragedy has its sources. To produce a theatre of violence: violently comic, violently tragic.

To avoid psychology, or, rather, to give it a metaphysical dimension.

---

**Source:** Eugene Ionesco, *Notes et contre-notes* (Paris: Gallimard, 1962), pp. 13–15. **Standard translation:** Eugene Ionesco, *Notes and Counter-Notes*, translated by Donald Watson (London: John Calder, 1964). **Further reading:** Martin Esslin, *The Theatre of the Absurd* (London: Eyre & Spottiswoode, 1964), pp. 94–150.

Drama consists in the extreme exaggeration of sentiment, exaggeration which dislocates the flatness of everyday reality. Dislocation also, and the disarticulation of language.

Moreover, if comedians annoyed me by not seeming natural enough, it is perhaps because they too were, or tried to be, too natural: by giving up such attempts, they might perhaps become such, but in another manner. It is important that they should not be scared of not being natural.

We need to be virtually bludgeoned into detachment from our banal existences, from habit, and from mental sluggishness, which conceal from us the strangeness of the world. Without a fresh virginity of mind, without a new, purified grasp of existential reality, there is no theatre, nor art either. But reality must be dislocated before it can be reintegrated.

To achieve this effect, one can sometimes employ a certain technique: playing against the script. A text that is crazy, absurd, comical can be provided with a production and an interpretation that is serious, solemn, and ceremonious. On the other hand, to avoid the ridiculous sentimentality of the tearjerker one might treat a dramatic text as a piece of buffoonery, and underscore its tragic sense through farce. Light makes shadow look even darker; shadow accentuates light. For my part, I have never understood the difference that people make between tragedy and comedy. Comedy, being an intuitive perception of the absurd, seems to me more despairing than tragedy. Comedy offers no way out. I say 'despairing', but in reality it lies beyond both hope and despair.

For some people, tragedy might seem comforting in a way, for even as it is attempting to express the impotence of man bruised and beaten by fate, tragedy acknowledges in the same gesture the existence of fate, of destiny, of those laws which rule the universe and which are often inscrutable but nevertheless objective. And this human impotence, the futility of our efforts might also, in one sense, appear comical.

I have called my comedies 'anti-plays', 'comic dramas', and my dramas 'pseudo-dramas' or 'tragic farces', because it seems to me that comedy is tragic, and human tragedy something risible. The modern critical mind takes nothing too seriously or too lightly. I tried in my *Victims of Duty* to infuse comedy into tragedy, and in *Chairs* tragedy into comedy, or, in other words, to set comedy and tragedy against each other, in order to produce a new theatrical synthesis of the two. But it is not a true synthesis, for these two modes cannot coalesce; but they can coexist, forever repelling one another, putting each other into relief, criticizing and negating one another, and finally arriving, therefore, thanks to this opposition, at a state of dynamic equilibrium and tension. Amongst my plays, I believe that *Victims of Duty* and *The New Tenant* have best met this requirement.

In a similar way, one can confront the prosaic with the poetic, and the normal with the unusual. That is what I tried to do in *Jacques, or the Submission*, which I also described as a 'Naturalist Comedy', because, after commencing in a Naturalist tone, I tried to go beyond Naturalism.

Likewise, *Amédée, or How to get rid of it*, in which the action takes place in the apartment of a petit-bourgeois family, is a Realist play, into which I introduced certain fantastic elements, which served both to destroy and, at the same time, to underline the realism of the play.

In my first play, *The Bald Prima-Donna* (which started off as an attempt to parody the theatre, and, through that, to parody a certain type of human behaviour), it was by plunging into banality, getting down to the depths, to the ultimate limits of the most hackneyed clichés of everyday language, that I tried to give full expression to that sense of strangeness that seems to me to bathe our entire existence.

5

---

# 'The book itself is only a tissue of signs'

## Roland Barthes: 'The death of the Author' (1968)

*Roland Barthes (1915–80) was one of the major voices of French Structuralism, a theoretical movement that sought to uncover those systems of signification that determine all forms of text, from everyday artefacts (see, for example, Barthes's analysis of the products of commodity culture in* Mythologies, *1957) through to canonic works of literature (*On Racine, *1960). Irrespective of its cultural status, Barthes argued, in his famous essay 'The death of the Author', the text has to be severed from its traditional dependency upon the constraining reference point of authorial intentionality for it to reveal its full semantic complexity.*

The removal of the Author (one could talk here with Brecht of a veritable 'distancing', the Author diminishing like a figurine at the far end of the literary stage) is not merely an historical fact or an act of writing; it utterly transforms the modern text (or – which is the same thing – the text is henceforth made and read in such a way that at all its levels the author is absent). The temporality is different. The Author, when believed in, is always conceived of as the past of his own book: book and author stand automatically on a single line divided into a *before* and an *after*. The Author is thought to *nourish* the book, which is to say that he exists before it,

**Source:** Roland Barthes, 'La mort de l'auteur', in *Images, Music, Text*, essays selected and translated by Stephen Heath (London: Flamingo, 1984), pp. 142–8. **Further reading:** Jonathan Culler, *Barthes* (London: Fontana, 1983).

thinks, suffers, lives for it, is in the same relation of antecedence to his work as a father to his child. In complete contrast, the modern scriptor is born simultaneously with the text, is in no way equipped with a being preceding or exceeding the writing, is not the subject with the book as predicate; there is no other time than that of the enunciation and every text is eternally written *here and now*. The fact is (or, it follows) that *writing* can no longer designate an operation of recording, notation, representation, 'depiction' (as the Classics would say); rather, it designates exactly what linguists, referring to Oxford philosophy, call a performative, a rare verbal form (exclusively given in the first person and in the present tense) in which the enunciation has no other content (contains no other proposition) than the act by which it is uttered – something like the *I declare* of kings or the *I sing* of very ancient poets. Having buried the Author, the modern scriptor can thus no longer believe, as according to the pathetic view of his predecessors, that this hand is too slow for his thought or passion and that consequently, making a law of necessity, he must emphasize this delay and indefinitely 'polish' his form. For him, on the contrary, the hand, cut off from any voice, borne by a pure gesture of inscription (and not of expression), traces a field without origin – or which, at least, has no other origin than language itself, language which ceaselessly calls into question all origins.

We know now that a text is not a line of words releasing a single 'theological' meaning (the 'message' of the Author-God) but a multi-dimensional space in which a variety of writings, none of them original, blend and clash. The text is a tissue of quotations drawn from the innumerable centres of culture. Similar to Bouvard and Pécuchet, those eternal copyists, at once sublime and comic and whose profound ridiculousness indicates precisely the truth of writing, the writer can only imitate a gesture that is always anterior, never original. His only power is to mix writings, to counter the ones with the others, in such a way as never to rest on any one of them. Did he wish to *express himself*, he ought at least to know that the inner 'thing' he thinks to 'translate' is itself only a ready-formed dictionary, its words only explainable through other words, and so on indefinitely; something experienced in exemplary fashion by the young Thomas de Quincey, he who was so good at Greek that in order to translate absolutely modern ideas and images into that dead language, he had, so Baudelaire tells us (in *Paradis Artificiels*), 'created for himself an unfailing dictionary, vastly more extensive and complex than those resulting from the ordinary patience of purely literary themes'. Succeeding the Author, the scriptor no longer bears within him passions, humours, feelings, impressions, but rather this immense dictionary from which he draws a writing that can know no halt: life never does more than imitate the book, and the book itself is only a tissue of signs, an imitation that is lost, infinitely deferred.

*Once the Author is removed, the text is freed from the tyranny of a single privileged meaning.*

In the multiplicity of writing, everything is to be *disentangled*, nothing *deciphered*; the structure can be followed, 'run' (like the thread of a stocking) at every point and at every level, but there is nothing beneath: the space of writing is to be ranged over, not pierced; writing ceaselessly posits meaning ceaselessly to evaporate it, carrying out a systematic exemption of meaning. In precisely this way literature (it would be better from now on to say *writing*), by refusing to assign a 'secret', an ultimate meaning, to the text (and to the world as text), liberates what may be called an anti-theological activity, an activity that is truly revolutionary since to refuse to fix meaning is, in the end, to refuse God and his hypostases – reason, science, law.

*The disclosure of meaning in a text now becomes the task not of the Author but of the reader, who is liberated from his or her role as a passive consumer of authorial intention.*

Thus is revealed the total existence of writing: a text is made of multiple writings, drawn from many cultures and entering into mutual relations of dialogue, parody, contestation, but there is one place where this multiplicity is focused and that place is the reader, not, as was hitherto said, the author. The reader is the space on which all the quotations that make up a writing are inscribed without any of them being lost; a text's unity lies not in its origin but in its destination. Yet this destination cannot any longer be personal: the reader is without history, biography, psychology; he is simply that *someone* who holds together in a single field all the traces by which the written text is constituted. Which is why it is derisory to condemn the new writing in the name of a humanism hypocritically turned champion of the reader's rights. Classic criticism has never paid any attention to the reader; for it, the writer is the only person in literature. We are now beginning to let ourselves be fooled no longer by the arrogant antiphrastical recriminations of good society in favour of the very thing it sets aside, ignores, smothers, or destroys; we know that to give writing its future, it is necessary to overthrow the myth: the birth of the reader must be at the cost of the death of the Author.

# 6

# 'This lost certainty, this absence of divine writing'

## Jacques Derrida: *Writing and Difference* (1967)

*The work of Jacques Derrida (b. 1930) represents the radicalization of elements within the thinking of the Structuralist school, most notably its concern with the dynamics of textuality and the free play of 'signification'. As such, Derrida went beyond Structuralism (whose main bent was to limit meaning to certain predetermined structures – hence the pervasive emphasis upon grammar and typology, particularly in the writing of A-J. Greimas) into Poststructuralism. Works such as* Writing and Difference *and* On Grammatology *stress the instability of the written sign, the fact that it is the result of a collision between the denotative and connotative potency of words, which allows it to occupy a semantic space that Derrida (himself playing on a pun) called 'difference'. In his* Writing and Difference, *Derrida speculated upon the dynamics of writing (and in a style which itself often seemingly enacts this famous process).*

To write is not only to know that the Book does not exist and that forever there are books, against which the meaning of a world not conceived by an absolute subject is shattered, before it has even become a unique meaning; nor is it only to know that the non-written and the non-read cannot be relegated to the status of having no basis by the obliging negativity of some dialectic, making us deplore the absence of the Book from under the burden of 'too many texts!' It is not only to have lost the theological certainty of seeing every page bind itself into the unique text of the truth, the 'book of reason' as the journal in which accounts (*rationes*) and experiences consigned for Memory was formerly called, the genealogical anthology, the Book of Reason this time, the infinite manuscript read by a God who, in a more or less deferred way, is said to have given us use of his pen. This lost certainty, this absence of divine writing, that is to say, first of all, the absence of the Jewish God (who himself writes, when necessary), does not solely and vaguely define something like 'modernity'. As the absence and haunting of the divine sign, it regulates all modern criticism and aesthetics. There is nothing astonishing about this. 'Consciously or not,' says Georges Canguilhem, 'the idea that man has of his poetic power corresponds to the idea he has about the creation of the world, and to the solution he gives to the

**Source:** Jacques Derrida, *Writing and Difference*, edited and translated by Alan Bass (London: Routledge & Kegan Paul, 1978), pp. 10–11, 12–13. **Further reading:** Christopher Norris, *Derrida* (London: Fontana, 1987).

problem of the radical origin of things. If the notion of creation is equivocal, ontological and aesthetic, it is not so by chance or confusion.' To write is not only to know that through writing, through extremities of style, the best will not necessarily transpire, as Leibniz thought it did in divine creation, nor will the transition to what transpires always be *willful*, nor will that which is noted down always infinitely *express* the universe, resembling and reassembling it. It is also to be incapable of making meaning absolutely precede writing: it is thus to lower meaning while simultaneously elevating inscription. The eternal fraternity of theological optimism and of pessimism: nothing is more reassuring, but nothing is more despairing, more destructive of our books than the Leibnizian Book. On what could books in general live, what would they be if they were not alone, so alone, infinite, isolated worlds? To write is to know that what has not yet been produced within literality has no other dwelling place, does not await us as prescription in some *topos ouranios*, or some divine understanding. Meaning must await being said or written in order to inhabit itself, and in order to become, by differing from itself, what it is: meaning. This is what Husserl teaches us to think in *The Origin of Geometry*. The literary act thus recovers its true power at its source. In a fragment of a book he intended to devote to *The Origin of Truth*, Merleau-Ponty wrote: 'Communication in literature is not the simple appeal on the part of the writer to meanings which would be part of an a priori of the mind; rather, communication arouses these meanings in the mind through enticement and a kind of oblique action. The writer's thought does not control his language from without; the writer is himself a kind of new idiom, constructing itself.' 'My own words take me by surprise and teach me what I think', he said elsewhere.

It is because writing is *inaugural*, in the fresh sense of the word, that it is dangerous and anguishing. It does not know where it is going, no knowledge can keep it from the essential precipitation toward the meaning that it constitutes and that is, primarily, its future. However, it is capricious only through cowardice. There is thus no insurance against the risk of writing. Writing is an initial and graceless resource for the writer, even if he is not an atheist but, rather, a writer. Did Saint John Chrysostom speak of the writer? 'It were indeed meet for us not at all to require the aid of the written Word, but to exhibit a life so pure, that the grace of the spirit should be instead of books to our souls, and that as these are inscribed with ink, even so should our hearts be with the Spirit. But, since we have utterly put away from us this grace, come let us at any rate embrace the second best course.' But, all faith or theological assurance aside, is not the experience of *secondarity* tied to the strange redoubling by means of which constituted – written – meaning presents itself as prerequisitely and simultaneously *read*: and does not meaning present itself as such at the point at which the other is found, the other who maintains both the vigil and the back-and-forth motion, the work, that comes between writing and reading, making this work irreducible? Meaning is neither before nor after the act. Is not that which is called God, that which imprints every human course and recourse with its secondarity, the passageway of deferred reciprocity between reading and writing? or the absolute witness to the dialogue in which what one sets out to write has already been read, and what one sets out to say is already a response, the third party as the transparency of meaning? Simultaneously part of creation and the Father of Logos. The circularity and traditionality of Logos. The strange labor of conversion and adventure in which grace can only be that which is missing.

*Derrida consolidates his argument with a discussion of the ideas of Raymond Roussel and Paul Valéry, before locating the emancipatory role of poetry in this scheme of the liberated Logos.*

This revelatory power of true literary language as poetry is indeed the access to free speech, speech unburdened of its signalizing functions by the word 'Being' (and this, perhaps, is what is aimed at beneath the notion of the 'primitive word' or the 'theme-word', *Leitwort*, of Buber). It is when that which is written is *deceased* as a sign-signal that it is born as language; for then it says what is, thereby referring only to itself, a sign without signification, a game or pure functioning, since it ceased to be *utilized* as natural, biological, or technical information, or as the transition from one existent to another, from a signifier to a signified. And, paradoxically, inscription alone – although it is far from always doing so – has the power of poetry, in other words has the power to arouse speech from its slumber as sign. By enregistering speech, inscription has as its essential objective, and indeed takes this fatal risk, the emancipation of meaning – as concerns any actual field of perception – from the natural predicament in which everything refers to the disposition of a contingent situation. This is why writing will never be simple 'voice-painting' (Voltaire). It creates meaning by enregistering it, by entrusting it to an engraving, a groove, a relief, to a surface whose essential characteristic is to be infinitely transmissible. Not that this characteristic is always desired, nor has it always been; and writing as the origin of pure historicity, pure traditionality, is only the *telos* of a history of writing whose philosophy is always to come. Whether this project of an infinite tradition is realized or not, it must be acknowledged and respected in its sense as a project. That it can always fail is the mark of its pure finitude and its pure historicity. If the play of meaning can overflow signification (signalization), which is always enveloped within the regional limits of nature, life and the soul, this overflow is the moment of the attempt-to-write. The attempt-to-write cannot be understood on the basis of voluntarism. The will to write is not an ulterior determination of a primal will. On the contrary, the will to write reawakens the willful sense of the will: freedom, break with the domain of empirical history, a break whose aim is reconciliation with the hidden essence of the empirical, with pure historicity. The will and the attempt to write are not the desire to write, for it is a question here not of affectivity but of freedom and duty. In its relationship to Being, the attempt-to-write poses itself as the only way out of affectivity. A way out that can only be aimed at, and without the certainty that deliverance is possible or that it is outside affectivity. To be affected is to be finite: to write could still be to deceive finitude, and to reach Being – a kind of Being which could neither be, nor affect me by *itself* – from without existence. To write would be to attempt to forget difference: to forget writing in the presence of so-called living and pure speech.

7

---

## *'Fiction is woven into all'*

### John Fowles: *The French Lieutenant's Woman* (1969)

*John Fowles (b. 1926) is an English novelist whose main works include* The Magus *(1966, revised 1977),* The French Lieutenant's Woman *(1969),* Daniel Martin *(1977) and* Mantissa *(1982). Set in Victorian middle-class England,* The French Lieutenant's Woman *largely employs a narrative line that is supported by traditional concerns for verisimilitude in plot and characterization. But at a point midway through the novel, the narrator asks, concerning one of his characters, 'Who is Sarah? Out of what shadows does she come?' Fowles (author/ narrator) answers with an abrupt intervention into the otherwise Realist discourse of the novel, which leads into an extended meditation upon the artifice of novel-writing, whose tenets and practices must, Fowles argues, be quite different in the age of Postmodernity.*

I do not know. This story I am telling is all imagination. These characters I create never existed outside my own mind. If I have pretended until now to know my characters' minds and innermost thoughts, it is because I am writing in (just as I have assumed some of the vocabulary and 'voice'

---

**Source:** John Fowles, *The French Lieutenant's Woman* (London: Jonathan Cape, 1969), pp. 97–9. **Further reading:** James Acherson, *John Fowles* (London: Macmillan, 1998).

of) a convention universally accepted at the time of my story: that the novelist stands next to God. He may not know all, yet he tries to pretend that he does. But I live in the age of Alain Robbe-Grillet and Roland Barthes; if this is a novel, it cannot be a novel in the modern sense of the word.

So perhaps I am writing a transposed autobiography; perhaps I now live in one of the houses I have brought into the fiction; perhaps Charles is myself disguised. Perhaps it is only a game. Modern women like Sarah exist, and I have never understood them. Or perhaps I am trying to pass off a concealed book of essays on you. Instead of chapter headings, perhaps I should have written 'On the Horizontality of Existence', 'The Illusions of Progress', 'The History of the Novel Form', 'The Aetiology of Freedom', 'Some Forgotten Aspects of the Victorian Age' . . . what you will.

Perhaps you suppose that a novelist has only to pull the right strings and his puppets will behave in a lifelike manner; and produce on request a thorough analysis of their motives and intentions. Certainly I intended at this stage (*Chap. Thirteen – unfolding of Sarah's true state of mind*) to tell all – or all that matters. But I find myself suddenly like a man in the sharp spring night, watching from the lawn beneath that dim upper window in Marlborough House; I know in the context of my book's reality that Sarah would never have brushed away her tears and leant down and delivered a chapter of revelation. She would instantly have turned, had she seen me there just as the old moon rose, and disappeared into the interior shadows.

But I am a novelist, not a man in a garden – I can follow her where I like? But possibility is not permissibility. Husbands could often murder their wives – and the reverse – and get away with it. But they don't.

You may think novelists always have fixed plans to which they work, so that the future predicted by Chapter One is always inexorably the actuality of Chapter Thirteen. But novelists write for countless different reasons: for money, for fame, for reviewers, for parents, for friends, for loved ones; for vanity, for pride, for curiosity, for amusement: as skilled furniture-makers enjoy making furniture, as drunkards like drinking, as judges like judging, as Sicilians like emptying a shotgun into an enemy's back. I could fill a book with reasons, and they would all be true, though not true of all. Only one same reason is shared by all of us: *we wish to create worlds as real as, but other than the world that is*. Or was. This is why we cannot plan. We know a world is an organism, not a machine. We also know that a genuinely created world must be independent of its creator; a planned world (a world that fully reveals its planning) is a dead world. It is only when our characters and events begin to disobey us that they begin to live. When Charles left Sarah on her cliff-edge, I ordered him to walk straight back to Lyme Regis. But he did not; he gratuitously turned and went down to the Dairy.

Oh, but you say, come on – what I really mean is that the idea crossed my mind as I wrote that it might be more clever to have him stop and drink milk . . . and meet Sarah again. That is certainly one explanation of what happened; but I can only report – and I am the most reliable witness – that the idea seemed to me to come clearly from Charles, not myself. It is not only that he has begun to gain an autonomy; I must respect it, and disrespect all my quasi-divine plans for him, if I wish him to be real.

In other words, to free myself, I must give him, and Tina, and Sarah, even the abominable Mrs Poulteney, their freedoms as well. There is only one good definition of God: the freedom that allows other freedoms to exist. And I must conform to that definition.

The novelist is still a god, since he creates (and not even the most aleatory avant-garde modern novel has managed to extirpate its author completely); what has changed is that we are no longer the gods of the Victorian image, omniscient and decreeing; but in the new theological image, with freedom our first principle, not authority.

I have disgracefully broken the illusion? No. My characters still exist, and in a reality no less, or no more, real than the one I have just broken. Fiction is woven into all, as a Greek observed some two and a half thousand years ago. I find this new reality (or unreality) more valid; and I would have you share my own sense that I do not fully control these creatures of my mind, any more than you control – however hard you try, however much of a latter-day Mrs Poulteney you may be – your children, colleagues, friends, or even yourself.

But this is preposterous? A character is either 'real' or 'imaginary'? If you think that, *hypocrite lecteur*, I can only smile. You do not even think of your own past as quite real; you dress it up, you gild it or blacken it, censor it, tinker with it . . . fictionalize it, in a word, and put it away on a shelf – your book, your romanced autobiography. We are all in flight from the real reality. That is a basic definition of *Homo sapiens*.

So if you think all this unlucky (but it *is* Chapter Thirteen) digression has nothing to do with your Time, Progress, Society, Evolution and all those other capitalized ghosts in the night that are rattling their chains behind the scenes of this book . . . I will not argue. But I shall suspect you.

# 8

## Against 'the tyranny of signification'

### Alain Robbe-Grillet: *Towards a New Novel* (1963)

*Alain Robbe-Grillet (b. 1922) was one of the leading exponents of the 'New French novel' (*nouveau roman*), an experimental fictional form practised by, apart from Robbe-Grillet, writers such as Michel Butor, Claude Simon and Nathalie Sarraute. Robbe-Grillet's novels, most notably* The Erasers *(1953),* The Voyeur *(1955) and* Jealousy *(1957), are sustained by the wish to see the all-embracing totality of the nineteenth-century novel (particularly as represented by Balzac), with its omniscient narration, its rounded characterization, its linear and closed narratives, replaced by a more open form of writing that can accommodate both the aleatory nature of human experience (its essential randomness), and its lack of metaphysical depth. In the work of the* nouveau roman, *the external world is granted a greater autonomy, and objects are allowed to exist in their own right rather than as signifiers of human intentionality. Robbe-Grillet outlines the consequences of his theory.*

In the place of that universe of 'signification' (psychological, social, and functional), it would, then, be necessary to try and construct a more solid, more immediate world. Let it be, above all, by their *presence* that objects and gestures impose themselves, and let that presence continue to hold sway over all analytical theories that would try to contain them within some referential system, whether they be sentimental, sociological, Freudian, metaphysical, or any other.

In the construction of future novels, gestures and objects will be simply *there*, before becoming *something*; and they will still be there afterwards, hard, unalterable, present for always, as if mocking their own meaning, this meaning that seeks in vain to reduce them to the precarious role of tools, of transitory and unworthy materials, which have been moulded exclusively – and in the most resolute fashion – by a superior human truth which, once it has used them as the vehicles for its expression, banishes them as embarrassing props into oblivion, into darkness.

Henceforth, however, objects will gradually lose their impermanence and their secrets, will renounce their false mystery, that suspect interiority which a recent commentator has described as 'the romantic heart of

**Source:** Alain Robbe-Grillet, *Pour un nouveau roman* (Paris: Gallimard, 1963), pp. 23–4 and 25–6. **Standard translation:** Alain Robbe-Grillet, *For a New Novel: Essays on Fiction*, translated by Richard Howard (New York: Grove Press, 1965), pp. 15–24. **Further reading:** Stephen Heath, *The Nouveau Roman: A Study in the Practice of Writing* (London: Elek, 1972), pp. 67–152.

things'. No longer will objects be the vague reflection of the vague soul of the hero, the mirror image of his torments, the shadow of his desires. Or, if they do momentarily continue to act as buttresses to human emotions, this will be a purely temporary state of affairs, which will accept the tyranny of signification only in appearance – almost derisively – only to more fully demonstrate the extent to which they remain alien to man.

As far as characters of the future novel are concerned, they might possibly be open to an abundance of likely interpretations; they might, according to the priorities of different readers, give rise to a variety of commentaries, psychological, psychiatric, religious or political. But one will soon discover how indifferent these characters are to this so-called abundance. Whereas the traditional hero is forever being solicited, way-laid, erased by these interpretations of the author, constantly displaced into an immaterial and unstable elsewhere, always more remote and indistinct, the hero of the future novel will, on the contrary, remain where he is. And it will be the commentaries that will be left elsewhere; faced with his irrefutable presence, they will seem useless, superfluous, even dishonest.

> *Robbe-Grillet invokes the genre of the detective story to demonstrate how close we are to this future novel, before concluding with a pithy critique of the notion of metaphysical 'depth' in fiction.*

All this might seem overly theoretical, even illusionary, if it were not for the fact that things are changing – and in a way that is total and definitive – in our relations with the universe. That is why we can glimpse an answer to that ironically put question: 'Why now?' Today we are, in fact, witnesses of a new development that separates us radically from Balzac, as it does from Gide or Madame de La Fayette: it is the abandonment of the old myths of 'depth'.

We know that the entire literature of the novel was based on such myths, and on them alone. The role of the author traditionally consisted in mining the depths of Nature, descending as far as possible, in order to reach increasingly deeper layers, and then finally bringing to light some fragment of a disturbing secret. Having descended into the abyss of human passions, he would send up to a world seemingly tranquil in appearance (the world on the surface) triumphant messages describing the mysteries that he had encountered. And the sacred vertigo the reader suffered on these occasions, far from causing anguish or nausea, would, on the contrary, reassure him of his power to dominate the world. There were chasms, certainly, but, thanks to these valiant explorers of the deep, their depths could be sounded.

It is not surprising, under these conditions, that the literary phenomenon par excellence should have resided in the form of the total and unique adjective, which sought to bring together all those traits of the internal world – the entire hidden soul of things. The word functioned, thus, as a snare in which the author could trap the universe, and then deliver it up to society.

The revolution that has taken place has the same proportions: not only do we no longer consider the world as ours, as our private property, as something designed to satisfy our needs and fully domesticated; but we no longer even believe in its depth. Whereas the essentialist conceptions of man are facing their extinction (with the notion of 'condition' from now on replacing that of 'nature'), the *surface* of things has ceased to be for us the mask of their heart. This is a sentiment that has acted as the first step to our 'going beyond' metaphysics.

It is, then, the entirety of literary language that must change, that is already changing. On a daily basis, we can observe the growing repugnance felt by the most sensitive commentators for words that are visceral, analogical or incantatory. On the other hand, adjectives that are optical and descriptive, words that are satisfied with measuring, placing, defining, are most likely to show the difficult way forward for the new art of the novel.

9

---

# 'The unwinding of these states in perpetual transformation'

## Nathalie Sarraute: 'What I am seeking to do' (1971)

*The novels of Nathalie Sarraute (b. 1902) – Tropisms (1939), Portrait of a Stranger (1948) and The Planetarium (1959) – are conventionally bracketed with those of the other exponents of the New French novel, such as Alain Robbe-Grillet and Michel Butor. But Sarraute does not follow the obsessive interest that these writers show in the pure externality of the phenomenal world. On the contrary, as the essays in her major theoretical work,* The Age of Suspicion *(1956), indicate, Sarraute remains centrally concerned with the Modernist exploration (and the influence of Virginia Woolf is vital here) of the fluid process of the mind, and most particularly (as she explains in the following extract) with those 'movements' that reveal themselves in the stirrings, tremors, inklings and other mental states that exist on the edge of consciousness.*

---

**Source:** Nathalie Sarraute, *Oeuvres complètes*, edited by Jean-Yves Tadie (Paris: Gallimard, 1996), pp. 1702–4. There is no standard translation. **Further reading:** Valerie Minogue, *Nathalie Sarraute and the War with Words: A Study of Five Novels* (Edinburgh: Edinburgh University Press, 1981), esp. pp. 7–29.

Please allow me now to speak to you – since this is the title of my paper and it is towards this that my preceding remarks have been directed – to speak to you of my own efforts in this area.

But I must declare right from the start (and with a sincerity that I hope you won't doubt), that I have never sought to offer a message in my writing, or to provide the slightest moral lesson, nor to set up as a rival to the psychologists or the psychiatrists by discovering any psychological truths. No, all that I have wanted to do is to explore through language, a part, however minute it might have been, of the unnamed.

The very vague and rough global designation that I gave to my first book, *Tropisms*, was an inadequate definition of those movements whose attraction for me resides in the fact that they do not carry, and can not carry, any name.

These movements belong, in fact, to those marshy and obscure regions towards which the child in *Between Life and Death* heads, in order to escape from 'poetic language', to those disdained regions to which [the character] Alain Guimier, in *The Planetarium*, tries to draw attention, and which Germain Lemaire turns away from, that writing that is so solidly installed in those vast domains which, to his eyes, belong to 'Literature'.

For what attracts me about these movements, these states (but these are inexact terms) is their shifting aspect, murky, and elusive. I felt, in fact, that in order to capture them in language it would be necessary to transport myself beyond those regions which had, in every way, already been occupied, and where literary language had set up its models, admirable and crushing. Here, in this little domain, I felt that I could finally make contact with my own feelings.

These movements, in order to come into existence, require the use of certain forms different from those used in the traditional novel. In order for them to unfold themselves in front of my eyes (and the eyes – I hope – of the reader), so that nothing should disturb us, they need to appear as if detached and, so to speak, in a pure state.

Characters in novels can do nothing other than divert our attention to themselves, to enclose in a mould that which cannot be contained, that fluid substance which flows within us all, passes from one to the other, in clearing those boundaries that have been arbitrarily fixed. Such characters can be nothing other than the bearers of states of being, anonymous vassals, hardly visible, simple constructs of chance.

Sometimes, it is across a group that this fluid substance circulates the most easily, a group often designated by 'the men' or 'the women' [*ils* or *elles*], but where the use of masculine or feminine designations was often determined only by a phonetic consideration or a desire for diversity.

The unwinding of these states in perpetual transformation forms a very precise dramatic action, whose vicissitudes have come to replace those that were offered to the reader by intrigue in the traditional novel. This dramatic action, which is always in the process of forming itself, inflates the present instant, and would not have been able to unfold within the framework of conventional chronology. In the final analysis, these movements transform those dialogues for me (which otherwise had no interest, other than as ways of making these movements visible), while sheltering them all the time under the covering of communication as a communal event. If we cut them off from the energies that propel them to the surface, these dialogues seem to be nothing more than examples of a crude reporting.

Starting from the most banal phrase in a dialogue that was as common as possible, I tried in *Martereau*, published in 1953, to construct four different dramatic actions. These had been chosen from the infinite mass of possible situations that the imagination can give rise to, none of which enjoyed the vantage point of a superior reality or a greater truth over any other.

The same scene repeated in four different variants (it might have been forty) formed a technique which today, employed with the remarkable results with which you are familiar and which are the result of a need that is very different from mine, is considered as one of the essential characteristics of the New French Novel.

To reach the reader, it was necessary to allow those unnamed, unnameable qualities to emerge through channels that would be immediately perceptible. Quite simple images, aimed at giving direct expression to familiar sensations, have thus come to occupy a more and more important place in my books. They have developed into imaginary scenes that have become longer and longer, which attract other scenes to themselves, amplify and bring to the light of day (without, however, any distortion) that which would remain without them a confused and obscure magma.

But these attempts, to make accessible to language that which unceasingly seeks to escape it, have presented great difficulties. These efforts, indeed, have encountered a formidable obstacle, the one that confronts them with language itself: a language which is installed everywhere, solidly established on positions which appear impregnable, as far as they are universally respected.

There, where language spreads its power, there rise up received notions, the denominations, the categories of psychology, of sociology, of morality. Language dries up, ossifies, and separates what is pure fluidity, a movement, something that spreads into infinity, and upon which language never ceases to prevail.

As soon as that formless thing has, shaking and trembling, tried to show itself in the light of day, then language, so powerful and so well-armed, which keeps itself at the ready to intervene and establish order – its order – leaps upon and crushes it.

I have tried to depict this struggle in my novels.

## 10

### *'Multiplying the potentiality of writing'*

#### Georges Perec: 'Writing and the mass media' (1967)

*The novels of Georges Perec (1936–82),* Things *(1965),* The Disappearance *(1969) and, most notably, his famous* Life, a User's Manual *(1978), a highly structured mosaic of literary puzzles and allusions, radio transcriptions, restaurant menus and acrostics, give shape to that exuberantly ludic and inter-textual idiom within Postmodernist writing. The textual eclecticism owes much to Perec's feel for the potential of multi-media interaction, whose creative energies (and their sources in the American Avant-Garde) he celebrated in an essay written early on in his career.*

The question that interests me might be formulated in this fashion: in what ways have the mass media modified the potentiality and the limits of writing? In other words: what has changed in writing since the advent of the mass media?

One might make two preliminary observations:

1  This problem is a problem of form, and not of content (to make use of a contrast which, although having lost any value, continues to remain influential in the minds of most people); one could perhaps say, just to remain with the individual perspective of the author, that what is at stake here is writing itself (the act of writing), and not the work produced: the question and not the response.

2  This problem is not one of choice. From the blank page to the published work, the writer (whether he wants to or not, or even whether he knows it or not) participates in the techniques and the practices of the mass media. One might describe the different ways in which this participation happens; for example: writing does not have the sole monopoly on narration; or again: there is no reason why the dictation machine should not overturn the techniques of writing, as the typewriter once did (Barthes, on this subject, might note that this

**Source:** Georges Perec, 'Écriture et mass-media', *Preuves*, 202 (1967), pp. 7, 8–9 and 9–10. There is no standard translation. **Further reading:** Warren F. Motte, Jr, *The Poetics of Experiment: A Study of the Work of Georges Perec* (Lexington, MA: French Forum Publishers, 1984).

would not necessitate any study of or enquiry into the *work* of the writer: one is still inclined to talk about inspiration, of the muse, of genius); or again: it is obviously not by accident that the science of messages and codes (I mean that branch of information theory that is called linguistics) today provides the theoretical base of all writing . . .

One can hardly talk about competition [between writing and the mass media]; it exists perhaps at the level of cultural consumption (but even here I believe, very little), but certainly not at the level of production: the mass media does not mean the death of writing, and nothing is more silly than to believe that the solution for the writer lies in writing pop songs or in making films, which are likely to turn out second-rate. It's my belief, rather, that the mass media acts as a challenge; that is to say, in the final analysis as an opportunity: that the problems of writing have an opportunity to illuminate themselves (to burst forth) in the light of the mass media.

*Perec goes on to consider the development of drama and the pictorial arts in the context of the impact of the mass media, before pointing to the literary opportunities inherent within this condition.*

This fortuitous coming together of a need (writing that was in search of new possibilities), and an occasion (mass media having arrived to undermine the continuation of linear narrative), provides writing with its greatest opportunity today. The mass media have brought about a new structure for the imaginary [*l'imaginaire*]. Can writing find there a new subject matter? The mass media both propose, and impose, a new sensibility, a new 'implication' (I am translating thus what Warhol, Cage and others call '*involvement*'; it is still far too early to refurbish the term 'engagement'): would writing know how to make use of it?

Implication, whether that be active participation (that is to say intervention) as in a Happening, where there is direction, as in, for example, *Votre Faust* of Pousseur and Butor; or the 'call to existence', as in, for example, the 'rotozaza' of Tinguely, which can only be described as 'people who throw balloons at a machine that returns them beneath the amused gaze of some pedestrians who finally make up their minds what to do with them'; or passive participation (that is to say connivance, a simultaneous knowledge of shared messages and codes). Implication, simultaneity and discontinuity form, then, it seems to me, the three axes of contemporary sensibility as they have been produced by the mass media. Their adaptation to writing allows us perhaps to sketch out an open structure for the work of literature, including the novel.

We still have few of the elements that would allow the implication of the reader into the text. His active participation seems to be precluded (the reader simply consumes what the author produces; his chances of intervention are slight; he might, through the reading that he retains for them, modify the narrative steps of a text ['*suites*'], allowing his participation there to take the place, step by step, of the hero, but that is virtually all). Connivance might materialize in the use of quotations that some authors integrate into their texts (in particular Michel Butor, but also Jean Ristat, Yann Gaillard, etc.). But I am overstating a little the notion of connivance, and exaggerating without doubt the function of quotations: their use resides in our contemporary need for a more secure and more subtle system of rhetoric than that of Classical rhetoric: quotations provide today one of the easiest (and most subtle) forms of connotation, that is to say, forms of literature, allowing writing to develop out of writing, that is to say, between the world and the work, the production of a language already literary.

*Perec concludes by speculating upon the potential of this interface between literature and the media.*

I am now at the heart of my subject. Simultaneity and discontinuity have made an intervention into writing. That image of the river, which is certainly more noble but equally turbulent, and which for such a long time presided over the structure of narration, has been replaced by those of the tree, the cluster, the drawer.

Models of discontinuity have the effect of multiplying the potentiality of writing: but one would be wrong to forget that they multiply equally the constraints: stereography, typographical inventions, variations in page-setting, the choices made possible by the present and simultaneous concurrence of several layers of reading, only have a chance of being effective if they can constitute a system. The problem is essentially one of elaborating on the basis of these elements a rhetoric, that is to say a code of constraints and of subversions that would allow the limits of the text to define itself between the overly aleatory and the overly deterministic. The impression that one frequently receives from reading works inspired by these models is of a system not exactly arbitrary but insufficiently conceptualized, and of an imperfect systematization, sometimes even rather naive (and I am here thinking of the recent work of Butor, or, to cite one of the more recent and more interesting examples, *Compact* by Maurice Roche). These works demonstrate well that, although such a rhetoric is in formation, it is still in its infancy. It is enough, however, to grant these works the potentiality of freedom and play (in the better sense of the term), something which one believed had long since been lost for writing.

# 11

# 'Over our lives preside the great twin leitmotifs of the 20th century – sex and paranoia'

## J. G. Ballard: Introduction to *Crash* (1974)

*J. G. Ballard (b. 1930) is one of the foremost writers of contemporary science fiction. The world he constructs in novels such as* Crash *(1974),* High Rise *(1976) and* The Drowned World *(1963) is one dominated by technological disaster (real or impending), destructive energy and violence. In the Introduction to the 1974 edition of his apocalyptic novel* Crash, *Ballard outlined his distinctive interpretation of the culture of modernity.*

The marriage of reason and nightmare which has dominated the twentieth century has given birth to an ever more ambiguous world. Across the communications landscape move the specters of sinister technologies and the dreams that money can buy. Thermonuclear weapons systems and soft drink commercials coexist in an overlit realm ruled by advertising and pseudoevents, science and pornography. Over our lives preside the great twin leitmotifs of the 20th century – sex and paranoia. Despite [Marshall] McLuhan's delight in high-speed information mosaics we are still reminded of Freud's profound pessimism in *Civilization and its Discontents*. Voyeurism, self-disgust, the infantile basis of our dreams and longings – these diseases of the psyche have now culminated in the most terrifying casualty of the century: the death of affect.

This demise of feeling and emotion has paved the way for all our most real and tender pleasures – in the excitements of pain and mutilation; in sex as the perfect arena, like a culture bed of sterile pus, for all the veronicas of our own perversions; in our moral freedom to pursue our own psychopathology as a game; and in our apparently limitless powers for conceptualization – what our children have to fear is not the cars on the highways of tomorrow but our own pleasure in calculating the most elegant parameters of their deaths.

To document the uneasy pleasures of living within this glaucous paradise has more and more become the role of science fiction. I firmly believe that science fiction, far from being an unimportant minor offshoot, in fact represents the main literary tradition of the 20th century,

**Source:** J. G. Ballard, *Crash* (New York: Vintage Books, 1974), pp. 1–2 and 4–6. **Further reading:** Michael Delville, *Ballard, J. G.* (Plymouth: Northcote House, 1998).

and certainly its oldest – a tradition of imaginative response to science and technology that runs in an intact line through H. G. Wells, Aldous Huxley, the writers of modern American science fiction, to such present-day innovators as William Burroughs.

The main 'fact' of the 20th century is the concept of the unlimited possibility. The predicate of science and technology enshrines the notion of a moratorium on the past – the irrelevancy and even death of the past – and the limitless alternatives available to the present. What links the first flight of the Wright brothers to the invention of the Pill is the social and sexual philosophy of the ejector seat.

Given this immense content of possibility, few literatures would seem better equipped to deal with their subject matter than science fiction. No other form of fiction has the vocabulary of ideas and images to deal with the present, let alone the future. The dominant characteristic of the modern mainstream novel is its sense of individual isolation, its mood of introspection and alienation, a state of mind always assumed to be the hallmark of the 20th century consciousness.

Far from it. On the contrary, it seems to me that this is a psychology that belongs entirely to the 19th century, part of a reaction against the massive restraints of bourgeois society, the monolithic character of Victorianism and the tyranny of the paterfamilias, secure in his financial and sexual authority. Apart from its marked retrospective bias and its obsession with the subjective nature of experience, its real subject matter is the rationalization of guilt and estrangement. Its elements are introspection, pessimism and sophistication. Yet if anything befits the 20th century it is optimism, the iconography of mass merchandising, naivety and guilt-free enjoyment of all the mind's possibilities.

*Ballard further extends his celebration of the genre of science fiction before concluding his essay with comments on the changed role of the writer in a period that no longer recognizes the ontological distinction between reality and fiction.*

In addition, I feel that the balance between fiction and reality has changed significantly in the past decade. Increasingly their roles are reversed. We live in a world ruled by fictions of every kind – mass merchandising, advertising, politics conducted as a branch of advertising, the instant translation of science and technology into popular imagery, the increasing blurring and intermingling of identities within the realm of consumer goods, the preempting of any free or original imaginative response to experience by the television screen. We live inside an enormous novel. For the writer in particular it is less and less necessary for him to invent the fictional content of his novel. The fiction is already there. The writer's task is to invent the reality.

In the past we have always assumed that the external world around us has represented reality, however confusing or uncertain, and that the inner world of our minds, its dreams, hopes, ambitions, represented the realm of fantasy and the imagination. These roles, too, it seems to me, have been reversed. The most prudent and effective method of dealing with the world around us is to assume that it is a complete fiction – conversely, the one small node of reality left to us is inside our own heads. Freud's classic distinction between the latent and manifest content of dream, between the apparent and the real, now needs to be applied to the external world of so-called reality.

Given these transformations, what is the main task facing the writer? Can he, any longer, make use of the techniques and conventions of the traditional 19th century novel, with its linear narrative, its measured chronology, its consular characters grandly inhabiting their domains within an ample time and space? Is his subject matter the sources of character and personality sunk deep in the past, the unhurried inspection of roots, the examination of the most subtle nuances of social behaviour and personal relationships? Has the writer still the moral authority to invent a self-sufficient and self-enclosed world, to preside over his characters like an examiner, knowing all the questions in advance? Can he leave out anything he prefers not to understand, including his own motives, prejudices and psychopathology?

I feel myself that the writer's role, his authority and licence to act, has radically changed. I feel that, in a sense, the writer knows nothing any longer. He has no moral stance. He offers the reader the contents of his own head, he offers a set of options and imaginative alternatives. His role is that of the scientist, whether on safari or in his laboratory, faced with a completely unknown terrain or subject. All he can do is to devise hypotheses and test them out against the facts.

*Crash* is such a book, an extreme metaphor for an extreme situation, a kit of desperate measures only for use in an extreme crisis.

# 12

# 'This dialectic of dream and existence'

## Yves Bonnefoy: 'Image and presence' (1983)

*In volumes such as* On the Motion and the Immobility of Douve *(1953)*,
Words in Stone *(1965) and* The Lure of the Threshold *(1975), the French
poet Yves Bonnefoy (b. 1923) attempted to realize the Symbolist dream of
transfiguring the quotidian world to allow the 'presence' (a key term in Bonnefoy's
poetic) of otherwise only dimly felt transcendent realities to shine through. The urge
here was not to attain mystical transcendence but to develop an aesthetic that could
keep alive the integrity of the object-world even as the poet was seeing it through
language. Indeed, the role of language in this process was addressed by Bonnefoy in
his inaugural address to the Collège de France in 1981, where in the face of the Post-
Structuralist deconstruction of poetic subjectivity, Bonnefoy charted out the complex
relationship between that essential sense of self retained by the poet and the more fluid
contours of the product of his or her writing.*

Ladies and gentlemen, I think that I can return, in any case, to the two
questions I asked myself at the outset.

The one regarded the contradiction which we observe today between,
on the one hand, the awareness one must have of the illusions of the
earlier cogito, and this fact, on the other hand, this fact which is just as
obvious – and is a question of such urgency! – that in order to simply
desire to survive we continue to need a meaning to give to life. To reflect
even a little on this immense challenge of our historic moment, it seemed
to me necessary to ask questions of poetry; or rather, having begun in
adult life in this way, I was unable to prevent myself from continuing to
do so, in spite of the suggestions to the contrary: but now I seem once
again to have found confirmed the reason for this confidence which once
was instinctive to me. Yes, there is in poets an attitude toward this
impasse, an answer to this uneasiness, and it is central in them and it is
clear. Whatever may be the driftings of the sign, the obviousness of
nothingness, to say 'I' remains for them the best of reality and a precise
task, the task of reorienting words, once beyond the confines of dream,
on our relationship to others, which is the origin of being. And as for the
way in which one might achieve this goal, it is not so unclear, even

**Source:** Yves Bonnefoy, *The Act and the Place of Poetry: Selected Essays*, translated and edited by
John T. Naughton and Jean Stewart (Chicago: University of Chicago Press, 1989), pp. 169–72.
**Further reading:** John T. Naughton, *The Poetics of Yves Bonnefoy* (Chicago: University of
Chicago Press, 1984).

beneath the level of the greatest contributions of which poetry is capable. For every being dreams his world, let us say at first; every being is imperiled by the words which shut themselves up in him – the writer is not the only one who abolishes, who becomes enchanted by a world-image; he simply runs the greatest risk because of his blank page. Therefore, if he is even slightly aware of his estrangement, and this is within his possibilities, he will feel himself close to others whose situation is the same. In fact, this awareness of enclosure within the sign is the only way which allows one speaking subject to rejoin another and to share – in the void perhaps, but fully and richly – a dimension of existence. It follows that to struggle in our intimate being against the allurements of universal writing, to criticize them, to undo them one by one, to refuse in short to say 'me' at the very moment when the 'I' is asserting itself, is, however negative this might seem, already to go forward toward the common ground. And along this path, which is the path of salvation, poems, the great poems at least, are examples, and more: not the silence characteristic of a 'text,' but a voice which spurs us on.

*Bonnefoy argues that the postmodern poet has arrived at a new maturity by attending to the deconstructionist attacks on notions of the poetic 'seer' or Romantic 'genius'; the way is now open for a reconciliation of theory with the transfiguring potential of the poetic discourse.*

And only a word now, to conclude, about the potential that is there. Up until now this evening I have seemed, I suppose, to define poetry, in its relation to the imaginary, as its refusal, its transgression. Without hesitation I defined truthfulness of speech as the war against the Image – the substitution of an image for the world – in favor of presence. But this was only a first approximation, justified I hope by the demonstration I assigned myself, and I would like now to evoke what was behind it in my mind – inasmuch as the few remarks which I have just made go straight toward it. What is this second level of the idea of poetry? Well, it is that to struggle in this way, for a better intuition of finitude, against the closing up of the self, against the denial of the other, can only be to love, since it is presence which opens, unity which already takes hold of consciousness, and thus it means loving as well this first network of naiveties, of illusions in which the will toward presence had become ensnared. At its highest point, of which one can at least have an intimation, poetry must certainly succeed in understanding that these images which, if made absolutes, would have been its lie are nothing more, once one overcomes them, than the forms, the simply natural forms, of desire, desire which is so fundamental, so insatiable that it constitutes in all of us our very humanity; and having refused the Image, poetry accepts it in a kind of circle which constitutes its mystery and from which flows, from which rises as if from a depths, its positive quality, its power to speak of everything – in a word, that joy which I said a moment ago poetry could be seen to feel even in its most dreadful hours of anguish. What dream opposes to life, what the analysts of the text study only to dissolve into the indifference of signs, what a more superficial poetry would have torn up with rage, even if perishing with its victim, poetry can refute but listen to, can condemn while absolving it of its fault; it reintegrates it, clarified, into the unity of life. In short, it has denounced the Image, but in order to love, with all its heart, images. Enemy of idolatry, poetry is just as much so of iconoclasm. Now what a resource this could be for responding to the needs of an unhappy society: illusion would reveal its richness, plenitude would be born from deficiency itself! But this dialectic of dream and existence, this third term of compassion, at the highest point of longing passion is, of course, the most difficult. On the level of these exalted representations, of these transfigurations, of these fevers which make up our literatures and which the wisdom of the East would call our delusions, one would need the capacity which the East seems to have – although simply beneath the leafy branches, whereas our place is history – to accept and to refuse at the same time, to make relative what appears absolute, and then to give new dignity, new fullness to this nonbeing. And indeed the Western world, which had a premonition of this deliverance with the agape of the early Christians, then for brief moments in the baroque period and on the peripheries of Romanticism, has, on the whole, made of it the very site of its failure, in unending wars between images. Poetry in Europe seems to have been the impossible: what eludes a man's lifelong search as immediacy does our words. But if it is true, as our time believes, that subjectivity is from now on fracturable, and that poetry and a science of signs may be able to unite in a new relationship between the 'I' which is and the 'me' which dreams, what unexpected richness for hope all at once! At the moment when so much night is gathering, could we be on the verge of the true light?

# 13

## 'An art of homing in tentatively on vital scarcely perceptible signals'

### Ted Hughes: Introduction to Vasko Popa, *Collected Poems* (1976)

*The Serbian poet, Vasko Popa (b. 1922), whose main works include* Bark *(1953),* The Unrest Field *(1956) and* Earth Erect *(1972), represents for Ted Hughes (whose own poetry, most notably* Crow *(1970), placed him among the most vital of voices in the English poetry of the 1960s and 1970s) that generation of Eastern Europe poets who have, through the very fact of their inner exile from their native societies, developed that close feel for personal anguish which all poetry seeks to uncover. The precarious position of these writers in Communist countries allowed them, Hughes argues in his Introduction to the poetry of Popa, to develop a style of writing that is without the self-conscious attitudinizing that Hughes sees marring the work of many Western writers, whose Postmodernism seems too much the product of a willed sense of alienation.*

We can guess at the forces which shaped their outlook and style. They have had to live out, in actuality, a vision which for artists elsewhere is a prevailing shape of things but only brokenly glimpsed, through the clutter of our civilized liberal confusion. They must be reckoned amongst the purest and most wide awake of twentieth-century poets.

In a way, their world reminds one of Beckett's world. Only theirs seems perhaps braver, more human and so more real. Beckett's standpoint is more detached, more analytical, and more the vision of an observer, or of the surgeon, arrived at through private perseverance. Their standpoint, in contrast, seems that of participants. It shows the positive, creative response to a national experience of disaster, actual and prolonged, with an endless succession of bitter events. One feels behind each of these poets the consciousness of a people. At bottom, their vision, like Beckett's, is of the struggle of animal cells and of the torments of spirit in a world reduced to that vision, but theirs contains far more elements than his. It contains all the substance and feeling of ordinary life. And one can argue that it is a step or two beyond his in imaginative truth, in that whatever terrible things happen in their work happen within a containing passion – Job-like – for the elemental final beauty of the created world. Their

**Source:** Vasko Popa, *Collected Poems, 1943–1976*, translated by Anne Pennington, with an Introduction by Ted Hughes (Manchester: Carcanet Press, 1978), pp. 2–3, 3–5 and 6–7.
**Further reading:** Anita Lekic, *The Quest for Roots: The Poetry of Vasko Popa* (New York: Peter Lang, 1993).

poetic themes revolve around the living suffering spirit, capable of happiness, much deluded, too frail, with doubtful and provisional senses, so undefinable as to be almost silly, but palpably existing, and wanting to go on existing – and this is not, as in Beckett's world, absurd. It is the only precious thing, and designed in accord with the whole universe. Designed, indeed, by the whole universe. They are not the spoiled brats of civilization disappointed of impossible and unreal expectations and deprived of the revelations of necessity. In this they are prophets speaking somewhat against their times, though in an undertone, and not looking for listeners. They have managed to grow up to a view of the unaccommodated universe, but it has not made them cynical, they still like it and keep all their sympathies intact. They have got back to the simple animal courage of accepting the odds.

*As Hughes goes on to explain:*

This helplessness in the circumstances has purged them of rhetoric. They cannot falsify their experience by any hopeful effort to change it. Their poetry is a strategy of making audible meanings without disturbing the silence, an art of homing in tentatively on vital scarcely perceptible signals, making no mistakes, but with no hope of finality, continuing to explore. Finally, with delicate manoeuvring, they precipitate out of a world of malicious negatives a happy positive. And they have created a small ironic space, a work of lyrical art, in which their humanity can respect itself.

*Combined from native folklore, Postmodern fabulation and historical insight, Popa has constructed his own distinctive idiom.*

Vasko Popa uses his own distinctive means. Like the others, he gives the impression of being well-acquainted with all that civilization has amassed in the way of hypotheses. Again, like the others, he seems to have played the film of history over to himself many times. Yet he has been thoroughly stripped of any spiritual or mental proprietorship. No poetry could carry less luggage than his, or be freer of predisposition and preconception. No poetry is more difficult to outflank, yet it is in no sense defensive. His poems are trying to find out what does exist, and what the conditions really are. The movement of his verse is part of his method of investigating something fearfully apprehended, fearfully discovered. But he will not be frightened into awe. He never loses his deeply ingrained humour and irony: that is his way of hanging on to his human wholeness. And he never loses his intense absorption in what he is talking about, either. His words test their way forward, sensitive to their own errors, dramatically and intimately alive, like the antennae of some rock-shore creature feeling out the presence of the sea and the huge powers in it. This analogy is not so random. There is a primitive pre-creation atmosphere about his work, as if he were present where all the dynamisms and formulae were ready and charged, but nothing created – or only a few fragments. Human beings, as visibly and wholly such, rarely appear in Popa's landscapes. Only heads, tongues, spirits, hands, flames, magically vitalized wandering objects, such as apples and moons, present themselves, animated with strange but strangely familiar destinies. His poetry is near the world of music, where a repository of selected signs and forms, admitted from the outer world, act out fundamental combinations that often have something eerily mathematical about their progressions and symmetries, but which seem to belong deeply to the world of spirit or of the heart. Again like music, his poems turn the most grisly confrontations into something deadpan playful: a spell, a riddle, a game, a story. It is the Universal Language behind language, and when the poetic texture of the verbal code has been cancelled (as it must be in translation, though throughout this volume the translations seem to me extraordinary in poetic rightness and freshness) we are left with solid hieroglyphic objects and events, meaningful in a direct way, simultaneously earthen and spiritual, plain-statement and visionary.

*Hughes bears out his discussion of Popa through a reading of two exemplary poems from Popa's first volume,* Kora. *He then concludes his assessment.*

It is all there, the surprising fusion of unlikely elements. The sophisticated philosopher is also a primitive, gnomic spellmaker. The desolate view of the universe opens through eyes of childlike simplicity and moody oddness. The wide perspective of general elemental and biological law is spelled out with folklore hieroglyphs and magical monsters. The whole style is a marvellously effective artistic invention. It enables Popa to be as abstract as man can be, yet remain as intelligible and entertaining and as fully human as if he were telling a comic story. It is in this favourite device of his, the little fable of visionary anecdote, that we see most clearly his shift from literary surrealism to the far older and deeper thing, the surrealism of folklore. The distinction between the two seems to lie in the fact that literary surrealism is always connected with an extreme remove from the business of living under practical difficulties and successfully managing them. The mind, having abandoned the struggle with circumstances and consequently lost the unifying focus that comes of that, has lost morale and surrendered to the arbitrary imagery of the dream flow. Folktale surrealism, on the other hand, is always urgently connected with the business of trying to manage practical difficulties so great that they have forced the sufferer temporarily out of the dimension of coherent reality into that depth of imagination where understanding has its roots and stores its X-rays. There is no sense of surrender to the dream flow for its own sake or of relaxation from the outer battle. In the world of metamorphoses and flights the problems are dismantled and solved, and the solution is always a practical one. This type of surrealism, if it can be called surrealism at all, goes naturally with a down-to-earth, alert tone of free enquiry, and in Popa's poetry the two appear everywhere together.

14

_____

# 'All language today tends to become a commodity'

## Alfredo Giuliani: Preface to *The Newest Voices* (1961)

*Alfredo Giuliani (b. 1924) was, with volumes such as* Images and Modes *(1965), one of the foremost experimental poets of his generation. He was also a major theoretician, editing volumes such as* The Newest Voices [I novissimi] *(1961), in which he introduced the work of a new group of poets, including Nanni Balestrini, Antonio Porta, Edoardo Sanguineti and Elio Pagliarani, to a wider public. As with these poets, Giuliani sought to break with the Modernist tradition of Hermeticist poetry written by Eugenio Montale and Salvatore Quasimodo, whose explorations of personal identity and straining after metaphysical depth Giuliani found both self-indulgent and politically irrelevant. As he argued in his Preface to* The Newest Voices, *poetry needs to develop a greater confrontational momentum and feeling for the discontinuity of the expressive act. Only by doing that will it be able to resist the pressures of commodification that surround all cultural forms in the age of late capitalism. Giuliani begins by sketching the radical group that he represents and how it differs from the preceding Modernists.*

Between the Modernist poets [*i nuovi*] and the newest generation of poets [*i novissimi*] there is no continuity, but rather rupture. Our coherence consists in the fact that we have moved on *in time* from the truly arid exercise of a 'style' to adventurous research and propositions for a 'way of writing' that is more impersonal and more extensive: the famous 'experimentalism'. A few years and everything has changed: the vocabulary, the syntax, the versification, the structure of the composition. *Tone* has changed too, and today, unlike yesterday, the perspective that is implicit in the very act of creating poetry. It seemed that the possibilities of 'speaking in verse' were restrictive: we have, however, opened them up, deploying, in fact, in the process that ability of which some of us are

**Source:** *I Novissimi: Poesie per gli Anni '60*, edited by Alfredo Giuliani (Turin: Giulio Einaudi, 1965), pp. 18–21. There is no standard translation. **Further reading:** *The New Italian Poetry 1945 to the Present: A Bilingual Anthology*, edited and translated by Lawrence R. Smith (Berkeley: University of California Press, 1981), pp. 1–37.

occasionally accused. It is true that, if the only rite still practised in our culture is the breaking of the mask, we have certainly gone a step further in the unmasking, challenging the silence which always follows, together with the prattle, the deterioration of a language, exasperating the meaninglessness, refuting the oppression of the meanings imposed, recounting with taste and with passion stories, thoughts and the oddities of this schizophrenic age.

Because all language today tends to become a commodity, neither words, grammatical constructions, nor syntagms can be taken at face value. The asperity and the sobriety, the analytic violence, the irreverent jump, the unruly use of the means of discourse, the prose, and nearly everything else which you are not accustomed to finding in poetry, but which you find in ours, is also to be considered from this perspective. The passion to speak in verse clashes, on the one hand, with the current of all-encompassing consumerism and commercial exploitation to which language is subjected, and, on the other hand, against the literary canon, which preserved the inertia of things, and institutes that *abuse of custom* (the fictitious 'that's how things are') in the construction of human relations. Therefore, before looking at abstract ideology, at cultural intention, we look at the concrete semantics of the poem, without forgetting that, above all, it is an art, a mythological force: for the ideologues, on the contrary, the poem is only a pretence and, as such, is forced to act either as Circe or the sow, secondary to the purpose it is meant to serve.

For us it goes without saying that an erroneous attitude towards the problems of language is not easily explained away with the desolation of society. Historically, there has always existed a correct position, even if this, precisely because it is 'correct', can perhaps lead us to an 'experimental' destiny. Indeed it will appear with clarity, once again, just how improbable is the return of the *neocrupuscolari* to the redundant and descriptive modes of a certain nineteenth-century person; just how futile, in the long term, is the solution of the eccentrics who take seriously their game of lucky dip, their tediously prepared tricks, in which you notice that there was only pedantry in the gesture or restlessness a little bitter from the display. But we ought to add, having said all of the above, that we do not share the neurotic, indiscriminate fear of some for contemporary common language. There are forms of this mechanical Esperanto of the imagination which, in spite of the class manipulation to which they are subjected, cannot be considered in themselves negative or positive, but are uniquely tailored; they are a part of the material, of the 'heteronomous semanticity', that the epoch offers to the writer. The techniques of mass culture entail a mental discomposition which we must take into consideration when we wish to produce a recomposition of the meanings of experience. Not only is it archaic to wish to use a *contemplative* language which pretends not to conserve the value and the possibility of contemplation, but instead its unreal syntax. It is also historically out of place to use that *discursive* language which was, in the Italian lyric, one of the great inventions of Leopardi. Therefore, the schizomorphic vision with which contemporary poetry takes possession of itself and of present life (and which has as typical characteristics the discontinuity of the imaginative process, the *asyntaxism*, the violence committed upon the sign) has no need to justify itself as the 'Avant-Garde', in the programmatic and marginal sense that one usually ascribes to this notion. We, instead, shall be at the 'centre' – and here I agree with Sanguinetti – of a precariousness that neither irrationally exalts us, nor makes us ashamed to be who we are.

For us, this linguistic acquisition has its value only inasmuch as it concerns that *how*, which, as we said above, we feel is coterminous with the 'content'. One writer can be rhetorically topical and altogether not increase but instead discourage our energy, and rather than communicate an experience he can use his astuteness to draw us into his private metaphors. Often the difference between the writer who is 'open' and another who is 'closed' is, apparently, to the disadvantage of the first. In fact, the 'open' writer himself draws, perhaps, knowledge from things and does not wish to teach anything; he does not give the impression of possessing a truth but rather of searching for it and of contradicting himself obscurely. He does not wish to capture benevolence or raise astonishment, because he is inclined to leave the initiative to the relationship which will be created at the meeting between the two semantic dispositions, that of the text and the other one which belongs, precisely, to the reader. And, indeed, how would one really locate the effect of that *new knowledge*, which a poem seems to impart, even if one had the patience to use it correctly? A poem is vital when it pushes us beyond the inevitable limits, when, that is, the things that have inspired its words (there are also those poor restless 'things' which are the words themselves) induce in us the sense of other things and other words, provoking our intervention. One should be able to profit from a poem just as from meeting something a little outside of the ordinary.

I should like to note two aspects of our poetry in particular: a real 'reduction of the I', that producer of meanings, and a corresponding versification, deprived of hedonism, free from that pseudo-ritual ambition which is proper to degraded syllabic versification and to some of its modern camouflagers. To the metrical problem, which one cannot avoid, which cannot be dealt with in a superficial manner, is dedicated an essay which you will find at the back of this book. With respect to the reduction of the 'I', there is a need for agreement. Also here, above all here, the artificial polemic concerning its 'contents' does not bring any clarification. Too frequently, in the poems that try to be the most distant from the personal, the 'I' hides itself with pride and obstinacy behind a presumption of objectivity. Appearances, as usual, deceive. In reality – which explains why we give importance to a certain metrical orientation – the *tone* not only makes music of the discourse, but also determines its operative, the meaning. And so the reduction of the 'I' depends more upon linguistic fantasy than upon ideological choice.

## 15

## *'When the true silence falls'*

### Harold Pinter: 'Writing for the theatre' (1962)

*The plays of Harold Pinter (b. 1930), such as* The Birthday Party *(1957),* The Dumb Waiter *and* The Caretaker *(both 1960), pointedly demonstrate the defining features of Postmodern dramaturgy: its break with the Realist stage and the distinctions between fact and illusion; its concern with the dramatic potential of gesture and personal ritual; its minimal focus upon silence and the absence of meaningful communication; its concern with time and identity; and its refusal to offer grandiose resolutions to moral or political issues. Pinter discussed the premises of this dramaturgy within the context of his own work in a speech given in 1962 at a National Student Drama Festival.*

We don't carry labels on our chests, and even though they are continually fixed to us by others, they convince nobody. The desire for verification on the part of all of us, with regard to our own experience and the experience of others, is understandable but cannot always be satisfied. I suggest there can be no hard distinctions between what is real and what is unreal, nor between what is true and what is false. A thing is not necessarily either true or false; it can be both true and false. A character on the stage who can present no convincing argument or information as to his past experience, his present behaviour or his aspirations, nor give a comprehensive analysis of his motives is as legitimate and as worthy of attention as one who, alarmingly, can do all these things. The more acute the experience the less articulate its expression.

Apart from any other consideration, we are faced with the immense difficulty, if not impossibility, of verifying the past. I don't mean merely years ago, but yesterday, this morning. What took place, what was the

**Source:** Harold Pinter, *Plays: One* (London: Methuen, 1976), pp. 11–12, 13–14 and 14–15.
**Further reading:** Martin Esslin, *The Peopled Wound: The Plays of Harold Pinter* (London: Methuen, 1970), esp. pp. 32–55.

nature of what took place, what happened? If one can speak of the difficulty of knowing what in fact took place yesterday, one can I think treat the present in the same way. What's happening now? We won't know until tomorrow or in six months' time, and we won't know then, we'll have forgotten, or our imagination will have attributed quite false characteristics to today. A moment is sucked away and distorted, often even at the time of its birth. We will all interpret a common experience quite differently, though we prefer to subscribe to the view that there's a shared common ground, a known ground. I think there's a shared common ground all right, but that it's more like quicksand. Because 'reality' is quite a strong firm word we tend to think, or to hope, that the state to which it refers is equally firm, settled and unequivocal. It doesn't seem to be, and in my opinion, is no worse or better for that.

> *What authors and characters alike use to escape from the fluid and inchoate nature of reality are the techniques of linguistic dissimulation: verbal games, rhetoric, comforting explanations, bland descriptions, happy predictions, a 'prison of empty definition and cliché'. Pinter goes on to explain his personal position on this matter.*

I have mixed feelings about words myself. Moving among them, sorting them out, watching them appear on the page, from this I derive a considerable pleasure. But at the same time I have another strong feeling about words which amounts to nothing less than nausea. Such a weight of words confronts us day in, day out, words spoken in a context such as this, words written by me and by others, the bulk of it a stale dead terminology; ideas endlessly repeated and permutated become platitudinous, trite, meaningless. Given this nausea, it's very easy to be overcome by it and step back into paralysis. I imagine most writers know something of this kind of paralysis. But if it is possible to confront this nausea, to follow it to its hilt, to move through it and out of it, then it is possible to say that something has occurred, that something has even been achieved.

Language, under these conditions, is a highly ambiguous business. So often, below the word spoken, is the thing known and unspoken. My characters tell me so much and no more, with reference to their experience, their aspirations, their motives, their history. Between my lack of biographical data about them and the ambiguity of what they say lies a territory which is not only worthy of exploration but which it is compulsory to explore. You and I, the characters which grow on a page, most of the time we're inexpressive, giving little away, unreliable, elusive, evasive, obstructive, unwilling. But it's out of these attributes that a language arises. A language, I repeat, where under what is said, another thing is being said.

> *Indeed, language, as a form of (non-) communication, as a form of repression and as a form of violence, constitutes the focus of many of Pinter's plays. He offers the following concluding words on the subject.*

There are two silences. One when no word is spoken. The other when perhaps a torrent of language is being employed. This speech is speaking of a language locked beneath it. That is its continual reference. The speech we hear is an indication of that which we don't hear. It is a necessary avoidance, a violent, sly, anguished or mocking smoke screen which keeps the other in its place. When the true silence falls we are still left with echo but are nearer nakedness. One way of looking at speech is to say that it is a constant stratagem to cover nakedness.

We have heard many times that tired, grimy phrase: 'Failure of communication' . . . and this phrase has been fixed to my work consistently. I believe the contrary. I think that we communicate only too well, in our silence, in what is unsaid, and that what takes place is a continual evasion, desperate rear-guard attempts to keep ourselves to ourselves. Communication is too alarming. To enter into someone else's life is too frightening. To disclose to others the poverty within us is too fearsome a possibility.

16

---

# Theatre: 'a laboratory for social fantasy'

## Heiner Müller: Letter (1975)

*Heiner Müller (1929–95) was one of the most radical playwrights in the former East Germany. His early works, such as* The Correction *(1957), largely follow the epic theatre of Bertolt Brecht; but in* Germania Death in Berlin *(1971),* Battle *(1975),* Hamletmachine *(1979) and* Macbeth *(1982), Müller developed a more aggressive experimental style, using dream-like short scenes constructed around sometimes brutal imagery to dramatize his increasingly pessimistic view of history and historical change. As the following letter indicates, it was a practice that alienated the conservative functionaries within the official state theatre.*

Dear Mr Linzer,
Reading your postscript to my essay on the play *Battle/Tractor*, I see that you feel unable to publish the piece because it is not accurate. The answers are, you say, imprecise, more an apology for the fact that art cannot be eaten than information on the work. At fault, I think, was my reluctance to talk about the pudding before it had been eaten (and

---

**Source:** Heiner Müller, *Theater-Arbeit* (Berlin: Rotbuch Verlag, 1975), pp. 124–6. There is no standard translation. **Further reading:** Jonathan Kalb, *The Theatre of Heiner Müller* (Cambridge: Cambridge University Press, 1998).

my politeness, which, in spite of this, made me do precisely that). Art legitimizes itself by attempting the new = is parasitical, when it can be described in categories taken from conventional aesthetics.

You ask me about the 'topical relevance' of *Battle/Tractor*. The very fact that you think such a question is necessary already indicates the answer: the undermining of historical consciousness through clichéd notions such as 'topicality'. The theme of fascism is topical and will remain so, I'm afraid, during our lifetime. The same is true of the problem of the working majority, which pays in to the system more than it gets out of it, particularly in the realm of material production; whereas the opposite is true for a minority, who cannot disappear fast enough.

Concerning the relationship of the play to *Fear and Misery*: Brecht was dependent upon documents and reports, secondary material, you might say. That gave rise to an image of fascism that was analytical – a sort of ideal construction. It was only with the preface to *Antigone*, which was written later in a different dramatic technique, that he came to grips with the concrete German form of fascism. Everyday fascism is once again interesting today: we also live with people for whom it represented normalcy, if not the norm – remaining innocent was a stroke of luck.

In its form, *Battle/Tractor* is a reworking of a number of early texts that date back more than twenty years. It is an attempt to synthetically reconstruct a fragment. No dramatic literature is as rich in fragments as the German. The reason for that lies in the fragmentary character of our (theatrical) history, in the continually severed link between literature, the theatre and the public (society), which comes from this. The most common relationship between these three related spheres was, until the historical windfall of Brecht, one of rupture, which, as is known, eventually weakened this connection through time. But the problems of yesteryear are the solutions of today; the fragmentation of an event highlights its nature as a process, prevents the disappearance of production into the product, interferes with its marketability, turns the image into an experimental area, in which the public can become the co-producers.

I don't believe that the so-called 'well-made' story (the classical fable) can ever get the better of reality. And in any case, this text deals with situations in which individual concerns figure only in a very specific way, undermined by the force of circumstance (which, of course, under certain conditions is the product of individual agency).

Regarding your accusation that this is an example of brutal madness (and that is the second most popular form of denunciation used by the frustrated censor, from which the academic journals, to which you don't belong, and with whom to argue bores me, today as yesterday, are recruited), I will say only this: I haven't got enough popular talent to pep up a weary public with the sort of good news that it can only dream about.

Coming on to your question about why our theatre 'has problems' with my plays (a euphemism, because actually they take no interest in my plays at all), and noting your reference to Naturalism (with which most plays today are saturated), I can only say that you have a point there, but that is only half of the matter. Naturalism means expelling the author from the text – the real presence of the author (and the producer, actors, and public) out of the theatre.

For example, if *Building* should be depicted as a 'construction of a building', then it could no longer be performed. The distance from the theme (the attitude that I adopt – I am not a construction worker, or an engineer, or a party functionary) is part of my approach, and belongs to the reality of the play, and must be represented in its performance. Or let's take this silly dispute about *Macbeth*. It's pure stupidity to read a chain of situations as the projection of the author. A text takes its life from the clash between intention and material, author and reality. Every author conceives of texts that are difficult to write; but he who surrenders to this problem, in order to avoid a collision with the public is, as Friedrich Schlegel once noted, a scoundrel who sacrifices having an effect to popular success, and condemns his text to death by applause.

Drama conducted in this fashion turns into a literary mausoleum instead of being a laboratory for social fantasy, and becomes simply a means for preserving antiquated values instead of an instrument for change. Talent is a privilege, but privileges must be paid for. With its expropriation under Socialist society, wisdom has become pigheadedness, the aphorism reactionary; the public persona of the great artist requires Homeric blindness.

That today, even after Brecht, we are still/once again being choked by Naturalism is the result of the (unresolved) dialectic between objective dispossession and subjective freedom. We can no longer keep a distance from our work, something that for Brecht, in the final period of his emigration, isolated from actual class struggles, might have been a real possibility. The *Caucasian Chalk Circle* has (and this secures its place within the repertoire) a closer affinity with Naturalism than either the *Fatzer* fragment or *Woyzeck*, whose spirit it continues.

I do not believe in theatre as a didactic tool. Historical crises deeply, even painfully, affect the individual who may still be an author, but who can no longer act as such. The rift between text and author, situation and self, emerges and provokes through a destruction of continuity. If the cinema depicts death within the work process (as Godard does), then the theatre deals with the joys/terrors of the transformation of birth and death into a single unity. That is why theatre is so important. The dead no longer have any significance, except for the civic planners.

Many thanks for your discussion of my work, with which you enticed me into this monologue.

17

---

# '*Irony has always been an explosion of liberation*'

## Dario Fo: 'Dialogue with an audience' (1979)

*With plays such as* Archangels Don't Play Pinball *(1959),* He Had Two Guns with Black and White Eyes *(1960) and, above all,* The Accidental Death of an Anarchist *(1970), Dario Fo (b. 1926) sought to communicate his radical political message through farce, slapstick and other forms of carnevalistic humour. That such a strategy, which fully accords with the turn to non-didactic political drama in the Postmodern period, runs the risk (for some of his readers) of trivializing its revolutionary mission, is clear from the following analysis made by a member of the audience after a performance of* Mistero Buffo *in Veneto: 'In my opinion,' the anonymous spectator argued, 'all of Fo's plays, as well as his specific criticisms of determining historical factors, [are] pre-Marxist in every sense. Any kind of culture that uses Marxism to create comedy and carries demystification on to the level of irony rather than criticism has nothing to do with Marxism and revolutionary praxis. . . . The aim of Marxist thought is to change the world. Fo's play raises doubts and poses problems and creates a sense of shock. But if these doubts are only used for the purposes of hilarity, this hilarity functions in a compensatory way. People leave the theatre satisfied by the play, they've seen a brilliant actor who criticizes certain things, but they haven't seen a political, revolutionary agent because a revolution doesn't just use irony, it tries to show the reality of class consciousness and organization through irony and criticism.' Fo countered this critique in the following manner.*

As far as a preoccupation with ridicule, laughter, sarcasm, irony, and the grotesque is concerned, I have to say – I'd be a liar if I said otherwise – it's my job. I've been teaching this lesson for years – the origins of the grotesque and the significance of the grotesque and Marxist and pre-Marxist culture and irony.

To take just one example – Brecht. Brecht says that the highest

---

**Source:** Dario Fo, 'Dialogue with an audience', translated by Tony Mitchell, *Theatre Quarterly,* 35 (1979), pp. 15–16. **Further reading:** David Hirst, *Dario Fo and Franca Rame* (London: Macmillan, 1989).

manifestation of satire – which is making people conscious, because it burns down to the deepest level – is precisely the manifestation of the grotesque. That is to say that nothing gets down as deeply into the mind and intelligence as satire. . . . The best didactic lessons of Marxism should be confronted by this fact. Brecht complained that there wasn't sufficient grotesqueness: Marxist didacticism didn't reach the heights of the grotesque. His best work in my opinion is *Puntila*, which is one of the best examples of didactic instruction about the meaning of struggle and the achievements of true Marxist consciousness.

Or take Mayakovsky – he was preoccupied with ridicule if anyone was, and see how he was the first person to be wiped out by Stalinism, obviously because he used a mechanism which reached a profound level, and cut through hypocrisy, really stirred things up.

Mao Tse-tung on the question of laughter used sarcasm and the grotesque as a means of destroying certain obtuse forms of tradition connected with feudalism and religion. I don't understand this fear of laughter. I think we should look closely at one of the results of this fear – if you go to Russia today you notice there's not a single satirical play on there. Not a single one. I've been around Moscow. I've been to Kiev and Stalingrad. I've been right up to the north, and I've never seen one.

But do you know what I did see? Pisshouse theatre. I mean vaudeville, operettas, plays for the play's sake, trifles, plays about trifles. But never any satire. A dramatic opera maybe, maybe something edifying, but never anything grotesque or satirical. Why? You tell me. The same reason there isn't anything in Poland, or Czechoslovakia, and very little in Hungary or other countries.

The end of satire is the first alarm bell signalling the end of real democracy. The person who said that really knew what he was talking about. That was Mayakovsky. He was censured to begin with, then he was banned, and then he was driven to suicide. And don't forget that Lenin was very fond of satire. He said 'I'm no theatregoer, but I do understand the importance of Mayakovsky's satire', in reference to one of his works, a lyric that really brought home the absurdity of conferences, debates, and meetings chasing themselves around in circles.

If you can only believe in the revolution if you keep a straight face, with no irony, grotesqueness, then I don't believe in it. Irony has always been an explosion of liberation. But if we want to be 'illuminated', and negate the importance of the *giullare*, of making people laugh about the conditions they are subject to . . . well, we're not even Marxists, because what Marx says about the potentials of human civilisation is something completely different.

# 18

## 'Speak-ins. . . do not want to revolutionize, they want to make aware'

### Peter Handke: Note on *Offending the Audience and Self-Accusation* (1965)

*With his* Offending the Audience *(1965),* Cries for Help *(1967) and* Kaspar *(1968), the Austrian playwright Peter Handke (b. 1942), became one of the most original voices on the European stage. Handke sought to develop an 'interventionist' dramaturgy that would provoke the audiences of his plays in the most direct way possible. This goal is most vividly realized in* Offending the Audience, *a so-called* Sprechstück *(vocal piece). The play contains neither dramatic action nor dramatis personae, but consists of a purely appellative process structured around a verbal confrontation between the 'actors' on the stage and the audience present in the auditorium, who are made the subject of a process of accelerating vilification. Handke outlined the terms of this studiously unemotive radicalism (which self-consciously breaks with the ideological gravitas cultivated by other radical playwrights) in his short Preface to the play.*

The speak-ins (*Sprechstücke*) are spectacles without pictures, inasmuch as they give no picture of the world. They point to the world not by way of pictures but by way of words; the words of the speak-ins don't point at the world as something lying outside the words, but to the world in the words themselves. The words that make up the speak-ins give no picture of the world but a concept of it. The speak-ins are theatrical inasmuch as they employ natural forms of expression found in reality. They employ only such expressions as are natural in real speech; that is, they employ the speech forms that are uttered *orally* in real life. The speak-ins employ natural examples of swearing, of self-indictment, of confession, of testimony, of interrogation, of justification, of evasion, of prophecy, of calls for help. Therefore they need a vis-à-vis, at least *one* person who listens; otherwise, they would not be natural but extorted by the author. It is to that extent that my speak-ins are pieces for the theatre. Ironically, they imitate the gestures of all the given devices natural to the theatre.

The speak-ins have no action, since every action on stage would only be the picture of another action. The speak-ins confine themselves, by

**Source:** Peter Handke, *Offending the Audience and Self-Accusation*, translated by Michael Roloff (London: Methuen, 1971). **Further reading:** Nicholas Hern, *Peter Handke* (New York: Frederick Ungar, 1971), esp. pp. 1–20.

obeying their natural form, to words. They give no pictures, not even pictures in word form, which would only be pictures the author extorted to represent an internal, unexpressed, wordless circumstance and not a *natural* expression.

Speak-ins are autonomous prologues to the old plays. They do not want to revolutionize, but to make aware.

19

---

## 'They project this "unbreakable core of night" into woman'

### Simone de Beauvoir: *The Second Sex* (1949)

*Simone de Beauvoir (1908–86), essayist and novelist (her major novel was* The Mandarins, *1954), was also, with her highly influential* The Second Sex, *one of the foremost voices in the early Feminist movement in Europe.* The Second Sex *is both an historical account of the traditional roles played by women in Western society (with a focus on the myths that have anchored those roles), and an analysis of the predicament of women in contemporary society. At one point in her study, de Beauvoir describes how women have been depicted and (mis)constructed through essentialist representations of 'womanhood' or 'the feminine' by male authors over the past two centuries. De Beauvoir discusses a number of examples, taken from writers such as D. H. Lawrence and André Breton. Her critique is all the more effective, given that many of these writers believed they were speaking on behalf of a liberated and woman-friendly sexuality.*

It is to be seen from these examples that each separate writer reflects the great collective myths: we have seen woman as *flesh*; the flesh of the male is produced in the mother's body and re-created in the embraces of the woman in love. Thus woman is related to *nature*, she incarnates it: vale of blood, open rose, siren, the curve of a hill, she represents to man the fertile soil, the sap, the material beauty and the soul of the world. She can hold the keys to *poetry*; she can be *mediatrix* between this world and the beyond: grace or oracle, star or sorceress, she opens the door to the supernatural, the surreal. She is doomed to *immanence*; and through her passivity she bestows peace and harmony – but if she declines this role,

**Source:** Simone de Beauvoir, *The Second Sex*, translated and edited by H. M. Parshley (New York: Alfred A. Knopf, 1976), pp. 278–80. **Further reading:** Karen Vintges, *Philosophy as Passion: The Thinking of Simone de Beauvoir* (Bloomington: Indiana University Press, 1966), pp. 21–45.

she is seen forthwith as a praying mantis, an ogress. In any case she appears as the *privileged Other*, through whom the subject fulfils himself: one of the measures of man, his counterbalance, his salvation, his adventure, his happiness.

But these myths are very differently orchestrated by our authors. The *Other* is particularly defined according to the particular manner in which the *One* chooses to set himself up. Every man asserts his freedom and transcendence – but they do not all give these words the same sense. For Montherlant transcendence is a situation: he is the transcendent, he soars in the sky of heroes; woman crouches on earth, beneath his feet; it amuses him to measure the distance that separates him from her; from time to time he raises her up to him, takes her, and then throws her back; never does he lower himself down to her realm of slimy shadows. Lawrence places transcendence in the phallus; the phallus is life and power only by grace of woman; immanence is therefore good and necessary; the false hero who pretends to be above setting foot on earth, far from being a demigod, fails to attain man's estate. Woman is not to be scorned, she is deep richness, a warm spring; but she should give up all personal transcendence and confine herself to furthering that of her male. Claudel asks her for the same devotion: for him, too, woman should maintain life while man extends its range through his activities; but for the Catholic all earthly affairs are immersed in vain immanence: the only transcendent is God; in the eyes of God the man in action and the woman who serves him are exactly equal; it is for each to surpass his or her earthly state: salvation is in all cases an autonomous enterprise. For Breton the rank of the sexes is reversed; action and conscious thought, in which the male finds his transcendence, seem to Breton to constitute a silly mystification that gives rise to war, stupidity, bureaucracy, the negation of anything human; it is immanence, the pure, dark presence of the real, which is truth; true transcendence would be accomplished by a return to immanence. His attitude is the exact opposite of Montherlant's: the latter likes war because in war one gets rid of women, Breton venerates woman because she brings peace. Montherlant confuses mind and subjectivity – he refuses to accept the given universe; Breton thinks that mind is objectively present at the heart of the world; woman endangers Montherlant because she breaks his solitude; she is revelation for Breton because she tears him out of his subjectivity. As for Stendhal, we have seen that for him woman hardly has a mystical value: he regards her as being, like man, a transcendent; for this humanist, free beings of both sexes fulfil themselves in their reciprocal relations; and for him it is enough if the *Other* be simply an other so that life may have what he calls 'a pungent saltiness'. He is not seeking a 'stellar equilibrium', he is not fed on the bread of disgust; he is not looking for a miracle; he does not wish to be concerned with the cosmos or with poetry, but with free human beings.

More, Stendhal feels that he is himself a clear, free being. The others – and this is a most important point – pose as transcendents but feel themselves prisoners of a dark presence in their own hearts: they project this 'unbreakable core of night' upon woman. Montherlant has an Adlerian complex, giving rise to his thick-witted bad faith: it is this tangle of pretensions and fears that he incarnates in woman; his disgust for her is what he dreads feeling for himself. He would trample underfoot, in woman, the always possible proof of his own insufficiency; he appeals to scorn to save him; and woman is the trench into which he throws all the monsters that haunt him. The life of Lawrence shows us that he suffered from an analogous though more purely sexual complex: in his works woman serves as a compensation myth, exalting a virility that the writer was none too sure of; when he describes Kate at Don Cipriano's feet, he feels as if he had won a male triumph over his wife, Frieda; nor does he permit his companion to raise any questions: if she were to oppose his aims he would doubtless lose confidence in them; her role is to reassure him. He asks of her peace, repose, faith, as Montherlant asks for certainty regarding his superiority: they demand what is missing in them. Claudel's lack is not that of self-confidence: if he is timid it is only in secret with God. Nor is there any trace of the battle of the sexes in his work. Man boldly takes to himself the burden of woman; she is a possibility for temptation or for salvation. It would seem that for Breton man is true only through the mystery that is within him; it pleases him for Nadja to see that star towards which he moves and which is like 'the heart of a heartless flower'. In his dreams, his presentiments, the spontaneous flow of his stream of consciousness – in such activities, which escape the control of the will and the reason, he recognizes his true self; woman is the visible image of that veiled presence which is infinitely more essential than his conscious personality.

# 20

# 'Where what is enounced disturbs, the wonder of being many things'

## Hélène Cixous: *The Newly Born Woman* (1975)

*Hélène Cixous (b. 1937) is a scholar (see, for example,* The Exile of James Joyce, *1968), novelist (*The Third Body, *1970 and* Portrait of Dora, *1976), and (with works such as 'Laugh of the Medusa', 1975) one of the leading theoreticians within the French Feminist movement. Her writing frequently focuses upon language, gender investments in language and the linguistic projections of the sexual self. Cixous, unlike de Beauvoir, accepts the designation of woman as Other, but she invests the latter category with a positive, indeed dynamic, quality. Cixous is able to do so (without falling into the essentialist trap) because she believes that sexuality and gender are distinct notions, that male and female partake of characteristics that flow between the crude binary oppositions that conventionally separate them. In her essay 'Sorties', from* The Newly Born Woman, *Cixous attempts to explain the ways in which the male, even when he is psychoanalytically at his most vulnerable, evades loss of identity but, at the same time, also his unique opportunity to address (particularly in writing) the great potential of non-identity.*

I will say: writing today belongs to women. This is not a provocation; it simply means that woman should admit that there is an Other. In her becoming-woman, she has not erased the latent bisexuality that dwells within the girl as it does within the boy. Femininity and bisexuality go together, in a combination that varies according to each individual, and they distribute their intensity differently, and, depending upon the way they develop, they privilege now this, now that component of the self. Man, he finds it immeasurably more difficult to allow the Other to pass through him. Writing, that is in me the passageway, the entrance, the exit, the dwelling place that is occupied by the Other that I both am and am not, the Other that I don't know how to be, but which I feel passes through me, which makes me live – that tears me apart, that disturbs me, that changes me; but who? – the masculine part, the feminine part, all the parts, some of them? – those which come from the unknown, and which

**Source:** Hélène Cixous, 'Sorties', in Hélène Cixous and Catherine Clement, *La Jeune Née* (Paris: Union Générale d'Editions, 1975), pp. 158–61 and 162–3. **Standard translation:** *The Newly Born Woman*, extracted in *The Hélène Cixous Reader*, edited by Susan Sellers and translated by Betsy Wing (London: Routledge, 1994), pp. 35–45. **Further reading:** Susan Sellers, *Hélène Cixous: Authorship, Autobiography and Love* (Oxford: Polity Press/Blackwell, 1996), esp. pp. 1–23.

precisely give me the desire to know, and from which all life springs forth. This peopling permits neither rest nor security, and problematizes one's relationship to 'the real', produces a feeling of uncertainty that acts as an obstacle to the socialization of the subject. It is exhausting, it wears you out; and for men, this permeability, this non-exclusion, that is the threat that all find intolerable.

In the past, when it was pushed to an extreme degree, it was called 'possession'. To be possessed, that was not desirable for the masculine mental projection of self [*l'imaginaire*], who would have experienced it as a form of passivity, as a threatening feminine attitude. It is true that what is 'feminine' involves a certain receptivity. One can certainly exploit, as history has always done, feminine receptivity in its alienated form. Through her openness, a woman is vulnerable to being 'possessed'; that is to say, to being dispossessed of herself.

But I am speaking here of a femininity that seeks to preserve in life the Other that is entrusted to her, that comes to her, that she can love as much as the Other. The desire to be the Other, an Other, without that necessarily leading to the diminution of self, of herself.

As for passivity, it is, in its excess, partly connected to death. But there exists a form of non-closure that is not submissiveness but a confidence and a way of knowing. And this is not a moment for destruction but for the marvellous extension of self.

Through the same openness that forms her vulnerability, she leaves herself to go to the Other, the explorer of unknown places, she does not hold back, she draws closer, not in order to annul the intervening space but to view it, to experience what is not, what is, and what might be.

Now, to write is to work; to be worked; (in) the between, to interrogate, (to be interrogated) the process itself *and of* the Other, without which nothing can live; to nullify the work of death, while desiring to bring together the-one-with-the-Other, infinitely dynamized by an incessant exchange between the one and the Other – not knowing them and beginning again only from what is most distant – from the self, from the Other, from the Other within me; a course that multiplies transformations by thousands.

And that does not happen without risk, without pain, without loss of the moments of self, of the persons that one has been, that one has gone beyond, that one has discarded. That does not happen without an investment – of sense, time, direction.

But is all of this specifically feminine? It is men who have inscribed, described, theorized the paradoxical logic without reserve. That they have done so is not a contradiction: it leads us back to interrogate *their* femininity. There are few men able to venture onto that brink where writing, liberated from laws, freed from restrictions, exceeds phallic authority, and where affective subjectivity becomes feminine.

Where, in writing, does difference emerge? If it does exist, it is in the modes of its output; in its valorization of what it owns; and in its way of thinking through the non-identical. In general, it lies in the way it thinks through every 'gain', if one understands this word in terms of 'return', of capitalization. Today, still, the masculine rapport with the identity [the '*propre*'] is narrower and more restricted than femininity's. Everything takes place as if man were more directly threatened in his being than woman by non-identity [the '*non-propre*']. Traditionally, this is exactly the culture that psychoanalysis has described; of someone who still has something to lose. And in the movement of desire, of exchange, it is he who is the one who pays: loss, expense, are involved in a commercial deal that always changes the gift into a gift-that-takes. The gift yields a return. At the end of a curved line, loss turns into its opposite, and returns in the form of profit.

But does woman escape this law of return? Can one speak of a different type of expense? In truth, there is no such thing as a 'free' gift. One never gives anything for nothing. But the decisive difference lies in the why and the how of the gift, in the values that the gesture of giving affirms and encourages; in the type of profit that the giver draws from the gift, and the use that is made of it.

*Cixous goes on to define what she understands by the self that is proper to woman.*

This does not mean that she is an undifferentiated magma, but simply that she does not oppress her body or her desires. Let masculine sexuality gravitate towards the penis, engendering this body (in terms of its political anatomy) under party dictatorship. Woman, she does not perform upon herself this regionalization that profits the combination of rationalist sexuality ('*tête-sexe*'), which only inscribes itself within frontiers. Her libido is cosmic, as her unconsciousness is universal. Her writing also cannot help but go into the future, without ever inscribing or recognizing contours, daring those vertiginous heights crossed by Others, and the ephemeral and passionate dwelling places that lie within him, with her, within them, which she inhabits just long enough to watch them as close as possible to the unconsciousness from which they arise, to love them as close as possible to their energies; and then, filled by these brief embraces of identification, she continues still further, journeying through to the infinite. She alone dares and wants to know from within that which exists before language, and which, excluding her, has never ceased to reverberate. She allows herself to speak the tongue of a thousand tongues, sound without obstruction or death. To life, she refuses nothing.

Her language is beyond capacity, it transports; it does not retain, it makes possible. Where what is enounced disturbs, the wonder of being many things, she does not protect herself against those unknown feminines which she is surprised to find herself becoming, taking joy in her gift of change. I am a spacious singing Flesh: onto which is grafted no one knows which I, more or less human. But it is, above all, a living I because it results in transformation.

# BIBLIOGRAPHY

## I. Romanticism

Abrams, M. H., *The Mirror and the Lamp: Romantic Theory and the Critical Tradition* (Oxford: Oxford University Press, 1953).

Abrams, M. H., *Natural Supernaturalism: Tradition and Revolution in Romantic Literature* (New York: Norton, 1971).

Behler, Ernst i.a., *Die europäische Romantik* (Frankfurt am Main: Athenäum, 1972).

Cranston, Maurice, *The Romantic Movement* (Oxford: Blackwell, 1994).

de Man, Paul, *The Rhetoric of Romanticism* (New York: Columbia University Press, 1984).

Eichner, Hans (ed.), *'Romantic' and Its Cognates: The European History of the Word* (Toronto: University of Toronto Press, 1972).

Furst, Lilian, *Romanticism in Perspective: A Comparative Study of Aspects of the Romantic Movement in England, France and Germany* (London: Macmillan, 1969).

Furst, Lilian, *Romanticism* (London: Methuen, 1976).

Furst, Lilian, *European Romanticism: Self-definition* (London: Methuen, 1980).

Halsted, John B., *Romanticism: Problems of Definition, Explanation and Evaluation* (Boston: Heath, 1965).

Hoffmeister, Gerhart, *Deutsche und europäische Romantik*, second edition (Stuttgart: Metzler, 1990).

Lovejoy, A. O., 'On the discriminations of romanticisms' (first published in 1924, and reprinted in Robert F. Gleckner and Gerald D. Enscoe (eds), *Romanticism: Points of View* (New York: Prentice-Hall, 1962, and in a second, heavily revised edition, 1970, pp. 66–81).

Löwy, Michael and Sayre, Robert, *Révolte et mélancolie: Le romantisme à contre-courant de la modernité* (Paris: Editions Payot, 1992).

Mumford Jones, Howard, *Revolution and Romanticism* (Cambridge, MA: Harvard University Press, 1974).

Peckham, Morse, *The Birth of Romanticism, 1790–1815* (Greenwood, FL: Penkevill, 1986).

Porter, Roy and Teich, Mikulas (eds), *Romanticism in National Context* (Cambridge: Cambridge University Press, 1988).

Prang, Helmut (ed.), *Begriffsbestimmung der Romantik* (Darmstadt: Wissenschaftliche Buchgesellschaft, 1972).

Praz, Mario, *The Romantic Agony* (Oxford: Oxford University Press, 1970).

Punter, David, *The Romantic Unconscious: A Study in Narcissism and Patriarchy* (Hemel Hempstead: Harvester Wheatsheaf, 1989).

Remak, H. H. H., 'West European Romanticism: definition and scope' (reprinted in Newton P. Stallknecht and Horst Frenz (eds), *Comparative Literature: Method and Perspective* (Carbondale: Southern Illinois Press, 1971), pp. 275–311).

Schenk, H. G., *The Mind of the European Romantics: An Essay in Cultural History* (London: Constable, 1966).

Thorlby, Anthony, *The Romantic Movement* (London: Longman, 1966).

Tieghem, Paul van, *Le Romantisme dans la littérature européenne* (Paris: Michel, 1948, second edition 1969).

Wellek, René, 'The concept of Romanticism in literary history' (first published in 1949, and republished in *Concepts of Criticism* (New Haven: Yale University Press, 1963), pp. 128–98).

## II. Realism

Auerbach, Erich, *Mimesis: The Representation of Reality in Western Literature* (Princeton, NJ: Princeton University Press, 1953).

Aust, Hugo, *Literatur de Realismus* (Stuttgart: Metzler, 1977).

Barthes, Roland, *Writing Degree Zero* (London: Jonathan Cape, 1967).

Barthes, Roland, *S/Z* (New York: Hill & Wang, 1974).

Becker, George J., *Documents of Modern Literary Realism* (Princeton, NJ: Princeton University Press, 1963).

Becker, George J., *Master European Realists of the Nineteenth Century* (New York: Ungar, 1982).

Borgerhoff, E. B. O., '*Réalisme* and kindred words', *PMLA*, 53 (1938), pp. 837–43.

Bornecque, J.-H. and Cogny, P., *Réalisme et naturalisme: l'histoire, la doctrine, les oeuvres* (Paris: Hachette, 1958).

Boyle, Nicholas and Swales, Martin (eds), *Realism in European Literature: Essays in Honour of J. P. Stern* (Cambridge: Cambridge University Press, 1986).

Brinkmann, Richard, *Begriffsbestimmung des literarischen Realismus* (Darmstadt: Wissenschaftliche Buchgesellschaft, 1969).

Dumesnil, René, *Le Réalisme et la naturalisme* (Paris: Del Duca, 1965).

Furst, Lilian, *Naturalism* (London: Methuen, 1971).

Furst, Lilian (ed.) *Realism* (London: Longman, 1992).

Grant, Damian, *Realism* (London: Methuen, 1970).

Hemmings, F. W. J. (ed.), *The Age of Realism* (Harmondsworth: Penguin Books, 1978).

Kearns, Katherine, *Nineteenth-Century Literary Realism: Through the Looking-Glass* (Cambridge: Cambridge University Press, 1996).

Larkin, Maurice, *Man and Society in Nineteenth Century Realism: Determinism and Literature* (London: Macmillan, 1977).

Levin, Harry, *The Gates of Horn: A Study of Five French Realists* (Oxford: Oxford University Press, 1966).

Lukács, Georg, *Studies in European Realism* (London: Merlin Press, 1950).

Lukács, Georg, *The Historical Novel* (London: Merlin Press, 1962).

Mahal, Günther, *Naturalismus* (Munich: Fink, 1975).

Martino, Pierre, *Le Naturalisme français, 1870–1895*, eighth edition (Paris: Colin, 1969).

Ruprecht, Erich, *Literarische Manifeste des Naturalismus, 1880–1892* (Stuttgart: Metzler, 1962).

Stern, J. P., *On Realism* (London: Routledge, 1973).

Walker, Dennis (ed.), *The Realist Novel* (London: Routledge, 1995).

Weinberg, Bernard, *French Realism: The Critical Reaction, 1830–1870* (London: Oxford University Press, 1937).

Wellek, René, 'The concept of realism in literary scholarship', in *Concepts of Criticism* (New Haven, CT: Yale University Press, 1963), pp. 222–55.

Williams, D. A., *The Monster in the Mirror: Studies in Nineteenth Century Realism* (Oxford: Oxford University Press, 1978).

## III. Modernism

Balakian, Anna (ed.), *The Symbolist Movement in the Literature of European Languages* (Budapest: Akadémiai Kiadó, 1982).

Berg, Christian (ed.) i.a., *The Turn of the Century/Le Tournant du siècle; Modernism and Modernity in Literature and the Arts/Le Modernisme et la modernité dans la littérature et les arts* (Berlin/New York: Walter de Gruyter, 1995).

Berman, Marshall, *All That Is Solid Melts into Air: The Experience of Modernity* (London: Verso, 1983).

Bradbury, Malcolm and McFarlane, James (eds), *Modernism, 1890–1930* (Harmondsworth: Penguin Books, 1976).

Bürger, Peter, *Theory of the Avant-Garde* (Manchester: Manchester University Press, 1984).

Calinescu, Matei, *Faces of Modernity: Avant-Garde, Decadence, Kitsch* (Bloomington: Indiana University Press, 1977).

Chiari, Joseph, *The Aesthetics of Modernism* (London: Vision, 1970).

Collier, Peter and Davis, Judy (eds), *Modernism and the European Unconscious* (Cambridge: Polity Press, 1990).

Eysteinsson, Astradur, *The Concept of Modernism* (Ithaca, NY: Cornell University Press, 1990).

Faulkner, Peter, *Modernism* (London: Methuen, 1977).

Faulkner, Peter (ed.), *A Modernist Reader: Modernism in England, 1910–1930* (London: Batsford, 1986).

Fokkema, Douwe W., *Literary History, Modernism, and Postmodernism* (Philadelphia: John Benjamins, 1984).

Giles, Steve (ed.), *Theorizing Modernism: Essays in Critical Theory* (London: Routledge, 1993).

Houston, John Porter, *French Symbolism and the Modernist Movement: A Study of Poetic Structures* (Baton Rouge: Louisiana University Press, 1980).

Lehmann, A. G., *The Symbolist Aesthetic in France, 1885–1895* (Oxford: Blackwell, 1950).

Levenson, Michael H., *A Genealogy of Modernism: A Study of English Literary Doctrine, 1908–1922* (Cambridge: Cambridge University Press, 1984).

Levenson, Michael (ed.), *The Cambridge Companion to Modernism* (Cambridge: Cambridge University Press, 1999)

Levin, Harry, 'What was Modernism?', in *Refractions: Essays in Comparative Literature* (New York: Oxford University Press, 1966).

Lodge, David, *The Modes of Modern Writing: Metaphor, Metonymy, and the Typology of Modern Literature* (London: Edward Arnold, 1977).

MacCabe, Colin, *James Joyce and the Revolution of the Word* (London: Macmillan, 1978).

Nicholls, Peter, *Modernisms: A Literary Guide* (London: Macmillan, 1995).

Peyre, Henri, *What Is Symbolism?* (Tuscaloosa: University of Alabama Press, 1980).

Pippin, Robert, *Modernism as a Philosophical Problem: On the Dissatisfactions of European High Culture* (Oxford: Blackwell, 1991).

Poggioli, Renato, *The Theory of the Avant-Garde* (Cambridge, MA: Belknap Press, 1968).

Quinones, Ricardo J., *Mapping Literary Modernism: Time and Development* (Princeton, NJ: Princeton University Press, 1985).

Ruprecht, Erich and Bänsch, Dieter, *Literarische Manifeste der Jahrhundertwende, 1890–1910* (Stuttgart: Metzler, 1970).

Russell, Charles, *Poets, Prophets and Revolutionaries: The Literary Avant-Garde from Rimbaud through Postmodernism* (Oxford: Oxford University Press, 1895).

Ryan, Judith, *The Vanishing Subject: Early Psychology and Literary Modernism* (Chicago: University of Chicago Press, 1991).

Spears, Monroe K., *Dionysus and the City: Modernism in Twentieth-Century Poetry* (New York: Oxford University Press, 1970, pp. 3–34).

Symons, Arthur, *The Symbolist Movement in Literature* (London: William Heinemann, 1899).

Wilson, Edmund, *Axel's Castle: A Study in the Imaginative Literature of 1870–1930*, second edition (London: Fontana, 1961).

## IV. The Literature of Political Engagement

Barnes, Hazel, *The Literature of Possibility: A Study in Humanistic Existentialism* (Lincoln: University of Nebraska Press, 1959).

Bisztray, George, *Marxist Models of Literary Realism* (New York, Columbia University Press, 1978).

Craig, David, *Marxists on Literature: An Anthology* (Harmondsworth: Penguin Books, 1975).

Ermolaev, Herman, *Soviet Literary Theories, 1917–1934*, second edition (New York: Octagon Books, 1977).

Flower, John (ed.), *The Writers and Politics* Series (London: Hodder & Stoughton, 1977–8).

Glicksberg, Charles I., *The Literature of Commitment* (Lewisburg, PA: Bucknell University Press, 1976).

Hamilton, Alastair, *The Appeal of Fascism: A Study of Intellectuals and Fascism, 1919–1945* (London: Blond, 1971).

Harrison, John, *The Reactionaries* (London: Gollancz, 1967).

James, C. Vaughan, *Soviet Socialist Realism: Origins and Theory* (London: Macmillan, 1973).

Jameson, Frederic, *Marxism and Form: Twentieth Century Dialectical Theories of Literature* (Princeton, NJ: Princeton University Press, 1971).

Kaes, Anton (ed.), *Weimarer Republik: Manifeste und Dokumente zur Deutschen Literatur, 1918–1933* (Stuttgart: Metzler, 1983).

Lawall, Sarah N., *Critics of Consciousness: The Existential Structures of Literature* (Cambridge, MA: Harvard University Press, 1968).

Lukács, Georg, *Essays on Realism*, edited by Rodney Livingstone (Cambridge, MA: MIT Press, 1981).

Mander, John, *The Writer and Commitment* (London: Secker & Warburg, 1961).

Milfull, John (ed.), *The Attractions of Fascism: Social Psychology and Aesthetics of the 'Triumph of the Right'* (New York and Oxford: Berg, 1990).

Montefiore, Janet, *Men and Women Writers of the 1930s: The Dangerous Flood of History* (London: Routledge, 1996).

New Left Books (eds), *Aesthetics and Politics* (London: Verso, 1980).

Panichas, George A. (ed.), *The Politics of Twentieth Century Novelists* (New York: Hawthorn Books, 1971).

Rühle, Jürgen, *Literature and Revolution: A Critical Study of the Writer and Communism in the Twentieth Century* (London: Pall Mall Press, 1969).

Slonim, Marc, *Soviet Russian Literature: Writers and Problems, 1917–1977* (Oxford: Oxford University Press, 1977).

Swingewood, Alan, *The Novel and Revolution* (London: Macmillan, 1975).

Winegarten, Renee, *Writers and Revolution: The Fatal Lure of Action* (New York: Franklin Watts, 1974).

Woodcock, George, *Writers and Politics* (London: Porcupine Press, 1948).

## V. Postmodernism

Barth, John, 'The literature of exhaustion', *Atlantic Monthly*, August 1967, pp. 29–34.

Belsey, Catherine and Moore, Jane (eds), *The Feminist Reader*, second edition (Oxford: Blackwell, 1997).

Butler, Christopher, *After the Wake: An Essay on the Contemporary Avant-Garde* (Oxford: Oxford University Press, 1980).

Calinescu, Matei and Fokkema, Douwe (eds), *Exploring Postmodernism* (Amsterdam: John Benjamins, 1987).

Docherty, Thomas (ed.), *Postmodernism: A Reader* (New York: Columbia University Press, 1993).

Esslin, Martin, *The Theatre of the Absurd* (London: Eyre and Spottiswoode, 1964).

Falck, Colin, *Myth, Truth and Literature: Towards a True Post-Modernism* (Cambridge: Cambridge University Press, 1989).

Fiedler, Leslie, 'Cross the border – close the gap: Post-Modernism', in *The Collected Essays of Leslie Fiedler*, 2 vols (New York: Stein and Day, 1971), vol. 1, pp. 461–85.

Hassan, Ihab, *The Dismemberment of Orpheus: Towards a Postmodern Literature* (New York: Oxford University Press, 1971).

Hassan, Ihab, *Paracriticisms: Seven Speculations of the Times* (Urbana: The University of Illinois Press, 1975).

Heath, Stephen, *The Nouveau Roman: A Study in the Practice of Writing* (London: Elek, 1972).

Howe, Irving, 'Mass society and Post-Modern fiction', in *Decline of the New* (New York: Harcourt Brace, 1970), pp. 190–207.

Hutcheon, Linda, *A Poetics of Postmodernism: History, Theory, Fiction* (London: Routledge, 1988).

Huyssen, Andreas, *After the Great Divide: Modernism, Mass Culture, Postmodernism* (Bloomington: Indiana University Press, 1986).

Jameson, Frederic, *Postmodernism, or, the Cultural Logic of Late Capitalism* (Durham, NC: Duke University Press, 1991).

Kearney, Richard, *The Wake of Imagination: Towards a Postmodern Culture* (Minneapolis: Minnesota University Press, 1988).

Kermode, Frank, 'The Modern', in *Continuities* (London: Routledge, 1968), pp. 1–32.

Lucy, Niall, *Postmodern Literary Theory: An Introduction* (Oxford: Blackwell, 1997).

Lyotard, Jean-François, *The Postmodern Condition: A Report on Knowledge* (Minneapolis: University of Minnesota Press, 1984).

McHale, Brian, *Postmodernist Fiction* (London: Methuen, 1987).

Moi, Toril, *Sexual/Textual Politics: Feminist Literary Theory* (London: Routledge, 1983).

Smyth, Edmund J. (ed.), *Postmodernism and Contemporary Fiction* (London: Batsford, 1991).

Waugh, Patricia (ed.), *Postmodernism: A Reader* (London: Edward Arnold, 1992).

Wilde, Alan, *Horizons of Assent: Modernism, Postmodernism, and the Ironic Imagination* (Baltimore: Johns Hopkins University Press, 1981).

Zurbrugg, Nicholas, *The Parameters of Postmodernism* (London: Routledge, 1993).

# INDEX